**CourseMate**

D0761425

CourseMate brings course concepts to life with interactive learning, study, and exam preparation tools that support SPEAK.

INCLUDES:
Interactive eBook, teaching and learning tools, and Engagement Tracker, a first-of-its-kind tool that monitors student engagement in the course.

ALSO AVAILABLE:
SPEAK is also available with Speech Studio™, where students can upload video files, peer-review speeches, and review grades and instructor feedback. Students can purchase Speech Studio at CengageBrain.com.

ON THE
WEB

SPEAK
Are you in?

ONLINE RESOURCES INCLUDED!

FOR INSTRUCTORS:
- First Day of Class Instructions
- Custom Options through 4LTR+ Program
- Instructor's Manual
- Test Bank
- PowerPoint® Slides
- Instructor Prep Cards
- Engagement Tracker

FOR STUDENTS:
- Interactive eBook
- Auto-Graded Quizzes
- Flashcards
- Games: Crossword Puzzles, Beat the Clock, & Quiz Bowl
- PowerPoint® Slides
- Interactive Video Activities
- Audio Study Tools
- Review Cards
- Speech Builder Express™
- InfoTrac® College Edition

Students sign in at **www.cengagebrain.com**

SPEAK
Rudolph K. Verderber,
Deanna D. Sellnow,
Kathleen S. Verderber

Senior Publisher: Lyn Uhl

Publisher: Monica Eckman

Senior Development Editor: Greer Lleuad

Development Editor: John Choi, B-books, Ltd.

Assistant Editor: Rebekah Matthews

Editorial Assistant: Colin Solan

Marketing Manager, 4LTR Press: Courtney Sheldon

Project Manager, 4LTR Press: Kelli Strieby

Media Editor: Jessica Badiner

Senior Marketing Manager: Amy Whitaker

Marketing Coordinator: Brittany Blais

Marketing Communications Manager:
    Courtney Morris

Production Director: Amy McGuire, B-books, Ltd.

Content Project Manager: Corinna Dibble

Art Director: Bruce Bond

Manufacturing Manager: Denise Powers

Rights Acquisition Specialist: Mandy Groszko

Production Service: B-books, Ltd.

Internal Designer: Beckmeyer Design

Cover Designer: Bruce Bond

Cover Image: Tom Kates Photography

Compositor: B-books, Ltd.

Inside cover flap images: Gears © C Squared Studios/
Photodisc/Getty Images; Chair © C Squared Studios/
Photodisc/Getty Images; Microscope © Siede Preis/
Photodisc/Getty Images; Dartboard © Photodisc/
Getty Images; Binoculars © Photodisc/Getty Images

Page i image: Computer © iStockphoto.com/CostinT

Back cover image: Computer © iStockphoto.com/
René Mansi

Outside flap image: © iStockphoto.com/brebca

For product information and technology assistance, contact us at
Cengage Learning Customer & Sales Support, 1-800-354-9706

For permission to use material from this text or product,
submit all requests online at **www.cengage.com/permissions**.
Further permissions questions can be emailed to
permissionrequest@cengage.com.

Library of Congress Control Number: 2011927443

ISBN-13: 978-1-111-83029-8
ISBN-10: 1-111-83029-0

Wadsworth
20 Channel Center Street
Boston, MA 02210
USA

Cengage Learning is a leading provider of customized learning solutions with office locations around the globe, including Singapore, the United Kingdom, Australia, Mexico, Brazil and Japan. Locate your local office at **international.cengage.com/region**

Cengage Learning products are represented in Canada by Nelson Education, Ltd.

For your course and learning solutions, visit **www.cengage.com**. Purchase any of our products at your local college store or at our preferred online store **www.cengagebrain.com**.

Instructors: Please visit login.cengage.com and log in to access instructor-specific resources.

Printed in the United States of America
1 2 3 4 5 6 7 15 14 13 12 11

SPEAK
Brief Contents

© ISTOCKPHOTO.COM/DIGITALSKILLET

© STEWART COHEN/DIGITAL VISION/GETTY IMAGES

© FUSE/JUPITERIMAGES

SPEAK Contents

PART 2 Principles 56

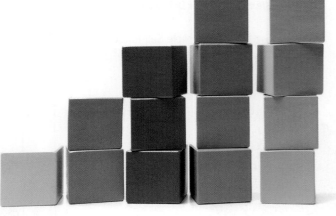

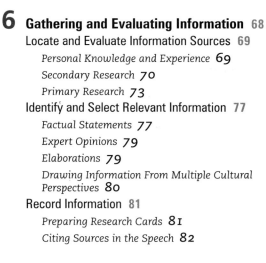

© ISTOCKPHOTO.COM/BLEND_IMAGES

© ISTOCKPHOTO.COM/EMIN OZKAN

© ISTOCKPHOTO.COM/MEHMET ALI CIDA

© ISTOCKPHOTO.COM/STEPHANIE HORROCKS

PART 3 Informative and Persuasive Speaking 166

© ISTOCKPHOTO.COM/PAVLEN

© ISTOCKPHOTO.COM/CHRIS SCHMIDT

Foundations of Public Speaking

When Sean Jones, a candidate for council, was invited to speak at the Riverside Community Center, he prepared and delivered a talk on his views about the proposed recreation center. As Marquez, Bill, and Gianna drove home from the movie they had seen, Bill said he thought the movie deserved an Academy Award nomination for Best Picture and asked the others if they agreed. Marquez listened carefully and then gave two reasons he thought the movie didn't deserve the honor.

In each of the situations described above, one person was talking to others. But in which of these situations was someone giving a "speech"? You probably recognized that Sean was giving a speech because he prepared beforehand, and you pictured him standing in front of an audience. But what about Marquez? Hadn't he also thought

about what he was saying and organized his thoughts in an effort to persuade his "audience"? In the broadest sense, he also was giving a speech. In this course, you will learn how to give speeches to an audience. But these skills will actually apply across a variety of personal, business, and community situations. In fact, public speaking, a sustained formal presentation by a speaker to an audience, is simply one form of human communication. So learning to be an effective public speaker will help you be more effective in other communication settings as well.

We begin this book by presenting some foundational communication concepts. In the first section of the chapter, we describe a basic model of human communication to help you understand how public speaking is similar to and different from other communication contexts. Because public speaking is one of the oldest liberal arts, we then provide a brief overview of the historical origins of the study of public address. Next, we present five principles that guide ethical communicators. Then, we introduce the concept of the rhetorical situation as a tool for analyzing a particular public speaking occasion. We conclude with a discussion of what makes a speech effective by previewing a speech-planning and -making process designed to help you become a confident and effective public speaker.

The Human Communication Process

Communication is the process of creating shared meaning. To understand how this process works, let's look at its essential elements: participants (who), messages (what), channels (how), interference/noise (distractions), feedback (reaction), and contexts (what kind).

Participants

Participants are the individuals who assume the roles of senders and receivers during an interaction (see Exhibit 1.1). As senders,

public speaking
a sustained formal presentation by a speaker to an audience

communication
the process of creating shared meaning

participants
the individuals who assume the roles of senders and receivers during an interaction

senders
participants who form and transmit messages using verbal symbols and nonverbal behaviors

receivers
participants who interpret the messages sent by others

messages
the verbal utterances, visual images, and nonverbal behaviors to which meaning is attributed during communication

meanings
the interpretations participants make of the messages they send and receive

encoding
the process of putting our thoughts and feelings into words and nonverbal behaviors

decoding
the process of interpreting the verbal and nonverbal messages sent by others

feedback messages
messages sent by receivers intended to let the sender know how the receiver made sense of the original message

channels
both the route traveled by a message and the means of transportation

interference/noise
any stimulus that interferes with the process of sharing meaning

feedback
the reactions and responses to messages that indicate to the sender whether and how a message was heard, seen, and interpreted

Exhibit 1.1

Model of Communication

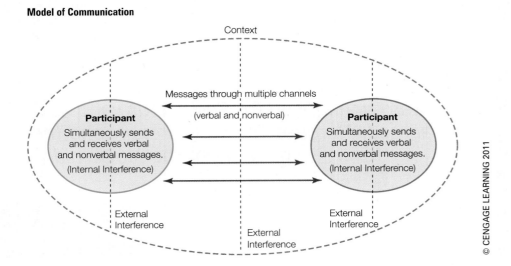

participants form and transmit messages using verbal symbols (words) and nonverbal behaviors. Receivers interpret the messages sent by others. Although all participants serve as both senders and receivers, in public speaking contexts, one participant acts primarily as sender and presents an extended message to which the other participants listen, interpret, and provide mostly nonverbal feedback.

Messages

Messages are the verbal utterances, visual images, and nonverbal behaviors to which meaning is attributed during communication. In public speaking situations, messages are typically speeches that are prepared beforehand and presented by one participant. **Meanings** are the interpretations participants make of the messages they send and receive. Messages are meant to convey the thoughts of the speaker but are easy to misinterpret. So the meaning that the sender intends may not be the meaning that the receiver understands. **Encoding** is the process of putting our thoughts and feelings into words and nonverbal behaviors, while **decoding** is the process of interpreting the verbal and nonverbal messages sent by others. **Feedback messages** sent by receivers are intended to let the sender know how the receiver made sense of the original message. As you can imagine, when you give a speech, you have to carefully encode many thoughts and pay attention to how you organize them so that your audience—the receivers of this complex message—will be able to decode it and understand as you intend.

Channels

Channels are both the route traveled by a message and the means of transportation. Messages are transmitted through sensory channels. We send and receive messages primarily through auditory (speaking and hearing) and visual (seeing) channels.

Interference/Noise

Interference, also referred to as **noise**, is any stimulus that interferes with the process of sharing meaning. Noise can be physical or psychological. Physical noise is any external sight or sound that distracts us from the message. For example, when a fire engine's siren roars by, a listener might not hear the message. Psychological noise refers to the thoughts and feelings you experience that compete with the sender's message for your attention. So when you daydream about what you have to do at work today, you are essentially distracted based on psychological noise.

Feedback

Feedback is the reactions and responses to messages that indicate to the sender whether and how a message was heard, seen, and interpreted. We can express feedback verbally by telling the sender what we understood or thought about a message, or we may simply indicate our understanding and reaction through nonverbal behavior, like nodding our heads to indicate agreement, raising eyebrows to register our surprise, or cocking our head and furrowing our eyebrows to indicate that we do not understand. When audiences listen to a speech, their feedback is usually nonverbal.

Contexts

Communication research reveals that there are specific contexts in which communication occurs. These differ by the number of participants and the balance of roles among them.[1] Let's briefly look at four of these. Intrapersonal communication (a.k.a. self-talk) is communicating with yourself. Usually this is done by thinking through choices, strategies, and the possible consequences of taking action. When you sit in class and consider what you'll have for dinner tonight, you are communicating intrapersonally. Much of our intrapersonal communication occurs subconsciously.[2] When you drive into your driveway "without thinking," you're communicating intrapersonally but at a subconscious level. When you are giving a speech and notice confused looks on your listeners' faces, you might communicate intrapersonally as you recognize the need to rephrase your explanation.

Interpersonal communication is communication between two people.[3] When you stop to chat with a friend between classes about weekend plans, how your family is, or what you did last night, you are engaging in interpersonal communication. Interpersonal communication sometimes occurs in a public speech setting when, during a question-and-answer session, a speaker directs remarks to one audience member.

Small group communication is communication that occurs among approximately three to 10 people.[4] There are many kinds of small groups, such as a family, a group of friends, or a management team in the workplace.[5] Small group communication occurs in a public speech setting when a team is asked to work together to research, prepare, and deliver a presentation on a particular topic.

Public communication is communication that occurs among more than 10 people where one message is presented to the participants who function as receivers whose own messages are limited primarily to feedback. One form of public communication is mass communication, which is communication produced and transmitted via media to massive audiences. Newspapers, magazines, books, blogs, TV programs, movies, websites, Facebook pages, and tweets are all examples of mass communication. Public speaking has been considered a separate

Intrapersonal Communication

Interpersonal Communication

Small Group Communication

Public Communication

intrapersonal communication communicating with yourself (a.k.a. self-talk)

interpersonal communication communication between two people

small group communication communication that occurs among approximately three to 10 people

public communication communication that occurs among more than 10 people where one message is presented to the participants who function as receivers whose own messages are limited primarily to feedback

mass communication communication produced and transmitted via media to massive audiences

liberal art
a body of general knowledge and skills needed to participate effectively in a democratic society

type of public communication because the intended audience is usually physically present to witness the speech. As media becomes more pervasive, however, the distinction between mass communication and public speaking has been somewhat blurred. For example, when President Obama gives a State of the Union address, he does so in the physical presence of the U.S. Congress, the Supreme Court justices, and other invited guests, but his speech is televised to a mass audience as well.

Public Speaking as a Liberal Art

When we say that public speaking is a liberal art, we mean that the knowledge and skills you gain by studying public speaking are general knowledge and essential skills that will help you participate effectively as an engaged citizen in our democratic society. This differs from the specialized knowledge you acquire when you study material in your major or when you develop skills specific to your profession. So that's why a course devoted in part or entirely to public speaking is often required in a general education curriculum.[6]

The Role of Public Speaking Education in Democracies

Since ancient times, liberal arts education has been at the center of study for free people in democracies. In fact, the word *liberal* means "free," and in ancient Greece it was the type of general education offered to free men (yes, back then it was restricted to men). Public speaking was central to a liberal education because it was the means by which free men conducted business, made public decisions, and gained and maintained power.[7] Today, effective public speakers continue to reap rewards in personal relationships, the work world, and the public sphere.[8]

Certainly, the formal study of public speaking equips you to give effective presentations; however, the process of preparing these speeches accomplishes something much more important. The study of public speaking teaches you not *what* to think but *how* to think—a central skill for a responsible citizen living in a democracy, especially the sound-bite-saturated, image-managed, political environment we live in today. Essentially, you learn to think critically about what you read, see, and hear.

You also learn how to behave ethically as both a sender and receiver of messages. As you prepare to speak about a topic, you must consider why you are speaking, what you know well enough, and what you think is important to present to others. You must assess how much you know about a topic and augment that knowledge with further study. When collecting additional information, you must critically evaluate the credibility of the information, the validity and reliability of the facts presented, and the logical reasoning offered. As you prepare your speeches, you must consider how best to organize your ideas and what words to use to be both clear and compelling. And, as you present your speeches, you must attend to the nonverbal behaviors of your listeners and adjust your message as needed to ensure they are getting the meaning you intend.

Learning to think critically and behave ethically as you prepare and present your own speeches also equips you to analyze the messages offered by others. You will be able to critically judge the information and arguments of others and identify flaws in their reasoning. You will be able to identify how others use emotion to try to persuade you. And you will be better equipped to realize when others are communicating unethically.

All of these activities are critical mental disciplines you can apply to a wide variety of issues and settings. Democracies only thrive in settings where citizens are capable of fulfilling their civic responsibilities to analyze, think about, and eloquently speak out about important issues. So public speaking is a liberal art—an essential skill for free, engaged citizens.

The Power of Effective Public Speaking for Free People

The ability to present your ideas in a speech effectively empowers you in several ways. First, public speaking skills empower you to participate in democratic processes. Free speech is a hallmark of democracy. The strategies and policies our government adopts are a direct result of the debate that occurs all across the nation, whether it's in the living room, in the media, or in the branches of government. When equipped with effective public speaking skills, you have the confidence to speak out and voice your ideas on important public issues.

Second, public speaking skills empower you to communicate complex ideas and information in ways that all audience members can understand. Most of us have had an unfortunate experience with a teacher who "talked over our heads." The teacher understood the material but was unable to express it clearly to us. When we can express our ideas clearly, we are more likely to share them. When others understand our ideas, they learn from us. This confidence equips us to share our knowledge to the benefit of others.

Third, public speaking skills empower you to achieve your career goals. Research shows that for almost any job, one of the most highly sought-after skills in new hires is oral communication skills.[9] So whether you aspire to a career in business, industry, government, the arts, or education, your success will depend on your ability to communicate what you know to others, including your manager, your clients, and your colleagues.

Ethical Principles for Public Speaking

Ethics are moral principles that a society, group, or individual holds that differentiate right from wrong and good behavior from bad behavior. In other words, ethics reflect what we believe we "ought to" and "ought not to" think and do. As audience members, we expect speakers to behave ethically. Likewise, as speakers, we expect audience members to behave ethically. What standards should we conform to as ethical communicators? Five generally agreed-upon ethical standards are honesty, integrity, fairness, respect, and responsibility. Let's look at each of these principles more closely as they relate to public speaking situations:

1. **Ethical communicators are honest.** Ethical public speakers tell the truth. An audience expects that what you tell them will be true—not made up, not your personal belief presented as fact, and not an exaggeration. If, during or after your speech, members of your audience doubt the accuracy of something you have said, they are likely to reject all of your ideas. To make sure that what you say is truthful, you will want to research your topic carefully and present both sides of controversial issues accurately.

   Honest speakers also credit the ideas of others they use in their speech and do not try to pass those ideas off as their own. Plagiarism is passing off the ideas, words, or created works of another as one's own by failing to credit the source. It is intellectual theft—stealing another's idea. Sadly, plagiarism is now commonplace. According to a 2002–2003 survey of 3,500 graduate students at U.S. and Canadian universities, "23 per-

cent to 25 percent of students acknowledged one or more instances of 'cutting and pasting' from Internet sources and/or published documents."[10] And results of a survey conducted by the Center for Academic Integrity indicate that as many as 80 percent of college students admit to having plagiarized.[11] In most colleges, plagiarism can result in failing an assignment or the entire course, and it can even lead to being suspended from school. In the world beyond the classroom, plagiarism has led to lawsuits and has ruined promising careers. How can you recognize if you are plagiarizing?

- If you change a few words at the beginning, in the middle, or at the end of a material but copy much of the rest, you are plagiarizing.
- If you completely paraphrase the unique ideas of another person and do not credit that person, you are plagiarizing.

ethics
moral principles that a society, group, or individual holds that differentiate right from wrong and good behavior from bad behavior

plagiarism
passing off the ideas, words, or created works of another as one's own by failing to credit the source

Being able to present your ideas effectively in a speech is empowering!

rhetorical situation
the composite of the occasion, speaker, and the audience that influences the speech that is given

- If you purchase, borrow, or use a speech or essay in part or in whole that was prepared by another and present it as original, you are plagiarizing.[12]

Honest speakers provide the sources for their material so audience members have the information they need to evaluate the truthfulness of what is being said. Where ideas originate is often as important as the ideas themselves. For example, if a statistic about global warming comes from an article by a renowned scientist in a respected peer-reviewed journal, it is likely to have more credibility than if it comes from a celebrity's blog.

2. **Ethical communicators have integrity.** They practice what they preach. A speaker who gives a speech on the need to quit smoking who then goes outside and lights up lacks integrity. A listener who espouses the importance of civil dialogue but interrupts the speech of someone who takes the opposite side of an issue lacks integrity.

3. **Ethical communicators are fair.** For speakers, behaving fairly means researching and accurately reporting all sides of an issue, even if some of the information runs contrary to their stand on a controversial issue. For listeners, it means considering all of the evidence that a speaker presents, even when that evidence contradicts what they believe.

4. **Ethical communicators demonstrate respect for others.** Behaving respectfully means being considerate of others and their feelings. For example, speakers show respect for their audience by choosing language and humor that is bias free, inoffensive, and inclusive. Listeners demonstrate respect by giving their undivided attention to the speaker. It is disrespectful to a speaker for audience members to send or read text or e-mail messages, read any other materials during the speech, hold side conversations, or in any other way "multitask" during a speech.

5. **Ethical communicators are responsible.** Being responsible means being accountable for your actions or your words. A well-settled point of law is that if someone yells "FIRE" in a crowded theater when there is no fire and someone is injured in the stampede for the door, the person who yelled is responsible for the injury caused. So, too, are speakers responsible for the foreseeable outcomes of what they advocate.

Ethical speakers only advocate for things that are in the best interest of audience members. When the organizers of the Hope for Haiti Now concert decided to ask only for small donations, they were being responsible. They recognized that many in the audience might be swept up in the moment and donate more than they could really afford. So they limited donations to $5 or $10. Similarly, listeners have the responsibility for critically evaluating the positions that speakers advocate so they do not blindly accept what may be inaccurate, dishonest information, or positions that are not in their best interest.

Throughout this book, we will elaborate on how these ethical principles should guide you as you prepare your speeches and listen to the speeches of others. To learn more about ethics, use the CourseMate for SPEAK at www.cengagebrain.com to access **Web Resource 1.1: The Basics of Ethics** and **Web Resource 1.2: Ethics Connection**. The first links to The Internet Encyclopedia of Philosophy, which provides an easy-to-read, thorough discussion about ethics. The second links to the website for the Markkula Center for Applied Ethics at Santa Clara University, a forum for research and discussion on ethical issues in American life.

Understanding the Rhetorical Situation

Public speaking is rooted in what we refer to as the rhetorical tradition.[13] The rhetorical tradition was conceived more than 2,000 years ago. The Greek philosopher Aristotle observed, "The audience is the end and object of the speech."[14] What he meant was that the eloquence of your words is irrelevant if the words are not heard by, are not understood by, or do not affect the people to whom you are speaking. Today, we recognize that the effectiveness of any speech depends not just on understanding the audience but also on how well the speaker gives a speech that fits the rhetorical situation.

In one sense, the rhetorical situation is the composite of the speaker, audience, and occasion. As shown in Exhibit 1.2, the **rhetorical situation** is the place where the speaker, audience, and occasion overlap. But Lloyd Bitzer, the rhetorical scholar who introduced the concept of the rhetorical situation, believed that the particular speech given by an individual to an audience on a specific occasion is the

Exhibit 1.2

The Rhetorical Public Speaking Situation

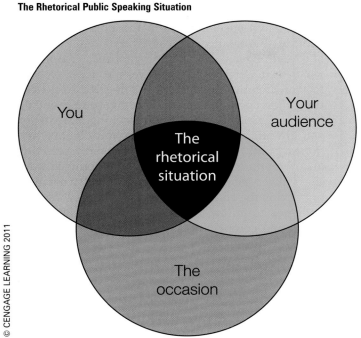

© CENGAGE LEARNING 2011

result of some real or perceived specific need that a speech might help to address.[15] Bitzer referred to this as the **exigence**.[16] The term can be defined as "something that a situation demands or makes urgently necessary and that puts pressure on the people involved."[17]

On January 12, 2010, a massive earthquake in Haiti created an exigence that led many people to speak out about the dire need for aid. In the United States, from President Obama's televised speech to the nation to the simple calls to action heard in grade school classrooms, individuals felt compelled to speak out and to help the victims of this disaster. The earthquake created an exigence that motivated speakers to seek an occasion and audience where a speech they would give could accomplish something.

Speaker

The **speaker** is the source or originator of the speech. As the speaker, what you discuss and the language you use to express those ideas will depend on your interests, beliefs, background, and public speaking skills. You will choose topics that you care about, know something about, and want to inform or persuade others about. Your personal experiences will influence the attitudes and beliefs you express, so what you say will be unique to you. For example, after her son was killed in Iraq, Cindy Sheehan began speaking out about the legitimacy of war and became a leader in the anti-war movement. Her speeches are informed

by her experience as a grieving mother. Leah Bolger, a leader of the Veterans for Peace organization, retired from the U.S. Navy after 20 years of service. Her military experiences influence her anti-war speeches. Each woman brings her own uniqueness to bear on what she says, so while both women share the same exigence, the speeches they give are informed by their unique backgrounds.

Audience

The **audience** is the specific group of people to whom your speech is directed. **Audience analysis** is a study made to learn about the diverse characteristics of audience members and then, based on these characteristics, to predict how audience members are apt to listen to, understand, and be motivated to act on your speech. Armed with an understanding of your specific audience, you are in a better position to develop a speech tailored to that audience and designed to motivate that specific audience to address the exigence as far as the audience is able. For example, the organizers of the Hope for Haiti Now concert recognized that a large part of their audience would be teens and young adults who were tech savvy, so they encouraged the audience to donate small amounts of money by text message. But because the organizers also expected a significant number of people in the audience to be encouraged to give larger donations and that many in this group were not tech savvy, they also had celebrities staffing toll-free phone lines.

Occasion

The **occasion** is the setting in which the speech is given. It encompasses the purpose for which the audience is gathered, their shared expectations about what is to happen there, and the physical location of the event, as well as potential constraints arising from these. When the congregation assembles at a church, synagogue, or mosque, they expect to hear sermons that elaborate on religious texts or principles. When physicians attend a professional meeting on "new treatment options for multiple sclerosis,"

exigence
some real or perceived need that a speech might help address

speaker
the source or originator of the speech

audience
the specific group of people to whom your speech is directed

audience analysis
a study made to learn about the diverse characteristics of audience members and then, based on these characteristics, to predict how audience members are apt to listen to, understand, and be motivated to act on your speech

occasion
the setting in which the speech is given

speech effectiveness
the extent to which audience members listen to, understand, remember, and are motivated to act on what a speaker has said

audience centered
offering ideas in ways that respond to a felt need, are appropriate to the occasion, reflect careful research, make sense, and sound interesting

ethos
everything you say and do to convey competence and good character

pathos
everything you say and do to appeal to emotions

logos
everything you say and do to appeal to logic and sound reasoning

macrostructure
the overall framework you use to organize your speech content

they expect to hear a scientific presentation about the efficacy of new treatments. Imagine what would happen if a local rabbi were to present his sermon to the physicians.

The location and the layout of the room where a speech is given are also important parts of the occasion. The speech you prepare to give in a large auditorium for an audience of more than a thousand is likely to be different from the speech you would prepare to give in a restaurant to an audience of 20.

Principles of Effective Public Speaking

When you give a speech, your goal is to communicate with your audience members. **Speech effectiveness** is the extent to which audience members listen to, understand, remember, and are motivated to act on what a speaker has said. Therefore, all effective public speakers and speeches are audience centered.

Effective Speakers Are Audience Centered

Audience centered speakers offer their ideas in ways that respond to a felt need, are appropriate to the occasion, reflect careful research, make sense, and sound interesting. You do so through the rhetorical appeals of ethos, pathos, and logos.[18] **Ethos** includes everything you say and do to

convey competence and good character. Dressing professionally, being poised as you speak, citing credible sources, and speaking within the time parameters allotted, for instance, convey ethos. **Pathos** consists of everything you say and do to appeal to emotions, which can range from negative emotions such as fear or dread to positive emotions such as adventure or joy. **Logos** includes everything you say and do to appeal to logic and sound reasoning. Essentially, you are audience centered when you demonstrate honesty and respect for your listeners by selecting an appropriate topic, developing your points in ways that reflect careful research and sound reasoning, organizing the content in a way that is easy for your audience to follow, rehearsing your delivery to be fluent and compelling, and presenting your speech so that it meets the expectations of the rhetorical situation.

An Effective Speech Includes Audience-Appropriate Content

The content of a speech is the information and ideas you present. It encompasses your purpose for giving the speech, the main ideas you will present, and the evidence you use to develop your main ideas. Evidence clarifies, explains, or supports your main ideas. It includes facts, expert opinions, and elaborations, and it comes from your own experiences as well as from research materials you collect. Effective evidence has sufficient breadth and depth. *Breadth* refers to the amount and types of evidence you use. *Depth* is the level of detail you provide from each piece of evidence. Evidence is effective when it is logically linked to the main idea it supports. The ideas you choose to present depend on what is appropriate for your audience and the occasion, and you adapt your content so that it includes listener relevance links, which are statements of how and why the ideas you offer are of interest to your listeners. Doing so makes the exigence of your ideas transparent.

An Effective Speech Is Well Structured

The structure of a speech is the framework that organizes the content. Clear structure helps your listeners follow your ideas so they can understand the points you are making.[19] Clear structure includes both macrostructure and microstructure.

Macrostructure is the overall framework you use to organize your speech content. It has four elements: the introduction, body, conclusion, and transitions. The introduction is the beginning segment of the

speech and should be structured so that you build audience interest in your topic and preview what you are going to say. The speech body contains the main ideas and supporting material you have decided to present; it is organized into a pattern that makes the ideas easy for the audience to understand and remember. The conclusion ends the speech, reminds the audience of your main ideas, and motivates them to remember or act upon what you have said.

The macrostructure of your speech also includes transitions, which are the phrases you use to move from one main point to the next. You have studied macrostructure throughout your education as you learned to write. Now, however, you will be learning how to adapt it to oral messages. You'll see that careful attention to macrostructure is more important when you craft a speech than when you write an essay. A reader can easily reread a poorly written essay to try to understand your intent, but an audience does not usually have the opportunity to rehear your speech. So as you prepare each of your speeches, you will need to develop an organizational framework that enables your audience to quickly understand and easily remember the ideas you present.

Whereas macrostructure is the overall framework you design for your speech, **microstructure** is the specific language and style choices you use as you frame your ideas and verbalize them to your audience. Pay careful attention to microstructure while practicing and delivering your speech so that you can present your ideas with words that are instantly intelligible and guide your audience to thoughts that are consistent with your own. Practicing and using words that are appropriate, accurate, clear, and vivid will help you accomplish your speaking goal.

As your practice wording, you can also plan to use **rhetorical devices**. These language techniques are designed to create audience attention, hold interest, and aid memory. Again, from your composition classes, you may be familiar with techniques such as alliteration, onomatopoeia, and personification. In Chapter 10, you will learn how to frame your ideas using effective rhetorical devices that make it easy for your audience to understand and remember the ideas in your speech.

An Effective Speech Is Delivered Expressively

Delivery is how you use your voice and body to present your message. The manner in which a speech is delivered can dramatically affect the audience's ability to listen to, understand, remember, and act on the ideas presented. Speakers whose voice and body actions have a conversational quality encourage audience members to listen. When speakers use appropriate volume, rate, pronunciation, and enunciation, they make their message easier for the audience to understand. When speakers are expressive and enthusiastic, listeners are more likely to remember and act on what has been said. In fact, listeners often are more persuaded by the manner in which a speech is delivered than by the words used.

Speaking conversationally means sounding as though you are having a spontaneous conversation with your audience rather than simply reading to them or performing in front of them. Speaking expressively means using various vocal techniques so you sound a bit more dramatic than you would in casual conversation. Some common vocal techniques used in speeches include speaking more quickly or loudly to underscore your attitudes or emotional convictions, stressing keywords or phrases, and pausing strategically to call attention to important ideas.

As you may already know, nonverbal communication is just as important as verbal communication in conveying messages. Effective speakers know this and use their eyes, face, stance, and hands to help them deliver a speech. For example, they make eye contact with audience members rather than focus solely on their notes, and they use appropriate facial expressions to reflect their conviction about their topic. They stand with poise and confidence, they avoid fidgeting, and they use gestures to reinforce important points.

microstructure
the specific language and style choices you use as you frame your ideas and verbalize them to your audience

rhetorical devices
language techniques designed to create audience attention, hold interest, and aid memory

delivery
how you use your voice and body to present your message

Speech Evaluation Checklist

General Criteria

You can use this checklist to critique a speech of self-introduction that you hear in class. (You can also use it to critique your own speech.) As you listen to the speaker, consider what makes a speech effective. Then answer the following questions.

Content

1. Were all main points addressed per the assignment? _____

2. Were two to three pieces of evidence provided for each main point? _____ *(breadth)*

3. Was one extended piece of evidence provided for each main point? _____ *(depth)*

4. Were listener relevance links provided for each main point? _____

5. Did the speech fall within the time constraints of the assignment? _____

Structure

1. Did the speech provide all the basic elements of an effective speech: introduction, body, conclusion, and transitions? _____ *(macrostructure)*

2. Did the introduction catch the audience's interest? _____ state the topic of the speech? _____ preview the main points of the speech? _____

3. Were the main points organized in a way that helped the audience understand and remember the ideas in the speech? _____

4. Were transitions provided between each main point? _____

5. Did the conclusion remind the audience of the main points? _____ motivate the audience to remember the main ideas of the speech? _____

6. Did the speaker use words that were accurate and clear? _____ vivid and emphatic? _____ appropriate and inclusive? _____ *(microstructure)*

7. Did the speaker use rhetorical devices that gained the audience's attention? _____ held the audience's interest? _____ *(microstructure)*

Delivery

1. Did the speaker use the appropriate volume? _____ rate of speaking? _____

2. Did the speaker use proper pronunciation? _____ enunciation? _____

3. Was the speaker's voice intelligible? _____ conversational? _____ expressive? _____

4. Did the speaker look up from his or her notes most of the time and make eye contact with the audience? _____

5. Did the speaker use appropriate facial expressions and gestures to reinforce important points? _____

6. Did the speaker appear poised and confident? _____

You can use the CourseMate for SPEAK at www.cengagebrain.com to access this checklist, complete it online and compare your feedback to that of the authors, or print a copy to use in class.

SAMPLE SELF-INTRODUCTION SPEECH

Mirror Image
By Kris Treinen[20]

Introduction

I. Have you ever looked into a mirror and seen your reflection and realized that the reflection in the mirror wasn't really you? I have, many times.

Attention getter

II. As you listen to my speech today, I believe you'll begin to understand how important I believe it is to believe in yourself, your family and friends, and, most important, your dreams.

Listener relevance link

III. Today, I'd like to introduce myself to you by talking about why my mirror image makes me unique, how where I grew up influenced my choice of majors, and how, ultimately, my major has helped shape my career goal.

Thesis statement with main point preview

Body

I. When I was a child, I had a mirror image that wasn't really me and I still have it today.

Thinking of my mirror image reminds me how important it is to have family and friends who love me.

Listener relevance link

   A. My mirror image isn't really an "it" but a "her."

   1. Her name is Karla, and she is my identical "mirror image" twin sister.

   2. Every day I am away from her, I realize how easy it was to take her and my family for granted.

   B. My sister and I were born right here at a local hospital in Fargo, North Dakota.

   1. We were born three minutes apart.

   2. I was born first, so I'm the oldest.

   C. We were known as the "good" twin and the "evil" twin.

   1. Here is a story about me as the "good" twin.

   2. Here is a story about her as the "evil" twin.

Now that you know how having my own mirror image—my twin—makes me unique, let's talk a bit about how where I grew up influenced my choice of a major.

Transition

II. I spent most of my life growing up in the lakes area of Brainerd, Minnesota.

Perhaps you'll want to visit this area after you hear about it today.

Listener relevance link

   A. I grew up in a small town called Nisswa, Minnesota.

   1. I moved to Nisswa when I was three years old.

   2. We lived in a house that was very special to me.

B. As I grew up in an area known for lots of snow in the winter, I got involved in snowboarding.

    1. I started snowboarding recreationally.

    2. Then I competed as a snowboarder.

    3. Eventually, I taught snowboarding as a part-time job.

Transition

So my upbringing led me to realize I love to snowboard and to teach snowboarding, which is why I chose to come to school here at North Dakota State University (NDSU).

III. I chose to further my education with a major in hospitality management.

Listener relevance link

I feel lucky every time I realize I can get a major and eventually earn a living doing something I love—working with people in the hospitality and recreation fields.

    A. NDSU has a reputable program.

    B. The winters in the Fargo area allow me to continue to pursue snowboarding.

    C. Ultimately, my degree will help me pursue my goal to work in a ski resort area and help children with disabilities learn to snowboard.

Conclusion

I. Now that you know a little bit about me as a twin and why I chose to major in hospitality management, I hope you'll be inspired to also follow your career dreams.

Thesis restatement with main point summary clincher

II. I hope you now see why I have learned to look beyond the reflection I see in the mirror to understand who I really am on the way to who I will one day become.

Test coming up? Now what?

With SPEAK you have a multitude of study aids at your fingertips. After reading the chapters, check out these ideas for further help.

Chapter in Review Cards include all learning outcomes, definitions, and summaries for each chapter.

Printable Flash Cards give you three additional ways to check your comprehension of key speech communication concepts.

Other great ways to help you study include **Interactive Quizzing**, **Crossword Puzzles**, **Games**, **Interactive Video Activities**, and **Audio Study Tools**.

You can find it all at the CourseMate for SPEAK at **www.cengagebrain.com**

Developing Confidence Through the Speech-Planning Process

Learning Outcomes

LO^1 What is public speaking apprehension? | LO^2 Why do we experience public speaking apprehension? | LO^3 What can we do to manage public speaking apprehension? | LO^4 In what ways does careful planning help reduce public speaking apprehension? | LO^5 What are the six steps in an effective speech action plan?

Professor Montrose begins class by saying, "Let's look at some of the key points of the chapter that you were assigned to read for today." He then points to Paul and asks, "What were the keys to solving the Kingston problem effectively?" Paul, sputtering and turning red, begins to sweat and stammers, "Well, uh, I guess that, well . . ." Professor Montrose then points to the next student and asks, "Sylvia, what would you say about this?" Sylvia looks at Professor Montrose and answers, "According to the text, there are three steps involved." She goes on to list the steps and then discusses each of the three.

You might think, "Poor, Paul. He just got so nervous when Professor Montrose pointed at him and asked him the question that he couldn't remember a thing." And perhaps he did suffer from severe public speaking apprehension—or stage fright. But then why was Sylvia able to look Professor Montrose in the eye, tell him there are three steps, and then discuss each? One answer might be, "Well, she doesn't suffer stage fright, so she was able to answer the question." Although that might be true, there's another possible answer: Paul hadn't prepared well for class, while Sylvia had not only read the text but had also outlined the key points and reviewed them over a cup of coffee before class.

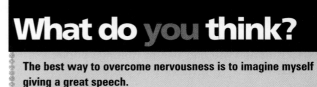

What do you think?

The best way to overcome nervousness is to imagine myself giving a great speech.

Strongly Disagree   Strongly Agree

1   2   3   4   5   6   7   8   9   10

Recall the title of this chapter: "Developing Confidence through the Speech-Planning Process." Although stage fright is normal in public settings, even the most frightened person whose heart is pounding will perform better when he or she is well prepared. In fact, as many as 76 percent of experienced public speakers claim to feel fearful before presenting a speech.[1]

We begin this chapter by explaining what scholars call public speaking apprehension. Then we discuss the causes and benefits of public speaking apprehension, as well as how you can manage anxiety successfully. And, finally, we explain how careful preparation can help you develop and display confidence when you speak. At the end of the chapter, we introduce the narrative/personal experience speech, a common early speech assignment.

Understanding Public Speaking Apprehension

Public speaking apprehension is the level of fear a person experiences when anticipating or actually speaking to an audience. Almost all of us have some level of public speaking apprehension, but about 15 percent of the U.S. population experiences high levels of apprehension.[2] Yet this apprehension hardly ever stops people from speaking!

public speaking apprehension
the level of fear a person experiences when anticipating or actually speaking to an audience

anticipation phase
the anxiety you experience prior to giving the speech, including the nervousness you feel while preparing and waiting to speak

confrontation phase
the surge of anxiety you feel as you begin delivering your speech

adaptation phase
the period during which your anxiety level gradually decreases

In fact, having some public speaking apprehension makes one a better public speaker than having none at all. Why? Because those feelings we label as fear are really a sign of the adrenaline boost that will help us perform at our best. Just as an adrenaline boost helps us perform better as athletes, musicians, and actors, it also helps us deliver better public speeches when we manage it effectively.[3] So if you are lackadaisical about giving a speech, you probably will not do a good job.[4] Because at least some tension is constructive, the goal is not to eliminate nervousness but to learn how to manage it.[5]

Now that we understand that some public speaking apprehension can actually help, let's identify the symptoms you may experience and the causes for speaking apprehension. Then we'll describe specific techniques you can use to manage public speaking in ways that will make you a more effective public speaker.

Symptoms of Public Speaking Apprehension

The symptoms of public speaking apprehension vary among individuals and range from mild to debilitating. Symptoms can be cognitive, physical, or emotional. Cognitive symptoms include negative self-talk (a.k.a. negative intrapersonal communication), which is also the most common cause of public speaking apprehension.[6] For example, a highly apprehensive person might dwell on thoughts such as "I'm going to make a fool of myself" or "I just know that I'll blow it." Physical symptoms may be stomach upset, flushed skin, sweating, shaking, light-headedness, rapid or pounding heartbeats, stuttering, and vocalized pauses ("like," "you know," "ah," "um"). Emotional symptoms include feeling anxious, worried, or upset.

Luckily, public speaking apprehension gradually decreases for most of us as we speak. Researchers have identified three phases through which we proceed: anticipation, confrontation, and adaptation.[7] Exhibit 2.1 depicts this cycle visually.

The **anticipation phase** is the anxiety we experience prior to giving the speech, including the nervousness we feel while preparing and waiting to speak. The **confrontation phase** is the surge of anxiety we feel as we begin delivering the speech. This begins to fall about a minute or so into the speech. The **adaptation phase** is the period during which our anxiety level gradually decreases. It typically begins about one minute into the presentation and tends to level off after about five minutes.[8] So it's normal to be nervous before you speak, and when understood and managed effectively it can result in a better speech than having no nervousness at all.

There are many ways to measure your level of public speaking apprehension. The table on the next page presents one short survey that is widely used by researchers. You can complete the six questions and score them to gauge your level of apprehension.

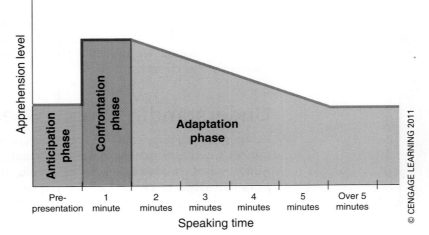

Exhibit 2.1

Phases of Public Speaking Apprehension

Apprehension level (vertical axis)

- Anticipation phase
- Confrontation phase
- Adaptation phase

Speaking time (horizontal axis): Pre-presentation — 1 minute — 2 minutes — 3 minutes — 4 minutes — 5 minutes — Over 5 minutes

These statements give you a chance to express how you feel about speaking in public. Please indicate in the space provided the degree to which each statement applies to you by marking whether you:

**1 = strongly agree; 2 = agree; 3 = are undecided;
4 = disagree; 5 = strongly disagree**

_____ **1.** I have no fear of giving a speech.

_____ **2.** Certain parts of my body feel very tense and rigid while giving a speech.

_____ **3.** I feel relaxed while giving a speech.

_____ **4.** My thoughts become confused and jumbled when I am giving a speech.

_____ **5.** I face the prospect of giving a speech with confidence.

_____ **6.** While giving a speech, I get so nervous I forget the facts I really know.

_____ **TOTAL**

Scoring: Begin by reversing the numbers you assigned to statements 2, 4, and 6 (1 = 5, 2 = 4, 3 = 3, 4 = 2, 5 = 1). Then add all six numbers.

Interpreting: If your total is more than 24, you may experience a high level of public speaking apprehension. People who are highly apprehensive will benefit most from applying techniques designed to reduce anxiety.

Source: Taken from the PRCA-24, subscale Public Speaking. See Rich, V. P., & McCroskey, J. C. (1997). *Communication apprehension, avoidance, and effectiveness.* Scottsdale, AZ: Gorsuch Scarisbrick.

Causes of Public Speaking Apprehension

Public speaking apprehension is most commonly caused by negative self-talk.[9] **Self-talk** is defined as intrapersonal communication regarding perceived success or failure in a particular situation. Negative self-talk about giving a speech increases anxiety. Negative self-talk generally focuses on a fear of being stared at, a fear of the unknown, a fear of failure, or a fear of becoming fearful. Where do these negative thoughts come from? Research suggests three common roots: biologically based temperament, previous experience, and level of skills.

Biologically Based Temperament

First, some public speaking apprehension may be inborn. This "communibiological" explanation suggests that for some, public speaking apprehension stems from our biologically based temperament. According to this theory, people who are extroverted tend to experience lower levels of public speaking apprehension than people who are introverted. Similarly, people who naturally experience elevated levels of general anxiety and shyness tend to experience higher levels of public speaking anxiety than people who do not.[10] Does this mean that if you are temperamentally predisposed toward high public speaking apprehension, you are doomed to be an ineffective speaker? Of course not. Many people are introverted and yet enjoy a great deal of public speaking success.

Previous Experience

Second, our level of apprehension may also result from our past experiences with public speaking. In other words, some of us actually learned to fear public speaking! Research tells us that most public speaking apprehension stems from such socialization.[11] We are socialized in two main ways: through modeling and reinforcement. **Modeling** is learning by observing and then imitating those you admire or are close to.[12] **Reinforcement** is learning from personal experiences so that past responses to our behavior shape our expectations about how our future behavior will be received.[13]

Consider your past. How did modeling affect your current communication behavior? What was oral communication like in your home when you were a child? Did your parents talk freely with each other in your presence? Did family or community members talk with each other a great deal, or were they quiet and reserved? Did any of your family members do much public speaking? What were their experiences? If your family tended to be quiet and reserved and avoided speaking in public or showed fear about it, your own preferences and fears may stem from modeling. Modeling an aversion to speaking freely in

self-talk
intrapersonal communication regarding perceived success or failure in a particular situation

modeling
learning by observing and then imitating those you admire or are close to

reinforcement
learning from personal experiences so that past responses to our behavior shape our expectations about how our future behavior will be received

public influenced noted *Boston Globe* columnist Diana White, who remarked, "In my family, looking for attention was one of the worst sins a child could commit. 'Don't make a spectacle of yourself' was a familiar phrase around our house."[14]

How you have been reinforced by others in your speaking efforts influenced how well you believe you performed in the past and affects how apprehensive you feel about future speaking occasions. We have all had many "public speaking" experiences, from reading aloud in class or accepting an award at a banquet. If the responses to your speaking in the past were generally positive, you probably learned to feel confident of your ability. If, on the other hand, the responses were negative, you probably learned to feel fearful of public speaking. So if your second-grade teacher humiliated you when you read aloud, or if friends laughed at your acceptance speech, you will probably be more apprehensive about speaking in public than if you had been praised for your efforts.

The public speaking apprehension you feel because of negative past experiences, though uncomfortable, does not have to influence your future performances. There are strategies you can use as you prepare to speak that will help you reduce your apprehension and be more effective. We will discuss some of these strategies in the next section.

Level of Skills

An important source of public speaking apprehension comes from having underdeveloped speaking skills. This "skill deficit" theory was the earliest explanation for apprehension and continues to receive the attention of researchers. It suggests that most of us become apprehensive because we don't know how to (or choose not to) plan or prepare effectively for a public presentation.

Effective speech planning is an orderly process based on a set of skills. If you do not know or apply these skills, you are likely to have higher anticipation reaction levels. On the other hand, as you become skilled at using the six-step speech-planning process

discussed later in this chapter, your preparation will give you confidence and your anticipation reaction will be lower than if you were not well prepared. The goal of this course is to help you become skilled and, in so doing, help you become a more confident public speaker.

Managing Public Speaking Apprehension

Because public speaking apprehension has multiple causes, there are both general methods and specific techniques that can help us reduce our anxiety and manage our nervousness.

General Methods

Some methods are targeted at reducing the apprehension that results from our worrisome thoughts and negative self-talk. Other methods are aimed at reducing our physical symptoms of anxiety. Still others focus on helping us overcome the skill deficiencies that lead to our anxiety. In this section, we consider six common methods for reducing public speaking apprehension.

1. **Communication orientation motivation (COM) techniques** are designed to reduce anxiety by helping us adopt a "communication" rather than a "performance" orientation toward our speeches.[15] According to communication researcher Michael Motley, public speaking anxiety increases when we hold a **performance orientation**, viewing public speaking as demanding special delivery techniques to impress our audience "aesthetically"[16] or viewing audience members as hypercritical judges who will not forgive even minor mistakes. When we approach public speaking with a performance orientation, our self-talk tends to focus on our fear of failing, which increases our anxiety. On the other hand, if we approach public speaking from a **communication orientation**, we view our speech as just an opportunity to talk with a number of people about an important topic. We focus on getting our message across to people in our audience rather than on how the people in our audience are judging us as a performer.

So one way to reduce public speaking apprehension is to view public speaking as a conversation with a group of people where we focus on getting our message across, not on how they might be judging our performance.

2. **Visualization** is a method that reduces apprehension by helping us develop a mental picture of ourselves giving a masterful speech. Doing so counters the fear of failure and the fear of becoming fearful. Like COM techniques, visualization helps us overcome the cognitive and emotional symptoms of apprehension. Joe Ayres and Theodore S. Hopf, two scholars who have conducted extensive research on visualization, have found that if people can visualize themselves going through an entire speech-preparation and speech-making process, they will have a much better chance of succeeding when they are speaking.[17]

By visualizing the process of speech making, not only do people seem to lower their general apprehension, but they also report fewer negative thoughts when they actually speak.[18] So, you will want to use visualization activities as part of your speech preparation. Use the CourseMate for SPEAK at www.cengagebrain.com to access **Web Resource 2.1: Visualizing Your Success**. This activity will guide you through a visualization in which you will imagine that you successfully accomplish the complete speech-preparation and speech-making process.

3. **Relaxation exercises** include breathing techniques and progressive muscle relaxation exercises that help reduce anxiety. For these exercises to be effective, you must learn how to do them and practice them regularly. With consistent practice, these will eventually become habitual, and you will be able to use them to calm yourself in the moments before your speech.

Let's take a closer look at breathing techniques. We were all born breathing correctly, using the muscles in our abdomen to draw air into and push air out of our lungs. But when we become anxious, the muscles in our abdomen tense and so we take shallower breaths, often raising our shoulders to get air into our lungs and dropping them to expel the air. Shallow breathing contributes to anxiety, depression, and fatigue.[19] Think of your lungs as balloons that fill up with air. Have you ever seen someone making balloon animals? If so, you probably noticed that when the artist wanted part of the balloon to remain uninflated, he or she squeezed that area off with the hand. Shallow breathing is like filling only the top half of the balloon because when your abdominal muscles tighten, you stop air from filling the bottom half of your lungs. Fortunately, we can retrain ourselves to breath from the abdomen and thereby reduce our anxiety.

We can also train our bodies relax by practicing progressive muscle relaxation exercises. Essentially, you systematically tense certain muscle groups for about 10 seconds and then relax them for another 10 seconds while focusing on what the relaxed state feels like.[20] Once you teach your body to relax on command, you can call it to do so before beginning to give your speech, again allowing the adrenaline rush to work for you. Exhibit 2.2 (p. 22) offers some suggestions for relaxation techniques.

4. **Systematic desensitization** is a method that reduces apprehension by gradually having people visualize and perform increasingly more frightening events while remaining in a relaxed state. Individuals first learn procedures for relaxation and then learn to apply these to each of the anxiety-producing

visualization
a method that reduces apprehension by helping speakers develop a mental picture of themselves giving a masterful speech

relaxation exercises
breathing techniques and progressive muscle relaxation exercises that help reduce anxiety

systematic desensitization
a method that reduces apprehension by gradually having people visualize and perform increasingly more frightening events while remaining in a relaxed state

© ISTOCKPHOTO.COM/RTIMAGES / © MOODBOARD/JUPITERIMAGES

Exhibit 2.2

Relaxation Techniques

Abdominal Breathing

Lie on the floor and place your hand on your abdomen. Consciously focus on filling your abdomen with air when you inhale by watching your hand rise. Then, as you release the air, watch your hand lower again.

Sighing

By sighing right before it is your turn to speak, you can release tension and lower you anxiety level, allowing the inevitable rush of adrenaline to work for you, not against you.[21]

Progressive Muscle Relaxation Exercises

Consciously tense and relax each of these muscle groups twice and then move on to the next group: hands, arms, shoulders, neck, lips, tongue, mouth, eyes and forehead, abdomen, back, midsection, thighs, stomach, calves, feet, and toes.

II. **Analyze the rationality of these fears.** Most fears about public speaking are, in fact, irrational because public speaking is not life threatening.

III. **Develop positive coping statements to replace each negative self-talk statement.** There is no list of coping statements that will work for everyone; you can develop positive coping statements to replace negative self-talk. Psychologist Richard Heimberg of the State University of New York at Albany asks his clients to consider just how many listeners in an audience of 100 would even notice or care if the clients did what they're afraid of doing when giving a speech. Ultimately, he concludes with the question, "Can you cope with the one or two people who [notice or criticize or] get upset?"[24]

IV. **Incorporate your positive coping statements into your life so that they're second nature.** You can do this by writing your statements down and reading them aloud to yourself each day, as well as before you give a speech. The more you repeat your coping statements to yourself, silently and aloud, the more natural they will become and the more unnatural your negative thoughts will seem.

Exhibit 2.3 is an example of how one student used this process to help her. For an activity that will help you develop positive coping statements to replace negative self-talk, use the CourseMate for SPEAK at

events that they visualize. Thus, they learn to remain relaxed when they encounter these anxiety-producing situations in real life.[22] Essentially, once you are in a relaxed state, you imagine yourself in successively more stressful speech-planning and speech-making situations—for example, researching a speech topic in the library, practicing the speech out loud in front of a roommate, and delivering the final speech to your audience. Once you can maintain a relaxed state while visualizing yourself in each event, you try performing each event while maintaining the learned state of calmness. The ultimate goal of systematic desensitization is to transfer the calm feelings we attain while visualizing to the actual speaking event. Calmness on command—and it works. Research tells us that more than 80 percent of those who try this method reduce their level of anxiety.[23]

5. **Cognitive restructuring** is a process designed to help you systematically change your intrapersonal communication about public speaking. The goal is to replace anxiety-arousing negative self-talk with anxiety-reducing positive self-talk. Effective speakers do so with regard to each of the fears we mentioned earlier: being stared at, the unknown, failure, and becoming fearful. The process consists of four steps:

I. **Identify your fears.** Write down all the fears that come to mind when you know you must give a speech.

cognitive restructuring
a process designed to help you systematically change your intrapersonal communication (self-talk) about public speaking

Exhibit 2.3

Negative Self-Talk Versus Positive Coping Statements

Negative Self-Talk	Positive Coping Statements
I'm afraid I'll stumble over my words and look foolish.	Even if I stumble, I will have succeeded as long as I get my message across.
I'm afraid everyone will be able to tell that I'm nervous.	They probably won't be able to tell I'm nervous, but as long as I focus on getting my message across, that's what matters.
I'm afraid my voice will crack.	Even if my voice cracks, as long as I keep going and focus on getting my message across, I'll succeed at what matters most.
I'm afraid I'll sound boring.	I won't sound boring if I focus on how important this message is to me and to my audience. I don't have to do somersaults to keep the audience's attention, because my topic is relevant to them.

www.cengagebrain.com to access **Web Resource 2.2: Restructure Your Expectations**.

6. Public speaking skills training is the systematic practicing of the skills associated with the processes involved in preparing and delivering an effective public speech with the intention of improving speaking competence and reducing public speaking apprehension. Skills training is based on the assumption that some of our anxiety about speaking in public is because we lack the knowledge and behaviors to be effective. Therefore, if we learn the processes and behaviors associated with effective speech making, then we will be less anxious.[25] Public speaking skills include those associated with the processes of goal analysis, audience and situation analysis, organization, delivery, and self-evaluation.[26]

All six of these methods for reducing public speaking apprehension have successfully helped people reduce their anxiety. If you think you'll experience public speaking apprehension in this course, which of these techniques do you think might help you? Have you already tried some of them in other situations? If they helped, do you think you could apply them to reduce your anxiety about giving a speech? For most people, using several of them yields the best results.[27]

Specific Techniques

Along with the six general methods just discussed, we recommend several specific anxiety-reducing techniques to employ in the days before you deliver your speech and on the day you actually give it.

1. **Allow sufficient time to prepare.** As soon as you know the day you are to give your speech and the expectations for it, identify the topic and begin to prepare. Ideally, you should spend at least a week to 10 days researching, organizing, and practicing your speech.

2. **Use presentational aids.** Recall that one of the major fears that increase public speaking anxiety is the fear of being stared at. Although it is human nature to enjoy being recognized for things we've done well, it is not human nature to be the constant center of attention for a prolonged amount of time.[28] When giving a public speech, that is exactly what happens. All eyes are focused constantly on us, and we can feel conspicuous. Using presentational aids allows you to direct your audience's attention to something else at carefully placed points during the speech,

which can diminish the sense of being constantly stared at and the anxiety that can accompany it.

3. **Practice your speech aloud.** When you practice your speech aloud, you get comfortable hearing yourself talk about your topic. You identify sections of the speech where your ideas may not flow and where you need to do additional preparation. By the third or fourth time you have practiced aloud, you will notice your delivery becoming easier, and you will gain confidence in your ability to present your ideas to others.

Many successful speakers not only practice aloud alone but also practice in front of trusted friends who serve as a "practice" audience and give the speaker feedback. If possible, practice your speech in the room where you'll ultimately deliver it. Hearing your voice in the room where you'll speak reduces anxiety that can arise as a result of the fear of the unknown because you now know what it will feel like to present your speech in that room. Finally, on the night before your speech, review your speech plan immediately before you go to sleep. That way, as you sleep, your mind will continue to prepare.[29]

4. **Dress up.** We tend to feel more confident when we know we look good. By dressing up for your speech, you'll reduce anxiety about being stared at because you feel good about how you look. Also, dressing up demonstrates good character and enhances credibility (ethos) because doing so sends a message that you care about the audience, the occasion, and the message.

5. **Choose an appropriate time to speak.** If you have a choice about whether you will give your speech first, last, or somewhere in between, pick the time that works best for you. Some speakers become more nervous when they sit and listen to others, so they are better off speaking early in the class period. Others find that listening to their peers calms them, so they are better off speaking later in the class period. If given a chance, choose to speak at the time that is optimal for you.

public speaking skills training systematic practicing of the skills associated with the processes involved in preparing and delivering an effective public speech with the intention of improving speaking competence and reducing public speaking apprehension

6. **Use positive self-talk.** Immediately prior to getting up to speak, coach yourself with a short "pregame pep talk." Remind yourself about the importance of what you have to say. Remember all the hard work you have done to be prepared, and recall how good you are when you are at your best. Remind yourself that nervousness is normal and useful. Tell yourself that you are confident and ready.

7. **Face the audience with confidence.** When it is time, walk purposefully to the front. Plant yourself firmly yet comfortably, and take a second or two to look at the audience. Take a deep breath (you might even silently count to five while reviewing the first lines of your speech in your head), and begin your well-rehearsed introduction.

8. **Focus on sharing your message.** Although you may feel nervous, your audience rarely "sees" it. Continue to focus on sharing your ideas with the audience rather than focusing on your nerves.

We tend to feel more confident when we know we look good.

Effective Speech Planning: The Key to Confidence

Whether you are a marketing account manager presenting an advertising campaign idea to your corporate clients, a coach trying to motivate your team for its game with your arch rival, or a student giving a speech in class, you will have more confidence in your likelihood of success when you have developed an effective speech plan—a strategy for achieving your goal.

In this text, you will learn a six-step process for planning your speeches that is grounded in the works of major speech scholars across the ages. Ancient Roman philosophers actually clarified five general rules for effective public speeches more than 2,000 years ago. These rules, known as the canons of rhetoric, which are commonly attributed to Cicero, still hold true today.[30] These five canons are invention (an effective speech has convincing content), arrangement (an effective speech is clearly organized), style (an effective speech uses appropriate language), delivery (an effective speaker delivers the speech with confidence, fluency, and strategic retention aids), and memory (an effective speaker rehearses the speech and creates prompts to remember the speech during delivery). While classical approaches to speech planning were speaker focused, later public speaking scholars recognized that effective speeches were audience centered and addressed the rhetorical situation.[31] In the chapters to come, you will be learning a process for speech planning that is both rooted in ancient wisdom and informed by contemporary understanding of how to prepare effective speeches. The steps in this process are as follows:

1. Select a speech goal that is appropriate to the rhetorical situation.

2. Understand your audience and adapt to it.

3. Gather and evaluate information to use in the speech.

4. Organize and develop ideas into a well-structured outline.

5. Choose, prepare, and use appropriate presentational aids.

6. Practice oral language and delivery style.

As you practice the skills, you will gain confidence in your ability to present your ideas effectively. Let's briefly preview what you will learn in each step.

Step 1: Select a Speech Goal That Is Appropriate to the Rhetorical Situation

Your speech goal is a specific statement of what you want your listeners to know, believe, or do. To arrive at an appropriate speech goal, you need to consider yourself as the speaker, the audience, and the occasion. Doing so will encourage your audience to pay attention because they will perceive your speech as relevant and timely.

You begin by selecting a topic that you know something about and that interests you or is important to you. Although there could be times in your life when you must speak on a topic that is unfamiliar to you, in the great majority of speaking experiences, you will speak on topics that meet these tests.

Because your speech will be given to a particular audience, before you get very far you need to think about your audience: Who are they? What do they need to know about your topic? What do they already know? To answer these questions, you need to make a preliminary audience analysis based on their gender, culture, average age, education level, occupation, income level, and group affiliation. Then you can assess the kinds of material the audience is likely to know and the information they are likely to respond to.

Likewise, you need to consider the occasion: What is the size of the audience? When will the speech be given? Where will the speech be given? Are there any peculiarities of the room? What is the time limit for the speech? What are the audience expectations for the speech?

Once you determine a topic based on your interest and expertise, the audience, and the occasion, you are ready to phrase your speech goal. Every speech has a general and a specific goal. For most classroom speeches, the general goal is usually either to inform, where your goal is shared understanding, or to persuade, where your goal is to convince your audience to believe something or persuade them to take action. Some other general goals, which Aristotle called ceremonial speeches, are called for on specific special occasions (e.g., to introduce, to entertain, and to celebrate).[32]

Your specific speech goal articulates exactly what you want your audience to understand, believe, or do. For instance, Gina, who is majoring in health and nutrition, might phrase her informative speech goal as, "I want the audience to understand three methods for ridding our bodies of harmful toxins." And Glen, a bioengineering major, might phrase his persuasive speech goal as, "I want to convince my audience of the value of genetic engineering."

Step 2: Understand Your Audience and Adapt to It

Once you have a clear and specific speech goal based on the speaker, audience, and occasion, you begin the task of understanding your audience more fully and how to adapt your speech to it. Audience adaptation is the process of tailoring your speech's information to the needs, interests, and expectations of your listeners. As you prepare for a speech, you will consider your specific audience's needs and seek to meet these needs continually throughout the speech-planning and -practicing process.

For any speech, it is important to consider the audience's initial level of interest in your goal, their ability to understand

> **speech goal**
> a specific statement of what you want your listeners to know, believe, or do
>
> **audience adaptation**
> the process of tailoring your speech's information to the needs, interests, and expectations of your listeners

The specific goal of your speech will depend on your audience.

the content of the speech, and their attitude toward you and your topic.

If you believe your audience has very little interest in your speech topic, you will need to adapt to them so that they understand why the topic is important. Not only will you need to adapt your speech by piquing audience interest, but if you believe that your audience doesn't know much about your topic, you will want to provide the basic information they need to understand your speech. Finally, you will need to adapt to your audience's initial attitudes toward your topic.

Step 3: Gather and Evaluate Information to Use in the Speech

When you select a topic, although you already know something about it, you will usually need additional information. In addition to drawing on material from your own knowledge and experiences, you can draw on the expertise of others by reading printed materials, as well as by conducting interviews and surveys. Regardless of the sources of your information, you will need to evaluate the information you gather and select the items you deem valid and truthful. The more you know about your topic, the easier it is to evaluate the information you uncover in your research. For instance, Nora, who is a member of the local volunteer Life Squad, will be able to give a better speech on CPR than a person with no practical experience who has learned about CPR from reading

and interviewing others. Why? Because, as a volunteer, Nora has actually used this skill and has real experiences to draw from.

Step 4: Organize and Develop Ideas Into a Well-Structured Outline

You begin the process of organizing your speech by identifying the two to four major ideas you want your audience to remember. You then turn each major idea into a complete sentence. These sentences will become the main points for the body of your speech. Next you combine your speech goal with each major idea into a succinct thesis statement that describes specifically what you want your audience to understand, believe, or do when you have finished speaking. This process provides the initial framework, or macrostructure, of your speech.

Main points must be carefully worded and then they must be arranged in an organizational framework that helps the audience understand and remember them. In later chapters, we'll consider several frameworks you may want to use in your speeches.

Having identified, phrased, and ordered the main points, you are now ready to outline the body of the speech. Although it is tempting to work out a speech as it comes to mind, speeches are not essays, and you will be more effective if you prepare a thorough outline.

After you have outlined the body of the speech, which includes noting elaborations, you can outline your introduction and conclusion. Your introduction should get attention, establish listener relevance and speaker credibility, and lead into the body of the speech. Because there are never any guarantees that your audience is ready to pay full attention to the speech, an effective introduction draws the audience into what you are saying.

In your conclusion, you will want to remind the audience of your main points and speech goal. You should do this in a creative way with a clincher that ties back to the attention catcher, which helps the audience remember.

When you think you are finished, review the outline to make sure that the parts are relevant to your goal. The length of your outline will depend on the length of your speech. In a speech of three to five minutes, the outline may contain up to 50 percent or more of the words in the speech; for a five- to eight-minute speech, 33 to 50 percent may be included. And in speeches of 30 to 45 minutes, the outline may contain as few as 20 percent of the words.

Although an expert who speaks frequently on a topic may be able to speak effectively from a mental outline or a few notes, most of us benefit from the discipline of organizing and developing a formal speech outline.

Step 5: Choose, Prepare, and Use Appropriate Presentational Aids

"A picture is worth a thousand words" is an old saying with a lot of wisdom. So, even for a very short speech, you may decide to use a visual aid that will help clarify, emphasize, or dramatize what you say. Because audiences understand and retain information better when they receive that information through more than one sense, objects, models, charts, pictorial representations, projections, and computer graphics that are well constructed and integrated smoothly maximize the effect of a speech. As you get ready to practice your speech, make sure you consider when to use presentational aids, how long to use them, and how to integrate them so that everyone can see and/or hear them.

Step 6: Practice Oral Language and Delivery Style

In your practice sessions, you need to choose the wording of main points and supporting materials carefully. If you have not practiced various ways of phrasing your key ideas, you run the risk of missing a major opportunity for communicating your ideas effectively. In practice sessions, work on the appropriateness, accuracy, clarity, and vividness of your wording. Recall that these language choices make up the microstructure of your speech.

Although a speech is composed of words, how effective you will be is also largely a matter of how well you use your voice and body in delivering your speech. You will want to present the speech intelligibly (understandably), conversationally, and expressively. You will also want to use good posture and eye contact (look at members of the audience while you are speaking) to appear confident and comfortable,

as well as facial expressions and gestures that emphasize emotional intentions and clarify structure.

Very few people can present speeches effectively without considerable practice. Practicing out loud gives you confidence that you can talk conversationally and comfortably with your audience and accomplish your speech goal within the time limit. Don't try to memorize the speech. Trying to memorize your speech is likely to add to your public speaking anxiety because you may also fear forgetting what you planned to say. Instead, deliver your speech extemporaneously—that is, practiced until the ideas of the speech are firmly in mind, even though the wording varies a bit from practice to practice and during the actual presentation.

Exhibit 2.4 (p. 28) summarizes the six action steps of an effective speech plan in outline form. These steps will be explained in more detail in later chapters of this book. As you read, you will see specific speech-preparation activities that are related to each action step. By completing all of these activities, you will gain confidence in your ability to be effective when you give your speech.

> **narrative/personal experience speech**
> a presentation in which you recount an experience or experiences you have had and the significance you attach to it or them
>
> **moral**
> a life lesson about right and wrong

Preparing a Narrative/ Personal Experience Speech

Walter R. Fisher, a professor of communication at the University of Southern California, claims that human beings understand and interpret the world around us through storytelling.[33] He and others propose narrative theory as a primary way in which we make sense of the world around us—that is, through stories. The **narrative/personal experience speech** is a presentation in which you recount an experience or experiences you have had and the significance you attach to it or them. In it, you talk about the setting, characters, and events as they serve as "good reasons" for accepting a moral you deem important. A **moral** is simply a life lesson about right and wrong. This speech is an excellent opportunity for you to try out the basic speech preparation action steps we have just introduced. Let's look at how Danelle applied these steps to prepare her speech "Me and My Aunt Barb."

The first step is to develop a speech goal appropriate to the public speaking situation. For her narrative/personal experience speech assignment, Danelle considered several experiences but finally chose the story of her and her Aunt Barb.

Exhibit 2.4

How to Create an Effective Speech Plan

I. Select a speech goal that is appropriate to the rhetorical situation (Chapter 4).
   A. Brainstorm and concept map to select a topic you know something about and that is important to you.
   B. Analyze your audience to assess their familiarity with and interest in your topic.
   C. Consider how the occasion affects what is appropriate for you to talk about.
   D. Develop a speech goal statement tailored to your audience and the occasion.

II. Understand your audience and adapt to it (Chapter 5).
   A. Understand audience diversity.
   B. Understand audience initial interest in and attitude toward your topic.
   C. Adjust content to be appropriate for your audience's current understanding of, interest in, and attitude toward your topic.
   D. Determine how you will establish your credibility with your audience.

III. Gather and evaluate information to use in the speech (Chapter 6).
   A. Examine what you know already about your topic and where you need additional information.
   B. Locate, evaluate, and select types and sources.
   C. Record relevant information on research cards.
   D. Cite sources.

IV. Organize and develop ideas into a well-structured outline (Chapters 7 and 8).
   A. Identify the two to four major ideas you want your audience to remember.
   B. Combine your speech goal with these major ideas to form a thesis statement with main point preview.
   C. Develop your main points.
   D. Develop and outline the speech body.
   E. Create an introduction that gets attention, establishes listener relevance and credibility, and states your thesis with main point preview.
   F. Create a conclusion that both summarizes your goal and main points and that leaves your audience with a vivid impression that provides a sense of closure.
   G. Compile a list of sources.
   H. Review and revise the outline as needed.

V. Choose, prepare, and use appropriate presentational aids (Chapter 9).
   A. Consider visual or other presentational aids that will help clarify, emphasize, or dramatize what you say.
   B. Make sure your aids use another symbol system (beyond just words alone).
   C. Make sure your visual aids are large enough to be seen.
   D. Make sure your audio aids are loud enough to be heard in the back of the room.
   E. Plan when to use presentational aids and how to integrate them during the speech.

VI. Practice oral language and delivery style (Chapters 10 and 11).
   A. Practice until the wording is accurate, clear, vivid, and appropriate.
   B. Practice until the delivery is intelligible, conversational, and expressive.
   C. Practice integration of presentational aids until you can do so confidently and smoothly.
   D. Continue practicing until you can deliver the speech extemporaneously within the time limit.

experiences. She also planned to use main points and statements within them that would encourage listeners to relate.

Because it was a personal experience narrative, Danelle didn't need additional research; she only needed to reconstruct the details of the stories she would share about her experiences growing up with her Aunt Barb.

Danelle began her speech with a description of her Aunt Barb, then recounted the story of her aunt as her babysitter, and concluded by reinforcing the point of her story.

When you use narratives/personal experiences as a speech or in a speech, remember the following elements:

- A narrative has a point to it, usually a life lesson about right and wrong. Think carefully about the point of your story and make sure it is appropriate.

- A narrative is developed with supporting details that give background to and embellish the story so that the point has maximum effect. Be sure to describe the character(s), setting(s), and events with vivid details to which listeners can relate.

- Narrative drama can be increased by using dialogue. Dialogue gives an audience the experience of "being there" and increases their interest and involvement.

- Most narratives dramatize because they recount emotional incidents. They may be funny, tragic, or frightening, but effectively told personal experiences establish an emotional bond between speaker and audience.

She knew that the speech would be for an audience of about 15 classmates who were all traditional-age college students, that the assignment was a narrative/personal experience speech, and that the time limit was three to five minutes.

Her general goal was to inform. Specifically, Danelle wanted the audience to appreciate how her experiences with her Aunt Barb as her babysitter shaped Danelle's morals.

Her strategy for audience adaptation included using personal pronouns and other means of creating common ground by telling about her personal

Danelle enhanced her speech with two photographs she displayed using the multimedia projector and screen in the front of the room. The first was of her and her Aunt Barb playing at the park when Danelle was a little girl. The second was a picture of her with her Aunt Barb, which was taken at a recent family reunion. Danelle used clear and vivid language to tell her story. She also practiced her speech several times until she was comfortable with her ability to tell the story.

Narrative/Personal Experience Speech Evaluation Checklist

General Criteria

You can use this checklist to critique a narrative/personal experience speech that you hear in class. (You can also use it to critique your own speech.) As you listen to the speaker, consider what makes a speech effective. Then, answer the following questions.

Content

1. Did the speaker's narrative make an important point? *(moral of the story)* _____

2. Did the speaker provide sufficient details about the setting(s), character(s), and event(s)? _____

3. Did the speaker dramatize the story with dialogue or emotional incidents? _____

4. Did the speaker offer listener relevance links? _____

5. Did the speech fall within the time constraints of the assignment? _____

Structure

1. Did the speech provide all of the basic elements of an effective speech: introduction, body, conclusion, and transitions? _____ *(macrostructure)*

2. Did the introduction catch the audience's interest? _____ state the goal of the speech? _____ preview the main points of the speech? _____

3. Were transitions provided between each main point? _____

4. Did the conclusion remind the audience of the main points? _____ motivate the audience to remember the main points of the speech? _____

5. Did the speaker use words that were accurate and clear? _____ vivid and emphatic? _____ appropriate and inclusive? _____ *(microstructure)*

Delivery

1. Was the speaker's voice intelligible? _____ conversational? _____ expressive? _____

2. Did the speaker look up from his or her notes most of the time and make eye contact with the audience? _____

3. Did the speaker use appropriate facial expressions to convey emotion? _____

4. Did the speaker use appropriate gestures to reinforce important points? _____

5. Did the speaker appear to be poised and confident? _____

You can use the CourseMate for SPEAK at www.cengagebrain.com to access this checklist, complete it online and compare your feedback to that of the authors, or print a copy to use in class.

THERE ARE EVEN MORE STUDY TOOLS FOR THIS CHAPTER
AT WWW.CENGAGEBRAIN.COM

- **Interactive Videos**
- **Speech Builder Express**
- **Printable Flash Cards**
- **Interactive Games**

- **Chapter Review Cards**
- **Online Quizzes with Feedback**
- **Speech Studio available upon instructor request**

Listening and Responding Effectively

Learning Outcomes

LO^1 Why is it important to study listening in a public speaking course? | LO^2 What is the difference between listening and hearing? | LO^3 What are five different types of listening? | LO^4 What strategies can you employ to improve your listening skills? | LO^5 How can you constructively critique speeches you hear?

As Ms. Fisher finished her remarks about improving restaurant service, she said, "And remember, the goal is to encourage customers to perceive their overall dining experience positively, not to move in and out too quickly. Return business is what is most important for success." As Brady, Jill, and Max were leaving the workshop, Brady said, "I was glad to hear that Ms. Fisher recognized the importance of moving customers in and out quickly." "That wasn't her point," said Jill. "She said that return business is the goal." "I'm sure she emphasized efficiency," responded Brady. "Max, what do you think she said?" "I don't have a clue. I was thinking about how I'm going to pay rent tomorrow because it cost a lot more to repair my car than I thought it would."

Listening

Have you had times when you'd swear that you heard right when you didn't? If your answer is "Not me," then we congratulate you, for this example illustrates two of the three most common listening problems: hearing what was said but misunderstanding, not remembering what was said, and missing what was said.

Recall that communication is the process of creating shared meaning. For communication to be effective, the *speaker* must present the message clearly and compellingly. Equally important, however, is that the *listener* understands and accurately remembers what was said.

Obviously, before you can listen, you must first hear what is said. Although listening depends on hearing, the two are not the same. **Hearing** is simply the biological process that occurs when the brain detects sound waves. In contrast to hearing, listening occurs after the brain has detected the sound waves and is sorting out what those waves mean. According to the International Listening Association, "**Listening** is the process of receiving, attending to, constructing meaning from, and responding to spoken or nonverbal messages."[1] Listening is important because 50 percent or more of our time in communication is spent listening.[2] Although all of us have spent a great deal of time learning to read and write, fewer than 2 percent of us have had any formal listening training.[3] In fact, even when they try to listen carefully, most people remember only about 50 percent of what they hear shortly after hearing it and only about 25 percent two days later.[4]

hearing
the biological process that occurs when the brain detects sound waves

listening
the process of receiving, attending to, constructing meaning from, and responding to spoken or nonverbal messages

© ISTOCKPHOTO.COM/NICOLAS HANSEN

Yet effective listening is a key to success in most occupations. One survey of North American executives revealed that 80 percent believe listening is one of the most important skills needed in the corporate environment.[5] Frankly, listening skill (or lack thereof) is often at the root of company success or failure. When employees fail to listen effectively to instructions, they usually make mistakes, which cost time and money. And when supervisors don't listen effectively to employees when they share concerns about potential problems or their creative ideas and solutions, again, the result may be lost time and money. Results of a study of more than 6,000 organizational crisis events revealed that in nearly every instance, employees and others had warned management repeatedly about potential problems. Had management listened effectively, the crises may have been avoided.[6] And, of course, when the employees of a company do not listen and respond to customers, they are bound to fail. So it simply makes sense to improve listening skills.

To be an effective communicator, you must understand and practice effective listening skills. During this course, you might give as many as six speeches, but you will probably listen to more than 60. As you listen, you can practice the skills you learn in this chapter.

In this chapter, we discuss five different types of listening, how you can improve your listening skills, and guidelines for providing a constructive and ethical speech critique.

Types of Listening

Although we spend most of the time we are communicating listening, the type of listening we engage in varies based on the situation. So in order to be an effective listener in different situations, you must consider your purpose for listening. Scholars have identified five types of listening based on five different purposes.[7] Each type requires a different degree of psychological processing.

In an **appreciative listening** situation, your goal is simply to enjoy the thoughts and experiences of others. When we listen to music for enjoyment and to speakers because we like their style, we are engaged in appreciative listening. In **discriminative listening**, your goal is to understand the speaker's meaning conveyed in other ways than the words themselves—for example, nonverbal cues such as rate, pitch, inflection, and gestures. So when a doctor is explaining the results of a test, a patient listens carefully not only to what the doctor is saying but also to the nonverbal cues that indicate whether the results are troubling or routine. In **comprehensive listening**, your goal is to understand, remember, and recall what has been said. We listen comprehensively, for example, to professors giving lectures or speakers at training seminars. In **empathic listening**, your goal is to be a sounding board to help another sort through feelings. We listen empathically, for example, when we listen to a close friend grieve over the death of a loved one. Finally, in **critical listening**, your ultimate goal is to evaluate the worth of a message. When we listen to salespeople trying to convince us that their brand is better than the others, we are listening critically. Because you need to hear, understand, evaluate, and assign worth to the message, as well as remember and recall it, critical listening requires more psychological processing than the others. We turn now to some techniques you can employ to improve your listening skills in both face-to-face and virtual settings.

Improving Your Listening Skills

Effective listening is a complex psychological process made up of five steps. These steps are attending, understanding, remembering, evaluating, and responding to the message (see Exhibit 3.1). In this section, we offer some techniques for improving your skills related to each step.

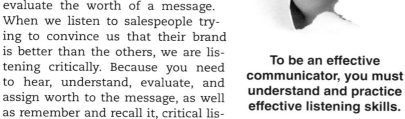

To be an effective communicator, you must understand and practice effective listening skills.

Attending

Attending is paying attention to what the speaker is saying regardless of extraneous interference. Poor listeners have difficulty exercising control over what they attend to, often letting their mind drift to thoughts totally unrelated to the speech. One reason for this stems from the fact that people typically speak at a rate of about 120 to 150 words per minute, but our brains can process between 400 and 800 words per minute.[8] This means we usually assume we know what a speaker is going to say before he or she finishes saying it. That gives our minds time to wander from the message.

Not only does the gap between speaking rate and processing create opportunities for inattention, but research suggests that the average attention span for adults today is 20 minutes or less.[9] Some reports even claim that our attention spans have become considerably shorter thanks to the Internet, satellite TV, DVR, and mobile phones.[10] Consider your own experiences listening to speeches, class lectures, and other extended presentations. Do you ever find yourself daydreaming, reading a text message, or updating Facebook? If you want to find out how long your attention span is, use the CourseMate for SPEAK at www.cengagebrain.com to access **Web Resource 3.1: Attention Span Self-Test**.

Exhibit 3.1

Effective and Ineffective Listening Behaviors

	Effective Listening Behavior	Ineffective Listening Behavior
Attending to the Speech	Physically and mentally focusing on what is being said, even when information doesn't seem relevant	Seeming to listen but looking out window and letting your mind wander
	Adjusting listening behavior to the specific requirements of the situation	Listening the same way regardless of type of material
Understanding/ Remembering Speech Information	Determining organization by identifying goals, main points, and supporting information	Listening to individual bits of information without regard for structure
	Asking yourself questions to help you identify key aspects of the speech	Seldom or never reconsidering what was said
	Silently paraphrasing to solidify understanding	Seldom or never paraphrasing
	Seeking out subtle meanings based on nonverbal cues	Ignoring nonverbal cues
	Taking good notes	Relying on memory alone
Evaluating and Responding	Assessing quality of content, structure, delivery	Relying on gut reactions

comprehensive listening
your goal is to understand, remember, and recall what has been said

empathic listening
your goal is to be a sounding board to help another sort through feelings

critical listening
your ultimate goal is to evaluate the worth of a message

attending
paying attention to what the speaker is saying regardless of extraneous interference

understanding
the ability to assign accurate meaning to what was said

To be an effective listener, then, you need to train yourself to focus on what people are saying regardless of potential distractions. Let's consider four techniques for doing so.

1. **Get physically ready to listen.** Good listeners create a physical environment that reduces potential distractions and adopt a listening posture. For example, you might turn off background music, your cell phone, and your computer. You can also adopt a listening posture by sitting upright in your chair, leaning slightly forward, stopping any random physical movement, and looking directly at the speaker.[11]

2. **Resist mental distractions while you listen.** Block out wandering thoughts when they creep into your head. These thoughts may stem from a visual distraction (such as someone entering the room while the speaker is talking), an auditory distraction (such as people chatting beside you during a speech), or a physical distraction associated with body aches, pains, or discomfort (such as wondering what you'll eat for lunch because your stomach is growling). Consciously attending to these mental distractions will help you focus on the message and improve your listening skills.

3. **Suspend judgment while you hear the speaker out.** Far too often, we let a person's

mannerisms and words "turn us off." If you find yourself upset by a speaker's ideas on a controversial topic, instead of tuning out or getting ready to argue, work that much harder to listen objectively so that you can understand the speaker's position before you react. Likewise, even when a speaker uses language that is offensive to you, you need to persevere and not be distracted. If we are not careful, we may become distracted when a speaker mumbles, stumbles over words, or fumbles with his or her notes. We need to focus instead on what is being said to be effective listeners.

4. **Identify the benefits of attending to the speaker's words.** At times, we do this when the speaker prompts us to, when a professor says something like, "Pay attention to this because it will be on the test." But you can also provide your own motivation. As you listen, ask yourself why and how you might use the information to improve some aspect in your own life—for instance, to help you solve a work-related problem or to improve personally.

Understanding and Remembering

Understanding is the ability to assign accurate meaning to what was said. Sometimes we may not fully understand a speaker's message because the

Ready!

Not Ready!

speaker uses unfamiliar words or complex concepts, and sometimes we might miss the emotional intent of the message. **Remembering** is being able to retain and recall information we have heard. Sometimes we have difficulty remembering because we fail to realize personal relevance while the message is being communicated. We can also have difficulty remembering because we are bombarded with so many messages all the time every day. Let's consider five listening techniques that can help you understand and remember the messages you hear.

1. **Determine the speaker's organization.** Determining the organization helps you establish a framework for understanding and remembering the information.[12] In any extended message, an effective speaker has an overall organizational macrostructure, which includes a goal, main points that develop the goal, and details that develop each main point. Effective listeners mentally (or physically) outline the organization so that when the speech is over, they can cite the goal, the main points, and some of the key details. To be an effective listener, ask yourself, "What does the speaker want me to know or do?" (goal); then ask, "What are each of the main points?" Finally, ask, "What details explain or support each of the main points?"

2. **Ask questions.** Although ethical listeners demonstrate respect by waiting until the speaker is finished to ask questions, you can make notes of any questions you have as you listen. Some of these questions may eventually be answered as the speaker moves through the presentation. However, others may not. If so, you can pose these questions during the question-and-answer period following the presentation, privately approach the speaker after the presentation, or use the questions to do additional research about the topic yourself later.

3. **Silently paraphrase key information.** A paraphrase is putting into your own words the meaning you have assigned to a message. It is not simply repeating what has been said. After you have listened to a message, you should be able to summarize your understanding of it. So after the speaker explains the criteria for selecting the best cell phone plan, you might say to yourself, "In other words, the key to deciding whether an unlimited plan is cost-effective depends on how many minutes I'm likely to spend talking on the phone each month."

4. **Observe nonverbal cues.** We interpret messages more accurately when we observe the nonverbal behaviors that accompany the words. Good speakers use their tone of voice, facial expressions, and gestures to emphasize important points and clarify structure. You can improve your listening skills by noticing where and how the speaker is attempting to emphasize or clarify points and then keying in on those comments.

5. **Take good notes.** Note taking is a powerful method for improving your memory of what you have heard in a speech. Not only does note taking provide a written record that you can go back to, but also by taking notes, you take a more active role in the listening process.[13]

What constitutes good notes varies by situation. For a short speech, good notes may consist of a statement of the goal, a brief list of main points, and a few of the most significant details. For a lengthy and rather detailed presentation, good notes will also include more detailed statements of supporting material, as well as questions that arise while listening. Review the basics of effective listening and note taking by using the CourseMate for SPEAK at www.cengagebrain.com to access **Web Resource 3.2: Effective Listening and Note Taking**.

remembering
being able to retain and recall information we have heard

paraphrase
putting into your own words the meaning you have assigned to a message

The Keys to Understanding and Remembering

- Determine the speaker's organization
- Ask questions
- Silently paraphrase key information
- Observe nonverbal cues
- Take good notes

© ISTOCKPHOTO.COM/CHRIS LAMPHEAR

evaluating
critically analyzing what is said to determine its truthfulness, utility, and trustworthiness

responding
providing feedback to the speaker about what is being said; usually occurs in the form of nonverbal behaviors

constructive critique
an analysis of a speech or presentation that evaluates how well a speaker meets a specific speaking goal while following the norms for good speaking and that recommends how the presentation could be improved

Evaluating and Responding

Evaluating is critically analyzing what is said to determine its truthfulness, utility, and trustworthiness. Critical analysis is especially important when the speaker expects you to believe, support, or act on what was said. If you don't critically analyze what you hear, you risk going along with ideas that violate your values. Responding is providing feedback to the speaker about what is being said. Responding to a speech usually occurs in the form of nonverbal behaviors such as smiling, nodding one's head in agreement, and applauding after the speaker finishes, though in some cultures audience members may give short verbal responses as well. Sometimes, however, you need to prepare a formal written evaluation, or critique, of a presentation by a classmate, colleague, or employee. Typically, a critique is based on your critical analysis of how well the speech and speaker performed on specific key criteria.

Preparing a Constructive Critique

A constructive critique is an analysis of a speech or presentation that evaluates how well a speaker meets a specific speaking goal while following the norms for good speaking and that recommends how the presentation could be improved. Essentially, a critique allows you to provide a speaker with *meaningful* feedback. Constructive critiques follow four guidelines.

First, effective critiques communicate specific observations. Comments like "great job" or "slow down" are too vague to truly help a speaker improve. Instead, describe specific things the speaker did to make you conclude that the speech was great. Did she use transitions in a way that helped you follow her train of thought? Or point out specific places where you would have liked the speaker to present the material at a slower pace.

Second, effective critiques begin with observations about what a speaker did well before turning to observations about what the speaker could do better. Begin with positive observations so that you reinforce what the speaker did well. When we are reinforced for what we have done, we are more likely to continue doing it. By the same token, there is room for improvement in any speech. Because the goal of a critique is to help the speaker improve, describe the specific problems you observe in the speech and then offer suggestions for overcoming them.

Third, effective critiques follow observation statements with explanations about how and why the observed behavior affected the speech. For example, if you suggest that the speaker slow down while previewing the speech's main points, your statement will be more helpful if you also explain that the speaker's rate did not allow the audience time to remember the points.

Finally, effective critiques are phrased so that it's clear they reflect your personal perceptions, not "truth." You can ensure this by using "I" rather than "you" language. For example, instead of using "you" language to say "You need to slow down," use "I" language. For example, "During the preview of main points, I had trouble listening because they were presented faster than I could understand and remember them."

Content of Constructive Critiques

A constructive critique offers observations about a speech's content, structure, and delivery. Comments on content focus on *what* the speaker said and an analysis of the topic and supporting material. For example, you might comment on how effectively the speaker used reasoning, or you might comment on the breadth and depth of the information used to develop each main idea. You might observe how relevant, recent, or credible the speaker's evidence seemed to be. Exhibit 3.2 illustrates ineffective and effective constructive critique comments regarding content.

Exhibit 3.2

Ineffective and Effective Comments About the Content of a Narrative/Personal Experience Speech

Ineffective	Effective
• Interesting stories • Too short	• I liked the story about your trip to the carnival. The many details you provided made it sound really fun. • I would have liked to hear another example for each main point. This would have helped me better understand why the carnival was so significant to you.

© CENGAGE LEARNING 2011

Comments on structure may be addressed to both the overall organization (macrostructure) and wording (microstructure) of the speech. You might provide feedback on the clarity of the speaker's goal, transitions, summary, or ordering of main ideas. You might also talk about the speaker's language and

Exhibit 3.3

Ineffective and Effective Comments About the Structure of a Narrative/Personal Experience Speech

Ineffective	Effective
• Nice transitions • Boring introduction	• Your transitions reminded me of the main point. • Because you finished one main point and introduced the upcoming main point in your transition, I found it easy to follow your ideas. • I would have tuned in to the speech more quickly if you had begun with a great story about the carnival to capture my attention before starting your thesis.

Exhibit 3.4

Ineffective and Effective Comments About the Delivery of a Narrative/Personal Experience Speech

Ineffective	Effective
• Great gestures! • Slow down.	• I really liked how you gestured while you stated your transitions. It made it even clearer to me that we were moving to the next main point. • When you previewed your main points, you were speaking so quickly that I didn't catch them. For me, it would be helpful if you had spoken more slowly so I could have processed the main points. That way, I would have followed along better throughout the speech.

style choices. Exhibit 3.3 offers some examples of ineffective and effective constructive critique comments regarding structure.

Comments on delivery focus on how the speaker used his or her voice and body. In commenting on voice, you might consider how intelligible, conversational, and emotionally expressive the speaker was. You may also comment on the speaker's use of body, poise, gestures, facial expressions, and eye contact. Consider if the speaker's mannerisms distracted you from the speech's message or enhanced it. Comment on the specific behaviors that contributed to your opinion of the speaker's use of body. Exhibit 3.4 provides a couple of examples of ineffective and effective constructive critique comments regarding delivery.

Certainly, you can help other speakers improve by offering effective constructive critiques. You can also help yourself by completing a self-critique after each speech you give using the same approach you use to critique others. Begin by noting one or two specific things you did well in terms of content, structure, and delivery. Then, consider one thing you'll focus on improving for your next speech. This self-critique approach is actually a form of cognitive restructuring that can help reduce your anxiety because it forces you to temper negative self-talk with positive self-talk immediately

after your speech. Exhibit 3.5 presents a list of general criteria that you may draw upon when preparing a constructive critique. You can use these criteria as a starting point for giving feedback to a speaker or critiquing your own speech.

Exhibit 3.5

General Criteria for a Constructive Critique

1. **Content of the speech**
   - Does the speaker establish common ground and adapt the content to the audience's interests, knowledge, and attitudes?
   - Does the speaker seem to have expertise in the subject areas?
   - Does the speaker have high-quality sources for the information given in the speech?
   - Does the speaker reveal the sources of the information?
   - Are the sources relevant? recent? varied? distributed throughout the speech?
   - Does the information presented explain or support each of the main points?
   - Are presentational aids appropriate and well used?
   - Is each main point supported with breadth? depth? listener relevance?

2. **Structure of the speech**
   - Does the introduction of the speech get attention, establish listener relevance and credibility, and lead into the topic?
   - Has the speaker stated a clear goal for the speech?
   - Are the main points of the speech clearly stated, parallel, and meaningful?
   - Do transitions lead smoothly from one point to another?
   - Does the information presented explain or support each of the main points?
   - Does the speaker use language that is appropriate, accurate, clear, and vivid?
   - Does the speaker use a compelling style?
   - Does the conclusion summarize the main points and end with a clincher?

3. **Delivery of the speech**
   - Does the speaker sound intelligible? conversational? expressive?
   - Is the presentation fluent?
   - Does the speaker look at the audience?
   - Does the speaker use appropriate facial expressions?
   - Were the pronunciation and articulation acceptable?
   - Does the speaker have good posture?
   - Does the speaker have sufficient poise?

As we will see later in this text, there are additional aspects of content, delivery, and structure you will want to consider in your constructive critique. We will provide additional criteria in speech-specific checklists that you can use to evaluate each type of speech you study in this text. These customized critique sheets will include the primary criteria (specific skills) your instructor is expecting speakers to demonstrate in the particular speech, as well as general criteria in Exhibit 3.5—skills that speakers will attempt to meet in all speeches.

Speech Evaluation Checklist

General Criteria Checklist for Providing Constructive Critique

1. Did you offer specific comments about your observations? _____ *(Consider what, where, and how.)*

2. Did you begin with observations about what the speaker did well, reinforcing positive behavior? _____

3. Did you offer specific suggestions for what the speaker could do to improve? _____ *(Consider what, where, and how.)*

4. Did you provide an explanation for each comment you made? _____

5. Did you focus on the *speech*, using "I" language to phrase each statement as a personal perception? _____

6. Did you avoid focusing on the *speaker personally* and avoid using "you" language, which can sound like a personal attack? _____

You can use the CourseMate for SPEAK at www.cengagebrain.com to access this checklist, complete it online and compare your feedback to that of the authors, or print a copy to use in class.

THERE ARE EVEN MORE STUDY TOOLS FOR THIS CHAPTER AT WWW.CENGAGEBRAIN.COM

- Interactive Videos
- Speech Builder Express
- Printable Flash Cards
- Interactive Games
- Chapter Review Cards
- Online Quizzes with Feedback
- Speech Studio available upon instructor request

Learning Your Way

89% of students surveyed found the interactive online quizzes valuable.

We know that no two students are alike. SPEAK was developed to help you learn speech communication in a way that works for you.

Not only is the format fresh and contemporary, it's also concise and focused. And, SPEAK is loaded with a variety of supplements, like chapter review cards, printable flash cards, and more.

At the CourseMate for SPEAK at **www.cengagebrain.com**, you'll also find **Interactive Quizzing**, **Crossword Puzzles**, **Games**, **Interactive Video Activities**, and **Audio Study Tools** to test your knowledge of key concepts, and plenty of resources to help you study no matter what learning style you like best!

Selecting an Appropriate Speech Goal

Learning Outcomes

LO[1] What strategies can you use to brainstorm for speech topics? | LO[2] What should you consider about your audience when determining your speech goal? | LO[3] How can you find out about your audience before giving your speech? | LO[4] In what ways might the occasion for your speech influence your speech goal? | LO[5] How should you phrase your specific speech goal?

Romeo Brown has been invited to speak to a student assembly at the inner-city middle school he attended. He has a lot he could say to these students who are so much like him, but he really wants them to understand what they need to do now to have a shot at going to college. Dan Wong is taking a public speaking class. His first speech is scheduled for two weeks from tomorrow. As of today, he doesn't have the foggiest idea what he is going to talk about.

In real-life settings, people are invited to speak because they have expertise on a particular subject or have some relationship to the audience. Nevertheless, choosing exactly what to speak about is usually left in the hands of the speaker. So, although Romeo may have an idea about what the audience expects, he, like Dan, will need to take the first action step, which is to determine a specific speech goal that is appropriate to the rhetorical situation.

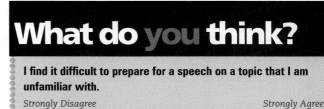

What do you think?

I find it difficult to prepare for a speech on a topic that I am unfamiliar with.

Strongly Disagree   *Strongly Agree*
1   2   3   4   5   6   7   8   9   10

You must determine your specific speech goal in light of the rhetorical situation, the reason your speech needs to be given (exigence). Recall from Chapter 1 (p. 9), and as Exhibit 4.1 (p. 42) reiterates, these circumstances include the speaker (you), the audience, and the occasion (the setting, including the purpose, audience, expectations, and location). Because the audience is a crucial component of the speaking situation, your specific speech goal must be based on audience analysis, the study of the intended audience for your speech, and audience adaptation, the process of tailoring your speech's information to the needs, interests, and expectations of your listeners. This step in the speech-making process is rooted in what communication scholars refer to as uncertainty reduction theory.[1] Of course, effective speakers continually adjust their analysis of their audience and adapt their speech accordingly throughout the speech-planning and speech-making process, but these steps begin at the point of determining your specific speech goal.

In this chapter, we explain each of the five substeps that help speakers determine a specific speech goal that is appropriate to the rhetorical situation. These five substeps are identifying possible topics, analyzing the audience, understanding the occasion, choosing a topic, and, finally, developing a specific speech goal statement. Although we discuss each task separately, in practice they overlap and can be completed in a different order.

ACTION STEP 1:
Select a Speech Goal That Is Appropriate to the Rhetorical Situation

A. Brainstorm and concept map for topics.
B. Analyze your audience.
C. Analyze the rhetorical situation.
D. Develop a speech goal statement tailored to your audience and the occasion.

Exhibit 4.1
The Rhetorical Situation

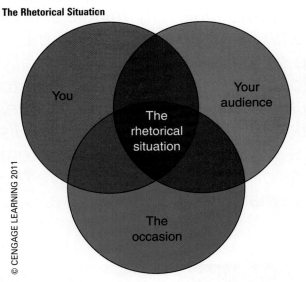

Identifying Potential Topics

Our speech topics should come from subject areas in which we already have some knowledge and interest. What is the difference between a subject and a topic? A **subject** is a broad area of expertise, such as movies, renewable energy, or the Middle East. A **topic** is a narrow, specific aspect of a subject. So if your broad area of expertise is movies, you might feel qualified to speak on a variety of topics such as how the Academy Awards nomination process works; the relationships among movie producers, directors, and distributors; or how technology is changing movie production.

In this section, you will learn how to identify subject areas that interest you and then, from those subject areas, to identify and select potential specific topics that you can use for the speeches you will present.

Listing Subjects

You can identify potential subjects for your speeches by listing those areas that (a) are important to you and (b) you know something about. These areas will probably include such things as your probable vocations or areas of formal study, your hobbies or leisure activities, and your special interests. So if sales and marketing are your actual or prospective vocations, skateboarding and snowboarding are your favorite activities,

subject
a broad area of expertise, such as movies, renewable energy, or the Middle East

topic
a narrow, specific aspect of a subject

and problems of illiteracy, substance abuse, and obesity are your special concerns, then these are subject areas from which you can identify topics for your speeches.

At this point, it is tempting to think, "Why not just talk on a subject I know an audience wants to hear about?" But in reality, all subject areas can interest an audience when speakers use their expertise or insight. If you speak on a topic that really interests you, you will find it easier to prepare for and be enthusiastic about presenting.

Holly, a beginning speech student, began thinking about subjects for upcoming class speeches. She chose to organize her subjects by using three broad headings: (a) major and career interests, (b) hobbies and activities, and (c) issues and concerns.

Brainstorming for Topic Ideas

Recall that a topic is a specific aspect of a subject, so from one subject you can list numerous top-

ics by **brainstorming**—an uncritical, nonevaluative process of generating associated ideas. When you brainstorm, you list as many ideas as you can without evaluating them. Brainstorming allows you to take advantage of the basic commonsense principle that just as it is easier to select a correct answer to a multiple-choice question than to think of the answer to the same question without the choices, so too is it easier to select a topic from a list than to come up with a topic out of the blue.

Holly decided she wanted to give a speech on the subject of birding. By brainstorming, she was able to come up with a list of possible topics that included the following: what is birding, how to identify birds, endangered birds, choosing and using binoculars for birding, keeping a bird list, and backyard birding. For practice brainstorming, use the CourseMate for SPEAK at www.cengagebrain.com to access **Web Resource 4.1: Brainstorming**.

Concept Mapping for Topic Ideas

You can use concept mapping to identify specific topics and related areas. **Concept mapping** is a visual means of exploring connections between a subject and related ideas.[2] To generate connections, you might ask yourself questions about your subject, focusing on who, what, where, when, and how. Holly decided that she wanted to give her speech on the topic of endangered birds, but then she felt that even that topic was too broad, so she used concept mapping to help her identify more specific topics on endangered birds. In Exhibit 4.2, you can see an example of what Holly's concept map looked like. Notice how concept mapping allowed Holly to think more deeply about a general topic idea that she had brainstormed and develop several more specific topics that could be used in shorter speeches or in speeches with different audiences.

Speech Planning Action Step 1, Activity 1A will help you develop a list of topic ideas to use for your speeches in this course. See the Student Response box immediately following the activity for a sample of how one student completed this exercise.

Exhibit 4.2

Holly's Concept Map

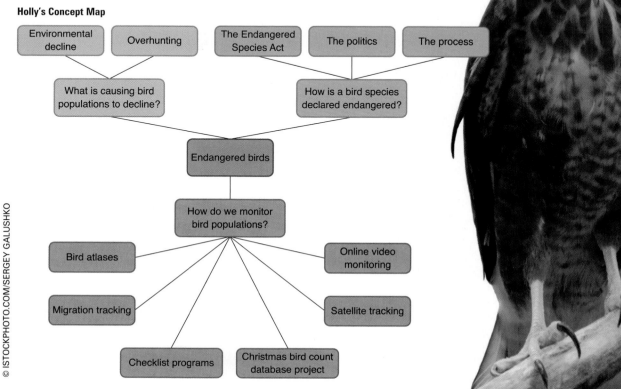

Action Step 1
Activity 1A

Using Brainstorming and Concept Mapping to Identify Speech Topics
The goal of this activity is to help you identify prospective topics for speeches.

1. Develop a subject list.
   a. Divide a sheet of paper into three columns. Label column 1 "major and career interests," label column 2 "hobbies and activities," and label column 3 "concerns and issues."
   b. Working on one column at a time, identify subjects of interest to you. Try to identify at least three subjects in each column.
   c. Place a check mark next to the one subject in each list that you would most enjoy speaking about.
   d. Keep the lists for future use in choosing a topic for an assigned speech.
2. For each subject you have checked, brainstorm a list of topics that relate to that subject.
3. Look at the topics you have brainstormed. In which do you have the most interest and expertise? Place a check mark beside one or two of these.
4. Then, for each item on the brainstorm list that you have checked, develop a concept map to identify smaller topic areas and related ideas that might be developed into future speeches.

You can go online to print a worksheet that will help you complete this activity. Go to the CourseMate for SPEAK at www.cengagebrain.com to access Action Step 1, Activity 1A.

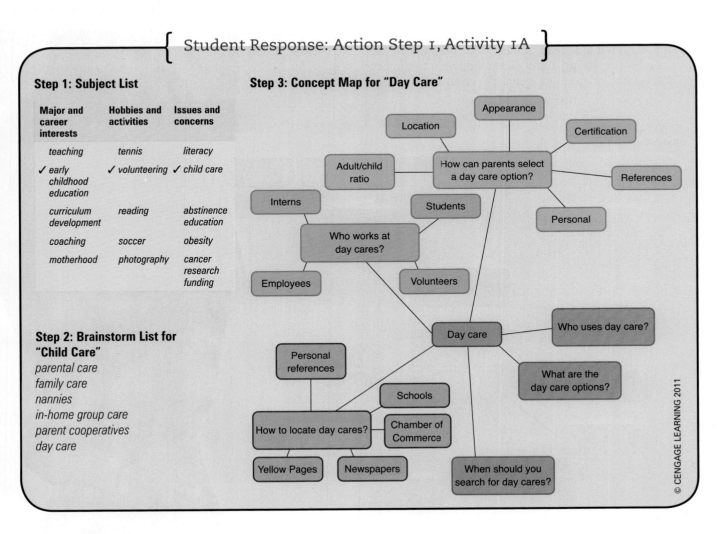

Student Response: Action Step 1, Activity 1A

Step 1: Subject List

Major and career interests	Hobbies and activities	Issues and concerns
teaching	tennis	literacy
✓ early childhood education	✓ volunteering	✓ child care
curriculum development	reading	abstinence education
coaching	soccer	obesity
motherhood	photography	cancer research funding

Step 2: Brainstorm List for "Child Care"
parental care
family care
nannies
in-home group care
parent cooperatives
day care

Step 3: Concept Map for "Day Care"

© CENGAGE LEARNING 2011

Analyzing the Audience

Because speeches are presented to a particular audience, before you can finally decide on your topic, you need to understand who will be in your prospective audience. Recall that audience analysis is the study of the intended audience for your speech. During your audience analysis, you will want to develop a demographic profile of your audience that includes age, gender, socioeconomic background, race, ethnicity, religion, geographic uniqueness, and language. You will also want to understand audience members' knowledge of and attitudes toward your topic. This information will help you choose from your topic list one that is appropriate for most audience members. You will use your audience analysis to tailor your speech to meet the needs, interests, and expectations of your listeners. To read an interesting article on the importance of careful audience analysis, use the CourseMate for SPEAK at www.cengagebrain.com to access **Web Resource 4.2: Defining Your Audience**.

Types of Audience Data Needed

The first step in analyzing the audience is to gather audience demographic data and subject-specific information to determine in what ways audience members are similar to and different from you and from one another.

Demographic Audience Data

Helpful demographic information about your audience includes each member's age, education, gender, income, occupation, race, ethnicity, religion, geographic uniqueness, and language. It is also important to know about your audience members' level of knowledge and attitude toward your subject (see Exhibit 4.3). You will use the demographic information you collect for several purposes.

First, demographic information helps you choose a specific topic and the main ideas you will present. The information you collect about your audience helps you make educated inferences about what they know about your subject area and what their attitudes are toward it. These inferences can then help you narrow your focus and choose an appropriate specific topic. For example, imagine that you want to talk about some aspect of the Internet, which is a very broad subject. Your audience analysis reveals that your audience is composed of college students, most under 21 years old, so you decide to talk about the dangers of blogging. You choose this topic based on the reasonable assumption that traditional-age college students are web savvy and understand what blogging is.

Second, demographic information can help you discover the ways in which your audience members are similar to and different from one another and from you. This information will help you tailor your speech to your audience. In planning your speech, it is just as important to recognize and adapt to differences as it is to acknowledge similarities. For example, while the majority of your audience may be under the age of 21, you may have several audience members who are "nontraditional" students and somewhat older. If you begin your speech on the dangers of blogging with the assumption that everyone in the audience is familiar with blogging and base all your examples on today's youth culture, older audience members may not relate to your speech.

Third, understanding who is in your audience will help later when you develop appropriate listener relevance links, which are statements of how and

listener relevance link statement alerting listeners about how a main point or subpoint relates to them or why they should care about it

---

Exhibit 4.3
Demographic Audience Analysis Questions

Age: What is the age range of your audience, and what is the average age?

Education: What percentage of your audience has a high school, college, or postgraduate education?

Sex: What percentage of your audience is male? female?

Socioeconomic background: What percentage of your audience comes from high-, middle-, or low-income families?

Occupation: Is a majority of your audience from a single occupational group or industry, or do audience members come from diverse occupational groups?

Race: Are most members of your audience of the same race, or is there a mixture of races?

Ethnicity: What ethnic groups are in the audience? Are most audience members from the same cultural background?

Religion: What religious traditions are followed by audience members?

Geographic uniqueness: Are audience members from the same state, city, or neighborhood?

Language: What languages do a significant number of members of the audience speak as a first language? What language (if any) is common to all audience members?

Knowledge of subject: What can I expect the audience already knows about my subject? How varied is the knowledge level of audience members?

Attitude toward subject: What can I expect my audience's feelings to be about my subject?

why the ideas you offer are of interest to your listeners. If your audience research indicated that about half of your audience has blogged, a fourth has only read blogs, and another fourth has never seen a blog, then during your speech, you would use listener relevance links that were appropriate for both those who are savvy and those who aren't. So, for example, you might pique everyone's interest with this link: "If you have blogged, you may not be aware of the long-term potential dangers in this practice. And if you have not yet blogged, you probably know and care about someone who has. So what I am about to say might prevent you or someone you care about from making a costly mistake." See Exhibit 4.3 for a list of questions to answer when acquiring demographic information about an audience.

Subject-Related Audience Data

Not only will you want to understand the demographic makeup of your audience, but you will also want to learn about the average knowledge level that your audience members have on your subject, their interest in the subject, their attitudes toward the subject, and their perceptions of your credibility. Knowing this information will help you reach your goals of (a) forming reasonable generalizations about your audience and (b) adapting your speech to embrace subject-related diversity. Let's take a closer look at each of these pieces of information.

1. **Audience knowledge.** What can you expect your average audience member to already know about your subject? What topics are likely to provide new information for most of them? It is important that you choose a topic geared to the background knowledge you can expect audience members to have. When you choose a topic that most audience members already know about, you will bore them if you are not really creative. On the other hand, if you choose a topic for which your audience has insufficient background, you will have to provide the background or risk confusing them.

2. **Audience interest.** How attracted are audience members likely to be to your subject? For instance, suppose you would like to speak on the subject of cancer drugs. If your audience is made up of health-care professionals, you can assume that because of their vocations they will be curious about the subject. But if your audience is this beginning public speaking class, then unless they have had a personal experience with cancer, they may not naturally relate to your subject. So you can either choose another topic or make an extra effort to determine why cancer drugs are important to your audience and articulate this relevance in your speech.

3. **Audience attitude toward the subject.** How does your audience feel about your subject? This is especially important when you want to influence their beliefs or move the audience members to action. You can determine your audience's attitudes toward your

subject directly by surveying them, which we will discuss in the next section. If you cannot survey the audience directly, you might try to see if published opinion polls related to your subject are available. Then you can estimate your audience members' attitudes by studying these opinion polls and extrapolating their results to your audience. To access links to one of the world's most respected polling organizations, use the CourseMate for SPEAK at www.cengagebrain.com to access **Web Resource 4.3: Public Opinion Polls**.

Finally, in some cases, you will be forced to estimate the audience's attitudes from the speaking occasion and the demographic information you have acquired. Once you understand your audience's attitude toward your subject, you can choose a topic that will allow you to influence rather than alienate the audience. For example, a speech calling for strict gun control is likely to be perceived differently by classmates who grew up in an urban environment where gang violence is a problem than by those who grew up in a suburb where gun crimes are relatively rare or in a rural area where many people are hunters.

4. **Audience attitude toward you as a speaker.** Will your audience recognize you as a subject matter expert? Will they know that beforehand, or will you have to establish your credibility as you speak? **Credibility** is based on the perception that you are knowledgeable (have the necessary understanding that allows you to explain the topic well), trustworthy (are honest, dependable, and ethical), and personable (show enthusiasm, warmth, friendliness, and concern for audience members). You will want to choose a topic that allows the audience to perceive you as credible and to believe that you know what you are talking about.

Methods for Gathering Audience Data

1. **You can collect data through surveys.** Although it is not always possible, the most direct way to collect audience data is to survey the audience. A **survey** is a questionnaire designed to gather information directly from people. Some surveys are done as interviews; others are written forms that are completed by the participants. The four kinds of items or questions most likely to be used in a survey are called two-sided, multiple-response, scaled, and open-ended.

- **Two-sided items** force the respondent to choose between two answers, such as yes/no, for/against, or pro/con. Suppose you wanted to understand your audience members' attitudes on the subject of TV. You might phrase several questions with two-sided answers, such as:

> Do you believe prime-time TV shows contain too much violence?
>
> _____ Yes _____ No

Two-sided items are easy to use in an interview, and the answers are easy to sort during analysis.

- **Multiple-response items** give the respondent several alternative answers from

credibility
the perception that you are knowledgeable, trustworthy, and personable

survey
questionnaire designed to gather information directly from people

two-sided items
survey items that force the respondent to choose between two answers, such as yes/no, for/against, or pro/con

multiple-response items
survey items that give the respondent several alternative answers from which to choose

What is your audience's attitude?

which to choose. These items are especially useful for gathering demographic data. For example:

> Which best describes your religious tradition?
> ____ Protestant
> ____ Evangelical
> ____ Catholic
> ____ Jewish
> ____ Buddhist
> ____ Muslim
> ____ Atheist
> ____ Other

Multiple-response items can also be used to assess the extent of knowledge that audience members have about a topic. For example, a speaker might assess audience members' knowledge about diamonds with the following question:

> Please indicate what you know about diamonds by placing an X next to each topic you already know about.
> ____ How to value a diamond
> ____ How diamonds are made
> ____ How to tell the difference between a real diamond and a fake
> ____ Blood diamonds

- **Scaled items** measure the direction and/or intensity of an audience member's feeling or attitude toward something. For example:

> Indicate the extent to which you agree or disagree with the following statement:
> There is too much violence on prime-time TV.
> ____ Strongly agree   ____ Agree
> ____ Neutral   ____ Disagree
> ____ Strongly disagree

Scaled items can also be used to assess audience interest in a subject. For example:

> Please indicate, by checking the appropriate response, how interested you are in learning about each of the following.

> How to value diamonds:
> ____ Very interested
> ____ Somewhat interested
> ____ Uninterested
> How diamonds are cut:
> ____ Very interested
> ____ Somewhat interested
> ____ Uninterested
> Blood diamonds:
> ____ Very interested
> ____ Somewhat interested
> ____ Uninterested

- **Open-ended items** encourage respondents to elaborate on their opinions without forcing them to answer in a predetermined way. These items yield rich information, but the wide variety of responses make them difficult to analyze. For example, to determine what you would need to do to establish your credibility on the subject of TV violence, you might ask:

> How can you tell if someone is an expert on TV violence?

2. **You can gather data through informal observation.** If you are familiar with members of your audience (as you are with members of your classroom audience), you can get much of the important data about them through informal observation. For instance, after being in class for even a couple of sessions, you should be able to estimate the approximate age or age range and the ratio of men to women. Because you are all in college, you know the educational level. As you listen to your classmates talk, you will learn more about their interest in, knowledge of, and attitudes about many issues.

3. **You can gather data by questioning the person who invited you to speak.** When you are invited to speak to a group you are unfamiliar with, ask your contact person to answer the demographic questions in Exhibit 4.4. Even when the person cannot provide answers to all of the questions, the information you get will be helpful. If necessary, probe your contact person to at least estimate answers for those demographics that are likely to be most important for your topic.

4. **You can make educated guesses about audience demographics and attitudes.** If you can't get information in any other way, you will have to make educated guesses based on indirect information such as the general makeup of the members of a community or organization. Suppose, for example, that you are asked by a nonprofit group to give a speech on volunteer opportunities to a meeting of high school guidance counselors. You can infer a number of things about the members of this audience. First, all will be college-educated high school counselors from your area. They will all speak English. There are likely to be more women than men. Their knowledge of the specific opportunities at your agency will vary.

Whether you survey your audience, rely on informal observation, question the person who invited you to speak, or make educated guesses about audience

---

Exhibit 4.4

Audience Analysis Summary Form

My subject is _____

Data were collected:

_____ by survey _____ by questioning the person who invited me

_____ by direct observation _____ by educated guessing

Demographic Data

1. The average audience member's education level is _____ high school _____ college _____ postgraduate.

2. The ages range from _____ to _____ . The average age is about _____ .

3. The audience is approximately _____ percent male and _____ percent female.

4. My estimate of the average income level of the audience is _____ high _____ moderate _____ low.

5. Most audience members are of _____ the same occupation/major (which is _____) _____ different occupations/majors.

6. Most audience members are of _____ the same race (which is _____) _____ a mixture of races.

7. Most audience members are of _____ the same religion (which is _____) _____ a mixture of religions.

8. Most audience members are of _____ the same nationality (which is _____) _____ a mixture of nationalities.

9. Most audience members are from _____ the same state _____ the same city _____ the same neighborhood _____ different areas.

10. Most audience members speak _____ English as their first language _____ English as a second language (ESL).

Subject-Specific Data

1. The average audience member's knowledge of the subject is likely to be _____ extensive _____ moderate _____ limited because _____ .

2. The average audience member's interest in this subject is likely to be _____ high _____ moderate _____ low because _____ .

3. The average audience member's attitude toward my subject is likely to be _____ positive _____ neutral _____ negative because _____ .

4. My initial credibility with the audience is likely to be _____ high _____ medium _____ low because _____ .

Conclusion

Based on these data _____
_____ ,

which relate to my speech topic in the following ways:
_____
_____

I will tailor my speech in the following ways: _____
_____
_____

demographics and subject-related information, you will want to record the information in a form that is convenient to use. Exhibit 4.4 presents an audience analysis summary form that you can use to summarize your findings.

Now that you understand audience analysis, you can complete Speech Planning Action Step 1, Activity 1B. See the Student Response box immediately following the activity for a sample of how one student completed this exercise.

Action Step 1
Activity 1B

Analyzing Your Audience

1. Decide on a method for gathering audience data.
2. Collect the data.
3. Copy or duplicate the Audience Analysis Summary Form (Exhibit 4.4).
4. Use the information you have collected to complete the form.
5. Write two short paragraphs to describe your initial impression of audience demographics, knowledge, and attitudes toward your subject.

6. Save the completed form. You will refer to this audience analysis information to address listener relevance throughout the speech-planning process.

You can download an online copy of this form. Go to the CourseMate for SPEAK at www.cengagebrain.com to access the chapter resources for Chapter 4 and then click Audience Analysis Summary Form.

{ Student Response: Action Step 1, Activity 1B }

Audience Analysis Summary Form
Demographic Data

1. The average audience member's education level is ___ high school _X_ college ___ postgraduate.
2. The ages range from _19_ to _24_. The average age is about _20_.
3. The audience is approximately _65_ percent male and _35_ percent female.
4. My estimate of the average income level of the audience is ___ high _X_ moderate ___ low.
5. Most audience members are of _X_ the same occupation/major (which is *communication students*) ___ different occupations/majors.
6. Most audience members are of _X_ the same race (which is *white*) ___ a mixture of races.
7. Most audience members are of _X_ the same religion (which is *Judeo-Christian tradition*) ___ a mixture of religions.
8. Most audience members are of _X_ the same nationality (which is *American*) ___ a mixture of nationalities.
9. Most audience members are from ___ the same state ___ the same city ___ the same neighborhood _X_ different areas.
10. Most audience members speak _X_ English as their first language ___ English as a second language (ESL).

Summary description of key audience characteristics: From these data, I conclude that most audience members are similar to one another and to me. We are all students at UC Most of us are around 20 years old, which suggests that we have a common generational view. Because UC is a commuter school, most of us

are probably in the middle to lower socioeconomic class. There are more men than women in the class, and we are mostly white middle-class Americans. Although we have some religious diversity, most of us come from Judeo-Christian religious traditions.

Subject-Specific Data

1. The average audience member's knowledge of the subject is likely to be ___ extensive ___ moderate _X_ limited because *my audience members are mostly communication students, not geology or mineralogy students*.
2. The average audience member's interest in this subject is likely to be ___ high _X_ moderate ___ low because *without encouragement, they have no need to know about this subject. Mineralogy is hardly a trendy subject*.
3. The average audience member's attitude toward my subject is likely to be ___ positive _X_ neutral ___ negative because *the audience doesn't really have any information about the topic*.
4. My initial credibility with the audience is likely to be ___ high ___ medium _X_ low because *this is our first speech and they don't know I am a geology major whose family owns a jewelry store*.

Summary: Most audience members don't know a lot about diamonds and have only a moderate interest in the subject, although it is not a controversial subject. So I will need to make sure to address listener relevance and include listener relevance links throughout the speech to maintain my audience's interest during the entire speech.

Using Audience Data Ethically

Once you have collected demographic and subject-related data from audience members, you can use what you have learned to tailor your speech to their interests, needs, and expectations. To demonstrate respect for everyone in your audience, you will want to avoid making inappropriate or inaccurate assumptions based on demographic or subject-related information you have collected. Two potential pitfalls you'll want to avoid are marginalizing and stereotyping.

Marginalizing is the practice of ignoring the values, needs, and interests of certain audience members, leaving them feeling excluded from the speaking situation. **Stereotyping** is assuming all members of a group have similar knowledge levels, behaviors, or beliefs simply because they belong to the group. For example, general demographic information like age and education can help you make reasonable assumptions about your audience. But if I find out most of my audience members are 20 to 25 years old and have blogged, I might marginalize the few members who have never blogged if I proceed as though everyone has done so. Similarly, if I find out that the average age of my audience is 65, I might stereotype and assume that most of the audience knows nothing about blogging when, in fact, several of them have done so.

You can minimize your chances of marginalizing or stereotyping by recognizing and acknowledging the demographic diversity your audience analysis reveals. **Demographic diversity** is the range of demographic characteristics represented in an audience. So while the average age of your audience may be 65, there may also be some in the audience who are much younger. Second, collecting audience data that are directly related to your subject can help you minimize stereotyping. For example, to gauge what your audience knows about blogging, you might include a few questions when collecting subject-related data that address what they know about this topic.

Understanding the Occasion

The occasion of the speech is its setting, which includes the purpose, audience expectations, and location. The answers to several questions about the occasion should guide your topic selection and other parts of your speech planning.

1. **What are the special expectations (i.e., the exigence) for the speech?** Why is this speech being given? Every speaking occasion is surrounded by expectations. At an Episcopalian Sunday service, for example, the congregation expects the minister's sermon to have a religious theme. For your classroom speeches, a major expectation is that your speech will meet the assignment requirements. Whether the speech assignment is defined by purpose (to inform or to persuade), by type (expository or demonstration), or by subject (book analysis or current event), your topic should reflect the nature of that assignment.

2. **What is the appropriate length for the speech?** The time limits for classroom speeches are usually quite short, so you will want to choose a topic that is narrow enough to be accomplished in the time allotted. "Three Major Causes of the Declining Honeybee Population" can be presented in five minutes, but "A History of Human Impact on the Environment" cannot. It is important to understand and adhere to audience expectations regarding time limits—this demonstrates respect for your listeners. For example, consider when a teacher kept you in class longer than the allotted time. You were likely frustrated because it seemed the instructor failed to respect your other classes, your job, or the other commitments you juggled along with that particular course.

3. **How large will the audience be?** If you will be speaking to a small audience (fewer than 50 people), you will be physically close enough to them to talk in a normal voice and to move about. In contrast, if you will be speaking to a large audience, you will probably need a microphone, and you'll be less likely to be able to move about.

4. **Where will the speech be given?** Because rooms vary in size, lighting, seating arrangements, and the like, consider the factors that may affect your presentation. In a long, narrow

marginalizing the practice of ignoring the values, needs, and interests of certain audience members, leaving them feeling excluded from the speaking situation

stereotyping assuming all members of a group have similar knowledge levels, behaviors, or beliefs simply because they belong to the group

demographic diversity the range of demographic characteristics represented in an audience

room, you may need to speak louder than usual to reach the back row. In a dark room, make sure the lights are on and the blinds or shades are open to bring in as much light as possible. Venues outside school settings offer even greater variations in conditions. Ask for specific information about seating capacity, shape, number of rows, nature of lighting, existence of a speaking stage or platform, distance between speaker and first row, and so on before you speak. If possible, visit the place and see it for yourself.

5. **When will the speech be given?** A speech given early in the morning requires a different approach from one given right after lunch or in the evening. If a speech is scheduled after a meal, for instance, the audience may be lethargic, mellow, or even on the verge of sleep. As a result, it helps to insert more "attention getters" (examples, illustrations, and stories) to counter potential lapses of attention.

6. **Where in the program does the speech occur?** If you are the only speaker or the featured speaker, you have an obvious advantage: You are the focal point of audience attention. In the classroom, however, or other events where there are many speeches, your place on the schedule may affect how you are received. If you go first, you may need to "warm up" the listeners and be prepared to meet the distraction of a few audience members' strolling in late. If you speak last, you must counter the tendency of the audience to be weary from listening to several speeches.

7. **What equipment is necessary to give the speech?** For some speeches, you may need a microphone, a flip chart, an LCD projector and screen, or a hookup for your laptop computer. In most instances, speakers have some kind of stand, but it is wise not to count on it. If the person who has invited you to speak has any control over the location and equipment, be sure to explain what you need, but always have alternative plans in case what you have asked for is unavailable. It is frustrating to plan a PowerPoint presentation, for example, and then discover that there's no place to plug in the computer!

Speech Planning Action Step 1, Activity 1C will help you understand the occasion so that you take into consideration your purpose, audience expectations, and location as you choose your topic and develop your speech. See the Student Response box immediately following the activity for a sample of how one student completed this exercise.

Action Step 1 Activity 1C

Understanding the Occasion

The goal of this activity is to help you understand your speech occasion. Fill in answers to the following questions:

1. What are the special expectations for the speech? _____
2. What is the appropriate length for the speech? _____
3. How large will the audience be? _____
4. Where will the speech be given? _____
5. When will the speech be given? _____
6. Where in the program does the speech occur? _____
7. What equipment is necessary to give the speech? _____

Write a short paragraph mentioning which aspects of the setting are most important for you to consider in speech preparation and why.

You can complete this activity online, print it, and, if requested, e-mail it to your instructor. Go to the CourseMate for SPEAK at www.cengagebrain.com to access Action Step 1, Activity 1C.

{ Student Response: Action Step 1, Activity 1C }

1. What are the special expectations for the speech? *an informative speech*
2. What is the appropriate length for the speech? *four to six minutes*
3. How large will the audience be? *13–15 people*
4. Where will the speech be given? *614 Dyer Hall*
5. When will the speech be given? *9:30 a.m., Tuesday*
6. Where in the program does the speech occur? *I will try to go first.*
7. What equipment is necessary to give the speech? *LCD projector, computer, and screen*

Time is certainly important: Four to six minutes is not very long. I plan to time my speech when I practice to make sure I stay within the expected time limits. Also, I want to make sure that I am one of the first speakers.

Choosing a Topic and Developing a Speech Goal Statement

Armed with your topic lists and the information you have collected on your audience and the occasion, you are ready to select a topic that will be appropriate to the public speaking situation.

As you review your list of topics, compare each to your audience profile. Are there some topics that are too simple for this audience's knowledge base? Too difficult? Are some topics likely to be more interesting to the audience? How do the audience's age, ethnicity, and other demographic features mesh with each topic? By asking these and similar questions, you will be able to identify topics that are appropriate for the audience. Then consider the occasion. Are some topics too broad for the time allotted? Are there topics that won't meet the special expectations? Answers to these and other questions will help you identify the topics that are appropriate to your setting.

Speech Planning Action Step 1, Activity 1D will help you select your topic. See the Student Response box immediately following the activity for a sample of how one student completed this exercise.

Action Step 1
Activity 1D

Choosing a Topic

Use your responses to Action Step Activities 1A, 1B, and 1C to complete this activity.

1. Look over the concept map you prepared in Activity 1A. List each of the specific topics that you generated:

    —————— —————— ——————
    —————— —————— ——————
    —————— —————— ——————

2. Using the information you compiled in Activity 1B, the audience analysis, compare each topic to your audience profile. Eliminate topics that seem less appropriate for this specific audience. Write each of the topics that remain:

    —————— ——————
    —————— ——————

3. Using the information you compiled in Activity 1C, your analysis of the occasion, compare each of the remaining topics to your setting profile. Eliminate topics that seem less appropriate. Write each of the topics that remain:

    —————— ——————

4. The remaining topics are appropriate to your public speaking situation; you can be confident that you can develop an appropriate speech from any of these. So, from this list, select the one that you are most excited about sharing with others. My topic will be:

    ——————

You can go online to the CourseMate for SPEAK at www.cengagebrain.com to complete this activity and print out a worksheet that will help you choose your topic.

© ISTOCKPHOTO.COM/NARVIKK

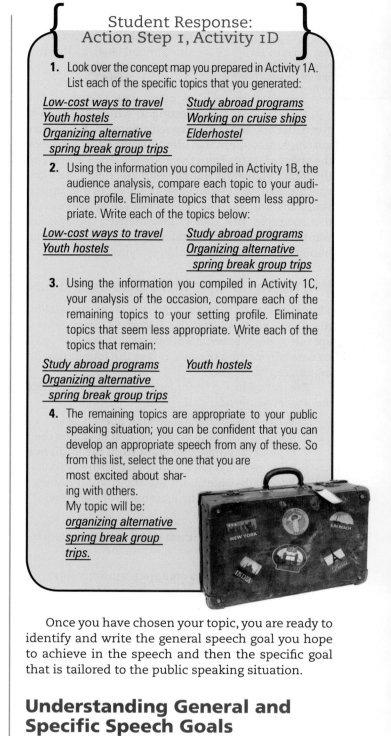

Once you have chosen your topic, you are ready to identify and write the general speech goal you hope to achieve in the speech and then the specific goal that is tailored to the public speaking situation.

Understanding General and Specific Speech Goals

The **general goal** is the overall intent of the speech. Most speeches intend to entertain, to inform, or to persuade, even though each type of speech may include elements of other types. The general goal is usually dictated by the occasion. (In this course, your instructor is likely to specify it.) Most speeches given by

general goal
the overall intent of the speech

adults as part of their job or community activities have the general goal of informing or persuading.

Whereas the general goal is often determined by the setting in which a speech is given, the **specific goal**, or specific purpose of a speech, is a single statement that identifies the exact response the speaker wants from the audience. For a speech on the topic "Vanishing Honeybees," one might state the specific goal as, "I would like the audience to understand the four reasons honeybees are vanishing." In this example, the goal is informative. The speaker wants the audience to understand the reasons that honeybees around the world are dying off.

Phrasing a Specific Speech Goal

The occasion (or in the case of this class, the assignment) usually dictates the nature of your general speech goal. A specific speech goal, however, must be carefully crafted because it lays the foundation for organizing the speech.

The following guidelines can help you craft a well-worded specific goal.

1. **Write a draft of your general speech goal using a complete sentence that specifies the type of response you want from the audience.** Julia, who has been concerned with and is knowledgeable about the subject of illiteracy, drafts the following statement of her general speech goal.

   I want my audience to understand the effects of illiteracy.

   Julia's draft is a complete sentence, and it specifies the response she wants from the audience: *to understand* the effects of illiteracy. Her phrasing tells us that she is planning to give an informative speech.

2. **Revise the statement (and the infinitive phrase) until it indicates the specific audience reaction desired.** If your objective is to explain (to inform), the infinitive that expresses your desired audience reaction could be "to understand," "to recognize," "to distinguish," or "to identify." If you see the goal of your speech as changing a belief or calling the audience to action, then your general goal is persuasive and can be reflected by the use of such infinitives as "to believe," "to accept," "to change," or "to do." If Julia wanted to convince her audience, her specific goal might be worded:

   I want my audience to believe that illiteracy is a major problem.

3. **Make sure that the goal statement contains only one idea.** Suppose Julia had first written:

   I would like the audience to understand the nature of illiteracy and its effects on the individual and society.

   This statement is not a good specific goal because it includes two distinct ideas: understanding the nature of illiteracy and understanding the specific effects that may follow from being illiterate. Either one is a worthy goal—but not both in one speech. Julia needs to choose one of these ideas. If your goal statement includes the word *and*, you have more than one idea.

4. **Revise your statement until it describes the precise focus of your speech (the infinitive phrase articulates the complete response you want from your audience).** Julia's draft "I want my audience to understand the effects of illiteracy" is a good start, but the infinitive phrase "to understand the effects of illiteracy" is vague. Exactly what about illiteracy is it that Julia wants her audience to understand? Here is where you need to consider your audience analysis and adapt your specific goal in ways that address listener relevance. What is it about illiteracy your particular audience should know and why?

   At this point, Julia may need to begin doing some research to focus her ideas and refine her goal statement. Because Julia knows her classmates all have the goal of becoming gainfully employed after graduating, and because she knows how illiteracy places people in the workplace at a disadvantage, she might rephrase her specific goal to read:

   I want the audience to understand three ways illiteracy hinders a person's effectiveness in the workplace.

   This statement meets the criteria for a good specific goal statement because it indicates the specific desired audience reaction and it contains only one explicit idea that is the focus of the speech.

A good specific goal statement is important because it will guide your research as you prepare the speech. Once you have completed your research, you will expand your specific goal statement into a thesis statement, which will be the foundation on which you will organize the speech. Exhibit 4.5 gives several additional examples of general and specific informative and persuasive goals.

Exhibit 4.5

General and Specific Goals

Informative Goals	
General goal:	To inform the audience about e-books
Specific goal:	I want the audience to understand the differences between the Kindle and the Sony/iPad approaches to electronic books.
General goal:	To inform the audience about forms of mystery stories
Specific goal:	I want the audience to be able to identify the three basic forms of mystery stories.

Persuasive Goals	
General goal:	To persuade the audience that saving for retirement is important
Specific goal:	I want the audience to begin a personal ROTH IRA funded this year with at least 2 percent of their income.
General goal:	To persuade the audience to get involved with the food bank
Specific goal:	I want to persuade the audience to volunteer to work on the campus food drive for our local food bank.

Speech Planning Action Step 1, Activity 1E will help you develop a well-written specific goal statement for your speech. See the Student Response box immediately following the activity for a sample of how one student completed this exercise.

Action Step 1
Activity 1E

Developing a Specific Goal

Type of speech: _____

1. Write a draft of your general speech goal using a complete sentence that specifies the type of response you want from the audience. _____
2. Revise the infinitive to make it reflect the specific audience response you desire. _____
3. Check the number of ideas expressed in the statement. If the statement contains more than one idea, select one and rewrite the statement. _____
4. Improve the statement so that it describes the precise focus of your speech as it relates to your intended audience. _____

Write the final draft of the specific goal:

_____

_____

_____

You can complete this activity online with Speech Builder Express, a speech outlining and development tool that will help you complete the action steps in this book to develop your speech. You can access Speech Builder Express through the CourseMate for SPEAK at www.cengagebrain.com.

Student Response:
Action Step 1, Activity 1E

Type of speech: *informative*

1. Write a draft of your general speech goal using a complete sentence that specifies the type of response you want from the audience.
   I want the audience to understand how a fire is lit without a match.
2. Revise the infinitive to make it reflect the specific audience response you desire.
   I want the audience to be able to light a fire without a match.
3. Check the number of ideas expressed in the statement. If the statement contains more than one idea, select one and rewrite the statement.
   I want my audience to recognize the basic steps necessary in lighting a fire without a match.
4. Improve the statement so that it describes the precise focus of your speech as it relates to your intended audience.
   I want my audience to recognize the three basic steps involved in lighting a fire without a match.

Write the final draft of the specific goal:

I want my audience to recognize the three basic steps involved in lighting a fire without a match.

THERE ARE EVEN MORE STUDY TOOLS FOR THIS CHAPTER AT WWW.CENGAGEBRAIN.COM

- **Interactive Videos**
- **Speech Builder Express**
- **Printable Flash Cards**
- **Interactive Games**
- **Chapter Review Cards**
- **Online Quizzes with Feedback**
- **Speech Studio available upon instructor request**

Adapting to Audiences

Learning Outcomes

LO[1] Why is it important to articulate the relevance of your speech to your audience? | LO[2] What should you do if your audience does not share your attitude about the topic of your speech? | LO[3] What can you do to help your audience see you as trustworthy and knowledgeable about your topic? | LO[4] Why is it important to address diverse learning styles in your speech? | LO[5] What can you do to overcome language and cultural differences between you and your audience?

Suzanne entered the studio to anchor the 5:00 evening news for the first time, thinking, "I can't believe I've landed my dream job of anchoring the nightly news in a major metropolitan market." Within moments of the start of the broadcast, however, telephones at the studio began ringing off the hook. Unfortunately, she had unintentionally offended a majority of the viewers before she even said a word. You see, Suzanne's post was with a television station in Boston, and she was wearing an orange suit on Saint Patrick's Day. After the broadcast, the assistant news director explained to Suzanne, "Orange is associated with Northern Irish Protestants. By wearing orange today, Saint Patrick's Day, you outraged and offended many of our Irish Catholic viewers."

This true story of award-winning news anchor Suzanne Bates illustrates how important it is to understand and adapt to your specific audience.[1] In the previous chapter, we saw how audience and occasion considerations help you to choose a speech topic and goal. In this chapter, we describe how you can use audience analysis to tailor what you say to the audience throughout the speech. The second Speech Planning Action Step is to understand your audience and adapt your speech to it.

Audience adaptation is the process of tailoring your speech's information to the needs, interests, and expectations of your listeners. Your concerns about adapting to your audience will inform your research efforts, your choice of main points, the supporting material that you will use to develop those points, and even the jokes you might want to tell. So recognizing audience adaptation needs during Action Step 2 lays the foundation for the work that follows. In the rest of this chapter, we describe the issues of adaptation, including demonstrating the relevance of your topic, acknowledging initial audience disposition toward your topic, establishing common ground, gaining credibility, ensuring information comprehension and retention, and managing language and cultural differences. Your consideration of these issues will enable you to formulate a specific blueprint to use as you plan your speech.

What do you think?

I find it easier to talk to a diverse audience.

Strongly Disagree								Strongly Agree	
1	2	3	4	5	6	7	8	9	10

relevance
adapting the information in a speech so that audience members view it as important to them

ACTION STEP 2:
Understand Your Audience and Adapt to It

A. Understand audience diversity.
B. Understand audience initial interest and attitude.
C. Adjust content to be appropriate for your audience.
D. Determine how you will establish your credibility with the audience.

Relevance

The first issue you face is demonstrating relevance—adapting the information in a speech so that audience members view it as important to them. Listeners pay attention to and are interested in ideas that have a personal impact and are bored when they don't see how a speech relates to them. Effective speakers demonstrate the timeliness, proximity, and personal impact that the ideas in their speech have for their audience.

Demonstrate Timeliness

Information has **timeliness** when it is useful now or in the near future. You can increase the relevance of the information you present by showing how it is timely for a particular audience. For example, in a speech about the hazards of talking on cell phones while driving, J. J. established the topic's relevance to the audience with this introduction:

> Most of us in this room, as many as 90 percent of us in fact, are a danger to society. Why? Because we talk or text message on our cell phones while driving. Although driving while phoning (DWP) seems harmless, a recent study conducted by the Nationwide Mutual Insurance Company reports that DWP is the most common cause of accidents today—even more common than driving under the influence (DUI). Did you know that when you talk on the phone when you're driving—even if you do so on a hands-free set—you're four times more likely to get into a serious crash than if you're not doing so? That's why several states have actually made doing so illegal. So this issue is far from harmless and is certainly one each of us should take seriously.

To see an excellent example of how timeliness can affect a message—President Ronald Reagan's 1986 speech on the *Challenger* space shuttle disaster—go

to the Coursemate for SPEAK at www.cengagebrain.com to access **Web Resource 5.1: Demonstrating Timeliness**.

Demonstrate Proximity

Listeners are more likely to be interested in information that has **proximity**, a relationship to their personal "space." Psychologically, we pay more attention to information that is related to our "territory"—to us, our family, our neighborhood, or our city, state, or country. You have probably heard speakers say, "Let me bring this close to home for you . . ." and then make their point by using a local example. As you research your speech, you will want to look for statistics and examples that have proximity for your audience.

Demonstrate Personal Impact

When you present information on a topic that can have a serious physical, economic, or psychological impact on audience members, they will be interested in what you have to say. For example, notice how your classmates' attention picks up when your instructor states that what is said next "will definitely be on the test." Your instructor understands that this "economic impact" (not paying attention can "cost") is enough to refocus most students' attention on what is said. As you prepare your speech, incorporate ideas that create personal impact for your audience.

© ISTOCKPHOTO.COM/SEAN LOCKE

Initial Audience Disposition

Initial audience disposition is the knowledge of and opinions about your topic that your listeners have before they hear you speak. Adapting to the initial audience disposition means creating a speech that takes into account how much audience members already know about your topic and what their attitudes are toward it. As part of your audience analysis, you identified the initial attitude you expected most of your audience members to have toward your topic. During your speech preparation, choose specific supporting material with these initial attitudes in mind.

Adapting to listeners' attitudes is obviously important for persuasive speeches, but it is also important for informative speeches. For example, a speech on refinishing wood furniture is meant to be informative. You might face two types of audiences—one that believes refinishing furniture is difficult, and another that is addicted to HGTV and really looking forward to your talk. Although the refinishing process you describe in both situations would be the same, your approach to explaining the steps would differ based on the audience. If you know your audience thinks refinishing furniture is complicated, you will need to pique their interest and convince them that the process is simpler than they initially thought. And if you know most of your audience enjoy watching HGTV, you can play upon their interest as you speak by making reference to some of the most popular shows on HGTV.

Common Ground

People in the audience are unique, with different knowledge, attitudes, philosophies, experiences, and ways of perceiving the world. They may or may not know others in the audience. So it is easy for them to assume that they have nothing in common with you or with other audience members. Yet when you speak, you will be giving one message to that diverse group. Common ground is the background, knowledge, attitudes, experiences, and philosophies that are shared by audience members and the speaker. Effective speakers use audience analysis to identify areas of similarity and then use the adaptation techniques of personal pronouns, rhetorical questions, and common experiences to create common ground.

Use Personal Pronouns

The simplest way to establish common ground is to use personal pronouns— "we," "us," and "our." For example, in a speech to an audience whose members are known to be sympathetic to legislation limiting violence in children's programming on TV, notice the effect of using a personal pronoun:

> I know that most people worry about the effects that violence on TV is having on young children.

> I know that most of us worry about the effects that violence on TV is having on young children.

By using "us" instead of "people," the speaker includes the audience members and thus gives them a stake in listening to what follows.

Ask Rhetorical Questions

A second way of developing common ground is to pose rhetorical questions—questions phrased to stimulate a mental response rather than an actual spoken response from the audience. Rhetorical

personal pronouns · rhetorical questions · common experiences

credibility
the perception that you are knowledgeable, trustworthy, and personable

knowledge and expertise
how well you convince your audience that you are qualified to speak on the topic

questions create common ground by alluding to information that is shared by audience members and the speaker. They are often used in speech introductions but can also be effective as transitions and in other parts of the speech. For instance, notice how this transition, phrased as a rhetorical question, creates common ground:

> When you have watched a particularly violent TV program, have you ever asked yourself, "Did they really need to be this graphic to make the point?"

Rhetorical questions are meant to have only one answer that highlights similarities between the speaker and audience members and leads them to be more interested in the content that follows.

Draw From Common Experiences

You can also develop common ground by sharing personal experiences, examples, and illustrations that embody what you and the audience have in common. For instance, in a speech about the effects of television violence, you might allude to a common viewing experience:

> You know how sometimes at a key moment when you're watching a really frightening scene in a movie you quickly shut your eyes? I vividly remember slamming my eyes shut over and over again during the scariest scenes in Texas Chainsaw Massacre, The Blair Witch Project, and Halloween.

To create material that draws on common experiences, you must first analyze how you and audience members are similar in the exposure you have had to the topic or in other areas that you can then compare to your topic.

Speaker Credibility

Credibility is the confidence that an audience places in the truthfulness of what a speaker says. The impact of credibility on speaker success has been a fundamental concept in public speaking since Aristotle described it as *ethos* more than 2,000 years ago. Having been understood as a key concept for so long, it is no wonder that several theories exist about how speakers develop credibility. You can read a summary of these theories by going to the CourseMate for SPEAK

at www.cengagebrain.com to access **Web Resource 5.2: Holistic Theory of Speaker Credibility**.

Some people are widely known as experts in a particular area and have proven to be trustworthy and likable. When these people give a speech, they don't have to adapt their remarks to establish their credibility. For example, in 2008, Nancy Nielsen, president of the American Medical Association, spoke to fellow physicians on patient advocacy—no one listening would have questioned her credibility.

However, most of us, even if we are given a formal introduction that attempts to acquaint the audience with our credentials and character, will still need to adapt our remarks to build audience confidence in the truthfulness of what we are saying. Three adaptation techniques can affect how credible we are perceived to be: demonstrating knowledge and expertise, establishing trustworthiness, and displaying personableness.

Demonstrate Knowledge and Expertise

When listeners perceive you to be a knowledgeable expert, they will perceive you as credible. Their assessment of your **knowledge and expertise** depends on how well you convince them that you are qualified to speak on the topic. You can demonstrate your knowledge and expertise through direct and indirect means.

You establish your expertise directly when you disclose your experiences with your topic, including formal education, special study, demonstrated skill, and your "track record." For example, in a speech on DWP, J. J. explained:

> I became interested in the issue of driving while phoning (DWP) after being involved personally in an accident caused by a driver who was talking on the phone. Since then, I've done a great deal of research on the subject and am involved in a grassroots organization devoted to passing legislation to ban driving while phoning in our state.

Of course, to make claims like this, you must have had experiences that give you "standing" to speak on your topic. This is why it is critical for you to choose a topic you know something about. When you can demonstrate your personal involvement with your topic, your audience begins to trust that you understand the material you are presenting.

Audience members will also assess your expertise through indirect means, such as how well prepared you seem and how much you demonstrate firsthand involvement by using personal examples and illustrations. Audiences have an almost instinctive sense of when a speaker is "winging it," and most audiences distrust a speaker who does not appear to have command of the material. Speakers who are overly dependent on their notes or who hem and haw fumbling to find ways to express their ideas undermine the confidence of the audience. On the other hand, when your ideas are easy to follow and clearly expressed, audience members perceive you to be more credible.

Similarly, when your ideas are developed through specific statistics, high-quality examples, illustrations, and personal experiences, audience members are more likely to view you as credible. Think about how impressed you are with instructors who always seem to have two or three perfect examples and illustrations and who are able to recall statistics without looking at their notes. Compare this with your experiences with instructors who seem tied to the textbook and don't appear to know much about the subject beyond their prepared lecture. In which instance do you perceive the instructor to be more knowledgeable?

Establish Trustworthiness

Your **trustworthiness** is the extent to which the audience can believe that what you say is accurate, true, and in their best interests. The more your audience sees you as trustworthy, the more credible you will be. People assess others' trustworthiness by judging their character and their motives. So you can establish yourself as trustworthy by following ethical standards and by honestly explaining what is motivating you to speak.

As you plan your speech, you need to consider how to demonstrate your character—that you are honest, industrious, dependable, and a morally strong person. For example, when you credit the source of your information as you speak, you confirm that the information is true and you signal your honesty by not taking credit for someone else's ideas. Similarly, if you present the arguments evenly on both sides of an issue instead of just the side you favor, audience members will see you as fair-minded.

How trustworthy you appear to be will also depend on how the audience views your motives. If people believe that what you are saying is self-serving rather than in their interests, they will be suspicious and view you as less trustworthy. Early in your speech, then, it is important to show how audience members will benefit from what you are saying.

Display Personableness

We have more confidence in people whom we like. Personableness is the extent to which you project an agreeable or pleasing personality. The more your listeners like you, the more likely they are to believe what you tell them. We quickly decide how much we like a new person based on our first impressions. This fact is actually based on a concept we refer to in the communication field as impression formation and management, which is rooted in the theory of symbolic

trustworthiness
the extent to which the audience can believe that what you say is accurate, true, and in their best interests

personableness
the extent to which you project an agreeable or pleasing personality

learning style
a person's preferred
way of receiving
information

interactionism.[2] These first impressions are based on what we infer about people from what we see, such as how they dress, how physically attractive we find them, how well they speak, whether they smile and appear friendly, and even how they carry themselves. Although first impressions are not always correct, we still use them. That's why a successful business professional might wear an oversize graphic T-shirt, baggy shorts, and a backward ball cap when hanging out with his friends but wear a formal blue suit to make a major presentation at a conference. In each case, he is adjusting his look to convey appropriate personableness in different settings. As a speaker trying to build credibility with an audience, you should look for ways to adapt your personal style to one that will help the audience like you and perceive you as credible.

Besides dressing appropriately for the audience and occasion, you can increase the chances that the audience will like you by smiling at individual audience members before beginning your remarks and by looking at individuals as you speak, acknowledging them with a quick nod. You can also demonstrate personableness by using appropriate humor. By appropriate humor, we mean humor that demonstrates respect for diverse listeners and is not sexist, ageist, or racist.

Information Comprehension and Retention

Although audience analysis helps you select a topic that is appropriate for your audience's current knowledge level, you will still need to adapt the information you present so that audience members can easily follow what you are saying and remember it when you are through. Six guidelines that can aid you are (a) appealing to diverse learning styles, (b) orienting the audience with transitions, (c) choosing specific and familiar language, (d) using vivid language and examples, (e) personalizing information, and (f) comparing unfamiliar ideas with those the audience recognizes.

Appeal to Diverse Learning Styles

A learning style is a person's preferred way of receiving information. Because people differ in how they prefer to learn, you should present your ideas in ways that make it easy for all audience members to under-

stand and remember what you are saying. Models for understanding learning styles have been developed by a number of scholars across many disciplines.[3] One prominent model, called Kolb's cycle of learning, conceptualizes these preferences along four dimensions: feeling, thinking, watching, and doing.[4] Kolb's model is actually rooted in John Dewey's experiential learning theory.[5] Exhibit 5.1 depicts how the watching–doing and feeling–thinking dimensions of the cycle of learning theory result in four types of learners.

Some people prefer to learn by "watching" and easily understand and remember things they see and hear. People who prefer to learn by watching relate to well-designed visual aids and vivid examples that they can picture. Others prefer to learn by "doing." For these people, hands-on activities aid their comprehension and memory. People who prefer to learn by doing relate well when speakers provide real-life applications and clearly state how the speech topic is relevant to their personal or professional lives.

Some people find it difficult to understand and remember factual material and learn better if their feelings are engaged. These people learn well from stories and other supporting material that appeals to their emotions or senses. Other people learn well by absorbing and considering factual material. People who prefer to learn by thinking connect well when your ideas are supported with detailed definitions, explanations, facts, and statistics.

Although each of us has a favored learning style, research reveals that all people learn most effectively when ideas are presented in ways that "round" the entire cycle of learning.[6] So as you consider what information you will provide, adapt to diverse learning styles by presenting new information in ways that appeal to watching and feeling and doing and thinking.

For example, suppose you are trying to make the point that for the large numbers of Americans who are functionally illiterate, understanding simple directions can be a problem. Here's an illustration that develops this idea:

> For instance, a person who is functionally illiterate might not be able to read or understand a label that says, "Take three times a day after eating."

Now look at how much richer this illustration becomes when we develop the statement by using supportive material that appeals to different learning styles:

> A significant number of Americans are functionally illiterate. That is, about 35 million people, 20 percent of the adult population, have serious difficulties with common reading tasks (thinking). That means that one of

Exhibit 5.1

Kolb's Cycle of Learning

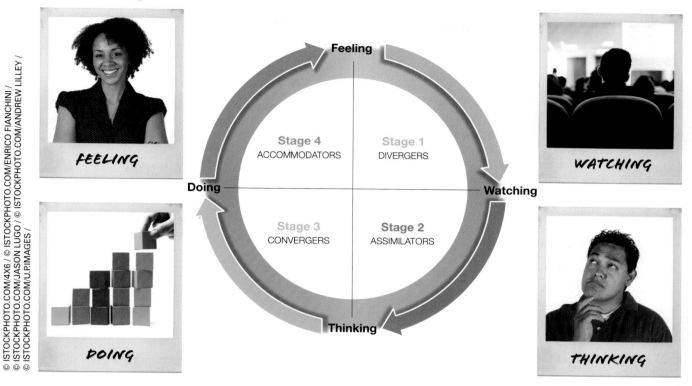

FEELING

WATCHING

DOING

THINKING

every five people you see today may struggle with basic reading tasks. They cannot read well enough to understand how to bake a frozen pizza, how to assemble their children's bicycle from the printed instructions, or which bus to catch from the signs at the stop (feeling). Many functionally illiterate people don't read well enough to follow the directions on this bottle [show an enlarged image of the label on a medicine bottle that reads, "Take three times a day after eating"] (watching). So the directions on a prescription bottle like this are basically meaningless (doing).

Bslo angtt moske h jec mleo h vrlaa rc kpoes. Vf xtaa hy sd catfs gntso.

Orient the Audience With Transitions

When listeners become confused or forget basic information, they lose interest in what is being said. If your speech is more than a couple of minutes long, you can use transitions to orient your audience. A **transition** is a sentence or two that summarizes one main point and introduces the next one. Suppose your goal is to explain the three phases of clinical trial a cancer drug must pass through to earn FDA approval. After explaining the goals of the first phase, you might use a transition like this: "So the goal of

the first phase is to see whether a drug that is safe in animals is also safe in humans. Phase I trials are not designed to determine whether or not the drug works; that is the goal in Phase II trials."

To see an excellent example of orienting listeners—former President Bill Clinton's speech outlining the reasons for NATO involvement in Kosovo—go to the Course-Mate for SPEAK at www.cengagebrain.com to access **Web Resource 5.3: Orienting Listeners**.

Choose Specific and Familiar Language

Words have many meanings, so you want to make sure your listeners understand the meaning you intend. You can do so by using specific language and choosing familiar terms. Specific words clear up the confusion caused by general words by narrowing the focus in some way. For example, "a banged-up 1994 baby blue Honda Civic" is more specific than "a car." Narrowing the meaning encourages your listeners to picture the same thing you are.

transition
a sentence or two that summarizes one main point and introduces the next one

It is also important to use familiar words. So avoid jargon and slang terms unless (a) you define them clearly the first time you use them and (b) they are central to your speech goal.

Use Vivid Language and Examples

Vivid examples help audience members understand and remember abstract, complex, and novel material. One vivid example can help us understand a complicated concept. So as you prepare your speech, you will want to adapt by finding or creating real or hypothetical examples and illustrations to help your audience understand new information you present. For example, the definition of *functionally illiterate people* as those "who have trouble accomplishing simple reading and writing tasks" can be made more vivid by adding the following example: "For instance, a functionally illiterate person could not read and understand the directions on a prescription label that states, 'Take three times a day with a glass of water. Do not take on an empty stomach.'"

Personalize Information

We personalize information by presenting it in a frame of reference that is familiar to the audience. Devon is to give a speech on how the Japanese economy affects U.S. markets at the student chapter of the American Marketing Association. He wants to help his audience understand geographic data about Japan. He could just quote the following statistics from the 2004 *World Almanac:*[7]

> *Japan is small and densely populated. The nation's 128 million people live in a land area of 146,000 square miles, giving them a population density of 877 persons per square mile.*

Although this would provide the necessary information, it is not adapted to an audience composed of college students in California, for example. Devon can easily adapt the information to the audience by personalizing it for this student audience:

> *Japan is a small, densely populated nation. Its population of 128 million is nearly half that of the United States. Yet the Japanese are crowded into a land area of only 146,000 square miles—roughly the same size as California. Just think of the implications of having half the population of the United States living here in California, where 30 million people—about one-fifth of that total—now live. In fact, Japan packs 877 persons into every square mile of land, whereas in the United States we average about 74 persons per square mile. Overall, then, Japan is about 12 times as crowded as the United States.*

This revision adapts the information by personalizing it for this audience. Most Americans don't know the total land area of the United States, only that it is quite large. Likewise, a California audience would have a sense of the size of their home state compared with the rest of the nation. Personalized information is easier for audience members to understand and remember, so as you research and prepare your speech, you will want to look for ways to personalize the information.

Compare Unknown Ideas With Familiar Ones

An easy way to adapt your material to your audience is to compare new ideas with ones the audience already understands. So as you prepare your speech, you will want to identify places where you can use comparisons. In a speech on functional illiteracy, if you want the audience of literates to sense what functionally illiterate people experience, you might compare it to the experience of surviving in a country where one is not fluent in the language:

> *Many of us have taken a foreign language in school. So we figure we can visit a place where that language is spoken and "get along," right? But when we get to the country, we are often appalled to discover that even the road signs are written in this "foreign" language. And we can't quite make the signs out, at least not at 60 kilometers an hour. I was in France last summer, equipped with my three years of high school French, and I saw a sign that indicated that the train station I was looking for was "à droit"—"to the right," or is it "to*

© POLKA DOT/JUPITERIMAGES

the left"? I knew it was one or the other. Unfortunately, I couldn't remember and took a shot that it was to the left. Bad move. By the time I figured it out, I was 10 miles in the wrong direction and ended up missing my train. At that moment, I could imagine how tough life must be for functionally illiterate people. So many "little details" of life require the ability to comprehend written messages.

Language and Cultural Differences

The approach to public speaking we discuss in this book is informed by Western European speaking traditions. However, public speaking is a social and cultural act, so as you would expect, public speaking practices and their perceived effectiveness vary across cultures. So when you address an audience composed of people from ethnic and language groups different from your own, you should make two adaptations: try to be understandable when speaking in a second language, and show respect by choosing culturally appropriate supporting material.

Work to Be Understood When Speaking in Your Second Language

When speaking to an audience in a second language, audience members may not be able to understand what you are saying because you may speak with an accent, mispronounce words, choose inappropriate words, and misuse idioms. Fear of making these mistakes can make second-language speakers self-conscious. But most audience members are more tolerant of mistakes made by a second-language speaker than they are of those made by a native speaker. Likewise, they will work hard to understand a non-native speaker.

Nevertheless, when you are speaking in a second language, you have an additional responsibility to make your speech as understandable as possible. You can help your audience by speaking more slowly and articulating as clearly as you can. By slowing your speaking rate, you give yourself additional time to pronounce difficult words. Also, you should give your audience members additional time to adjust their ears so they can more easily process what you are saying. You can also use visual aids to reinforce key terms and concepts as you move through your speech.

One of the best ways to improve is to practice the speech in front of friends and associates who are native speakers of your second language. Ask them to take note of words and phrases that you mispronounce or misuse. They can then work with you to correct your pronunciation or help you choose other words that better express your ideas. They can also review your visual aids to make sure they are appropriate. Also, keep in mind that the more you practice speaking the language, the more comfortable you will become with it and with your ability to relate to audience members.

Choose Culturally Appropriate Supporting Material

Much of your success in adapting to the audience hinges on establishing common ground and drawing on common experiences. When you are speaking to audiences who are different from you, it will take work to find out about the culture and experiences of your audience so you can adapt to them. This may mean conducting additional research to find statistics, examples, and other supporting material that will be meaningful to the audience. Or it may require you to elaborate on ideas that would be self-explanatory in your own culture. For example, suppose that Maria, a Mexican-American student, was giving a narrative/personal experience speech for her speech class at Yeshiva University in Israel on the *quinceañera* party she had when she turned 15. Because students in Israel probably don't have experience with *quinceañera* parties, they would have trouble understanding the significance of this event unless Maria was able to use her knowledge of the bar mitzvah and bat mitzvah coming-of-age ritual celebrations in Jewish culture and relate it to them.

Forming a Specific Plan of Audience Adaptation

You now understand the challenges speakers face in developing and maintaining audience interest and understanding, and you have read about the adaptation techniques that can overcome these challenges. You have also completed your own audience analysis. So you are ready to think about the adaptation challenges you will face in your speech, as well as how you might adapt to them. At this point in your preparation process, identifying the challenges you face with your audience and planning how you might meet them will provide a guide to direct your research efforts and aid you as you develop the speech. Your adaptation plan should answer the following questions:

1. **How relevant will the audience find this material?** How can I demonstrate that the material is timely, proximate, and has personal impact for audience members?

2. **What is my audience's initial disposition toward my speech topic likely to be?** What can I do to create or enhance audience interest in my topic or sympathy for my argument?

3. **What common ground do audience members share with one another and with me?** How and where can I use personal pronouns, rhetorical questions, and common experiences to enhance the perception of common ground?

4. **What can I do to enhance my credibility?** How did I develop my expertise on this topic, and how can I share that with the audience? How can I demonstrate my trustworthiness as I speak? What will I do to help the audience find me personable so they will like me?

5. **How can I make it easier for audience members to comprehend and remember the information I will share?** What types of material can I find and use to appeal to different learning style preferences? Given my topic and audience, to what ideas will the audience

need to be oriented? What key terms will I need to define? What new concepts might I develop with vivid language and examples? How can I personalize the information so it is familiar to my audience? What new ideas might I want to compare to ones the audience is already familiar with?

6. **What language or cultural differences do audience members have with one another and with me?** If I will be speaking in a second language, how do I plan to increase the likelihood that the audience will understand me? What cultural differences do I need to be sensitive to, and what culturally appropriate material might I search for and use?

Speech Planning Action Step 2, Activity 2 will help you identify opportunities for audience adaptation as you develop your speeches in this course. See the Student Response box immediately following the activity for a sample of how one student completed this exercise.

ACTION STEP 2
Activity 2

Recognizing Opportunities for Audience Adaptation

To identify opportunities for audience adaptation and lay a groundwork for applying information from the next several chapters, state your potential topic and then answer the following questions.

Potential topic: _____

1. How relevant will the audience find this material? How can I demonstrate that the material is timely, proximate, and has personal impact on the members of this audience?

2. What is my audience's initial disposition toward my speech topic likely to be?

3. What common ground do audience members share with one another and with me?

4. What can I do to enhance my credibility?

5. How can I make it easier for audience members to comprehend and remember the information I will share?

6. What language or cultural differences do audience members have with one another and with me?

You can complete this activity online, view another student sample of this activity, and, if requested, e-mail your completed activity to your instructor. Go to the CourseMate for SPEAK at www.cengagebrain.com to access Action Step 2, Activity 2.

Student Response: Action Step 2, Activity 2

Potential topic: *The overall effects of hurricanes*

1. How relevant will the audience find this material?
Initially, since they don't live on a coast, they are not likely to see it as relevant.
How can I demonstrate that the material is timely, proximate, and has personal impact on the members of this audience?
I can make the information timely and demonstrate personal impact by talking about Hurricane Katrina, a fairly recent hurricane that most people are aware of, that affected many people, and that even affected the weather in Kentucky.

2. What is my audience's initial disposition toward my speech topic likely to be?
Most audience members will be only mildly interested in and not well informed about this topic when I begin. I hope to pique and maintain their interest by using vivid language and examples, as well as graphic photos.

3. What common ground do audience members share with one another and with me?
Because most audience members are my age and are from the same national culture, we share areas of common ground that I can draw on. First, hurricanes occur every year and affect weather patterns throughout the country when they do. I should also be able to use personal pronouns and rhetorical questions to create common ground. We are different in that I have actually lived through the devastation of a hurricane in my hometown, so I'll have to keep in mind that most of my listeners have not. That means I'll have to be careful not to assume they know more than general facts about hurricanes.

4. What can I do to enhance my credibility?
I will build credibility through solid research and oral citations of sources. Early in my introduction, I'll mention where I live on the Gulf Coast and the fact that I've lived through several hurricanes.

5. How can I make it easier for audience members to comprehend and remember the information I will share?
I will round the cycle of learning by talking about my personal experiences (feeling), showing photographs (watching), offering facts and statistics about the effects of hurricanes (thinking), and providing clear instructions about how to categorize hurricanes and act appropriately to ensure safety (doing). I'll also describe the effects using vivid language and examples, and I'll compare them to other natural disasters my audience members may have experienced such as thunderstorms, tornados, and floods.

6. What language or cultural differences do audience members have with one another and with me?
I will not be speaking in a second language, but I will need to be careful not to use too many technical terms that may be "jargon" to my audience, and, when I do, I need to be sure to define them clearly. Although most audience members are U.S. nationals, there are three international students in class. I will do some research to see if any of them live in a country that experiences hurricanes, and, if so, I'll include some examples from their countries as well.

THERE ARE EVEN MORE STUDY TOOLS FOR THIS CHAPTER AT WWW.CENGAGEBRAIN.COM

- **Interactive Videos**
- **Speech Builder Express**
- **Printable Flash Cards**
- **Interactive Games**
- **Chapter Review Cards**
- **Online Quizzes with Feedback**
- **Speech Studio available upon instructor request**

Gathering and Evaluating Information

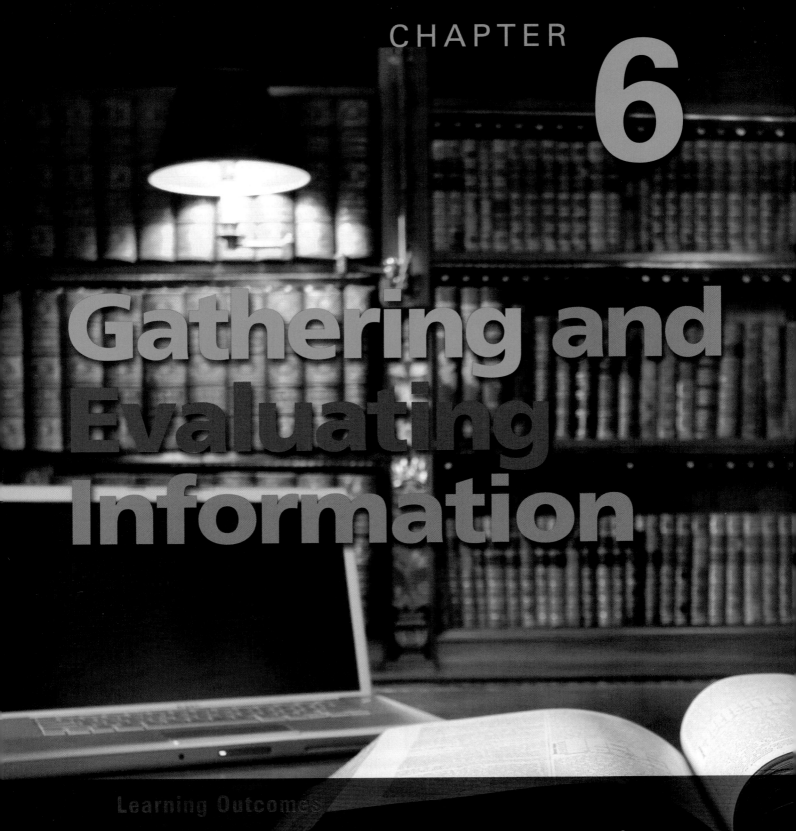

Learning Outcomes

LO^1 What are the differences between primary and secondary research? | LO^2 Where can you locate information for your speech? | LO^3 How will you evaluate information and sources? | LO^4 How will you select and record relevant information for your speech? | LO^5 How and why do you cite sources in a speech?

Justin was concerned. He was scheduled to give his speech in a week, but he hadn't begun to find information. A couple of months ago, he had read a magazine article about the vanishing honeybees while in the doctor's office, but he couldn't remember the name of magazine the article was in. He was still really interested in the subject. But he wondered what to do to find reliable information for a speech.

Justin's experience is not unusual. Most of us have formed opinions about a variety of subjects based on our personal experiences, interactions with others, and things we've read or watched either online or on TV. But when it comes to presenting our ideas in a public forum, we need to do research to find evidence to support them. **Evidence** is essentially any information that clarifies, explains, or otherwise adds depth or breadth to a topic. In this chapter, we explain how to locate and evaluate a variety of information types and sources, identify and select relevant information, and cite key sources appropriately in your speech.

What do you think?

The best way to prepare for an interview is to write out every question in advance.

Strongly Disagree   *Strongly Agree*
1   2   3   4   5   6   7   8   9   10

evidence
any information that clarifies, explains, or otherwise adds depth or breadth to a topic

secondary research
the process of locating information that has been discovered by other people

primary research
the process of conducting your own study to acquire the information you need

Locate and Evaluate Information Sources

How can you quickly find the best information related to your specific speech goal? You can start by assessing your own knowledge, experience, and personal observations. Then you can move to **secondary research**, which is the process of locating information about your topic that has been discovered by other people. If the information you find from secondary sources is insufficient and doesn't answer all of the questions you are seeking answers for, you may need to do **primary research**, which is the process of conducting your own study to acquire the information you need.

ACTION STEP 3: Gather and Evaluate Information to Use in the Speech

A. Examine what you know already and areas where you need additional information.
B. Locate, evaluate, and select a variety of information types and sources.
C. Prepare research cards.
D. Cite sources.

Personal Knowledge and Experience

If you have chosen to speak on a topic you know something about, you are likely to have some personal examples and experiences you can use in your speech. For instance, musicians have special knowledge about music and instruments, entrepreneurs about starting their own businesses, and dieticians about healthy diets. So Diane, a skilled long-distance runner, can draw on material from her own knowledge and experience for

credentials
your experiences or education that qualifies you to speak with authority on a specific subject

her speech on "How to Train for a Marathon." Sharing your personal knowledge and experience can also bolster your credibility if you share your credentials—your experiences or education that qualifies you to speak with authority on a specific subject. For Diane, establishing her credentials means briefly mentioning her training and expertise as a long-distance runner before she launches into her speech.

Secondary Research

The process of locating information about your topic that has been discovered by other people is called secondary research. To conduct secondary research, you'll need to know how to locate sources and what types of sources you can draw from, as well as how to skim and evaluate them.

Locating Sources

First, you'll need to conduct a search to locate potential sources for your speech. You can do so by searching the Internet, searching online libraries and databases, and searching at a local library. Today, most of us typically begin by searching the Internet via a search engine like Google, Yahoo, or Bing. This is a great place to start because the Internet stores so much information from a variety of sources. Searching the Internet can also be overwhelming because a general search will typically reveal thousands of links. However, you can begin to collect general facts about your topic, as well as ideas as to the kinds of sources that publish material on your topic. You can also locate material on websites, blogs, YouTube, and discussion boards that might prove useful to your speech and that cannot be located elsewhere.

You can also search online libraries and databases for secondary sources about your topic. Whereas we were once limited to the sources housed in local libraries, we can now search hundreds of libraries across the country and the world to find material we might use in our papers and speeches.

Types of Secondary Sources

As you conduct your search for secondary sources, you'll want to draw from a variety of types. You can find pertinent information in encyclopedias, books, articles in academic journals and magazines, newspapers, statistical sources, biographies, quotation books and websites, and government documents.

1. **Encyclopedias.** Encyclopedia entries can serve as a good starting point for your research.

Diane, a skilled-long distance runner, can draw from her own experiences for her speech on marathons.

Encyclopedias give an excellent overview of many subjects and can acquaint you with the basic terminology and ideas associated with a topic. But because encyclopedias provide only overviews, they should never be the only source for your speech. General encyclopedias contain short articles about a wide variety of subjects. In addition, there are many specialized encyclopedias to choose from in areas such as art, history, religion, philosophy, and science. For instance, a college library is likely to have the *African American Encyclopedia*, *Latino Encyclopedia*, *Asian American Encyclopedia*, *Encyclopaedia Britannica*, *Encyclopedia Americana*, *World Book Encyclopedia*, *Encyclopedia of Computer Science*, *Encyclopedia of Women*, *Encyclopedia of Women in American Politics*, and many more. The online collaborative encyclopedia, *Wikipedia*, has become a popular research tool, but it is also a controversial source of information. Because there is no way to confirm the credibility of the people posting information in *Wikipedia* entries, you might use it as a starting point but not as a main source. You can also use the Notes section at the end of the articles to find links to published sources that support and inform the entry. Then you can locate the published pieces to determine if they provide relevant and reliable evidence for your speech.

2. **Books.** If your topic has been around for more than six months, there are likely to be books written about it. Although books are excellent

sources of in-depth material about a topic, most of the information in a book is likely to be at least two years old by the time it is published. So books are not a good resource if your topic is very recent or if you're looking for the latest information on a topic. You can also use the call number for one book to physically locate other books on the same subject.

3. **Articles.** Articles, which may contain more current or highly specialized information on your topic than a book would, are published in periodicals—magazines and journals that appear at fixed periods. The information in articles is often more current than that published in books because many periodicals are published weekly, biweekly, or monthly. Most libraries subscribe to electronic databases that index periodical articles. Check with your librarian to learn what electronic indexes your college or university subscribes to. The following are four widely available databases that index many popular magazines and academic journals:

   - **InfoTrac College Edition** is the electronic index that you can access from the Internet this semester through the CourseMate for SPEAK at www.cengagebrain.com. InfoTrac College Edition indexes millions of articles in popular magazines and academic journals.

   - **InfoTrac University Library** is an expanded version of InfoTrac College Edition. Available online through most college and university libraries, it provides access to several hundred additional popular magazines and academic journals.

   - **Periodical Abstract**, another electronic database available online in most college and university libraries, provides access to articles in more than 1,000 popular magazines and academic journals.

   - **EBSCO**, also available online at many college and university libraries, is another database that provides access to many popular magazines and academic journals.

4. **Newspapers.** Newspaper articles are excellent sources of facts about and interpretations of both contemporary and historical issues, and they provide information about local issues and perspectives. Keep in mind, however, that most authors of newspaper articles are journalists who are not experts on the topics they write about. So it is best not to rely solely on newspaper articles for your speech. Today, most newspapers are available online,

which makes them very accessible. Two electronic newspaper indexes that are most useful if they are available to you are the *National Newspaper Index*, which indexes five major newspapers—the *New York Times*, *Wall Street Journal*, *Christian Science Monitor*, *Washington Post*, and *Los Angeles Times*—and *Newsbank*, which provides not only the indexes but also the text of articles from more than 450 U.S. and Canadian newspapers. If you don't have access to an electronic newspaper index, you may be able to access articles about your topic at the websites of specific newspapers.

periodicals
magazines and journals that appear at fixed periods

5. **Statistical sources.** Statistical sources present numerical information on a wide variety of subjects. When you need facts about demography, continents, heads of state, weather, or similar subjects, access one of the many single-volume sources that report such data. *The Statistical Abstract of the United States*, which provides numerical information on various aspects of American life, is available online. For links to other web-based statistical sources, go to the CourseMate for SPEAK at www.cengagebrain.com to access **Web Resource 6.1: Online Statistics**. To read an interesting essay on the improper uses of statistics, access **Web Resource 6.2: Bad Uses of Statistics and Polling**.

6. **Biographies.** When you need an account of a person's life, from thumbnail sketches to reasonably complete essays, you can use a biographical reference source. Although you can access some biographical information online, you will find information of more depth and breadth by reading full-length biographies and by consulting biographical references such as *Who's Who in America* and *International Who's Who*. Your library is also likely to carry *Contemporary Black Biography*, *Dictionary of Hispanic Biography*, *Native American Women*, *Who's Who*

of *American Women, Who's Who Among Asian Americans,* and many more. For links to web-based collections of biographical references, go to the CourseMate for SPEAK at www.cengagebrain.com to access **Web Resource 6.3: Online Biographical References**.

7. **Quotation books and websites.** A good quotation can be especially provocative as well as informative, and there are times you want to use a quotation from a respected person. *Bartlett's Familiar Quotations* is a popular source of quotes from historical as well as contemporary figures. But many other collections of quotations are also available. Some others include *The International Thesaurus of Quotations; Harper Book of American Quotations; My Soul Looks Back, 'Less I Forget: A Collection of Quotations by People of Color; The New Quotable Woman;* and *The Oxford Dictionary of Quotations*. Some popular quotation websites include *The Quotations Page* and *Quoteland.com*. For links to web-based collections of quotations, go to the CourseMate for SPEAK at www.cengagebrain.com to access **Web Resource 6.4: Online Quotations**.

8. **Government documents.** If your topic is related to public policy, government documents may provide useful information. The *Federal Register* publishes daily regulations and legal notices issued by the U.S. executive branch and all federal agencies. It is divided into sections, such as rules and regulations and Sunshine Act meetings. Of special interest are announcements of hearings and investigations, committee meetings, and agency decisions and rulings. The *Monthly Catalog of United States Government Publications* covers publications of all branches of the federal government. It has semiannual and annual cumulative indexes by title, author/agency, and subject. For links to several frequently used U.S. federal government documents, go to the CourseMate for SPEAK at www.cengagebrain.com to access **Web Resource 6.5: Online Government Publications**.

Skimming to Determine Source Value

Because your search of secondary sources is likely to uncover far more information than you can use, you will want to skim sources to determine whether or not to read them in full. Skimming is a method of rapidly going through a work to determine what is covered and how.

If you are evaluating an article, spend a minute or two finding out whether it really presents information on the exact topic you are exploring and whether it contains any documented statistics, examples, or quotable opinions. You can often do so by reading the abstract—a short paragraph summarizing the research findings. If you are evaluating a book, read the table of contents carefully, look at the index, and skim pertinent chapters, asking the same questions as you would for a magazine article. Skimming helps you decide which sources should be read in full, which should be read in part, and which should be abandoned.

Evaluating Sources

Secondary sources vary in their accuracy, reliability, and validity. Accurate sources do not distort information or demonstrate bias by not reporting conflicting pieces of information. Reliable sources can be counted on to present accurate information. Valid sources contain information that has been demonstrated to be true. So before you use the information from a source in your speech, you will want to evaluate it. Four criteria you can use to determine the accuracy, reliability, and validity of sources are authority, objectivity, currency, and relevance.

1. **Authority.** The first test of a resource is the expertise of its author and/or the reputation of the publishing or sponsoring organization. When an author is listed, you can check the author's credentials through biographical references or by seeing if the author has a home page listing professional qualifications. Use the electronic periodical indexes or check the Library of Congress to see what else the author has published in the field.

   On the Internet, you will find information that is anonymous or credited to someone whose background is not clear. In these cases, your ability to trust the information depends on evaluating the qualifications of the sponsoring organization. On the Internet, URLs ending in ".gov," ".edu," and ".org" are noncommercial sites with institutional publishers. The URL ".com" indicates that the sponsor is a for-profit organization. In general, if you do not know whether you can trust the sources, then do not use the information.

2. **Objectivity.** Although all authors have a viewpoint, you will want to be wary of information that is overly biased. Documents that have been published by business, government, or public interest groups should be carefully scrutinized for obvious biases or good public relations fronts. To evaluate the potential

biases in articles and books, read the preface or identify the thesis statement. These often reveal the author's point of view. When evaluating a website with which you are unfamiliar, look for its purpose. Most home pages contain a purpose or mission statement (sometimes in a link called "About Us"). Armed with this information, you are in a better position to recognize potential biases in the information.

3. **Currency.** In general, newer information is more accurate than older. So when evaluating your sources, be sure to consult the latest information you can find. One of the reasons for using web-based sources is that they can provide more up-to-date information than printed sources.[1] But just because a source is found online does not mean that the information is timely. To determine how current the information is, you will need to find out when the book was published, the article was written, the study was conducted, or the article was placed on the web or revised.

4. **Relevance.** During your research, you will likely come across a great deal of interesting information. Whether that information is appropriate for your speech is another matter. Relevant information is directly related to your topic and supports your main points, making your speech easier to follow and understand. Irrelevant information will only confuse listeners, so you should avoid using it no matter how interesting it is.

Web Resource 6.6: Analyzing Information Sources provides information on additional criteria you can use to evaluate your sources. Go to the CourseMate for SPEAK at www.cengagebrain.com to access this resource. And for more information on evaluating websites as sources of information, access **Web Resource 6.7: Evaluating Internet Sources**.

© ISTOCKPHOTO.COM/BARIS SIMSEK

Authority Objectivity Currency Relevance

> **ethnography**
> a form of primary research based on fieldwork observations
>
> **survey**
> a canvassing of people to get information about their ideas and opinions, which are then analyzed for trends

Primary Research

When there is little secondary research available on your topic or on a main idea you want to develop in your speech, or when you wonder whether what you are reading about is true in a particular setting, consider doing primary research, which is the process of conducting your own study to acquire the information you need. But keep in mind that primary research is much more labor intensive and time consuming than secondary research—and, in the professional world, much more costly. If after making an exhaustive search of secondary sources you cannot locate the information you need, try getting it by conducting fieldwork observations, surveys, interviews, original artifact or document examinations, or experiments.

Fieldwork Observations

Sometimes you might question whether what you are reading in secondary research actually happens in a particular setting or with a particular group, or you might wonder whether something that was true in the past is still true today. To find out, you might conduct *fieldwork observations*, also known as **ethnography**. If, for instance, you are planning to talk about how social service agencies help the homeless find shelter and job training, you can learn more by visiting or even volunteering for a period of time at a homeless shelter. By focusing on specific behaviors and taking notes on your observations, you will have a record of specifics that you can use in your speech.

Surveys

A **survey** is a canvassing of people to get information about their ideas and opinions, which are then analyzed for trends. Surveys are especially effective for discovering the attitudes, values, and beliefs generally held by a group of people. Surveys may be conducted in person, over the phone, online, or in writing. At times, your secondary research will reveal publications that summarize findings from surveys that have been conducted by other people or organizations. At other times, you may want to conduct your own survey. If you decide to conduct your own survey, go to the CourseMate for SPEAK at www.cengagebrain.com to access **Web Resource 6.8: Conducting Surveys**, which will provide you with important tips for collecting good information.

Interviews

Like media reporters, you may get some of your best information from an interview—a planned, structured conversation where one person asks questions and another answers them. To be effective, you'll want to select the best person to interview, prepare a solid interview protocol (the list of questions you plan to ask), and adhere to several ethical guidelines when conducting and then processing the actual interview.

1. **Selecting the best person.** Somewhere on campus or in the larger community are people who have expertise in the topic area of your speech and who can provide you with information. Usually, a few telephone calls and a bit of research will lead you to that person. For instance, for a speech on how to get a music recording contract, you might begin by asking a professor in the music department for the name of a music production agency in your community or nearby. Or you could find one by searching online. Once you find a website, you can usually find an "About Us" or "Contact Us" link on it, which will offer names, titles, e-mail addresses, and phone numbers. You should be able to find someone appropriate to your purpose from this list. Once you have identified a potential interviewee, you should contact the person to make an appointment. Today, it is generally best to do so by both e-mail and telephone. Be forthright in your reasons

for scheduling the interview. You should also tell the person how long you expect the interview to take and suggest several dates and time ranges so the person can select the date and time that works best for him or her.

At the end of the conversation to set up the interview, thank the person, repeat the date and time of the interview, and confirm the office location. If you make the appointment more than a few days in advance, it is usually wise to call the day before the interview to confirm the appointment.

Finally, before interviewing the expert, make sure that you have done other research on the topic, especially anything he or she has written about it. Likewise, do your research to understand the expert's credentials. Interviewees are more likely to talk with you if you appear informed, and being informed will ensure that you ask better questions. You don't want to waste the interviewee's time by asking questions you could find elsewhere.

2. **Preparing the interview protocol.** The heart of an effective interview is a list of good questions. How many questions you plan to ask depends on how much time you have for the interview. Keep in mind, however, that you never know how a person will respond. Some people may answer every question you were planning to ask in response to your first question; other people will answer each question with just a few words.

Early in the interview, you will want to establish rapport by asking some questions that can be answered easily and that will show your respect for the person you are interviewing. The goal is to get the interviewee to feel at ease and talk freely. Then you can ask the major questions you have prepared. You may not ask all the questions you planned, but you don't want to end the interview until you have the important information you intended to get. A good interview protocol will consist of a mix of primary and secondary questions that are phrased to be neutral rather than leading.

Primary questions are the lead-in questions about one of the major topics of the interview, typically related to the main points for the speech. **Secondary questions** are follow-up questions designed to probe the answers given to primary questions. Although some follow-ups are planned ahead by anticipating possible answers, more often than not they are composed as the interview goes along. Some simply encourage the interviewee to continue ("And then?" "Is there more?"); others probe into what the person has said ("What were you thinking at the time?"); and some probe the feelings of the interviewee ("Were you worried when you didn't find her?").

Open questions are broad-based questions that ask the interviewee to provide perspective, ideas, information, or opinions as he or she wishes, which gives the interviewee more control, but take longer to answer ("What research studies are you working on next?").[2]

Closed questions are narrowly focused and require very brief (one- or two-word) answers. Some require a simple yes or no; others need only a short response. By asking closed questions, interviewers can control the interview and obtain specific information quickly. But the answers cannot reveal the nuances behind responses, nor are they likely to yield much voluntary information.[3]

For the most part, questions should be phrased neutrally. **Neutral questions** are phrased in ways that do not direct a person's answers—for example, "What can you tell me about your work with Habitat for Humanity?" By contrast, **leading questions** are phrased in a way that suggests the interviewer has a preferred answer—for example, "What do you like about working for Habitat for Humanity?"

Exhibit 6.1 lists some of the questions you might ask in an interview with a music producer.

3. **Conducting the interview.** The following ethical guidelines characterize the "best practices" for ensuring an effective interview.

- **Dress professionally.** Doing so sends a message to the interviewee that you *respect* the time he or she is giving and take the interview seriously.

- **Be prompt.** You also demonstrate *respect* by showing up prepared to begin at the time you have agreed to. Remember to allow enough time for potential traffic or parking problems.

- **Be courteous.** Begin the interview by introducing yourself and the purpose for the interview and by thanking the person for

primary questions
lead-in questions about one of the major topics of the interview, typically related to the main points for the speech

secondary questions
follow-up questions designed to probe the answers given to primary questions

open questions
broad-based questions that ask the interviewee to provide perspective, ideas, information, or opinions

closed questions
narrowly focused questions that require only very brief answers

neutral questions
questions phrased in ways that do not direct a person's answers

leading questions
questions phrased in a way that suggests the interviewer has a preferred answer

Exhibit 6.1

Sample Interview Questions

Rapport Building Opener

How did you get interested in becoming a music producer?

Major Topic Questions

Primary Question #1:	How do you find artists to consider for contract?
Secondary Question:	Is this different from the methods used by other producers?
Secondary Question:	Do artists ever come to you in other ways?
Primary Question #2:	Once an artist has been brought to your attention, what course of action follows?
Secondary Question:	Did you ever just see artists or bands and sign them?
Secondary Question:	What's the longest period of time you "auditioned" an artist or band before signing them?
Primary Question #3:	What criteria do you use in deciding to offer a contract?
Secondary Question:	How important is the artist's age, sex, or ethnicity?
Primary Question #4:	Can you tell me the story of how you came to sign one of your most successful artists?
Secondary Question :	What do you think made the artist so successful?
Primary Question #5:	Can you tell me the story of an artist you signed who was not successful?
Secondary Question:	Why do you think this artist failed?
Secondary Question:	Do you think it was a mistake to sign this artist?

taking the time to talk to you. Remember, although the interviewee may enjoy talking about the subject, may be flattered, and may wish to share knowledge, that person has nothing to gain from the interview. So you should let the interviewee know you are grateful to him or her for taking the time to talk with you. Most of all, *respect* what the person says regardless of what you may think of the answers.

- **Ask permission to record.** If you want to record the interview, ask permission. If the interviewee says "no," *respect* his or her wishes and take careful notes instead.
- **Listen carefully.** At key places in the interview, repeat what the interviewee has said in your own words to ensure that you really understand him or her and to assure the interviewee that you will report the answers *truthfully* and *fairly* during your speech.
- **Keep the interview moving.** You do not want to rush the person, but you do want to behave *responsibly* by getting your questions answered during the allotted time.
- **Monitor your nonverbal reactions.** You demonstrate *integrity* when your facial expressions and your gestures match the tone you want to communicate. Maintain good eye contact with the person. Nod to show understanding, and smile occasionally to maintain the friendliness of the interview. How you look and act is likely to determine whether the person will warm up to you and give you an informative interview.
- **Get permission to quote.** Be sure to get permission for exact quotes. Doing so demonstrates that you *respect* the interviewee and want to report his or her ideas *honestly* and *fairly*. Doing so also communicates that you have *integrity* and strive to act *responsibly*. You might even offer to let the person see a copy of the formal outline for your speech before you actually give it or invite him or her to attend the presentation.
- **Confirm credentials.** Before you leave, be sure to confirm your interviewee's professional title and the company or organization he or she works with. Doing

If you want to record the interview, ask permission.

so is acting *responsibly* because you'll need these details when explaining why you chose to interview this person.
- **End on time.** As with arriving promptly, ending the interview when you said you would demonstrates *respect* for the interviewee and his or her valuable time and that you act *responsibly* and with *integrity*.
- **Thank the interviewee.** Always close the interview by thanking the interviewee. This closure leads to positive rapport should you need to follow up with the interviewee later, and it demonstrates that you recognize the person gave up valuable time to visit with you. You may even follow up with a short thank-you note after you leave.

4. **Processing the interview.** Because your interview notes were probably taken in an outline or shorthand form and may be difficult to translate later, sit down with your notes as soon as possible after the interview and make individual research cards of the information you may want to use in the speech. (Research cards will be discussed in detail later in this chapter.) If at any point you are not sure whether you have accurately transcribed what the person said, take a minute to telephone or e-mail the person to double-check.

Original Artifact or Document Examinations

Sometimes the information you need may not have been published. Rather, it may exist in an original unpublished source, such as an ancient manuscript, a diary, personal correspondence, or company files. Alternatively, you may need to view an object to get the information you need, such as a geographic feature, a building, a monument, or an artifact in a museum.

Experiments

You can design a study to test a hypothesis you have. Then, you can report the results of your experiment in your speech. Keep in mind that experimenting takes time, and you must understand the principles of the scientific process to be able to trust results of a formal experiment. However, sometimes you can do an informal experiment to test the results of a study you learn about elsewhere.

Speech Planning Action Step 3, Activity 3A will help you evaluate and compile a list of potential sources for your speeches in this course. See

ACTION STEP 3
Activity 3A

Gathering and Evaluating Information Sources

The goal of this activity is to help you compile a list of potential sources for your speech.

1. Brainstorm a list of keywords that are related to your speech goal.
2. Identify gaps in your current knowledge that you would like to fill.
3. Use a search engine to identify sponsored and personal websites that may be sources of information for your speech.
4. Work with a library database (either physically located at the library or electronically) to list specific resources that appear to provide information for your speech.
5. Gather and skim the resources you have identified to decide which are likely to be the most useful.
6. Evaluate each resource to determine how much faith you can place in the information.
7. Determine what primary research you might conduct to fill gaps in the information you have collected.

You can complete this activity online, print it, and, if requested, e-mail it to your instructor. Go to the CourseMate for SPEAK at www.cengagebrain.com to access Action Step 3, Activity 3A.

{ Student Response: Action Step 3, Activity 3A }

Speech goal: I would like the audience to understand why honeybees are vanishing.

1. Brainstorm a list of keywords that are related to your speech goal. _honeybees, bumblebees, beekeepers, colony collapse disorder_
2. Identify gaps in your current knowledge that you would like to fill. _**Because I'm a biology major and have done an eight-week internship in the field, I am familiar with the kinds of works I'll need to seek out in order to fill any gaps in my knowledge.**_
3. Use a search engine to identify sponsored and personal websites that may be sources of information for your speech. _I searched using Google and found a Wikipedia entry that I used as a starting point to locate other websites and an interview with a beekeeper I could use in my speech._
4. Work with a library database (either physically located at the library or electronically) to list specific resources that appear to provide information for your speech. _Journal of Bee Biology, Science, Biology Quarterly, Journal of Entomology_
5. Gather and skim the resources you have identified to decide which are likely to be the most useful.
6. Evaluate each resource to determine how much faith you can place in the information.
7. Determine what primary research you might conduct to fill gaps in the information you have collected. _I will interview my adviser, who has been studying the vanishing bees since 2006._

---

the Student Response box immediately following the activity for a sample of how one student completed this exercise.

Identify and Select Relevant Information

The information you find in your sources that you will want to use in your speech may include factual statements, expert opinions, and elaborations.

Factual Statements

Factual statements are those that can be verified. One way to verify whether the information is factual is to check it against other sources on the same subject. Never use any information that is not carefully documented unless you have corroborating sources. Factual statements may come in the form of statistics or real examples.

Statistics

Statistics are numerical facts. Statistical statements, such as, "Only five of every 10 local citizens voted in the last election" can provide impressive support for a point, but when they are poorly used in a speech, they may be boring and, in some instances, downright deceiving. Here are some ethical guidelines for using statistics effectively.

1. **Use only statistics you can verify to be reliable and valid.** Taking statistics from only the most reliable sources and double-checking any startling statistics with another source will guard against the use of faulty statistics.

2. **Use only recent statistics so your audience will not be misled.**

3. **Use statistics comparatively.** When we present comparative statistics, they are easier to understand and interpret. For example, according to the U.S. Department of Labor, the national unemployment rate in

factual statements
information that can be verified

statistics
numerical facts

examples
specific instances that illustrate or explain a general factual statement

hypothetical examples
specific instances based on reflections about future events

definition
a statement that clarifies the meaning of a word or phrase

February 2011 was 9.8 percent. This statistic is more meaningful when you also mention that this figure has held steady for three months or when you compare it with 8.5 percent in March 2009 and with 5.1 percent in March 2008.

4. **Use statistics sparingly.** Although statistics may be an excellent way to present a great deal of material quickly, be careful not to overuse them. A few pertinent numbers are far more effective than a battery of statistics. When you believe you must use many statistics, your audience is likely to understand them better if you also show them via a chart or graph on a visual aid.

5. **Remember that statistics are biased.** Mark Twain once said there are three kinds of lies: "lies, damned lies, and statistics."[4] Not all statistics are lies, of course, but consider the source of statistics you'd like to use, what that source may have been trying to prove with these data, and how that situation might have influenced the way the data were collected and interpreted. No statistic can represent the truth perfectly, so evaluate the source thoughtfully and cross-check the method used to collect and interpret the data.[5]

Examples

Examples are specific instances that illustrate or explain a general factual statement. Because you can usually find an example to make any point, ethical speakers are careful to use only examples that are typical of the more general case. One or two short examples, such as the following, are often enough to help make a generalization meaningful.

One way a company increases its power is to acquire another company. Recently, Delta bought out Northwest Airlines and is now the world's largest airline company.

Professional figure skaters practice many long hours every day. Adam Rippon practices 20 to 25 hours per week.

Examples are useful because they provide concrete details that make a general statement more meaningful to the audience.

Although most of the examples you find will be real, you may find a hypothetical example you can use or you might create one yourself. **Hypothetical examples** are specific instances based on reflections about future events. They develop the idea "What if . . . ?" In the following excerpt, John A. Ahladas presents some hypothetical examples of what it will be like in the year 2039 if global warming continues.

In New York, workers are building levees to hold back the rising tidal waters of the Hudson River, now lined with palm trees. In Louisiana, 100,000 acres of wetland are steadily being claimed by the sea. In Kansas, farmers learn to live with drought as a way of life and struggle to eke out an existence in the increasingly dry and dusty heartland. . . . And reports arrive from Siberia of bumper crops of corn and wheat from a longer and warmer growing season.[6]

Because hypothetical examples are not themselves factual, you must be very careful to check that the facts on which they are based are accurate.

Three principles should guide your use of examples. First, the examples should be clear and specific enough to create a picture the audience can understand. Consider the following generalization and supporting example.

Generalization: Electronics is one of the few areas in which products are significantly cheaper today than they were in the 1980s.

Supporting example: In the mid-1980s, Motorola sold cell phones for $5,000 each; now a person can buy a cell phone for under $50.

With this single example, the listener has a vivid picture of the tremendous difference in about a 30-year period.

Second, the examples you use should be representative. If cell phones were the *only* electronics product whose prices had dropped so much over that same period, this vivid example would be misleading and unethical. Any misuse of data is unethical, especially if the user knows better.

Third, use at least one example to support every generalization.

Definitions

A **definition** is a statement that clarifies the meaning of a word or phrase. Definitions are often used in speeches to clarify a topic or some aspect of it. Definitions serve to clarify in three ways.

First, definitions clarify the meaning of terminology that is specialized, technical, or otherwise likely to be unfamiliar to your audience. For example, when Dan talked about bioluminescence, he clarified the meaning of the word *bioluminescence* with the following definition: "According to *Encyclopaedia Britannica Online*, bioluminescence is the emission of visible light by living organisms like fireflies." Although dictionaries and encyclopedias contain definitions, your speech topic might be such that you have to find definitions through prominent researchers or professional practitioners.

Second, definitions clarify words and terms that have more than one meaning and might be misconstrued. For example, because *child abuse* is a term that encompasses a broad range of behaviors, you might choose to define it in a way that acknowledges which behaviors you intend to focus on in your speech.

Third, particularly with controversial subjects, definitions clarify your stance on a subject in an effort to draw listeners to interpret it as you do. For example, in a speech about domestic violence against women, former U.S. Secretary of Health and Human Services Donna Shalala defined such violence as "terrorism in the home."[7]

Expert Opinions

Expert opinions are interpretations and judgments made by authorities in a particular subject area. They can help explain what facts mean or put them in perspective. "Having a Firewire port on your computer is absolutely necessary" is an opinion. Whether they are expert opinions or not depends on who made the statements.

How do you tell if a source is an expert? An expert is someone who has mastered a specific subject, usually through long-term study, and is recognized by other people in the field as being a knowledgeable and trustworthy authority. When you use expert opinions in your speech, you should always cite the credentials of the expert. You should also identify comments from the expert as opinions. For instance, an informative speaker might say, "Temperatures throughout the 1990s were much higher than aver-

age. Paul Jorgenson, a space biologist, believes that these higher-than-average temperatures represent the first stages of the greenhouse effect, but the significance of these temperatures is still being debated."

Elaborations

Both factual information and expert opinions can be elaborated on through anecdotes and narratives, comparisons and contrasts, or quotable explanations and opinions.

Anecdotes and Narratives

Anecdotes are brief, often amusing stories; **narratives** are accounts, personal experiences, tales, or lengthier stories. Because holding audience interest is important and because audience attention is likely to be captured by a story, anecdotes and narratives are worth looking for or creating. In a five-minute speech, you have little time to tell a detailed story, so one or two anecdotes or a very short narrative would be preferable.

The key to using stories is to make sure that the point of the story directly states or reinforces the point you are making in your speech. In the following speech excerpt, John Howard uses a story to make a point about failure to follow guidelines.

> The knight was returning to the castle after a long, hard day. His face was bruised and badly swollen. His armor was dented. The plume on his helmet was broken, and his steed was limping. He was a sad sight.
>
> The lord of the castle ran out and asked, "What hath befallen you, Sir Timothy?"
>
> "Oh, Sire," he said, "I have been laboring all day in your service, bloodying and pillaging your enemies to the West."
>
> "You've been doing what?" gasped the astonished nobleman. "I haven't any enemies to the West!"
>
> "Oh!" said Timothy. "Well, I think you do now."
>
> There is a moral to this little story. Enthusiasm is not enough. You need to have a sense of direction.[8]

> **expert opinions**
> interpretations and judgments made by authorities in a particular subject area
>
> **anecdotes**
> brief, often amusing stories
>
> **narratives**
> accounts, personal experiences, tales, or lengthier stories

© ISTOCKPHOTO.COM/OSTILL

comparison
illuminating a point by
showing similarities

contrast
illuminating a point by
highlighting differences

plagiarism
the unethical act of
representing another
person's work as your
own

Comparisons and Contrasts

One of the best ways to give meaning to new ideas is through comparison and contrast. **Comparisons** illuminate a point by showing similarities. Although you can easily create comparisons using information you have found, you should still keep your eyes open for creative comparisons developed by the authors of the books and articles you have found.

Comparisons may be literal or figurative. Literal comparisons show similarities of real things:

> The walk from the lighthouse back up the hill to the parking lot is equal to walking up the stairs of a 30-story building.

Figurative comparisons express one thing in terms normally denoting another:

> I always envisioned myself as a four-door sedan. I didn't know she was looking for a sports car!

Comparisons make ideas both clearer and more vivid. Notice how Steven Joel Trachtenberg, in a speech to the Newington High School Scholars' Breakfast, uses a figurative comparison to demonstrate the importance of a willingness to take risks even in the face of danger. Although the speech was given years ago, the point is timeless:

> The eagle flying high always risks being shot at by some hare-brained human with a rifle. But eagles and young eagles like you still *prefer the view from that risky height* to what is available flying with the turkeys far, far below.[9]

Whereas comparisons suggest similarities, **contrasts** highlight differences. Notice how the following humorous contrast dramatizes the difference between "participation" and "commitment."

> If this morning you had bacon and eggs for breakfast, I think it illustrates the difference. The eggs represented "participation" on the part of the chicken. The bacon represented "total commitment" on the part of the pig![10]

Quotations

When you find an explanation, an opinion, or a brief anecdote that seems to be exactly what you are looking for, you may quote it directly in your speech. Because audiences want to listen to your ideas and arguments, they do not want to hear a string of long quotations. Nevertheless, a well-selected quotation may be perfect in one or two key places.

Quotations can both explain and enliven. Look for quotations that make a point in a particularly clear or vivid way. For example, in his speech "Enduring Values for a Secular Age," Hans Becherer, executive officer at Deere & Company, quoted Henry Ford to show the importance of enthusiasm to progress:

> Enthusiasm is at the heart of all progress. With it, there is accomplishment. Without it, there are only alibis.[11]

> ## " Quotations can both explain and enliven. "

Frequently, historical or literary quotations can reinforce a point vividly. Cynthia Opheim, chair of the Department of Political Science at Southwest Texas State University, quoted Mark Twain to express the frustration of witnessing legislative decision making:

> There are two things you should never watch being made: sausage and legislation.[12]

When you use a direct quotation, you need to verbally acknowledge the person it came from. Using any quotation or close paraphrase without crediting its source is **plagiarism**, the unethical act of representing another person's work as your own.

Drawing Information From Multiple Cultural Perspectives

How we perceive facts and what opinions we hold often are influenced by our cultural background. Therefore, it is important to draw your information from culturally diverse perspectives by seeking sources that have differing cultural orientations and

© FRANS LEMMENS/PHOTOGRAPHER'S CHOICE/GETTY IMAGES

by interviewing experts with diverse cultural backgrounds. For example, when Carrie was preparing for her speech on proficiency testing in grade schools, she purposefully searched for articles written by noted Hispanic, Asian, and African-American, as well as European-American, authors. In addition, she interviewed two local school superintendents—one from an urban district and one from a suburban district. Because she consciously worked to develop diverse sources of information, Carrie had greater confidence that her speech would more accurately reflect all sides of the debate on proficiency testing.

Record Information

As you find the facts, opinions, and elaborations that you want to use in your speech, you need to record the information accurately and keep a careful account of your sources so that they can be cited appropriately during your speech. Although some people try to record information in files on their computers, we propose here a proven method for organizing your information on research cards.

Preparing Research Cards

How should you keep track of the information you plan to use? Although it may seem easier to record all material from one source on a single sheet of paper (or to photocopy source material), sorting and arranging material is much easier when each item is recorded separately. Recording each piece of information on its own research card allows you to easily find, arrange, and rearrange each item of information as you prepare your speech.

In the research card method, each factual statement, expert opinion, or elaboration, along with the bibliographical information on its source, is recorded on a four- by six-inch or larger index card containing three types of information. First, each card should have a heading or key-words that identify the subcategory to which the information belongs. Second, the specific fact, opinion, or elaboration statement should be recorded on the card. Any part of the information item that is quoted directly from the source should be enclosed in quotation marks. Third, the bibliographical publication data related to the source should be recorded.

The bibliographical information you will record depends on whether the source is a book, a periodical, a newspaper, an interview, or a website. For a book, include the names of authors, the title of the book, the place of publication and the publisher, the date of publication, and the page or pages from which the information is taken. For a periodical or newspaper, include the name of the author (if given), the title of the article, the name of the publication, the date, and the page number from which the information is taken. For online sources, include the URL for the website, the credentials of the site host, and the heading under which you found the information. Be sure to record enough source information so that you can relocate the material if you need to and cite the source appropriately during your speech. Exhibit 6.2 shows a sample research card.

As your stack of research cards grows, you can sort the material and place each item under the heading to which it is related. For instance, for a speech on bioluminescence, you might have a stack of research cards related to the biological process of bioluminescence, species that are bioluminescent, and causes of bioluminescence. The card in Exhibit 6.2 would be indexed under the heading "Uses."

The number of sources you will need depends in part on the type of speech you are giving and your own expertise. For a narrative/personal experience speech, you obviously will be the main, if not the only, source. For informative reports and persuasive speeches, however, speakers ordinarily draw from multiple sources. Moreover, the research cards should come from at least three different sources. Avoid using only one source for your information, because this often leads to plagiarism; furthermore, basing your speech on one or two sources suggests that you have not done sufficient research. Selecting and using information from several sources allows you to develop an original approach to your topic, ensure a broader research base, and make it more likely that you will have uncovered various opinions related to your topic.

Exhibit 6.2

A Sample Research Card

Topic: Bioluminescence

Heading: Uses

Fireflies blink to communicate, and each fly has a distinctive blink. Males and females also blink during mating season.

Johnson, K. L. (2006). Things that go "blink" in the night. *American Gardener, 85*(4) 46–47.

Speech Planning Action Step 3, Activity 3B will help you prepare research cards for the sources you compiled in Activity 3A. See the Student Response box immediately following the activity for a sample of how one student completed this exercise.

ACTION STEP 3
Activity 3B

Record Relevant Information on Research Cards

The goal of this activity is to review the source material that you identified in Action Step Activity 3A and to record on research cards specific items of information that you might wish to use in your speech.

1. Carefully read all print and electronic sources (including website material) that you have identified and evaluated as appropriate sources for your speech. Review your notes and tapes from all interviews and observations.

2. As you read an item (fact, opinion, example, illustration, statistic, anecdote, narrative, comparison–contrast, quotation, definition, or description) that you think might be useful in your speech, record the item on a research card or on the appropriate electronic research card form available at your CourseMate for SPEAK at www.cengagebrain.com. (If you are using an article that appeared in a periodical source that you read online, use the periodical research card form.)

You can complete this activity online and, if requested, e-mail it to your instructor. You can also use online forms to prepare your own research cards and print them for use in preparing your speech. Go to the CourseMate for SPEAK at www.cengagebrain.com to access Action Step Activity 3B.

{ **Student Response:**
Action Step 3, Activity 3B }

Speech goal: *I would like the audience to agree that domestic violence is a problem, realize some of its underlying causes, and be convinced of strategies to reduce domestic violence in the United States today.*

Card 1
Topic: *The problem*
Heading: *Scope*
Three million women per year are physically abused by their husbands or boyfriends. And about 31 percent of American women report being sexually or physically abused by a male partner during their lifetime.

(In other words, of the 20 women in my speech class, about six will be assaulted by a male partner during their lifetime!)
Family Violence Prevention Fund. (2007). Domestic violence is a serious, widespread social problem in America: The facts. Retrieved from http://www.endabuse.org/resources/facts.

Card 2
Topic: *The problem*
Heading: *Severity*
There were 248,300 rapes/sexual assaults in 2007, more than 500 per day, up from 190,600 in 2005.
Goodman, A. (2010, March 2). Domestic violence: A pre-existing condition? TruthDig.com. Retrieved from http://www.truthdig.com/report/item/domestic_violence_a_pre-existing_condition_20100302/

Card 3
Topic: *Causes*
Heading: *Power and control*
Men often resort to violence to gain power over women when they feel threatened and subordinate and want to maintain a sense of control.
Johnson, M. P., & Ferraro, K. J. (2000). Research on domestic violence in the 1990s: Making distinctions. Journal of Marriage and Family, 62(4), 948–963.

Card 4
Topic: *Causes*
Heading: *Power and control*
Most abused women would leave if human capital such as housing and employment were more readily available to them.
Christy-McMullin, K., & Shobe, M. A. (2007). The role of economic resources and human capital with woman abuse. Journal of Policy Practice, 6(1), 3–26.

Citing Sources in the Speech

In your speeches, as in any communication in which you use ideas that are not your own, you need to acknowledge the sources of your ideas and statements. Specifically mentioning your sources not only helps the audience evaluate the content but also adds to your credibility. In addition, citing sources will give concrete evidence of the depth of your research. Failure to cite sources, especially when you are presenting information that is meant to substantiate a controversial point, is unethical. Furthermore, failure to cite sources orally during your speech constitutes plagiarism. Just as you would provide footnotes in a written document, you must provide oral footnotes

Exhibit 6.3

Appropriate Speech Source Citations

Books

Cite the title of the book and the name of its author. You may cite the book's publication date or the author's credentials if doing so boosts credibility.

> *Thomas Friedman, noted international editor for the* New York Times*, stated in his book* Hot, Flat, and Crowded . . .

> *But to get a complete picture, we have to look at the statistics. According to the 2007* Statistical Abstract*, the level of production for the European economic community rose from . . .*

Journal or Magazine Articles

Cite the name of the publication in which you found the article. You may cite the article's author and title if doing adds credibility.

> *According to an article about the Federal Reserve in last week's* Newsweek . . .

> *In the latest Gallup poll cited in the February 10 issue of* Newsweek . . .

> *Timothy Sellnow, professor of communication at the University of Kentucky, wrote in an article published in 2009 in the* Journal of Applied Communication *that . . .*

Newspapers

Cite the name of the newspaper and date of the article. You may cite the article's author and his or her credentials if it adds credibility.

> *According to a May 2010 article in the* Washington Post . . .

Interviews

Cite the name and credentials of the person interviewed and the date the interview took place. If you cite the interview more than once, you need only cite the interviewee's name in subsequent oral footnotes.

> *In an interview with the* Wall Street Journal *on February 22, 2010, Treasury Secretary Timothy Geithner said . . .*

> *In my telephone interview on September 29 with Dr. Susan Nissen, physican for physical medicine in Kansas City, Kansas, I learned that . . .*

Internet Sources

Cite the website's author, his or her credentials, and the date of the site's most recent revision. If there is no author, cite the credentials of the website's sponsoring organization. Do not cite the URL as part of your oral footnote.

> *According to a January 2010 posting on the official website of the American Heart Association . . .*

Television Programs

Cite the name of the program and the date of the original broadcast. You may also cite the name of the reporter for news programs if it boosts credibility.

> *According to an October 2009 CNN special broadcast called "Latino in America" . . .*

Public Speeches

Cite the name and credentials of the speaker, as well as the occasion and date of the speech.

> *In a speech on the need for financial education during times of financial crises delivered to the Kansas City Federal Reserve Interagency Consumer Complaint Conference in April 2009, Susan C. Keating, president of the National Foundation of Credit Counseling, stated . . .*

---

during your speech. Oral footnotes are references to an original source made at the point in the speech where information from that source is presented. The key to preparing oral footnotes is to include enough information for listeners to access the sources themselves and to offer enough credentials to enhance the credibility of the information you are citing. Exhibit 6.3 gives several examples of appropriate speech source citations.

oral footnote reference to an original source made at the point in the speech where information from that source is presented

Speech Planning Action Step 3, Activity 3C, will help you prepare oral citations for the sources you recorded in Activity 3B. See the Student Response box immediately following the activity for a sample of how one student completed this exercise.

ACTION STEP 3
Activity 3C

Citing Sources

On the back of each research card, write a short phrase that you can use in your speech as an oral footnote for the material on this card.

Student Response: Action Step 3, Activity 3C

According to J. S. Gordon in Helping Survivors of Domestic Violence: The Effects of Medial, Mental Health, and Community Services*, domestic violence is the number one reason for emergency room visits by women.*

THERE ARE EVEN MORE STUDY TOOLS FOR THIS CHAPTER AT WWW.CENGAGEBRAIN.COM

- **Interactive Videos**
- **Speech Builder Express**
- **Printable Flash Cards**
- **Interactive Games**
- **Chapter Review Cards**
- **Online Quizzes with Feedback**
- **Speech Studio available upon instructor request**

Organizing and Outlining the Speech Body

Learning Outcomes

LO[1] Why is it important to limit your speech to two to four main points? | LO[2] Why should you construct a clear thesis statement? | LO[3] How might you arrange your points in your speech? | LO[4] What are some types of supporting material you can use to elaborate your main points? | LO[5] Why are transitions important?

"Troy, Mareka gave an awesome speech about recycling paper. I didn't realize the efforts that other universities are making to help the environment, and I haven't heard so many powerful stories in a long time."

"Yeah, Brett, I agree, the stories were interesting. But, you know, I had a hard time following the talk. I couldn't really get a hold of what the main ideas were. Did you?"

"Well, she was talking about recycling and stuff, . . . but now that you mention it, I'm not sure what she really wanted us to think or do about it. I mean, it was really interesting but kind of confusing too."

Troy and Brett's experience is not that unusual; even well-known speakers can give speeches that aren't as tightly organized as they could or should be. Yet if your speeches are well organized, you are more likely to achieve your speech goal. A well-organized speech has three identifiable parts: an introduction, a body, and a conclusion. In this chapter and the next, we explain the fourth speech plan action step: Organize and develop your ideas into a well-structured outline. This chapter focuses on developing the body of your speech by describing how to (a) identify main points that are implied in the specific goal statement and write them into a thesis statement for the speech; (b) organize the body of your speech by carefully wording and ordering your main points, developing each main point with supporting material that is appropriate to the audience; and (c) create transitions that move the speech smoothly from one main point to the next. In the next chapter, we describe how to create introductions and conclusions that pique audience interest, aid understanding, and help the audience remember what you spoke about.

What do you think?

The best way to arrange the main points of a speech is with stories.

Strongly Disagree								Strongly Agree	
1	2	3	4	5	6	7	8	9	10

main points
complete sentence statements of the two to four central ideas the audience needs to understand for your speech goal to be realized

Main Points

Once you have analyzed your audience, identified your general goal, created a specific goal, and assembled a body of information on your topic, you are ready to identify the main ideas you wish to present in your speech.

Identify Main Points

The **main points** of a speech are complete sentence statements of the two to four central ideas the audience needs to understand for your speech goal to be realized.

ACTION STEP 4:
Organize and Develop Ideas Into a Well-Structured Outline (the Body)

A. Identify two to four main points.
B. Write a thesis statement with main point preview.
C. Develop your main points.
D. Outline the speech body.

You need to limit the number of main points you present so audience members can easily understand what you are saying, remember the major ideas you present, and understand the speech's importance.

With some speech goals, identifying the main points is easy. For example, if your goal is to demonstrate how to create a web page, your main points will likely be the steps involved in developing it. Most times, however, you will need to do some further work to identify the main points that audience members need to understand if you are to achieve your speech goal. How can you identify these main ideas? First, begin by listing the ideas you have found that relate to your specific goal. You may be able to list as many as nine or more. Second, eliminate ideas that your audience analysis suggests this audience already understands. Third, check to see if some of the ideas can be grouped together under a broader theme. Fourth, eliminate any ideas that might be too complicated or too broad for this audience to comprehend in the time allotted for your speech. Finally, from the ideas that remain, choose two to four that are the most important for your audience to understand if you are to accomplish your specific speech goal.

Let's look at how Katie used these steps to identify the main points for a speech whose goal was to "inform my classmates of the growing problem of Adderall use among college students." To begin, Katie listed ideas she had discovered while doing her research.

what is a prescription drug
what is Adderall
what are the ingredients in Adderall
how is Adderall made
what is the history of Adderall
who takes Adderall
why is it prescribed
benefits
risks
how many college students take Adderall without a prescription
demographics of college students who take Adderall without a prescription
why college students who don't have a prescription take it (perceived benefits)
benefit myths
actual results/consequences

~~what is a prescription drug~~
what is Adderall
~~what are the ingredients in Adderall~~
~~how is Adderall made~~
~~what is the history of Adderall~~
who takes Adderall
why is it prescribed
benefits
risks

1) understanding the nature and purpose of Adderall as a prescription drug

how many college students take Adderall without a prescription
demographics of college students who take Adderall without a prescription
why college students who don't have a prescription take it (perceived benefits)

2) its growing popularity as a study aid among college students

benefit myths
actual results/consequences

3) problems involved with using Adderall as a study aid

Second, Katie eliminated the idea "what is a prescription drug" because she knew her audience already understood this. Third, Katie noticed that several of the ideas seemed to be related: what is Adderall, why is it prescribed, and who takes it, as well as its benefits and risks, seemed to go together. How many take it, demographics, and perceived benefits of college students who take Adderall without a prescription also seemed to be related. And benefit myths and actual results/consequences could be grouped together. Fourth, Katie decided the ingredients, history, and how Adderall is made were too broad to cover adequately in the time she was allotted and were not directly related to her goal. Finally, Katie decided her main points would be (a) understanding the nature and purpose of Adderall as a prescription drug, (b) its growing popularity as a study aid among college students, and (c) problems involved with using Adderall as a study aid. This process left Katie with three broad-based points that she could develop in her speech. See the figure on page 86 for what Katie's list looked like after she finished her analysis and synthesis.

Speech Planning Action Step 4, Activity 4A will help you identify main points to use for your speeches in this course. See the Student Response box immediately following the activity for a sample of how one student completed this exercise.

ACTION STEP 4
Activity 4A

Identifying Main Points

1. List all of the ideas you have found that relate to the specific purpose of your speech.
2. If you have trouble limiting the number, do the following:
   a. Draw a line through each of the ideas that you believe the audience already understands, that you have no information to support, or that just seem too complicated.
   b. Combine ideas that can be grouped together under a single heading.
3. From those ideas that remain, choose the two to four you will use as main points in your speech.

You can complete this activity online with Speech Builder Express and, if requested, e-mail your completed activity to your instructor. Go to the CourseMate for SPEAK at www.cengagebrain.com to access Action Step Activity 4A.

General goal: I want to inform my audience.

Specific goal: I want my audience to understand seasonal affective disorder (SAD).

1. List all of the ideas you have found that relate to the specific purpose of your speech.
   what is SAD
   symptoms
   causes of SAD
   historical background
   discoverer
   types of depression
   vitamin deficiencies
   locations and prevalence
   diagnoses
   medical treatments
   organic treatments
   therapeutic treatments
   the role of sunshine
   light therapy
   myths
   realities
2. If you have trouble limiting the number, do the following:
   a. Draw a line through each of the ideas that you believe the audience already understands, that you have no information to support, or that just seems too complicated.
   b. Combine ideas that can be grouped together under a single heading.
3. From those ideas that remain, choose the two to four you will use as main points in your speech.

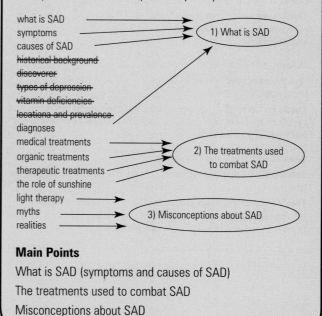

Main Points

What is SAD (symptoms and causes of SAD)

The treatments used to combat SAD

Misconceptions about SAD

thesis statement
a one- or two-sentence summary of the speech that incorporates the general and specific goals and previews the main points

Write the Thesis Statement

A thesis statement is a one- or two-sentence summary of your speech that incorporates your general and specific goals and previews the main points. Not only will you write this sentence on your speech outline, but you will also use this sentence as a basis for the transition from the introduction to the body of your speech. Thus, your thesis statement provides a blueprint from which you will organize the body of your speech. Exhibit 7.1 provides several examples of specific speech goals and thesis statements.

Katie crafted the following thesis statement for her speech on Adderall: "I want to inform my audience about the growing problem of college students taking Adderall without a prescription by explaining the nature and purpose of Adderall as a prescription drug, its growing popularity as a study aid among college students, and problems associated with using Adderall without a prescription." For more guidance on writing thesis statements, go to the CourseMate for SPEAK at www.cengagebrain.com to access **Web Resource 7.1: Writing Different Types of Thesis Statements**.

Exhibit 7.1

Sample Speech Goals and Thesis Statements

General goal: I want to inform my audience.

Specific goal: I want my audience to understand how to improve their grades in college.

Thesis statement: Three proven techniques for improving test scores in college are to attend classes regularly, develop a positive attitude, and study efficiently.

General goal: I want to inform my audience.

Specific goal: I want the audience to understand the benefits of volunteering.

Thesis statement: Some important benefits of volunteering include helping underprivileged populations, supporting nonprofit organizations, and improving your own self-esteem.

General goal: I want to persuade my audience.

Specific goal: I want my audience to believe that parents should limit the time their children spend viewing television.

Thesis statement: Parents should limit the time their children spend viewing television because heavy television viewing desensitizes children to violence and increases violent tendencies in children.

Speech Planning Action Step 4, Activity 4B will help you write a thesis statement for your speech. See the Student Response box immediately following the activity for a sample of how one student completed this exercise.

ACTION STEP 4
Activity 4B

Writing a Thesis Statement

The goal of this activity is to use your general and specific goals and the main points you have identified to develop a well-worded thesis statement for your speech.

1. Write the general and specific goals you developed in Action Step 1 Activity 1E.
2. List the main points you identified in Activity 4A.
3. Now write one or two complete sentences that combine your specific goal with your main point ideas.

You can complete this activity online with Speech Builder Express, view a student sample of this activity, and, if requested, e-mail your completed activity to your instructor. Go to the CourseMate for SPEAK at www.cengagebrain.com to access Action Step Activity 4B.

Student Response: Action Step 4, Activity 4B

1. Write the general and specific goals you developed in Activity 1E.
   General goal: I want to inform my audience.
   Specific goal: I want my audience to enjoy symphonic music.
2. List the main points you identified in Activity 4A.
   The characteristics of symphonic music
   How to listen to symphonic music
   The influence of symphonic music on popular music
3. Now write one or two complete sentences that combine your specific goal with your main point ideas.
   My goal is to increase the audience's enjoyment of symphonic music by describing the characteristics of symphonies, by explaining how to listen to a symphony, and by discussing the influence that symphonic music had and continues to have on popular music.

Outline the Body of the Speech

Once you have a thesis statement, you can begin to outline your speech. A **speech outline** is a sentence representation of the hierarchical and sequential relationships among the ideas presented in the speech. In a way, it is a diagram that organizes the information you will present. Your outline may have three hierarchical levels of information: main points (noted by the use of Roman numerals: I, II, III, . . .), subpoints that support a main point (noted by the use of capital letters: A, B, C, . . .), and sometimes sub-subpoints to support subpoints (noted by Arabic numerals: 1, 2, 3, . . .).

You will want to write your main points and subpoints in complete sentences to clarify the relationship between main points and subpoints. Exhibit 7.2 shows the general form of how a formal speech outline system looks.

The length of your speech is not determined by the number of main points you have but by how thoroughly you develop each of them. The same two to four main points can be developed into a speech that will last for three to five minutes, eight to 10 minutes, or even into a 50-minute major presentation. As you will see, a complex main point may have two, three, or even more subpoints. Each subpoint will be developed through one or more sub-subpoints. And subpoints and/or sub-subpoints may be elaborated with definitions, examples, statistics, personal experiences, stories, quotations, and other items. It's often the number and length of elaborations that determine the length of the speech. In a five-minute speech, you may be limited to only two or three elaborations for each subpoint. But an hour-long speech may allow you to include more elaborations and longer ones for each subpoint.

Exhibit 7.3 shows how Katie developed one of her main points. Notice that all main points, subpoints, and sub-subpoints are written in complete sentences.

> **speech outline**
> a sentence representation of the hierarchical and sequential relationships among the ideas presented in the speech

Exhibit 7.2

General Form for a Speech Outline

I. **Main point one**
  A. Subpoint A for main point one
    1. Sub-subpoint one
      a. Elaboration material (if needed)
      b. Elaboration material (if needed)
    2. Sub-subpoint two
      a. Elaboration material (if needed)
      b. Elaboration material (if needed)
  B. Subpoint B for main point one
    1. Sub-subpoint one
      a. Elaboration material (if needed)
      b. Elaboration material (if needed)
    2. Sub-subpoint two
      a. Elaboration material (if needed)
      b. Elaboration material (if needed)
II. **Main point two**
  A. Subpoint A for main point two
    1. Sub-subpoint one
      a. Elaboration material (if needed)
      b. Elaboration material (if needed)
    2. Sub-subpoint two
      a. Elaboration material (if needed)
      b. Elaboration material (if needed)
  B. Subpoint B for main point two
    1. Sub-subpoint one
      a. Elaboration material (if needed)
      b. Elaboration material (if needed)
    2. Sub-subpoint two
      a. Elaboration material (if needed)
      b. Elaboration material (if needed)
. . . etc.

© CENGAGE LEARNING 2011

Exhibit 7.3

Katie's Sample Outline

I. Adderall is a psychostimulant prescribed to treat three conditions.
  A. Adderall, the brand name for amphetamine-dextroamphetamine is a psychostimulant, one of a class of drugs intended to promote concentration, suppress hyperactivity, and promote healthy social experiences for patients.
    1. Adderall stimulates the central nervous system by increasing the amount of dopamine and norepinephrine in the brain. These chemicals are neurotransmitters that help the brain send signals between nerve cells.
    2. Mentally, Adderall brings about a temporary improvement in alertness, wakefulness, endurance, and motivation.
    3. Physically, it can increase heart rate and blood pressure and decrease perceived need for food or sleep.
  B. Adderall is prescribed for the medical treatment of attention deficit hyperactivity disorder (ADHD) in children and adults as well as for narcolepsy and clinical depression.
    1. ADHD is a neurobehavioral developmental disorder characterized by problems of attention coupled with hyperactivity.
      a. Since the mid-1990s, there has been a documented increase in the number of American children diagnosed and treated for ADHD.
      b. According to the *Diagnostic and Statistical Manual of Mental Disorders* (2000), symptoms must be present for at least six months for diagnosis, and symptoms must be excessive for medicinal treatment.
      c. The drugs Ritalin and Dexedrine are also used to treat ADHD. Adderall, however, remains the most widely prescribed of these drugs.
      d. According to the Centers for Disease Control and Prevention, approximately 4.4 million American children have been diagnosed with ADHD, and more than 2.5 million of those patients have been prescribed medicine to treat the condition.
    2. Adderall is also prescribed to treat narcolepsy, which occurs when the brain can't normally regulate cycles of sleep and waking, so sufferers experience excessive daytime sleepiness that results in episodes of suddenly falling asleep.
    3. Adderall can also be used to treat clinical depression, a disorder that is characterized by low mood, a loss of interest in normal activities, and low self-esteem.

© ISTOCKPHOTO.COM/KYOSHINO

preparation outline
provides a starting point of main points but doesn't specify clearly how each main point is related to the goal

parallel
when wording of points follows the same structural pattern, often using the same introductory words

Outline Main Points

Once you have a thesis statement, you can begin outlining the main points that will make up the body of your speech. It is important to write main points, subpoints, and sub-subpoints as complete sentences because only complete sentences can fully express the relationship among the main points and subpoints, and between each main point and the specific speech goal. Once you have worded each main point, you will choose an organizing pattern.

Wording Main Points

Recall that Katie determined that her main points would be to understand the nature and purpose of Adderall as a prescription drug, its growing popularity as a study aid among college students, and the risks involved in doing so, and that her thesis statement was "I want to inform my audience about the growing problem of college students taking Adderall without a prescription by explaining the nature and purpose of Adderall as a prescription drug, its growing popularity as a study aid among college students, and problems associated with using Adderall without a prescription." Suppose she wrote her first draft of main points as follows:

I. *What is Adderall, and why is it prescribed?*

II. *College student use*

III. *Risks*

From this wording, Katie would have drafted some ideas of the main points she was going to talk about, which is essentially what you need to do in the preliminary draft of your formal outline. This version is also known as a **preparation outline** because it provides a starting point of main points but doesn't specify clearly how each main point is related to her goal. To make the relationships clear, Katie needs to create complete sentences for each. So she might clarify her main points like this:

I. *What is Adderall?*

II. *An increasing number of American college students are using Adderall.*

III. *Abusing Adderall is risky.*

Look at these statements. Do they seem a bit vague? Notice that we have emphasized that this is a first draft. Sometimes, the first draft of a main point is well expressed and doesn't need additional work. More often, however, we find that our first attempt doesn't quite capture what we want to say. So we need to rework our points to make them clearer. Let's consider Katie's draft statements more carefully. Katie has made a pretty good start. Her three main points are complete sentences. Now let's see how Katie might use two test questions to assure herself that she has achieved the best wording for her points.

1. **Is the relationship between each main point statement and the goal statement clearly specified?** Katie's first main point statement doesn't indicate what purposes Adderall serves as a prescription medicine. So she could improve this statement by saying:

   What is Adderall, and what is it prescribed for?

   Similarly, she can improve the second main point statement by saying:

   Adderall abuse is becoming increasingly popular among American college students.

   The third point might be redrafted to state:

   Abusing Adderall as a study aid is dangerous.

2. **Are the main points parallel in structure?** Main points are **parallel** to one another when their wording follows the same structural pattern, often using the same introductory words. Parallel structure is not a requirement, but it can help the audience recognize main points when you deliver your speech. Katie notices that she could make her main points parallel with a small adjustment:

   I. *First, what is Adderall, and why is it prescribed?*

   II. *Second, a growing number of American college students are using Adderall.*

   III. *Third, abusing Adderall as a study aid is dangerous.*

   Parallelism can be achieved in many ways. Katie used numbering: "first . . . second . . . third." Another way is to start each sentence with an active verb. Suppose Adam wants his audience to understand the steps involved in writing an effective job application cover letter. He might write the following first draft of his main points:

   I. *Format the heading elements correctly.*

   II. *The body of the letter should be three paragraphs long.*

   III. *When concluding, use "sincerely" or "regards."*

   IV. *Then you need to proofread the letter carefully.*

   After further consideration, Adam might revise his main points to make them parallel

First . . .

Second . . .

Third . . .

in structure by using active verbs (shown in bold):

I. **Format** *the heading elements correctly.*

II. **Organize** *the body into three paragraphs.*

III. **Conclude** *the letter with "sincerely" or "regards."*

IV. **Proofread** *the letter carefully.*

Notice how the similarity of structure clarifies and strengthens the message. The audience can immediately identify the key steps in the process.

Selecting an Organizational Pattern for Main Points

A speech can be organized in many different ways. Your objective is to find or create the structure that will help the audience make the most sense of the material. Although speeches may follow many types of organization, beginning speakers should learn four fundamental patterns: time order, narrative order, topic order, and logical reasons order.

1. **Time order.** Time order, sometimes called *sequential order* or *chronological order*, is a frequently used pattern in informative speeches. When you use **time order**, you organize your main points in a chronological sequence or by steps in a process. Thus, time order is appropriate when you are explaining how to do something, how to make something, how something works, or how something happened. Adam's speech on the *steps* in writing a job application cover letter is an example of time order. As the following example illustrates, the order of main points is as important for audiences to remember as the ideas themselves.

General goal: I want to inform my audience.

Specific goal: *I want the audience to understand the four steps involved in developing a personal network.*

Thesis statement: *The four steps involved in developing a personal network are to analyze your current networking potential, to position yourself in places for opportunity, to advertise yourself, and to follow up on contacts.*

I. *First, analyze your current networking potential.*

II. *Second, position yourself in places for opportunity.*

III. *Third, advertise yourself.*

IV. *Fourth, follow up on contacts.*

Although the use of "first," "second," and so on is not required when using time order,

using them helps audience members understand that the *sequence* is important.

> **time order**
> organizing the main points of the speech in a chronological sequence or by steps in a process
>
> **narrative order**
> organizing the main points of the speech as a story or series of stories

2. **Narrative order.** A second pattern for arranging your main points is narrative order, which conveys your ideas through a story or series of stories. Narrative order conveys your ideas through a story or series of stories. Narrative order is rooted in narrative theory, which suggests that one important way people communicate is through storytelling. We use stories to teach and to learn, to entertain, and to make sense of the world around us.[1] This pattern is similar to time order because the main points are usually presented in chronological order, but with narrative order, the entire speech consists of one or more stories that include characters, settings, and plots. Narrative order is particularly effective when you tell stories that are emotionally compelling. The goal of using this pattern is for listeners to accept your conclusion by showing them the validity of what you are saying through description rather than simply telling them. Lana shared her story about having anorexia to help listeners understand the impact of the condition on one's life.

General goal: I want to inform my audience.

Specific goal: *I want my audience to understand how anorexia nervosa affects the lives of its victims and their loved ones.*

Thesis statement: *Today, I want to share my story as a person living with anorexia by sharing my weight obsession experiences as a high school gymnast, as a college sophomore, and as a young adult today.*

I. *I recall first becoming weight conscious when I was captain of the high school gymnastics team.*

II. *What might have been described merely as obsessive dieting turned into full-blown anorexia during my sophomore year of college.*

III. *Thanks to loving help from my family and friends, as well as doctors and therapists, I am alive and well today.*

IV. *Living with anorexia nervosa means being forever cognizant of eating enough so I never go back into that horrible place where I nearly died.*

topic order
organizing the main points of the speech by categories or divisions of a subject

logical reasons order
organizing the main points of a persuasive speech by the reasons that support the speech goal

3. **Topic order.** A third, often used organization for informative speeches is **topic order**, which organizes the main points of the speech by categories or divisions of a subject. This is a common way of ordering main points because nearly any subject can be subdivided or categorized in many different ways. The order of the topics may go from general to specific, move from least important to most important, or follow some other logical sequence.

In the example that follows, the topics are presented in the order that the speaker believes is most suitable for the audience and specific speech goal, with the most important point at the end.

General goal: I want to inform my audience.

Specific goal: I want the audience to understand three proven methods for ridding our bodies of harmful toxins.

Thesis statement: Three proven methods for ridding our bodies of harmful toxins are reducing intake of animal foods, hydrating, and eating natural whole foods.

I. *One proven method for ridding our bodies of harmful toxins is reducing our intake of animal products.*

II. *A second proven method for ridding our bodies of harmful toxins is keeping well hydrated.*

III. *A third proven method for ridding our bodies of harmful toxins is eating more natural whole foods.*

Whereas time order suggests a sequence that must be followed, topic order suggests that of any possible ideas or methods, two to four are particularly important, valuable, or necessary. Katie's speech on the uses and abuses of Adderall is another example of a speech using topic order.

4. **Logical reasons order.** Logical reasons order organizes the main points by the reasons that

support the speech goal. It emphasizes why the audience should believe something or behave in a particular way. Logical reasons order is most appropriate for a persuasive speech.

General goal: I want to persuade my audience.

Specific goal: I want the audience to donate money to the United Way.

Thesis statement: Donating to the United Way is appropriate because your one donation covers many charities, you can stipulate which specific charities you wish to support, and a high percentage of your donation goes to charities.

I. *When you donate to the United Way, your one donation covers many charities.*

II. *When you donate to the United Way, you can stipulate which charities you wish to support.*

III. *When you donate to the United Way, you know that a high percentage of your donation will go directly to the charities you've selected.*

These four organizational patterns are the most common. There are others, and we'll talk about some of them in later chapters. As you develop your public speaking skills, you may find that you will need to revise one of these patterns or create a totally different one to meet the needs of your particular subject matter or audience.

In summary, then, to organize the body of your speech, (a) turn your speech goal into a one- or two-sentence thesis that combines the general goal and specific goal with a preview of the main points; (b) state the main points in complete sentences that are clear, parallel, meaningful, and limited to no more than four; and (c) organize the main points in the pattern best suited to your material and the needs of your specific audience.

Exhibit 7.3, shown earlier, shows what Katie's outline would look like at this stage of preparation. Notice that her general and specific speech goals are written at the top of the page. Her thesis statement comes right after the goals because later it will become part of her introduction.

Speech Planning Action Step 4, Activity 4C will help you develop well-written main points for your speech. See the Student Response box immediately following the activity for a sample of how one student completed this exercise.

ACTION STEP 4
Activity 4C

Developing the Main Points of Your Speech

The goal of this activity is to help you phrase and order your main points.

1. Write your thesis statement.
2. Underline the two to four main points identified in your thesis statement.
3. For each underlined item, write one sentence that summarizes what you want your audience to know about that idea.
4. Review the main points as a group.
   a. Is the relationship between each main point statement and the goal statement clearly specified? If not, revise.
   b. Are the main points parallel in structure? If not, consider why and revise.
5. Choose an organizational pattern for your main points.
6. Identify the type of pattern you have used.

You can complete this activity online with Speech Builder Express, view a student sample of this activity, and, if requested, e-mail your completed activity to your instructor. Go to the CourseMate for SPEAK at www.cengagebrain.com to access Activity 4C.

Student Response:
Action Step 4, Activity 4C

1. Write your thesis statement.
   The three tests that you can use to determine whether a diamond is real are the <u>acid test</u>, <u>the streak test</u>, and the <u>hardness test</u>.
2. Underline the two to four main points identified in your thesis statement.
3. For each underlined item, write one sentence that summarizes what you want your audience to know about that idea.
   I. *<u>One way to identify a diamond is by using the acid test.</u>*
   II. *<u>You can also identify a diamond by using the streak test.</u>*

III. *<u>You can also identify a diamond by using the hardness test.</u>*
4. Review the main points as a group.
   a. Is the relationship between each main point statement and the goal statement clearly specified? If not, revise.
   No. The purpose of testing is to identify whether the diamond is real. The following revision puts emphasis in the right place.
   Revision:
   I. *<u>One way to identify whether a diamond is real is by using the acid test.</u>*
   II. *<u>You can also identify whether a diamond is real by using the streak test.</u>*
   III. *<u>You can also identify whether a diamond is real by using the hardness test.</u>*
   b. Are the main points parallel in structure? If not, consider why and revise.
   Revision:
   I. *<u>One way to determine whether a diamond is real is to use the acid test.</u>*
   II. *<u>A second way to determine whether a diamond is real is to use the streak test.</u>*
   III. *<u>A third way to determine whether a diamond is real is to use the hardness test.</u>*
5. Choose an organizational pattern for your main points.
   I. *<u>One way to determine whether a diamond is real is to use the acid test.</u>*
   II. *<u>A second way to determine whether a diamond is real is to use the streak test.</u>*
   III. *<u>A third way to determine whether a diamond is real is to use the hardness test.</u>*
6. Identify the type of pattern you have used.
   <u>Topic order</u>

Identify and Outline Subpoints

Just as you must identify the main points of your speech, you must also identify the subpoints. One subpoint should be a **listener relevance link**, a statement alerting listeners about how this point relates to them or why they should care about it. As stated earlier, your outline will include complete sentence statements of each of your subpoints. A main point may have two, three, or even more subpoints depending on the complexity of the main point.

Identifying Subpoints

You can identify subpoints by sorting the research cards you prepared earlier into

listener relevance link
a statement alerting listeners about how a main point or subpoint relates to them or why they should care about it

piles that correspond to each of your main points. The goal at this point is to see what information you have that supports each of your main points. Once you have listed the items of information that make the point, look for relationships between and among ideas. As you analyze, you can draw lines connecting items of information that fit together logically, cross out information that seems irrelevant or doesn't really fit, and combine similar ideas using different language.

Outlining Subpoints

Subpoints should also be represented on the outline in full sentences. Be sure to also include internal references for items of information you found in secondary sources. Doing so will remind you to cite them during the speech, which will enhance your credibility and help you avoid unintentional plagiarism. As with main points, they should be revised until they are clearly stated. The items of information listed for Katie's first main point might be grouped as follows:

I. Adderall is a psychostimulant prescribed to treat three conditions.

Listener relevance link: Understanding the intended medical uses of the drug Adderall may help you understand why the drug is so widely abused by collegians.

A. Adderall, the brand name for amphetamine-dextroamphetamine is a psychostimulant, one of a class of drugs intended to promote concentration, suppress hyperactivity, and promote healthy social experiences for patients (Willis, 2001).

1. Adderall stimulates the central nervous system by increasing the amount of dop-

amine and norepinephrine in the brain. These chemicals are neurotransmitters that help the brain send signals between nerve cells (Daley, 2004).

2. Mentally, Adderall brings about a temporary improvement in alertness, wakefulness, endurance, and motivation.

3. Physically, it can increase heart rate and blood pressure and decrease perceived need for food or sleep.

B. Adderall is prescribed for the medical treatment of attention deficit hyperactivity disorder (ADHD) in children and adults as well as for narcolepsy and clinical depression.

1. ADHD is a neurobehavioral developmental disorder characterized by problems of attention coupled with hyperactivity.

   a. Since the mid-1990s, there has been a documented increase in the number of American children diagnosed and treated for ADHD (McCabe, Teter, & Boyd, 2004).

   b. According to the *Diagnostic and Statistical Manual of Mental Disorders* (2000), symptoms must be present for at least six months for diagnosis, and symptoms must be excessive for medicinal treatment.

   c. The drugs Ritalin and Dexedrine are also used to treat ADHD. Adderall, however, remains the most widely prescribed of these drugs (Willis, 2001).

   d. According to the Centers for Disease Control and Prevention (2005), approximately 4.4 million American children have been diagnosed with ADHD, and more than 2.5 million of those patients have been prescribed medicine to treat the condition (2005).

2. Adderall is also prescribed to treat narcolepsy, which occurs when the brain can't normally regulate cycles of sleep and waking.

   a. Sufferers of narcolepsy experience excessive daytime sleepiness that results in episodes of suddenly falling asleep.

   b. A chronic sleep disorder, narcolepsy affects 1 in every 2,000 Americans (American Academy of Sleep Medicine, 2005).

3. Adderall can also be used to treat clinical depression, a disorder that is characterized by low mood, a loss of interest in normal activities,

Main point III

Main point II

Main point I

and low self-esteem. According to the National Institute of Mental Health, 9.5 percent of the adult population—that is, nearly 1.8 million American adults—suffer from clinical depression.

List Supporting Material

A good outline also includes short outline statements of **supporting material**—developmental material that will be used in the speech—for example, personal experiences, examples, illustrations, anecdotes, statistics, and quotations. You will choose these items to meet the needs of your specific audience. Be sure to include internal citations and develop a reference list as you go along. Doing so will help you remember what research to cite and when during your speech to enhance your credibility and to demonstrate ethical communication behavior by avoiding plagiarism.

Create Transitions

Once you have outlined your main points, subpoints, and potential supporting material, you will want to consider how you will move smoothly from one main point to another. **Transitions** are words, phrases, or sentences that show the relationship between, or bridge, two ideas. Transitions act like tour guides leading the audience from point to point through the speech. There are two types of transitions: section transitions and signposts.

Section transitions are complete sentences that show the relationship between, or bridge, major parts of a speech. They typically summarize what has just been said in one main point and preview the next main idea. Essentially, section transitions are the glue that holds the macrostructure of your speech together.

For example, suppose Adam has just finished the introduction of his speech on creating a cover letter and is now ready to launch into his main points. Before stating his first main point, he might say, "Creating a good cover letter is a process that has four steps. Now let's consider the first one." When his listeners hear this transition, they are signaled to mentally prepare to listen to and remember the first main point. When he finishes his first main point, he will use another section transition to signal that he is finished speaking about step one and is moving on to discuss step two: "Now that we have seen what is involved in creating the heading elements, we can move on to the second step."

You might be thinking that this sounds repetitive or patronizing, but section transitions are important for two reasons. First, they help the audience follow the organization of ideas in the speech by signaling that you are moving to the next point. In writing, you may use verbal transitions, but you also use paragraph notation (either through indenting the first sentence of a new paragraph or double spacing between paragraphs) to indicate a change of topic. In speaking, we use section transitions and perhaps body language to signal that we are moving on to a different point. Second, section transitions help audience members remember information. We may well remember something that was said once in a speech, but our retention is likely to increase markedly if we hear something more than once. In a speech, if we preview main points, then state each main point, and also provide transitions between points, audiences are more likely to follow and remember the organization. To help you remember to use section transitions, write them in complete sentences on your speech outline.

supporting material
developmental material that will be used in the speech, including personal experiences, examples, illustrations, anecdotes, statistics, and quotations

transition
a sentence or two that summarizes one main point and introduces the next one

section transitions
complete sentences that show the relationship between, or bridge, major parts of a speech

signposts
words or phrases that connect pieces of supporting material to the main point or subpoint they address

Signposts are words or phrases that connect pieces of supporting material to the main point or subpoint they address. While section transitions are complete sentences, signposts are usually one-word references. Sometimes, signposts highlight numerical order: "first," "second," "third," or "fourth." Sometimes, they help the audience focus on a key idea: "foremost," "most important," or "above all." They can also be used to signify an explanation: "to illustrate," "for example," "in other words," "essentially," or "to clarify." Signposts can also signal that an important idea, or even the speech itself, is coming to an end: "in short," "finally," "in conclusion," or "to summarize." Just as section transitions serve as the glue that holds your macrostructure together, signposts serve as the glue that holds your subpoints and supporting material together within each main point.

Speech Planning Action Step 4, Activity 4D will help you complete the outline for the body of your speech. See the Student Response box immediately following the activity for a sample of how one student completed this exercise.

ACTION STEP 4
Activity 4D

Outlining the Speech Body

The goal of this exercise is to help you get started on the outline for the body of your first speech. Using complete sentences, write the following:

1. The specific goal you developed in Action Step 1 Activity 1E.
2. The thesis statement you developed in Activity 4B.
3. A transition to the first main point.
4. The first main point you developed in Activity 4C.
5. The outline of the listener relevance link, subpoints, and support for your first main point, similar to the sample shown earlier under "Outlining Subpoints."
6. A transition from your first main point to your second.
7. The other points, subpoints, support, section transitions, and signposts. Use the format for numeration, spacing, and so on shown in the Student Response to Activity 4D. For a sample of a completed outline, see pages 112–115 of Chapter 8. (Note that the labels Introduction, Conclusion, and Sources are included just to help you understand the requirements for your final outline.)

You can complete this activity online with Speech Builder Express and, if requested, e-mail your completed activity to your instructor. Go to the CourseMate for SPEAK at www.cengagebrain.com to access Activity 4D.

{ Student Response: Action Step 4, Activity 4D }

Here is Katie's outline of her main points, including her goals, thesis statement, and section transitions.

General goal: I want to inform my audience.

Specific speech goal: I would like the audience to understand the uses and abuses of Adderall.

Thesis statement: I want to inform my audience about the growing problem of college students taking Adderall without a prescription by explaining the nature and purpose of Adderall as a prescription drug, its growing popularity as a study aid among college students, and problems associated with using Adderall without a prescription.

Body

I. Adderall is a psychostimulant prescribed to treat three conditions.
   Listener relevance link: Understanding the intended medical uses of the drug Adderall may help you understand why the drug is so widely abused by collegians.
   A. Adderall, the brand name for amphetamine-dextroamphetamine, is a psychostimulant, one of a class of drugs intended to promote concentration, suppress hyperactivity, and promote healthy social experiences for patients (Willis, 2001).
      1. Adderall stimulates the central nervous system by increasing the amount of dopamine and norepinephrine in the brain. These chemicals are neurotransmitters that help the brain send signals between nerve cells (Daley, 2004).
      2. Mentally, Adderall brings about a temporary improvement in alertness, wakefulness, endurance, and motivation.
      3. Physically, it can increase heart rate and blood pressure and decrease perceived need for food or sleep.
   B. Adderall is prescribed for the medical treatment of attention deficit hyperactivity disorder (ADHD) in children and adults as well as for narcolepsy and clinical depression.
      1. ADHD is a neurobehavioral developmental disorder characterized by problems of attention coupled with hyperactivity.
         a. Since the mid-1990s, there has been a documented increase in the number of American children diagnosed with and treated for ADHD (McCabe, Teter, & Boyd, 2004).
         b. According to the *Diagnostic and Statistical Manual of Mental Disorders* (2000), symptoms must be present for at least six

months for diagnosis, and symptoms must be excessive for medicinal treatment.

   c. The drugs Ritalin and Dexedrine are also used to treat ADHD. Adderall, however, remains the most widely prescribed of these drugs (Willis, 2001).

   d. According to the Centers for Disease Control and Prevention, approximately 4.4 million American children have been diagnosed with ADHD, and more than 2.5 million of those patients have been prescribed medicine to treat the condition (2005).

2. Adderall is also prescribed to treat narcolepsy, which occurs when the brain can't normally regulate cycles of sleep and waking.

   a. Sufferers of narcolepsy experience excessive daytime sleepiness that results in episodes of suddenly falling asleep.

   b. A chronic sleep disorder, narcolepsy affects 1 in every 2,000 Americans (American Academy of Sleep Medicine, 2005).

3. Adderall can also be used to treat clinical depression.

   a. Clinical depression is a disorder characterized by low mood, a loss of interest in normal activities, and low self-esteem.

   b. According to the National Institute of Mental Health, 9.5 percent of the adult population— that is, nearly 1.8 million American adults— suffer from clinical depression.

Transition: Now that we understand the basic properties and medical uses of the drug Adderall, let's now assess the increasing level of abuse of the drug by college students.

II. Unfortunately, Adderall has become popular among college students who use it "off label" as a study aid and for recreational purposes.

Listener relevance link: As college students, we need to be aware of what students believe about Adderall and why they are abusing it.

   A. College students who don't suffer from ADHD, narcolepsy, or depression will take it with no prescription because they believe that it will improve their focus and concentration, allowing them to perform better on academic tasks (Teter, McCabe, Crandford, Boyd, & Gunthrie, 2005).

   1. Adderall abuse among college students occurs especially at stressful times of the semester when students get little sleep.

      a. DeSantis, Webb, and Noar (2007) found that 72 percent of the students they surveyed reported using the drug to stay awake so that they could study longer when they had many assignments due.

      b. Katherine Stump, a Georgetown University student, reported in the school newspaper: "During finals week here at Georgetown, campus turns into an Adderall drug den. Everyone from a cappella singers to newspaper writers become addicts, while anyone with a prescription and an understanding of the free market becomes an instant pusherman" (Jaffe, 2006).

      c. Collegians report using the drug frequently during stressful times of the semester. One student said, "I use it every time I have a major paper due" (Daley, 2004).

   2. Students also use Adderall for purposes other than academic ones.

      a. A survey of undergraduate and graduate students revealed that students engage in Adderall abuse for partying at a frequency just slightly less than taking the drug for academic purposes (Prudhomme White, Becker-Blease, & Grace-Bishop, 2006).

      b. DeSantis, Webb, and Noar (2007) report that students take the drug for its energizing effects. Other students report taking the drug to make them more social and outgoing at parties.

      c. Some college students, especially women, report using the drug for its use as an appetite suppressant for dieting purposes (Daley, 2004).

   B. Adderall abuse is pervasive at the University of Kentucky, and the medication is easily obtained on campus.

   1. I lived on campus my freshman year of college, and I currently still live in the dorms. By living in close proximity with other students, I learned a great deal about the individuals on my floor. I personally knew several students who used Adderall without a prescription. One student obtained the medication from a younger sibling diagnosed with ADHD, and another student purchased the pills from a friend on campus. The students would take the medicine to focus more intently when they had a short amount of time to complete a task. Both told me that they had used the drug as a study aid whenever they had several assignments to complete around the same time.

   2. Adderall is easily obtained at the University of Kentucky. A male friend of mine told me that he had no problem finding someone to sell him the medication once he approached his first exam week as a college freshman. He told me that he merely had to ask around, and within no time, he was able to find a fellow student who agreed to sell him Adderall.

As with any major university, the University of Kentucky is not impervious to the widespread abuse of Adderall by its students.

Transition: Now that we understand that Adderall abuse is prevalent on university campuses among students, it is important to understand the detrimental effects that can accompany the illegal use of Adderall.

III. Whether students acknowledge the dangers or not, there are great risks involved in illegally using Adderall.

Listener relevance link: As we have now discussed the pervasiveness of Adderall abuse, statistically, it is likely that several of you have used this substance without a prescription to either enhance your academic performance or your social outings. Thus, it is important that we all recognize the adverse effects that result from taking Adderall without a prescription.

A. Adderall abuse can cause negative health effects for individuals not diagnosed with ADHD (Daley, 2004, April 20).

  1. Adderall is reported to cause a heightened risk for heart problems when used inappropriately. Problems include sudden heart attack or stroke, sudden death in individuals with heart conditions, and increased blood pressure and heart rate (FDA, 2010).

  2. Adderall abuse also can result in a myriad of mental problems including manifestation of bipolar disorder, an increase of aggressive thoughts, and a heightened risk for psychosis similar to schizophrenia (FDA, 2010).

B. Adderall is highly addictive.

  1. Adderall is an amphetamine, and while amphetamines were once used to treat a variety of ailments including weight loss in the 1950s and '60s, the drugs began to be much more closely regulated once their addictive nature was realized (Daley, 2004).

  2. Adderall has similar properties to cocaine, and, as a result, abuse of the drug can lead to substance dependence (FDA, 2010).

C. Though clear risks are associated with the illegal use of Adderall, unlike other drugs, collegians do not view the inappropriate use of Adderall as harmful or illegal.

  1. College students typically view stimulant abuse as morally acceptable and physically harmless. In a 2010 study, DeSantis and Hane found that students were quick to justify their stimulant abuse by claiming its use was fine in moderation.

  2. *The Kentucky Kernel*, the student newspaper at the University of Kentucky, published an editorial of a student who flippantly described the use of Adderall among college students. He states, "If you want to abuse ice cream, amphetamines or alcohol, then there are going to be serious problems; however, let's not pretend a person using Adderall twice a semester to help them study is in any way likely to die a horrible death or suffer terrible side effects" (Riley, 2010).

  3. In a study assessing the attitudes of college students toward the inappropriate use of stimulants, the authors found that "the majority of students who reported misuse or abuse were not concerned about the misuse and abuse of prescription stimulants, and a number of students thought that they should be more readily available" (Prudhomme White, Becker-Blease, & Grace-Bishop, 2006, p. 265).

Transition: Now that we understand the risks involved in illegally using Adderall, hopefully you have a better understanding of why using the drug without a prescription is so dangerous.

THERE ARE EVEN MORE STUDY TOOLS FOR THIS CHAPTER AT
WWW.CENGAGEBRAIN.COM

- **Interactive Videos**
- **Speech Builder Express**
- **Printable Flash Cards**
- **Interactive Games**

- **Chapter Review Cards**
- **Online Quizzes with Feedback**
- **Speech Studio available upon instructor request**

Speak Up!

SPEAK was built on a simple principle: to create a new teaching and learning solution that reflects the way today's faculty teach and the way you learn.

Through conversations, focus groups, surveys, and interviews, we collected data that drove the creation of the current version of SPEAK that you are using today. But it doesn't stop there—in order to make SPEAK an even better learning experience, we'd like you to SPEAK UP and tell us how SPEAK worked for you. What did you like about it? What would you change? Are there additional ideas you have that would help us build a better product for next semester's speech communication students?

At the CourseMate for SPEAK at **www.cengagebrain.com**, you'll find all of the resources you need to succeed—**Printable Flash Cards**, **Interactive Quizzing**, **Crossword Puzzles**, **Games**, **Interactive Video Activities**, **Audio Study Tools**, and more!

Speak Up! Go to the CourseMate for SPEAK at **www.cengagebrain.com**

The Introduction and Conclusion

Learning Outcomes

LO¹ Why are solid introductions and conclusions so important to effective public speaking? | LO² How can you get your audience's attention in your introduction? | LO³ Why should you summarize your main points again in the conclusion? | LO⁴ How might you motivate listeners to remember your speech in your conclusion? | LO⁵ How do you determine which sources to include in your outline and reference list?

Courtney asked April to listen to her rehearse her speech. As she stood in front of the room where she was practicing, she began, "According to Merriam-Webster's online dictionary, organic food is 'relating to, yielding, or involving the use of food produced with the use of feed or fertilizer of plant or animal origin without employment of chemically formulated fertilizers, growth stimulants, antibiotics, or pesticides.' In my speech, I'd like to offer three reasons to eat organic food. First, organic food is healthier than mass-produced food. Let me explain why."

"Whoa, Courtney," April said. "That's your introduction?"

"Yes," Courtney replied. "I've got a lot of information to share and don't have a lot of time to say it. So, I don't want to waste any more time than necessary on my introduction."

Courtney's response sounds reasonable at first. But what she is failing to realize is that not everyone in the audience may be ready to listen to a speech about eating organic food. People might think the topic is boring, irrelevant to them, or for some other reason not worth their time. They might also wonder what makes Courtney a credible speaker on the subject. For most speeches, how well you start the speech may determine whether most members of the audience even listen, and how well you start and finish your speech can play a major role in the speech's overall success.

One reason a speech's introduction and conclusion are so important is based on what psychologists call the **primacy-recency effect**: We are more likely to remember the first and last items conveyed orally in a series than the items in between.[1] Another reason stems from the need for listeners to quickly grasp your goal and main points as they listen to your speech and to remember them after you've finished. You can give listeners a preview of the macrostructure of your speech by using the introduction to highlight your goal and preview the main points, and you can reinforce them by restating them in the conclusion.

In the previous chapter, we described the first few tasks involved in organizing the body of your speech. In this chapter, we describe how to complete the process by creating an introduction that both gets attention and leads into the body of the speech, creating a conclusion that both summarizes the material and leaves the speech on a high note, writing a title, and completing a list of the sources you used to develop the speech.

What do you think?

A really good conclusion should leave the audience wanting to learn more about the topic.

Strongly Disagree									Strongly Agree
1	2	3	4	5	6	7	8	9	10

primacy-recency effect
the tendency to remember the first and last items conveyed orally in a series rather than the items in between

ACTION STEP 4:
Organize and Develop Ideas Into a Well-Structured Outline

E. Create the speech introduction.
F. Create the speech conclusion.
G. Compile the list of sources used.
H. Complete the formal speech outline.

Creating the Introduction

Once you have developed the body of your speech, you can decide how to begin your speech. Because the introduction is so important to your success, you will want to develop two or three different introductions and then select the one that seems best for this particular audience. Although your introduction may be very short, it needs to motivate your audience to want to listen to what you have to say. An introduction is generally about 10 percent of the length of the entire speech, so for a five-minute speech, an introduction of about 30 seconds is appropriate.

Goals of the Introduction

An effective introduction has four primary goals: to get audience attention, establish listener relevance, begin to establish speaker credibility and goodwill, and identify your thesis statement (speech goal and main point preview). In our opening scenario, Courtney didn't achieve any of these goals. Rather, she simply identified and defined the topic and then moved right into her first main point.

Get Attention

An audience's physical presence does not guarantee that people will actually listen to your speech. Your first goal, then, is to create an opening that will win your listeners' attention by arousing their curiosity and motivating them to want to know more about what you have to say about your topic. Some rhetorical devices for doing so include startling statements, questions, stories, jokes, personal references, quotations, action, and suspense. You can determine which attention-getting device to use by considering what emotional tone is appropriate for your topic. A humorous attention getter will signal a light-hearted tone; a serious one signals a more thoughtful or somber tone.

1. **Make a startling statement.** A startling statement is a sentence or two that grabs your listeners' attention by shocking them in some way. Chris used a startling statement to get his listeners' attention for his speech about how automobile emissions contribute to global warming:

Look around. Each one of you is sitting next to a killer. That's right. You are sitting next to a cold-blooded killer. Before you think about jumping up and running out of this room, let me explain. Everyone who drives an automobile is a killer of the environment. Every time you turn the key to your ignition, you are helping to destroy our precious surroundings.

Once Chris's startling statement grabbed the attention of his listeners, he went on to state his speech goal and preview his main points.

2. **Ask a question.** Questions are requests for information that encourage your audience to get involved with your topic. Questions can be *rhetorical* or *direct*. A rhetorical question seeks a mental rather than a direct response. Here's an example of how a student began his speech on counterfeiting with three short rhetorical questions:

What would you do with this $20 bill if I gave it to you? Take your friend to a movie? Treat yourself to a pizza and drinks? Well, if you did either of these things, you could get in big trouble—this bill is counterfeit!

Unlike a rhetorical question, a direct question demands an overt response from the audience, usually by a show of hands. Here's how author and motivational speaker Harvey Mackay started his commencement address at the University of Southern California on May 15, 2009:

Let me start by asking all of you in the audience this question: How many people talk to themselves? Please raise your hands. I count approximately 50 percent. To the other 50 percent who didn't raise your hands, I can just hear you now, saying to yourself: "Who me? I don't talk to myself!"[2]

Direct questions can be helpful in getting audience attention because they require a physical response. However, getting listeners to actually comply with your request can also pose a challenge.

© ISTOCKPHOTO.COM/MEHMET ALI CIDA

3. **Tell a story.** A story is an account of something that has happened or could happen. Most people enjoy a well-told story, so it makes a good attention getter. One drawback of stories is that they are often lengthy and can take more time to tell than is appropriate for the length of your speech. Use a story only if it is short or if you can abbreviate it so that it is just right for your speech length.

4. **Tell a joke.** A joke is an anecdote or a piece of wordplay designed to be funny and make people laugh. A joke can be used to get audience attention when it meets the *three R's test*: It must be realistic, relevant, and repeatable.[3] In other words, it can't be too far-fetched, unrelated to the speech purpose, or potentially offensive to some listeners. In his speech about being a person of integrity, for example, an inspirational speaker offered this joke to get attention:

A lady went up to a butcher to purchase a chicken to roast for dinner. The butcher looked in the cooler and discovered he had only one left. He put it on the scale for her to consider. She said, "I think I'd like a bigger one." The butcher cleverly put the chicken back in the cooler and then took it out again. This time, he placed the chicken and his thumb on the scale to make it appear a bit heavier. After contemplating for a moment, the woman responded, "Oh heck, I'll take both of them!"

When jokes work, they adhere to the three R's test, but if you decide to use one, be sure to consider how you will handle the situation if nobody laughs.

5. **Supply a personal reference.** A personal reference is a brief story about something that happened to you or a hypothetical situation that listeners can imagine themselves in. In addition to getting attention, a personal reference can be especially effective at engaging listeners as active participants.

For longer speeches, you can build personal references that tie together the speaker, the audience, and the occasion. Let's see how Bruce Cole, chairman of the National Endowment for the Humanities, used a personal reference in the opening of his speech at New York University's "Art in an Age of Uncertainty" conference:

Good morning. It is an honor and pleasure to be here today. It's been said that a picture is worth a thousand words; as an art historian, I ardently believe this is true. And so I freely confess that nothing I say here today is as meaningful, as momentous, or as memorable as the sight of what lies nearby. We are on hallowed ground. The magnitude of the horrific events of September 11 is still being realized, the aftershocks still felt. But even in an age of uncertainty there are truths to be discovered, lessons to discern, and hope to share.

Today, I'd like to talk to you about the centrality of the humanities to democratic and civic life; the danger of American amnesia; and the possibilities of recovering our memory and protecting the best of our culture.[4]

Notice how smoothly Cole moves from personal reference into his thesis and main point preview.

6. **Recite a quotation.** A quotation is a comment made by and attributed to someone other than the speaker. A particularly vivid or thought-provoking quotation can make an excellent attention getter as long as it relates to your topic. Although it is common to quote famous people, a good quotation from *any* source can create interest in your topic. For instance, notice how Sally Mason, provost at Purdue University, used the following quotation to get the attention of her audience, the Lafayette, Indiana, YWCA:

story
an account of something that has happened (actual) or could happen (hypothetical)

joke
an anecdote or a piece of wordplay designed to be funny and make people laugh

personal reference
a brief story about something that happened to you or a hypothetical situation that listeners can imagine themselves in

quotation
a comment made by and attributed to someone other than the speaker

There is an ancient saying, "May you live in interesting times." It is actually an ancient curse. It might sound great to live in interesting times. But interesting times are times of change and even turmoil. They are times of struggle. They are exciting. But, at the same time, they are difficult. People of my generation have certainly lived through interesting times and they continue today.[5]

As the introduction progressed, she introduced her topic about the gender gap in technology.

7. **Perform or motivate an action.** You can introduce your topic and gain attention through an action, an attention-getting act designed to highlight your topic or purpose. You can perform an action yourself, or you can ask volunteers from the audience to perform the action. For example, Cindria used three audience members to participate in breaking a piñata to create interest in her speech on the history of the piñata. If you choose to use audience members, consider soliciting participants ahead of time to avoid the possibility of having no volunteers when you ask during your speech. Finally, you can ask your entire audience to perform some action related to your speech topic. If you'd like to ask your whole audience to perform an action, realistically assess whether what you are asking is something your audience is likely to comply with.

8. **Create suspense.** When you create suspense, you word your attention getter so that what is described generates uncertainty or mystery during the first few sentences and excites the audience. When you get the audience to ask, "What is she leading up to?" you hook them for the entire speech. The suspenseful opening is especially valuable when your audience is not particularly interested in hearing about your topic. Consider this suspenseful statement:

It costs the United States more than $116 billion per year. It has cost the loss of more jobs than a recession.

It accounts for nearly 100,000 deaths a year. I'm not talking about cocaine abuse—the problem is alcoholism. Today I want to show you how we can avoid this inhumane killer by abstaining from it.

Notice that by introducing the problem, alcoholism, at the end of the statement, the speaker encourages the audience to try to anticipate the answer. And because the audience may well be thinking that the problem is narcotics, the revelation that it is alcoholism is likely to be that much more effective.

For more tips about how to use these and other types of attention getters, go to the CourseMate for SPEAK at www.cengagebrain.com to access **Web Resource 8.1: Strategies for Introducing Speeches**.

Establish Listener Relevance

Even if you successfully get the attention of your listeners, to *keep* their attention you will need to motivate them to listen to your speech. You can do this by creating a clear listener relevance link, a statement of how and why your speech relates to or might affect your audience. Doing this in the introduction and again for each main point helps your audience realize its exigence.[6] Sometimes your attention-getting statement will serve this function, but if it doesn't, you will need to provide a personal connection between your topic and your audience. When creating a listener relevance link, answer these questions: Why should my listeners care about what I'm saying? In what way(s) might they benefit from hearing about it? How might my speech relate to my listeners' needs or desires for health, wealth, well-being, self-esteem, success, and so forth?

Establish Your Credibility and Goodwill

If someone hasn't formally introduced you before you speak, audience members are going to wonder who you are and why they should pay attention to what you say. So another goal of the introduction is to begin to build your credibility. The theoretical grounding for this goal actually dates back to the work of Aristotle in his treatise *The Rhetoric.*[7] In it, he asserted that listeners would be motivated to both listen to and believe a speaker based on their perception of his or her *ethos* (competence, good character, and goodwill), *pathos* (appeals to emotions), and *logos* (perception of truth through evidence and reasoning).

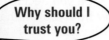

Why should I trust you?

© ISTOCKPHOTO.COM/SHARON MEREDITH

To be successful, you need to begin to establish ethos during your introductory remarks. This initial ethos responds to the questions listeners may be thinking, such as Why should I trust you? What makes you an authority on the subject? Do you seem sincere? Do your words and actions demonstrate respect for me and this occasion? Remember, though, that your goal is to highlight how you are a credible speaker on this topic, one who respects the audience and occasion, not that you are *the* or even *a* final authority on the subject. Carmen Mariano, principal of Archbishop Williams High School, established credibility and goodwill in a "welcome back, students" speech in September 2009 this way:

> *Ladies and gentlemen, you will hear one word many times this morning. That word is* welcome. *Please know how much we mean that word. Please know how much I mean that word.*
>
> *Why will we mean that word so much?*
>
> *Because without you, this is just a building on 80 Independence Avenue. And with you, this is Archbishop Williams High School. That's right. When you walked through those doors this morning, you made this building a school again.*
>
> *So welcome back.*
>
> *And welcome to your school.*[8]

State Your Thesis

Because audiences want to know what your speech is going to be about, it's important to state your thesis. Recall from Chapter 7 that your thesis statement introduces your audience to your general goal, specific goal, and main points. Stating your main points in the introduction is necessary unless you have some special reason for not revealing the details of the thesis. For instance, during a commencement address at Stanford, Steve Jobs specified the number of main points he would have but left out the details in a preview statement by saying, "Today I want to tell you three stories from my life. That's it. No big deal. Just three stories."[9]

Selecting the Best Introduction

Because the introduction is critical in establishing your relationship with your audience, it's worth investing the time to compare different openings. Try working on two or three different introductions; then, pick the one you believe will work best for your specific audience and speech goal.

Your speech introduction should meet all four of the goals discussed above and be long enough to put listeners in a frame of mind that will encourage them to hear you out, without being so long that it leaves too little time to develop the substance of your speech. Of course, the shorter the speech, the shorter the introduction.

Speech Planning Action Step 4, Activity 4E will help you develop three choices for your speech introduction. See the Student Response box immediately following the activity for a sample of how one student completed this exercise.

ACTION STEP 4
Activity 4E

Creating Speech Introductions

The goal of this activity is to create choices for how you will begin your speech.

1. For the speech body you outlined earlier, write three different introductions—using different rhetorical devices (a startling statement, a question, a story, a personal reference, a joke, a quotation, an action, or suspense) to get attention—that you believe meet the primary goals of effective introductions and would be appropriate for your speech goal and audience.

2. Of the three introductions you drafted, which do you believe is the best? Why?

3. Write that introduction in outline form, indicating in parentheses where you are meeting each goal.

You can complete this activity online with Speech Builder Express, view a student sample of this activity, and, if requested, e-mail your completed activity to your instructor. Go to your CourseMate for SPEAK at www.cengagebrain.com to access Activity 4E.

Student Response:
Action Step 4, Activity 4E

1. For the speech body you outlined earlier, write three different introductions—using different rhetorical devices (a startling statement, a question, a story, a personal reference, a joke, a quotation, an action, or suspense) to get attention—that you believe meet the goals of effective introductions and would be appropriate for your speech goal and audience.

Specific goal: I would like the audience to understand the three ways to tell if a diamond is real.

(1) We are at an age where buying diamonds might be on our minds. I would like to tell you how you can know for sure if your diamond is real.

(2) Have you ever wondered if you would know if the diamond the jeweler is trying to sell you

continued

The Conclusion

Shakespeare once said, "All's well that ends well." A strong conclusion can heighten the impact of a good speech. Even though the conclusion will be a relatively short part of the speech—seldom more than 5 percent (35 to 45 words for a five-minute speech)—your conclusion should be carefully planned.

Goals of the Conclusion

The conclusion of a speech has two major goals. The first is to review the goal and main points of the speech. The second is to provide a sense of closure that leaves the audience with a vivid impression of your message. Just as with your speech introduction, prepare two or three conclusions, and then choose the one you believe will be the most effective for your audience and speaking occasion.

clincher
a one- or two-sentence statement in a conclusion that provides a sense of closure by driving home the importance of your speech in a memorable way

appeal to action
a statement in a conclusion that describes the behavior you want your listeners to follow after they have heard your arguments

Summarize the Speech Goal and Main Points

Any effective speech conclusion will include a summary of your speech goal and main points. A summary for an informative speech on how to improve your grades might be, "So I hope you now understand [*informative goal*] that three techniques for helping you improve your grades are to attend classes regularly, to develop a positive attitude toward the course, and to study systematically [*main points*]." Likewise, a short summary for a persuasive speech on why you should lift weights might be, "So remember the three major reasons why you should consider [*persuasive goal*] lifting weights are to improve your appearance, to improve your strength, and to improve your bone density [*main points*]."

Clinch

Although summaries help you achieve the first goal of an effective conclusion, you'll need to develop additional material designed to achieve the second goal: leaving your audience with a vivid impression. You can achieve this second goal with a clincher—a one- or two-sentence statement that provides a sense of closure by driving home the importance of your speech in a memorable way. Very often, effective clinchers also achieve closure by referring back to the introductory comments in some way. Two effective strategies for developing effective clinchers are using vivid imagery and appealing to action.

To develop vivid imagery in your clincher, you can use any of the devices we discussed for getting your audience's attention: a startling statement, a question, a story, a personal reference, a joke, a quotation, an action, or suspense. Clinchers that foster vivid imagery are appropriate for both informative and persuasive speeches because they leave listeners with a vibrant picture imprinted in their minds.

The appeal to action is a common way to end some persuasive speeches. The appeal to action describes

© ISTOCKPHOTO.COM/STEVEN WYNN / © ISTOCKPHOTO.COM/RUDI WAMBACH

"All's well that ends well."

the behavior you want your listeners to follow after they have heard your arguments. Notice how Matthew Cossolotto, president and founder of Study Abroad Alumni International, concludes his speech on global awareness and responsibility with a strong appeal to action:

So, yes, you should have this re-entry program. Yes, you should network and explore international career opportunities. That's all good. But I also encourage you to Globalize Your Locality. I urge you to Think Global. . . . Act Global. . . . Be Global.

This is an urgent call to action . . . for you and other study abroad alumni . . . to help us reduce the global awareness deficit.

I'd like to leave you with this image . . . just picture in your mind's eye that iconic photograph of planet earth. I'm sure you've seen it. Taken over four decades ago . . . in December 1968 . . . on the Apollo 8 mission to the moon.

The photograph—dubbed Earthrise—shows our small, blue planet rising above a desolate lunar landscape. This photo was a true watershed in human history . . . marking the first time earthlings . . . fellow global citizens had traveled outside earth's orbit and looked back on our lonely planet.

The widespread publication of Earthrise had a lot to do with launching the worldwide environmental movement. It's no accident that the first Earth Day—on April 22, 1970—took place so soon after the publication of this remarkable photograph.

We're all privileged to inhabit this same planet— truly an island in space. And voices to the contrary notwithstanding . . . whether we want to admit it or not . . . we are all, undeniably and by definition, citizens of the world.

The only question is: will we accept the responsibilities of global citizenship?

Your future . . . and perhaps the survival of the planet . . . just may depend on how many of us answer yes to that question.[10]

Selecting the Best Conclusion

To determine how you will conclude your speech, create two or three conclusions; then, choose the one you believe will best reinforce your speech goal with your audience.

For her short speech on Adderall, Katie created the following three variations of summaries for consideration. Which do you like best?

Adderall is a prescription stimulant that is being used more and more among college students especially as a study aid, and there are serious risks associated with using the drug illegally. The next time you or a friend considers taking Adderall as a study aid, think again. The potential harm that the drug could cause to your body is not worth even a perfect grade point average.

Adderall is a prescription drug that is being abused by college students across the country. The stimulant is meant to treat medical conditions but is now being used illegally as a study aid. The harms in doing so are alarming. So if you've considered taking Adderall as a study aid, I hope you consider what we've talked about today before you do. Not taking it is not only better for you in the long run, just like wearing your seat belt and not drinking and driving, but it's also obeying the law.

So, Adderall is a stimulant that is prescribed to treat real problems but is now being abused by more and more college students as a study aid, which is, quite frankly, breaking the law. I won't ask for a show of hands this time, but I will ask the question once more. If you've used Adderall illegally as a study aid, will you think twice before you do it again? If you know someone who uses it illegally as a study aid, will you share what you've learned today with that person? I sincerely hope so. It really is a matter of life and health.

For speeches that are no longer than five minutes, a one- to three-sentence conclusion is often appropriate. You're likely to need as much time as possible to do a good job presenting your main points. But as speech assignments get longer, you'll want to consider supplementing the summary to give the conclusion more impact.

Speech Planning Action Step 4, Activity 4F will help you develop choices for your speech conclusion. See the Student Response box immediately following the activity for a sample of how one student completed this exercise.

Creating Speech Conclusions

The goal of this activity is to help you create choices for how you will conclude your speech.

1. For the speech body you outlined earlier, write three different conclusions that review important points you want the audience to remember, and include a clincher that provides closure by leaving the audience with a vivid impression.
2. Which do you believe is the best? Why?
3. Write that conclusion in outline form.

You can complete this activity online with Speech Builder Express, view a student sample of this activity, and, if requested, e-mail your completed activity to your instructor. Go to the CourseMate for SPEAK at www.cengagebrain .com to access Activity 4F.

{ **Student Response:**
Action Step 4, Activity 4F }

1. For the speech body you outlined earlier, write three different conclusions that review important points you want the audience to remember, and include a clincher that provides closure by leaving the audience with a vivid impression.

   Specific goal: I would like the audience to understand the three ways to tell if a diamond is real.

   (1) So, the next time you buy or receive a diamond, you will know how to do the acid, streak, and hardness tests to make sure the diamond is real.

   (2) Before making your final diamond selection, make sure it can pass the acid test, streak test, and hardness test. Remember, you want to make sure you're buying a diamond—not paste!

   (3) You now know how to tell if your diamond is real. So, folks, if you discover that the gem you're considering effervesces in acid, has a streak that is not clear, or can be scratched, you will know that the person who tried to sell it to you is a crook!

2. Which do you believe is the best? Why?

formal outline
a full sentence outline of your speech that includes internal references and a reference list

The third one, because it restates the characteristics and leaves a vivid impression.

---

3. Write that conclusion in outline form.
   I. You now know how to tell if your diamond is real.
   II. If it effervesces, streaks, or scratches, the seller is a crook.

Completing the Outline

At this point, you have a draft outline of your speech. To complete the formal outline, you will want to compile a list of the source material you will be drawing from in the speech, create a title (if required), and review your outline to make sure that it conforms to a logical structure.

Listing Sources

Regardless of the type of speech or how long or how short it will be, you'll want to prepare a list of the sources you use in it. This list will enable you to direct audience members to the specific source of the information you have used and will allow you to quickly find the information at a later date. You will also want to use internal references throughout the formal speech outline to help you remember what to cite and where during your speech. Doing so will ultimately enhance your credibility and help you avoid unintentional plagiarism. The two standard methods of organizing source lists are alphabetically by author's last name and by content category, with items listed alphabetically by author within each category. For speeches with a short list, the first method is efficient. But for long speeches with a lengthy source list, it is helpful to group sources by content categories.

Many formal bibliographical styles can be used in citing sources (e.g., MLA, APA, Chicago, CBE); the "correct" form differs by professional or academic discipline. Check to see if your instructor has a preference about which style you use in class.

Regardless of the particular style, the specific information you need to record differs depending on whether the source is a book, a periodical, a newspaper, or an Internet source or website. The elements that are essential to all are author, title of article, name of publication, date of publication, and page numbers. Exhibit 8.1 gives examples of Modern Language Association (MLA) and American Psychological Association (APA) citations for the most commonly used types of sources.

Speech Planning Action Step 4, Activity 4G will help you compile a list of sources used in your speech. See the Student Response box immediately following the activity for a sample of how one student completed this exercise.

Exhibit 8.1

Examples of the MLA and APA Citation Forms

	MLA Style	APA Style
Book	Miller, Roberta B. *The Five Paths to Persuasion: The Art of Selling Your Message*. New York: Warner Business Books, 2004. Print.	Miller, R. B. (2004). *The five paths to persuasion: The art of selling your message*. New York: Warner Business Books.
Edited book	Janzen, Rod. "Five Paradigms of Ethnic Relations." *Intercultural Communication*. 10th ed. Eds. Larry Samovar and Richard Porter. Belmont, CA: Wadsworth, 2003. 36–42. Print.	Janzen, R. (2003). Five paradigms of ethnic relations. In L. Samovar & R. Porter (Eds.), *Intercultural communication* (10th ed., pp. 36–42). Belmont, CA: Wadsworth.
Academic journal	Barge, J. Kevin. "Reflexivity and Managerial Practice." *Communication Monographs* 71 (Mar. 2004): 70–96. Print.	Barge, J. K. (2004, March). Reflexivity and managerial practice. *Communication Monographs, 71*, 70–96.
Magazine	Krauthammer, Charles. "What Makes the Bush Haters So Mad?" *Time* 22 Sept. 2003: 84. Print.	Krauthammer, C. (2003, September 22). What makes the Bush haters so mad? *Time*, 84.
Newspaper	Cohen, Richard. "Wall Street Scandal: Whatever the Market Will Bear." *The Cincinnati Enquirer* 17 Sept. 2003: C6. Print.	Cohen, R. (2003, September 17). Wall Street scandal: Whatever the market will bear. *The Cincinnati Enquirer*, p. C6.
Electronic article based on print source	Friedman, Thomas L. "Connect the Dots." *The New York Times*. 25 Sept. 2003. Web. 20 Aug. 2004.	Friedman, T. L. (2003, September 25). Connect the dots. *The New York Times*. Retrieved from http://www.nytimes.com/2003/09/25/opinion/25FRIED.html
Electronic article from Internet-only publication	Osterweil, Neil, and Michelle Smith. "Does Stress Cause Breast Cancer?" *Web M.D. Health*. WebMD Inc. 24 Sept. 2003. Web. 20 Aug. 2004.	Osterweil, N., & Smith, M. (2003, September 24). Does stress cause breast cancer? *Web M.D. Health*. Retrieved from http://my.webmd.com/contents/article/74/89170.htm?z3734_00000_1000_ts_01
Electronic article retrieved from database	Grabe, Mark. "Voluntary Use of Online Lecture Notes: Correlates of Note Use and Note Use as an Alternative to Class Attendance." *Computers and Education* 44 (2005): 409–21. *ScienceDirect*. Web. 28 May 2006.	Grabe, M. (2005). Voluntary use of online lecture notes: Correlates of note use and note use as an alternative to class attendance. *Computers and Education, 44*, 409–421. Retrieved from ScienceDirect.
Movie	*Pirates of the Caribbean: Dead Man's Chest*. Dir. Gore Verbinksi. Perf. Johnny Depp, Orlando Bloom, Keira Knightley. 2006. The Walt Disney Company, 2007. DVD.	Bruckheimer, J. (Producer), & Verbinksi, G. (Director). (2006). *Pirates of the Caribbean: Dead man's chest* [Motion picture]. United States: Walt Disney Pictures.
Television program episode	"Truth Be Told." *Dexter*. Showtime. 10 Dec. 2006. Television.	Gordon, K. (Director). (2006, December 10). Truth be told. [Television series episode]. In J. Manos Jr. (Executive producer), *Dexter*. New York, NY: Showtime Networks Inc.
Music recording	Nirvana. "Smells Like Teen Spirit." *Nevermind*. Geffen, 1991. CD.	Nirvana. (1991). Smells like teen spirit. On *Nevermind* [CD]. Santa Monica, CA: Geffen.
Personal interview	Mueller, Bruno. Personal interview. 19 March 2004.	APA style dictates that no personal interview is included in a reference list. Rather, cite this type of source orally in your speech, mentioning the name of the person you interviewed and the date of the interview.

© CENGAGE LEARNING 2011

ACTION STEP 4
Activity 4G

Compiling a List of Sources

The goal of this activity is to help you record the list of sources you used in your speech.

1. Review your research cards, separating those whose information you have used in your speech from those whose information you have not used.

2. Note on your research card or your outline where you'll reference the source during your speech.

3. List the sources whose information was used in the speech by copying the bibliographical information recorded on the research card.

4. For short lists, organize your list alphabetically by the last name of the first author. Be sure to follow a form given in the text. If you did not record some of the bibliographical information on your notecard, you will need to revisit the library, database, or other source to find it.

You can complete this activity online with Speech Builder Express, view a student sample of this activity, and, if requested, e-mail your completed activity to your instructor. Go to the CourseMate for SPEAK at www.cengagebrain.com to access Activity 4G.

{ **Student Response:**
Action Step 4, Activity 4G }

1. Review your research cards, separating those whose information you have used in your speech from those whose information you have not used.

2. Note on your outline where you'll reference the source during your speech.

3. List the sources whose information was used in the speech by copying the bibliographical information recorded on the research card.

4. For short lists, organize your list alphabetically by the last name of the first author. Be sure to follow a form given in the text. If you did not record some of the bibliographical information on your notecard, you will need to revisit the library, database, or other source to find it.

Sources

Dixon, D. (1992). The practical geologist. NY: Simon & Schuster.

Klein, C. (1993). Manual of mineralogy (2nd ed). New York: John Wiley & Sons.

Montgomery, C. W. (1997). Fundamentals of geology. (3rd ed). Dubuque, IA: Wm. C. Brown.

America's Destiny
Are Farmers on the Way Out?
Promises to Keep: Broadcasting and the Public Interest

Writing a Title

In most speech situations outside the classroom, it helps to have a title that lets the audience know what to expect. A title is probably necessary when you will be formally introduced, when the speech is publicized, or when the speech will be published. A good title helps to attract an audience and build interest in what you will say. Titles should be brief, descriptive of the content, and, if possible, creative. Most speakers don't settle on a title until the rest of the speech preparation is complete.

Three kinds of titles can be created: a simple statement of subject, a question, or a creative title.

1. **Simple statement of subject.** This straightforward title captures the subject of the speech in a few words.

   Selling Safety
   America's Destiny

2. **Question.** To spark greater interest, you can create a title by phrasing your speech goal as a question. A prospective listener may then be motivated to attend the speech to find out the answer.

   Do We Need a Department of Play?
   Are Farmers on the Way Out?

3. **Creative title.** A more creative approach is to combine a familiar saying or metaphor with the simple statement of subject.

   Promises to Keep: Broadcasting and the Public Interest
   Freeze or Freedom: On the Limits of Morals and Worth of Politics

The simple statement of the subject gives a clear idea of the topic but is not especially eye- or ear-catching. Questions and creative titles capture interest but may not give a clear idea of content. Creative titles often require subtitles.

Reviewing the Outline

Now that you have created all of the parts of the outline, it is time to put them together in complete outline form and edit them to make sure the outline is well organized and well worded. Use this checklist to complete the final review of your formal outline before you move into adaptation and rehearsal.

1. **Have I used a standard set of symbols to indicate structure?** Main points should be indicated by Roman numerals, major subdivisions by capital letters, minor subheadings by Arabic numerals, and further subdivisions by lowercase letters.

2. **Have I written main points and major subdivisions as complete sentences?** Complete sentences help you to see (a) whether each main point actually develops your speech goal and (b) whether the wording makes your intended point. Unless the key ideas are written out in full, it will be difficult to follow the next guidelines.

3. **Do main points and major subdivisions each contain a single idea?** This guideline ensures that the development of each part of the

speech will be relevant to the point. Thus, if your outline contains a point like this:

I. *Organically produced food is good for the environment and for animals.*

Then divide the sentence so that the two parts are separate:

I. *Organically produced food is good for the environment.*

II. *Organically produced food is good for animals.*

Sort out distinct ideas so that when you line up supporting material you can have confidence that the audience will see and understand its relationship to the main points.

4. **Does each major subdivision relate to or support its major point?** This principle, called subordination, ensures that you don't wander off point and confuse your audience. For example:

I. *Proper equipment is necessary for successful play.*
   A. *Good gym shoes are needed for maneuverability.*
   B. *Padded gloves help protect your hands.*
   C. *A lively ball provides sufficient bounce.*
   D. *And a good attitude doesn't hurt.*

In this outline, A, B, and C (shoes, gloves, and ball) all relate to the main point. But D, attitude, is not equipment and should appear somewhere else, if at all.

5. **Are potential subdivision elaborations indicated?** Recall that it is the subdivision elaborations that help to build the speech. Because you don't know how long it might take you to discuss these elaborations, it is a good idea to include more than you are

likely to use. During rehearsals, you may discuss each a different way.

Now that we have considered the various parts of an outline, let us put them together for a final look. The outline in Exhibit 8.2 on pages 112–115 illustrates the principles in practice.

Speech Planning Action Step 4, Activity 4H will help you write and review a complete sentence outline of your speech. For this activity, refer to Katie's complete outline (Exhibit 8.2) as the student response.

ACTION STEP 4
Activity 4H

Completing the Formal Speech Outline

Write and review a complete sentence outline of your speech using material you've developed so far with the Action Steps in Chapters 4 through 8. You can complete this activity online with Speech Builder Express, view a student sample of this activity, and, if requested, e-mail your completed activity to your instructor. Go to your CourseMate for SPEAK at www.cengagebrain.com to access Activity 4H.

THERE ARE EVEN MORE STUDY TOOLS FOR THIS CHAPTER AT WWW.CENGAGEBRAIN.COM

- **Interactive Videos**
- **Speech Builder Express**
- **Printable Flash Cards**
- **Interactive Games**
- **Chapter Review Cards**
- **Online Quizzes With Feedback**
- **Speech Studio available upon instructor request**

Exhibit 8.2
Sample Complete Formal Outline

Using and Abusing Adderall: What's the Big Deal?
by Kate Anthony
University of Kentucky

General goal: I want to inform my audience.

Specific goal: I would like the audience to understand the uses and abuses of Adderall by college students.

Thesis statement: I want to inform you about the growing problem of off-label Adderall usage by college students, explaining the nature and legal uses of Adderall, its growing popularity as a study aid for college students, and the problems associated with abusing Adderall.

Introduction

I. *Attention getter:* Raise your hand if anyone you know has taken the drug Adderall. Keep your hand raised if the person you know to be taking Adderall is doing so without a prescription for the drug.

II. *Listener relevance link:* The illegal use of stimulants like Adderall among college students has increased dramatically over the past decade. The latest National Study on Drug Use and Health found that nearly 7 percent of full-time college students reported using Adderall without a prescription. So if you know 10 people who are in college, it is likely that you know someone who is abusing Adderall.

III. *Speaker credibility:* I became interested in this topic my freshman year when my roommate received a call from her mother telling her that her best friend, who was a sophomore at a different college, had died suddenly from an Adderall-induced heart attack. Because I had several friends who were also using Adderall without a prescription but who thought it was safe to do so, I began to read all I could about the drug, its use, and its risks. Not only have I become versed in the written information on Adderall, but I have also interviewed several faculty here who are studying the problem, and I have become an undergraduate research assistant helping one faculty member to collect data on this problem. Today, I want to share with you some of what I have learned.

IV. *Thesis statement:* Specifically, I want to inform you about the growing problem of off-label Adderall usage by college students, explaining the nature and legal uses of Adderall, its growing popularity as a study aid for college students, and the problems associated with abusing Adderall.

Body

I. Adderall is a psychostimulant prescribed to treat three conditions.

Listener relevance link: Understanding the intended medical uses of the drug Adderall may help you understand why the drug is so widely abused by collegians.

A. Adderall, the brand name for amphetamine-dextroamphetamine, is a psychostimulant, one of a class of drugs intended to promote concentration, suppress hyperactivity, and promote healthy social experiences for patients (Willis, 2001).

1. Adderall stimulates the central nervous system by increasing the amount of dopamine and norepinephrine in the brain. These chemicals are neurotransmitters that help the brain send signals between nerve cells (Daley, 2004).

2. Mentally, Adderall brings about a temporary improvement in alertness, wakefulness, endurance, and motivation.

3. Physically, it can increase heart rate and blood pressure and decrease perceived need for food or sleep.

continued

© ISTOCKPHOTO.COM/KYOSHINO

B. Adderall is prescribed for the medical treatment of attention deficit hyperactivity disorder (ADHD) in children and adults as well as for narcolepsy and clinical depression.

   1. ADHD is a neurobehavioral developmental disorder characterized by problems of attention coupled with hyperactivity.

      a. Since the mid-1990s, there has been a documented increase in the number of American children diagnosed and treated for ADHD (McCabe, Teter, & Boyd, 2004).

      b. According to the *Diagnostic and Statistical Manual of Mental Disorders* (2000), symptoms must be present for at least six months for diagnosis, and symptoms must be excessive for medicinal treatment.

      c. The drugs Ritalin and Dexedrine are also used to treat ADHD. Adderall, however, remains the most widely prescribed of these drugs (Willis, 2001).

      d. According to the Centers for Disease Control (2005), approximately 4.4 million American children have been diagnosed with ADHD, and over 2.5 million of those patients have been prescribed medicine to treat the condition.

   2. Adderall is also prescribed to treat narcolepsy, which occurs when the brain can't normally regulate cycles of sleep and waking.

      a. Sufferers of narcolepsy experience excessive daytime sleepiness that results in episodes of suddenly falling asleep.

      b. A chronic sleep disorder, narcolepsy affects between 50,000 and 2.4 million Americans. (National Heart, Lung, and Blood Institute, 2008).

   3. Adderall can also be used to treat clinical depression.

      a. Clinical depression is a disorder characterized by low mood, a loss of interest in normal activities, and low self-esteem.

      b. According to the National Institute of Mental Health, 9.5% of the adult population—that is nearly 1.8 million American adults—suffer from clinical depression.

Transition: Now that we understand the basic properties and medical uses of the drug Adderall, let's now assess the increasing level of abuse of the drug by college students.

II. Unfortunately, Adderall has become popular among college students who use it as a study aid and for recreational purposes.

Listener relevance link: As college students, we need to be aware of what students believe about Adderall and why they are abusing it.

  A. College students who don't suffer ADHD, narcolepsy, or depression will take it with no prescription because they believe that it will improve their focus and concentration, allowing them to perform better on academic tasks (Teter, McCabe, Crandford, Boyd, & Gunthrie, 2005).

   1. Adderall abuse among college students occurs especially at stressful times of the semester when students get little sleep.

      a. DeSantis, Webb, and Noar (2008) found that 72 percent of the students they surveyed reported using the drug to stay awake so that they could study longer when they had many assignments due.

      b. Katherine Stump, a Georgetown University student, reported in the school newspaper: "During finals week here at Georgetown, campus turns into an Adderall drug den. Everyone from

continued

a cappella singers to newspaper writers become addicts, while anyone with a prescripttion and an understanding of the free market becomes an instant pusherman" (Jaffe, 2006).

      c. Collegians report using the drug frequently during stressful times of the semester. One student said, "I use it every time I have a major paper due" (Daley, 2004).

  B. Students also use Adderall for purposes other than academic ones.

    1. A survey of undergraduate and graduate students revealed that students engage in Adderall abuse for partying at a frequency just slightly less than taking the drug for academic purposes (Prudhomme White, Becker-Blease, & Grace-Bishop, 2006).

    2. DeSantis, Webb, and Noar (2007) report that students take the drug for its energizing effects. Other students report taking the drug to make them more social and outgoing at parties.

    3. Some college students, especially women, report using the drug for its use as an appetite suppressant for dieting purposes (Daley, 2004).

Transition: Now that we understand that Adderall abuse is prevalent on university campuses among students, it is important to understand the detrimental effects that can accompany the illegal use of Adderall.

III. Whether students acknowledge the dangers or not, there are great risks involved in illegally using Adderall.

Listener relevance link: As we have now discussed the pervasiveness of Adderall abuse, statistically, it is likely that several of you have used this substance without a prescription to either enhance your academic performance or your social outings. Thus, it is important that we all recognize the adverse effects that result from taking Adderall without a prescription.

  A. Adderall abuse can cause negative health effects for individuals not diagnosed with ADHD (Daley, 2004).

    1. Adderall is reported to cause a heightened risk for heart problems when used inappropriately. Problems include sudden heart attack or stroke, sudden death in individuals with heart conditions, and increased blood pressure and heart rate (FDA, 2010).

    2. Adderall abuse also can result in a myriad of mental problems, including manifestation of bipolar disorder, an increase of aggressive thoughts, and a heightened risk for psychosis similar to schizophrenia (FDA, 2010).

  B. Adderall is highly addictive.

    1. Adderall is an amphetamine, and while amphetamines were once used to treat a variety of ailments including weight loss in the 1950s and '60s, the drugs began to be much more closely regulated once their addictive nature was realized (Daley, 2004).

    2. Adderall has similar properties to cocaine, and, as a result, abuse of the drug can lead to substance dependence (FDA, 2010).

  C. Though clear risks are associated with the illegal use of Adderall, unlike other drugs, collegians do not view the inappropriate use of Adderall as harmful or illegal.

    1. College students typically view stimulant abuse as morally acceptable and physically harmless. In a 2010 study, DeSantis and Hane found that students were quick to justify their stimulant abuse by claiming its use was fine in moderation.

    2. The *Kentucky Kernel*, the student newspaper at the University of Kentucky, published an editorial of a student who flippantly described the use of Adderall among college students. He states, "If you want to abuse ice cream, amphetamines or alcohol, then there are going to be serious problems; however, let's not pretend people using Adderall twice a semester to help them study is in any way likely to die a horrible death or suffer terrible side effects" (Riley, 2010).

continued

3. In a study assessing the attitudes of college students toward the inappropriate use of stimulant, the authors found that "the majority of students who reported misuse or abuse were not concerned about the misuse and abuse of prescription stimulants, and a number of students thought that they should be more readily available" (Prudhomme White, Becker-Blease, & Grace-Bishop, 2006, p. 265).

Transition: Now that we understand the risks involved in illegally using Adderall, hopefully you have a better understanding of why using the drug without a prescription is so dangerous.

Conclusion

I. *Restatement of thesis:* Adderall is a prescription stimulant that is increasingly being abused by college students primarily as a study aid.

II. *Main point review:* We have examined today what the drug Adderall is, its growing popularity among college students especially as a study aid, and the risks associated with using the drug illegally.

III. *Clincher:* The next time you or a friend consider taking Adderall as a study aid, think again. The potential harm that the drug could cause to your body is not worth even a perfect grade point average.

References

American Psychiatric Association. (2000). *Diagnostic and statistical manual of mental disorders*. Arlington, VA: Author.

Centers for Disease Control and Prevention. (2005). *Morbidity and mortality weekly report (MMWR)*. Retrieved from http://www.cdc.gov

Daley, B. (2004). Perspective: Miracle drug? Adderall is prescribed for individuals with ADD and ADHD; for nonprescribed users there can be some serious risks. *Daily Pennsylvanian*. Retrieved from http://www.vpul.upenn.edu

DeSantis, A. D., & Hane, A. C. (2010). "Adderall is definitely not a drug": Justifications for the illegal use of ADHD stimulants. *Substance Use & Misuse, 45*, 31–46.

DeSantis, A. D., Webb, E. M., & Noar, S. M. (2008). Illicit use of prescription ADHD medications on a college campus: A multi-methodological approach. *Journal of American College Health, 57*, 315–324.

Food and Drug Administration. (2010). *Drugs @ FDS: FDA approved drug products*. Retrieved from http://www.access data.fda.gov.

Jaffe, H. (2006). ADD and abusing Adderall. *The Washingtonian*. Retrieved from http://www.washingtonian.com

McCabe, S. E., Teter, C. J., & Boyd, C. J. (2004). The use, misuse and diversion of prescription stimulants among middle and high school students. *Substance Use and Misuse, 39*, 1095–1116.

National Heart, Blood, and Lung Institute (2008). "What is narcolepsy?" *National Heart, Blood, and Lung Institute diseases and conditions index*. Retrieved from http://www.nhlbi.nih.gov/health/dci/Diseases/nar/nar_what.html

Prudhomme White, B., Becker-Blease, K. A., & Grace-Bishop, K. (2006). Stimulant medication use, misuse, and abuse in an undergraduate and graduate student sample. *Journal of American College Health, 54*, 261–268.

Riley, T. (2010). Prescription drug abuse is a personal choice. *Kentucky Kernel*. Retrieved from http://kykernel.com

Substance Abuse and Mental Health Services Administration, Office of Applied Studies. (2009). *The NSDUH report: Nonmedical use of Adderall among full-time college students*. Rockville, MD: Author.

Teter, J. C., McCabe, S. E., Crandford, J. A., Boyd, C. J., & Gunthrie, S. K. (2005). Prevalence and motives for illicit use of prescription stimulants in an undergraduate student sample. *Journal of American College Health, 53*, 253–262.

Willis, F. (2001). Attention deficit disorder. *Modern Drug Discovery, 4*, 84–86.

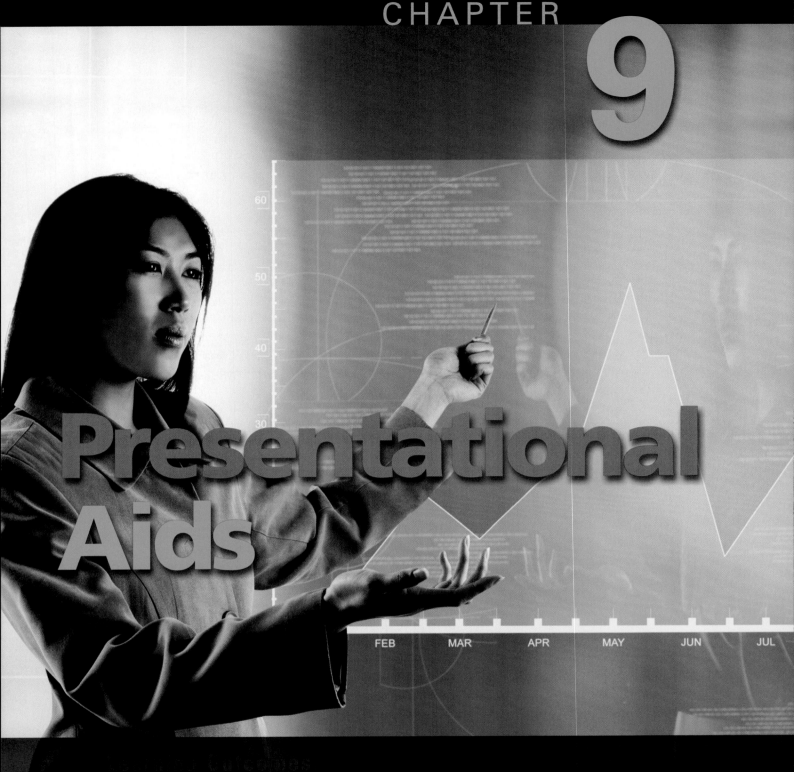

Presentational Aids

Learning Outcomes

LO^1 Why should you incorporate presentational aids into your speech? | LO^2 What are some types of presentational aids you can choose from? | LO^3 What are some common mistakes speakers make when constructing and using presentational aids? | LO^4 What are some important considerations to keep in mind when choosing presentational aids? | LO^5 What are some important considerations to keep in mind when preparing presentational aids? | LO^6 What are some important considerations to keep in mind when presenting with your presentational aids?

As Scott and Carrie drove home, Carrie exclaimed, "Wow! Dominic's speech was really great. I learned so much about what we could do to develop more sustainable electronics."
"Yeah, I know what you mean," Scott replied. "I've even got some ideas for reducing the e-waste he talked about."
"You know, what's really amazing to me is how much I learned from such a short talk!"
"I know what you mean. When I heard these were going to be PowerPoint presentations, all I could think was 'Oh no! Here we go again! Beer or no beer, it's going to be Death by PowerPoint: a darkened room and a faceless speaker talking to an oversized screen.' Thank goodness I was wrong. Dominic's visuals really helped me, but he was still the center of my focus. And the slides just helped me visualize and reinforced the important points he was making. My manager could benefit from watching someone like Dominic."
"I know. I can't believe we learned so much in five minutes! Tomorrow when I get into the office, I'm going to check out Dominic's blog."

This conversation might have occurred between two people who attended the Ignite Seattle 6 event on April 29, 2009, when industrial designer Dominic Muren gave a five-minute PowerPoint-aided presentation titled "Humblefacturing a Sustainable Electronic Future."[1] Begun by Brady Forrest of O'Reilly Radar in 2006, Ignite has become a worldwide speaking movement. During an Ignite event, speakers give five-minute presentations, often on technical topics, aided by 20 PowerPoint slides. Unlike the "death by PowerPoint" speeches Scott alluded to and we've all had to suffer through, the speeches given at these events are adapted to people today—people for whom interacting on several different social networking sites while talking or texting on cell phones and eating dinner is the norm. We live in an era when the written, oral, visual, and digital modes of communicating are merging. Whether it is a TV news program, your professor's lecture, or a sermon you hear at a place of worship, audiences have come to expect computer-enhanced presentations. This means that when you are preparing your speech, you will need

What do you think?

A really good speech should have a strong visual component.

Strongly Disagree   *Strongly Agree*
1   2   3   4   5   6   7   8   9   10

ACTION STEP 5:
Choose, Prepare, and Use Appropriate Presentational Aids

A. Consider presentational aids that will clarify, emphasize, or dramatize your message.
B. Use another symbol system (beyond words alone) in your aids.
C. Make sure your visual aids are large enough to be seen.
D. Make sure your audio aids are loud enough to be heard.
E. Plan when to use aids and integrate them during your speech.

presentational aid
any visual, audio, audiovisual, or other sensory material used in a speech

visual aid
a form of speech development that allows the audience to see as well as hear the speaker present the information

audio aid
a presentational aid that enhances the speaker's verbal message with additional sound

audiovisual aid
a presentational aid that enhances the speech using a combination of sight and sound through video

other sensory aids
presentational aids that enhance the ideas offered verbally by appealing to smell, taste, or touch

Speakers who use presentational aids are almost twice as likely to persuade listeners than those who do not.

to decide what presentational aids to include and how to do so in ways that will motivate your audience to both pay attention and remember your message.

A presentational aid is any visual, audio, audiovisual, or other sensory material used by the speaker in a speech. A **visual aid** is a form of speech development that allows the audience to see as well as hear the speaker present the information. Examples of visual aids include actual objects, models, photographs, drawings and diagrams, maps, charts, and graphs. An **audio aid** is one that enhances the speaker's verbal message with additional sound. Examples include music clips, recorded conversations or interviews, and nature sounds. **Audiovisual aids** enhance the speech using a combination of sight and sound through video. **Other sensory aids** include materials that enhance the ideas offered verbally by appealing to smell, taste, or touch. For example, a verbal description of a perfume's fragrance can be clarified by allowing audience members to smell it.

There are several benefits to using presentational aids. First, they enable you to adapt to an audience's level of knowledge by clarifying and dramatizing your verbal message. Second, presentational aids help audiences retain the information they hear.[2] Third, presentational aids allow you to address the diverse learning styles of your audience.[3] Fourth, they can increase the persuasive appeal of your speech. In fact, some research suggests that speakers who use presentational aids are almost twice as likely to persuade listeners than those who do not.[4] Finally, using presentational aids may help you to feel more competent. Speakers report that when they use presentational aids, they tend to be less anxious and have more confidence.[5]

Today, presentational aids are usually developed into computerized slide shows using presentation software such as PowerPoint, MediaPro, Adobe Acrobat, or Photodex and are projected onto a large screen via a computer and LCD projector. These programs allow you to embed audio and audiovisual links from local files and the Internet, which makes it fairly simple to create effective multimedia presentations. Whether creating multimedia presentations or developing simpler presentational aids, the principle is the same: effective aids enhance the speaker's message without overpowering the speaker or the verbal message. When speakers violate this principle, they end up with what Scott called "death by PowerPoint," a situation where the speaker is extraneous and the audience is overwhelmed with the technology being used. The result is that the message gets lost. In this chapter, we describe various types of presentational aids, criteria you should consider when choosing them, which and how many presentational aids to use, ways you can create aids, methods for displaying your aids to the audience, and guidelines for using them effectively when you are speaking.

Types of Presentational Aids

Before you can choose what presentational aids you might want to use for a specific speech, you need to recognize the various types of aids that you can choose from. Presentational aids range from those that are simple to use and readily available from some existing source to those that must be custom produced for your specific speech and require practice to use effectively. In this section, we describe types of presentational aids to consider using as you prepare your speech.

Visual Aids

Visual aids can include actual objects and models, photographs, drawings, diagrams, maps, charts, and graphs. They enhance the verbal message by allowing audiences to see what it is you are describing or explaining in your speech.

Actual objects are inanimate or animate physical samples of the idea you are communicating. Using them allows audience members to see precisely what you are talking about. Inanimate objects make good visual aids if they are (a) large enough to be seen by all audience members, (b) small enough to carry to the site of the speech, (c) simple enough to understand visually, and (d) safe. A volleyball or Muslim prayer rug would be appropriate in size for audiences of 20 to 30. An iPhone or BlackBerry might be okay if the speech goal is simply to show what one looks like, but these would probably be too small if you want to demonstrate how to use any of their specialized functions.

Some animate objects also make effective visual aids. On occasion, *you* can be an effective visual aid. For instance, you can use posture and movement to show the motions involved in swinging a golf club.

Sometimes, it can be appropriate to use another person as a visual aid, such as when Jenny used a friend of hers to demonstrate the Heimlich maneuver. Animals can also be effective visual aids. For example, Josh used his AKC Obedience Champion dog to demonstrate the basics of dog training. But keep in mind that animals placed in unfamiliar settings can become difficult to control and can distract from your message.

When an object is too large or too small, too complex to understand visually, potentially unsafe, or uncontrollable, a model of the object can be an effective visual aid. A **model** is a three-dimensional scaled-down or scaled-up version of an actual object that may be simplified to aid understanding. In a speech on the physics of bridge construction, a scale model of a suspension bridge would be an effective visual aid.

If an exact reproduction of material is needed, photographs can be excellent visual aids. When choosing photographs, be sure that the image is large enough for the audience to see and that the object of interest in the photo is clearly identified and, ideally, in the foreground. For example, if you are giving a speech about your grandmother and show a photo of her with her college graduating class, you might circle her image so she's easily seen.

Simple drawings and **diagrams** (a type of drawing that shows how the whole relates to its parts) are easy to prepare and can be effective because you can choose how much detail to include. To make sure they look professional, you can prepare them using a drawing program or find them already prepared using an Internet search engine like Google Images. If you do this, however, be sure to credit the source during your speech to enhance your credibility and avoid plagiarism. If you use a drawing or diagram, be sure to keep it simple so it doesn't obscure the point you wish to make. Andria's representation of the human body and its pressure points is an example of an effective diagram that clarified her message and helped her meet her speech goal (see Exhibit 9.1 on page 120).

actual object
an inanimate or animate sample of the idea you are communicating

model
a three-dimensional scaled-down or scaled-up version of an actual object

diagram
a type of drawing that shows how the whole relates to its parts

Exhibit 9.1

Diagram

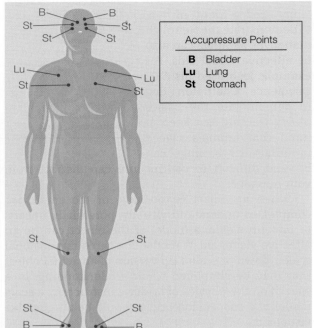

Accupressure Points

B	Bladder
Lu	Lung
St	Stomach

Exhibit 9.2

Map

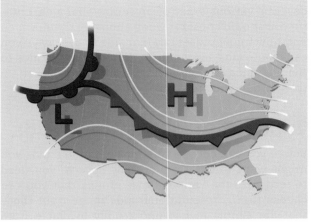

chart
a graphic representation that distills a lot of information and presents it to an audience in an easily interpreted visual format

flowchart
a chart that diagrams a sequence of steps through a complicated process

organizational chart
a chart that shows the structure of an organization in terms of rank and chain of command

pie chart
a diagram that shows the relationships among parts of a single unit

graph
a diagram that presents numerical comparisons

bar graph
a diagram that uses vertical or horizontal bars to show relationships between or among two or more variables at the same time or at various times on one or more dimensions

line graph
a diagram that indicates changes in one or more variables over time

Like drawings and diagrams, maps are relatively easy to prepare or find on the Internet. Simple maps allow you to orient audiences to landmarks (mountains, rivers, and lakes), states, cities, land routes, weather systems, and so on. Remember to include only the details that are relevant to your purpose. Exhibit 9.2 on page 120 shows a map that focuses on weather systems.

A **chart** is a graphic representation that distills a lot of information and presents it to an audience in an easily interpreted visual format. Flowcharts, organizational charts, and pie charts are the most common types. A **flowchart** uses symbols and connecting lines to diagram a sequence of steps through a complicated process. Tim used a flowchart to help listeners move through the sequence of steps to assess their weight (see Exhibit 9.3). An **organizational chart** shows the structure of an organization in terms of rank and chain of command. The chart in Exhibit 9.4 on page 122 illustrates the organization of a student union board. A **pie chart** is a diagram that shows the relationships among parts of a single unit. Ideally, pie charts have two to five "slices," or wedges—more than eight wedges clutter a pie chart. If your chart includes too many wedges, use another kind of chart unless you can consolidate several of the less important wedges into the category of "other," as Tim did to show the percentage of total calories that should come from the various components of food (see Exhibit 9.5 on page 122).

A **graph** is a diagram that presents numerical comparisons. Bar graphs and line graphs are the most common forms of graphs. A **bar graph** is a diagram that uses vertical or horizontal bars to show relationships between or among two or more variables at the same time or at various times on one or more dimensions. For instance, Jacqueline used a bar graph to compare the amounts of caffeine found in one serving each of brewed coffee, instant coffee, tea, cocoa, and cola (see Exhibit 9.6 on page 122). A **line graph** is a diagram that indicates changes in one or more variables over time (see Exhibit 9.7 on page 122).

Audio Aids

Audio aids enhance a verbal message through sound. They are especially useful when it is difficult, if not impossible, to describe a sound in words. For example, in David's speech about the three types of trumpet mutes and how they alter the sound of the instrument, he played his trumpet so listeners could hear what he meant. If you don't want to make your own sounds, you can use recorded excerpts from various sources,

Exhibit 9.3

Flowchart

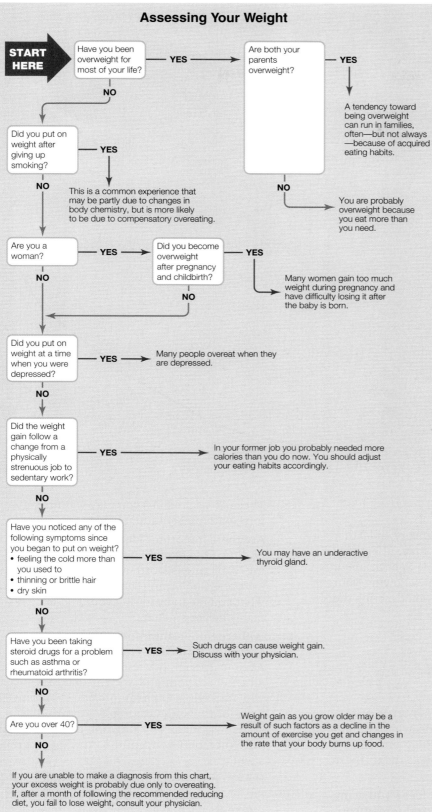

Assessing Your Weight

START HERE → Have you been overweight for most of your life? — YES → Are both your parents overweight? — YES → A tendency toward being overweight can run in families, often—but not always—because of acquired eating habits.

Are both your parents overweight? — NO → You are probably overweight because you eat more than you need.

Have you been overweight for most of your life? — NO → Did you put on weight after giving up smoking? — YES → This is a common experience that may be partly due to changes in body chemistry, but is more likely to be due to compensatory overeating.

Did you put on weight after giving up smoking? — NO → Are you a woman? — YES → Did you become overweight after pregnancy and childbirth? — YES → Many women gain too much weight during pregnancy and have difficulty losing it after the baby is born.

Are you a woman? — NO →

Did you become overweight after pregnancy and childbirth? — NO →

Did you put on weight at a time when you were depressed? — YES → Many people overeat when they are depressed.

Did you put on weight at a time when you were depressed? — NO →

Did the weight gain follow a change from a physically strenuous job to sedentary work? — YES → In your former job you probably needed more calories than you do now. You should adjust your eating habits accordingly.

Did the weight gain follow a change from a physically strenuous job to sedentary work? — NO →

Have you noticed any of the following symptoms since you began to put on weight?
- feeling the cold more than you used to
- thinning or brittle hair
- dry skin

— YES → You may have an underactive thyroid gland.

— NO →

Have you been taking steroid drugs for a problem such as asthma or rheumatoid arthritis? — YES → Such drugs can cause weight gain. Discuss with your physician.

— NO →

Are you over 40? — YES → Weight gain as you grow older may be a result of such factors as a decline in the amount of exercise you get and changes in the rate that your body burns up food.

— NO →

If you are unable to make a diagnosis from this chart, your excess weight is probably due only to overeating. If, after a month of following the recommended reducing diet, you fail to lose weight, consult your physician.

© CENGAGE LEARNING 2011

---

which may convey information better than describing the material or reading it as a quotation. For example, Susan chose to begin her speech on the future of the NASA space program with a recording of Neil Armstrong's first words as he stepped on the surface of the moon: "That's one small step for a man, one giant leap for mankind." Before using audio material, make sure you have enough time to present it (it should make up no more than about 5 percent of your speaking time) and that you have access to a quality sound system.

Audiovisual Aids

Audiovisual aids enhance the verbal message through sight and sound. You can use short clips from films and videos to demonstrate concepts or processes and to expose audiences to important people. They are relatively easy to access on Internet sites such as YouTube. For example, during his speech about the use of robots in automobile production, Chad, who worked as a technician at the local Ford plant, showed a 20-second video clip of a car being painted in a robotic paint booth. As with audio clips, keep video and film clips short (no more than 5 percent of your speaking time). It can be challenging to keep clips this short, particularly in short classroom speeches, so choose clips that are to the point and really enhance your message. Because computerized slide show software programs like PowerPoint make it so easy to import sounds and visual images, as well as to insert hyperlinks to websites, most effective speakers today enhance their speeches with slide shows that incorporate visual, audio, and audiovisual material.

Exhibit 9.4

Organizational Chart

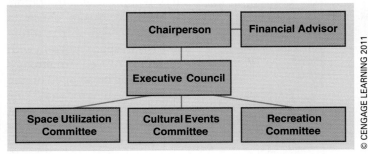

© CENGAGE LEARNING 2011

Exhibit 9.5

Pie Chart

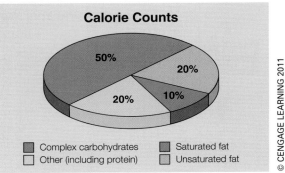

© CENGAGE LEARNING 2011

Exhibit 9.6

Bar Graph

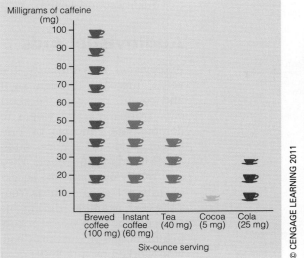

© CENGAGE LEARNING 2011

Exhibit 9.7

Line Graph

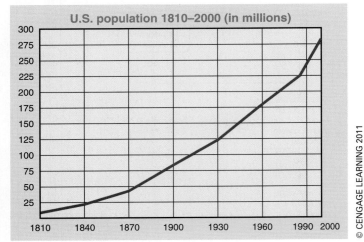

© CENGAGE LEARNING 2011

Other Sensory Aids

Depending on your topic, other sensory aids that appeal to smell, touch, or taste may effectively enhance your speech. For example, a speech about making perfume might benefit from allowing your audience to smell some samples as you describe the ingredients used to make the scents.

Criteria for Choosing Presentational Aids

Now that you understand the various types of presentational aids, you have to decide what content you want to highlight and how. Your answers to the following questions can help you make these decisions.

1. **What are the most important ideas you want your audience to understand and remember?** These ideas are ones you may want to reinforce with presentational aids.

2. **Are there important ideas that are complex or difficult to explain verbally?** The old saying "A picture is worth a thousand words" is true. The same thing can be said for clarifying what you mean by letting your audience hear, taste, feel, or smell it.

3. **Is there important information in your speech that the audience may find boring?** At times, you may want to use presentational aids to help your audience attend to what you are saying. For example, it's sometimes hard for the audience to pay attention to statistics, but a colorful graph can help audience members concentrate on what you're saying.

4. **How many presentational aids should I use?** Presentational aids should supplement the oral message of your speech, not replace,

overshadow, or distract from it. While the Ignite speech referred to in the chapter opener was a five-minute speech that used 20 slides, most speakers find that one good aid for about one minute of speaking time is sufficient. So in a five-minute presentation, you might aim for between three and seven presentational aids.

5. **How large is the audience?** Presentational aids should be large enough to be seen and loud enough to be heard by those in the back and corners of the room.

6. **Are my presentational aids easy to use and transport?** Choose aids that you feel comfortable using and that are easy to transport from home to your speaking site. You want to focus on the content and delivery of your speech, not on how nervous you are using a new technology or transporting a cumbersome or fragile presentational aid.

7. **Is the necessary equipment readily available?** At times, you may be speaking in an environment that is not equipped for certain displays. In any situation in which you have scheduled equipment from an outside source, you need to prepare for the possibility that the equipment may not arrive on time or may not work the way you anticipated. Call ahead, get to your speaking location early, practice using your presentational aids with the available equipment, and have a backup plan, just in case. This is especially true when using computers and projection units from an outside source. Being prepared in this case means you might bring your own laptop and cable cords, an extra extension cord, and handouts in case the equipment still fails you.

8. **Is there sufficient time to show the aid without having it overtake the speech itself?** Remember that presentational aids are meant to supplement and enhance your speech, not replace it. If sharing the aid will take too much time, consider a different sort of aid.

9. **Is the time involved in making or getting the presentational aid and equipment cost-effective?** Presentational aids are supplements. Their goal is to supplement what you are doing verbally. If you believe that a particular aid will help you better achieve your goal, then the time spent is well worth it. Otherwise, the best advice we can offer is to "keep it simple."

Preparing Effective Presentational Aids

However simple you plan to make your presentational aids, keep in mind that you still have to take the time to design and produce them carefully. You may need to find or create charts, graphs, diagrams, maps, or drawings. You may need to search for and prepare photographs. You may need to look for audio, video, or audiovisual clips and then need to convert them to a format that you can use at your speech site.

As you prepare, you must first determine whether you will design your aids by hand or by using presentation software. What you decide may depend on the resources available at your speech site. If you are artistic, can print clearly, and work neatly, then hand-designed aids would be a good choice. If you are comfortable using software, then this method may be more efficient. The goal, however, is to prepare professional-looking presentational aids that will enhance your ethos (perceived competence, credibility, and character) in addition to clarifying your message and making it more memorable. Regardless of the method you choose, there are several guidelines you will want to follow.

1. **Limit the reading required of the audience.** The audience should not spend a long time reading your visual aid; you want them listening to you. So write points as short phrases rather than complete sentences.

2. **Customize presentational aids from other sources.** We often get ideas and information for visual aids from other sources, and the tendency is to include everything that was in the original source. But if the original source includes information that is irrelevant to your purpose or audience, simplify your aid so that it includes only the information you want to present.

3. **Use a photo, print, or type size that can be seen easily and a volume and sound quality that can be heard easily by your entire audience.** Regarding visual materials, check your photo, charts, and lettering for size by moving as far away from the presentational aid as the farthest person in your audience will be sitting. If you can see the image, read the lettering, and see the details from that distance, your aid is large enough; if not, create a larger draft and check it again. Check audio materials for volume and sound quality in a similar way.

4. **Use a consistent print style that is easy to read.** Avoid fancy print styles; your goal is presentational aids that are easy to read.

There are a number of strategies that we can pursue in order to increase current profits and ensure the growth of revenue streams. First, we should expand into the emerging markets in which we currently do not have significant presence. This will require us to invest heavily in overseas partners and facilities. Second, we should diversify our product line so that we can appeal both to a broader domestic customer base, as well as provide goods that will be attractive to foreign consumers. Third, we should analyze the strategies that our direct competitors are using to expand their domestic and overseas business so that we can replicate and improve upon their successes.

- **Expansion**
- **Diversification**
- **Success**

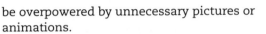

Likewise, stick to one print style throughout the aid or computerized slide show. In addition, some people think that printing in all capital letters creates emphasis, but the combination of uppercase and lowercase letters is easier to read than uppercase only—even when the ideas are written in short phases.

5. **Make sure information is laid out in a way that is aesthetically pleasing.** Leave sufficient white space around the whole visual so that it's easy to identify each component (white space is the areas of a page without print or pictures). Also, use typefaces and indenting to visually represent relationships between ideas.

6. **Add pictures or other visual symbols to add interest.** To truly enhance a verbal message, a presentational aid should consist of more than just words.[6] Visual symbols can increase retention by appealing to diverse learning styles.[7] If you are working with computer graphics, consider adding clip art. Most computer graphics packages have a wide variety of clip art that you can import to your document. You can also buy relatively inexpensive software packages that contain thousands of clip art images. A relevant piece of clip art can make the image look both more professional and more dramatic. Be careful, though; clip art can be overdone. Don't let your message

be overpowered by unnecessary pictures or animations.

7. **Use color strategically.** Although black and white can work well for your visual aids, consider using color strategically to emphasize points. Here are some suggestions for incorporating color in your presentational aids:

- Use the same background color for all your presentational aids and theme for the slides on your computerized slide show.
- Use the same color to show similarities, and use opposite colors (on a color wheel) to show differences between ideas.
- Use bright colors, such as red, to highlight important information. Be sure to avoid using red and green together, however, because audience members who are color-blind may not be able to distinguish between them.
- Use dark colors for lettering on a white background and light colors for lettering on black or deep blue backgrounds.
- Use no more than two or three colors on any presentational aid that is not a photograph or video clip.
- Pretend you are your audience. Sit as far away as they will be sitting, and evaluate the colors you have chosen for their readability and appeal.

8. **Use presentation software to prepare professional-looking presentational aids.** Presentation software is a computer program that enables you to electronically prepare and store your presentational aids using a computer. Microsoft's PowerPoint, Adobe's Captivate, and Apple's Keynote are popular commercial presentation software programs. The visuals you create on a computer can become overhead transparencies or handouts, or they can be displayed directly on a screen as a computerized slide show. Aids developed with presentation software give a very polished look to your speech and allow you to develop and deliver the complex multimedia presentations that are expected in many professional settings.

Computerized slide shows have quickly become the presentational aid of choice today. However, too often, these shows do not adhere to the most important function of effective presentational aids, which is to enhance the verbal message, not replace it.[8] The speaker should not be relegated to the role of projectionist. Effective computerized slide shows adhere to all of the fundamental criteria we have addressed regarding presentational aids. Well-designed and well-presented slide shows greatly enhance audience interest, understanding, and memory, as well as the audience's perceptions of the speaker's credibility.

Let's see if we can put all of these principles to work. Exhibit 9.8 contains a lot of important information, but notice how unpleasant it is to the eye. As you can see, this visual aid ignores all the principles we've discussed. However, with some thoughtful simplification, this speaker could produce the visual aid shown in Exhibit 9.9, which sharpens the focus by emphasizing the keywords (reduce, reuse, recycle), highlighting the major details, and adding clip art for a professional touch.

Exhibit 9.8

A Cluttered and Cumbersome Visual Aid

I WANT YOU TO REMEMBER THE THREE Rs OF RECYCLING
Reduce the amount of waste people produce, like overpacking or using material that won't recycle.
Reuse by relying on cloth towels rather than paper towels, earthenware dishes rather than paper or plastic plates, and glass bottles rather than aluminum cans.
Recycle by collecting recyclable products, sorting them correctly, and getting them to the appropriate recycling agency.

Methods for Displaying Presentational Aids

Once you have decided on the specific presentational aids for your speech, you will need to choose the method to display them. Methods for displaying aids vary in the type of preparation they require, the amount of specialized training needed to use them effectively, and the professionalism they convey. Some methods, such as writing on a chalkboard, require little advance preparation. Sometimes, computerized slide shows can require extensive preparation. Finally, the quality of your presentational aid will affect your ethos. A well-run slide show is impressive, but technical difficulties can make you look unprepared. Hand-drawn charts and graphs that are hastily or sloppily developed mark you as an amateur, whereas professional-looking visual aids enhance your credibility. Speakers can choose from the following methods for displaying presentational aids.

Posters

The easiest method for displaying simple drawings, charts, maps, photos, and graphs is by preparing them on or attaching them to stiff cardboard or foamcore. Then the visual can be placed on an easel or in a chalk tray when it is referred to during the speech. Because poster boards tend to be fairly small, use them only with smaller audiences (30 people or fewer).

Whiteboards or Chalkboards

Because a whiteboard or chalkboard is a staple in every college classroom, many novice (and ill-prepared) speakers rely on this method for displaying their visual aids. Unfortunately, a whiteboard or chalkboard is easy to misuse and to overuse. Moreover, they are not suitable for depicting complex material. Writing on a whiteboard or chalkboard is appropriate only for very short items

Exhibit 9.9

A Simple but Effective Visual Aid

presentation software
a computer program that enables you to electronically prepare and store your visual aids using a computer

of information that can be written in a few seconds. Nevertheless, being able to use a whiteboard or chalkboard effectively should be a part of any speaker's repertoire.

Whiteboards or chalkboards should be written on prior to speaking or during a break in speaking. Otherwise, the visual is likely to be either illegible or partly obscured by your body as you write. Or you may end up talking to the board instead of to the audience. Should you need to draw or write on the board while you are talking, you should practice doing it first. If you are right-handed, stand to the right of what you are drawing. Try to face at least part of the audience while you work. Although it may seem awkward at first, your effort will allow you to maintain contact with your audience and will allow the audience to see what you are doing while you are doing it.

"Chalk talks" are easiest to prepare, but they are the most likely to result in damage to speaker credibility. It is the rare individual who can develop well-crafted visual aids on a whiteboard or chalkboard. More often, these presentations signal a lack of preparation.

Flipcharts

A flipchart, a large pad of paper mounted on an easel, can be an effective method for presenting visual aids. Flipcharts (and easels) are available in many sizes. For a presentation to four or five people, a small tabletop version works well; for a larger audience, a larger pad (30 by 40 inches) is needed.

Flipcharts are prepared before the speech using colored markers to record the information. At times, a speaker may record some of the information before the speech begins and then add information while speaking.

When preparing flipcharts, leave several pages between each visual on the pad. If you discover a mistake or decide to revise, you can tear out that sheet without disturbing the order of other visuals you may have prepared. After you have the visuals, tear out all but one sheet between each chart. This blank sheet serves as both a transition page and a cover sheet. Because you want your audience to focus on your words and not on visual material that is no longer being discussed, you can flip to the empty page while you are talking about material not covered by charts. Also, the empty page between charts ensures that heavy lines or colors from the next chart will not show through.

For flipcharts to be effective, the information that is handwritten or drawn must be neat and appropriately sized. Flipchart visuals that are not neatly done detract from speaker credibility. Flipcharts can be comfortably used with smaller audiences (fewer than 100 people) but are not appropriate for larger settings. It is especially important when creating flipcharts to make sure that the information is written large enough to be easily seen by all audience members.

LCD multimedia projector
a projection unit that connects to a VCR player, a DVD player, or a computer and projects images from them onto a screen

Handouts

At times, it may be useful for each member of the audience to have a personal copy of the visual aid. In these situations, you can prepare a handout. On the plus side, you can prepare handouts (material printed on sheets of paper) quickly, and all the people in the audience can have their own professional-quality material to refer to and take with them from the speech. On the minus side is the distraction of distributing handouts and the potential for losing audience members' attention when you want them to be looking at you.

Before you decide to use handouts, carefully consider why they would be better than some other method. Handouts are effective for information you want listeners to refer to after the speech, such as a set of steps to follow later, useful telephone numbers and addresses, or mathematical formulas.

If you decide to use handouts, distribute them at the end of the speech. If you want to refer to information on the handout during the speech, create another visual aid that you can reveal only when discussing it for use during the actual speech.

Document Cameras

Another simple way to display drawings, charts, photos, and graphs is with a document camera, such as an Elmo. A document camera allows you to project images without transferring them to an acetate film. Transfer drawings, charts, photos, and graphs from original sources onto sheets of 8- by 11-inch paper so you can display them smoothly and professionally.

DVD Players and LCD Projectors

To show TV, film, and video clips for a classroom speech, a DVD player and a television monitor should be sufficient. For larger audiences, however, you will need multiple monitors or, ideally, an LCD multimedia projector, which is a projection unit that connects to a DVD player or a computer and projects images from them onto a large screen, which makes them easy to see, even in a large auditorium. An LCD projector is also ideal for displaying computerized slide shows, such as PowerPoint presentations.

Computerized Slide Shows

You can present computerized slide shows using an LCD projector or a large monitor connected to an onsite computer that has presentation software compatible with the software you used to make your aids. Because you can't always anticipate problems with onsite projection equipment, come with backup aids, such as handouts. When you present your slide show, ensure that the audience focuses their attention on you when you're not talking about one of your slides. To redirect their attention from your slide show to you, insert blank screens between your slides or press the B key on your computer to display a blank screen.

For more about how to use Microsoft PowerPoint, the most popular presentation software, go to the CourseMate for SPEAK at www.cengagebrain.com to access **Web Resource 9.1: PowerPoint Tutorial**.

Guidelines for Using Presentational Aids During the Speech

Many speakers think that once they have prepared good presentational aids, they will have no trouble using them in the speech. However, many speeches with good aids have become shambles because the speaker neglected to *practice with them*. You will want to make sure that you practice using presentational aids in your speech rehearsals. During practice sessions, indicate on your notes exactly when you will reveal each aid (and when you will conceal it). Work on statements for introducing the aids, and practice different ways of showing your aids until you are comfortable using them and satisfied that everyone in the audience will be able to see them. Following are several other guidelines for using presentational aids effectively in your speech.

1. **Plan carefully when to use presentational aids.** As you practice your speech, indicate on your outline when and how you will use each aid. Avoid displaying aids before you begin talking about the specific information to which they relate, as they may distract your audience's attention from important information that precedes the aid. Likewise, if you find that a presentational aid does not contribute directly to the audience's attention to, understanding of, or retention of information on your topic, then reconsider whether to use it at all.

2. **Position presentational aids and equipment before beginning your speech.** Make sure your aids and equipment are where you want them and that everything is ready and in working order. Test to make sure visual, audio, or audio-visual equipment works and that excerpts are cued correctly. Taking time to position your aids will make you feel more confident and look more professional and at ease.

3. **Show or play presentational aids only when talking about them.** Because presentational aids will draw audience attention, the basic rule of thumb for using them is this: When the aid is no longer the focus of attention, cover it up, remove it, turn it off, or get rid of it.

4. **Talk about the visual aid while showing it.** Because you already know what you want your audience to see in a presentational aid, tell your audience what to look for, explain the various parts of the aid, and interpret figures, symbols, and percentages. For an audio presentational aid, point out what you want your audience to listen for before you play the aid. When showing a visual aid, use the following "turn-touch-talk" technique:
   - When you display the visual, walk to the screen—that's where everyone will look

anyway. Slightly turn to the visual and point to it with your arm or a pointer. Then, with your back to the screen and your body still at a slight 45–degree angle to the group, talk to your audience about the visual.
   - When you finish making your comments, return to the lectern or your speaking position and turn off the projector or otherwise conceal the visual.

5. **Talk to your audience, not to the presentational aid.** You may need to look at the visual aid occasionally, but it is important to maintain eye contact with your audience as much as possible—in part so that you can gauge how they are reacting to your visual material. When speakers become too engrossed in their visual aids, looking at them instead of the audience, they tend to lose contact with the audience entirely.

6. **Display visual aids so that everyone in the audience can see them.** If you hold the visual aid, position it away from your body and point it toward the audience. If you place your visual aid on an easel or mount it in some way, stand to one side and point with the arm nearest the visual aid. If it is necessary to roll or fold the visual aid, bring some transparent tape to mount it to a board or wall so that it does not roll or wrinkle. If the visual aid is projected onto a screen, point with your hand or a pointer to the screen.

7. **Avoid passing objects around the audience.** People look at, read, handle, and think about whatever they hold in their hands. While they are so occupied, they are not likely to be listening to you. This is why it's best to distribute a handout after your speech, not during it.

To see video clips of student speakers presenting visual aids effectively, go to the CourseMate for SPEAK at www.cengagebrain.com to access chapter resources for Chapter 12. The speeches "Flag Etiquette," "Making Ethanol," and "The Three C's of Down Syndrome" all feature students using presentational aids. For more about how and when to use visual aids in a speech, access **Web Resource 9.2: Enhancing Written and Spoken Presentations.**

ACTION STEP 5
Activity 5A

Choosing, Preparing, and Using Presentational Aids
The goal of this activity is to identify information where a presentational aid would increase audience interest, understanding, and retention.

1. Identify the key ideas in your speech where a presentational aid would increase audience interest, facilitate understanding, or increase retention.
2. For each idea you have identified, list the type of presentational aid you think would be most appropriate to develop and use.
3. For each aid you have identified, decide how you will design it.
4. For each aid you have identified, decide on the method you will use to display it and how you will reference it during the speech.

You can complete this activity online with Speech Builder Express, download a Presentational Aids Planning Chart to help you organize your aids, and, if requested, e-mail your completed activity to your instructor. Go to the CourseMate for SPEAK at www.cengagebrain.com to access Activity 5A.

THERE ARE EVEN MORE STUDY TOOLS FOR THIS CHAPTER AT WWW.CENGAGEBRAIN.COM

- **Interactive Videos**
- **Speech Builder Express**
- **Printable Flash Cards**
- **Interactive Games**
- **Chapter Review Cards**
- **Online Quizzes With Feedback**
- **Speech Studio available upon instructor request**

Student Response:
Action Step 5, Activity 5A

Speech goal: I would like my audience to learn to identify common poisonous plants that grow in our area.

1. Identify the key ideas in your speech where a presentational aid would increase audience interest, facilitate understanding, or increase retention.
   Leaf shape, size, and color; habitat; signs of contact
2. For each idea you have identified, list the type of presentational aid you think would be most appropriate to develop and use.
   I will use two color photographs of each type of plant. The first will show the entire plant; the second will be a close-up of the leaves. I will also use photos to show the habitat in which each plant is usually found. Finally, I will use photographs to show the reactions that occur as a result of contact with the plants. I will have actual plant samples available for closer inspection after my speech.
3. For each aid you have identified, decide how you will design it.
   I will use my digital camera to take photographs of each plant and the habitats in which I found them. These will be transferred to my computer, and then I will create a computerized slide show using PowerPoint. I will locate images of reactions to each plant online, download them, and add them to the computerized slide show. I will also collect samples of each type of plant and bring them with me to the speech.
4. For each aid you have identified, decide on the method you will use to display it and how you will reference it during the speech.
   I will bring a memory stick with the PowerPoint presentation on it with me and use the computer and LCD projector that is available at the speaking site. I will also have backup overheads of all my photos and slides. I will reference it using a pointer because I will be speaking to an audience of at least 50 people.

Language and Oral Style

As Rhonda replayed the recording she had made of her first speech practice session, she listened carefully to the section on the effects of Rohypnol. She stopped the tape after she heard herself saying, "Rohypnol leaves many bad effects on people. And a lot of these are really, really terrible. I mean, you can be totally out of it for a long time."

"Yuck," thought Rhonda. "That sounds so vague. I say, 'leaves bad effects,' but I don't specifically state any of the effects. And calling the effects 'really, really terrible' isn't very descriptive. What could I say instead?"

With an outline in hand and your presentational aids prepared, you are ready to practice your speech, switching your focus from the macrostructure (the overall framework you use to organize your speech content) to the microstructure (the specific language and style choices you use to frame your ideas and verbalize them to your audience). In the chapter opening, Rhonda is working on developing appropriate, accurate, clear, and vivid language for sharing her ideas. Once she does this, she will continue to rehearse until she is conversational and animated, as well as intelligible and expressive.

In written communication, an effective style evolves through an iterative process of reading and revising. In a speech, an effective style develops through an iterative process of practicing aloud and revising. To prepare for your rehearsals, you begin by creating **speaking notes** that consist of a keyword outline adapted from your formal outline with delivery cues and reference citations you will use as you deliver your speech. During each rehearsal, you orally elaborate on the points on your keyword outline until the finished speech is the appropriate length. With each rehearsal, you also revise your language choices until your ideas are presented appropriately, accurately, clearly, and vividly.

When a written sentence is unclear, the reader can reread it to figure out its meaning, but when a sentence in a speech is unclear, the listener cannot go back, and the meaning may be misunderstood or lost. So as a speaker, you must focus on how to help the audience understand the meaning *as the speech is given*. In this chapter, you will learn to use the kind of language that is instantly intelligible to the *ear* so the audience receives the same meanings you intend.

Let's begin our discussion by briefly describing oral style and how it differs from written style. Then we'll offer some specific strategies you can employ to ensure that your speech is appropriate, accurate, clear, and vivid.

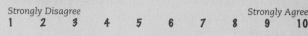

What do you think?

A speaker who uses offensive language does not care about his or her audience.

Strongly Disagree   Strongly Agree
1   2   3   4   5   6   7   8   9   10

speaking notes
a keyword outline with delivery cues and reference citations you will use as you deliver your speech

ACTION STEP 6:
Practice Oral Language and Delivery Style

A. Practice to develop an oral style using language that is appropriate, accurate, clear, and vivid.

Oral Style

Oral style refers to the manner in which one conveys messages through the spoken word. An effective oral style differs quite a bit from written style, though when giving a speech, your oral style is still more formal than everyday talk. In fact, the degree of formality required to be an effective public speaker is based on the rhetorical situation. In other words, your goal is to adapt your language to the audience and occasion.

Although the language you use when speaking to a small audience at a business meeting will be more formal than when conversing with a friend, it will not be as formal as when speaking to an audience of 100 or more at a professional conference. As the speaker, however, your primary goal is to establish a relationship with your listeners, so your language in any of these situations should reflect a personal tone that encourages listeners to feel you are having a conversation with them. There are four primary characteristics that distinguish an effective oral style from an effective written style.

1. **An effective oral style tends toward short sentences and familiar language.** Because listeners have only one opportunity to hear your idea, work to ensure your words are ones that your audience is likely to understand.

2. **An effective oral style features plural personal pronouns.** Using personal pronouns such as "we," "us," and "our" creates a sense of relationship with the audience, showing respect for them as participants in the rhetorical situation.

3. **An effective oral style features descriptive words and phrases that appeal to the ear and are designed to sustain listener interest and promote retention.** By using colorful adjectives and adverbs, you can draw your listeners into your message and motivate them to stay focused on it.

4. **An effective oral style incorporates clear section transitions and signposts.** Because listeners hear a speaker's message only once, section transitions that verbally signal moving from one major section of the speech to the next provide oral markers that help listeners follow your train of thought as the speech progresses.

Now, let's turn our attention to some specific things to consider when making language choices as you practice your speech. These strategies focus on speaking appropriately, accurately, clearly, and vividly.

Speaking Appropriately

Speaking appropriately means using language that adapts to the needs, interests, knowledge, and attitudes of your listeners and avoiding language that alienates audience members. In the communication field, we use the term **verbal immediacy** to describe language used to reduce the psychological distance between you and your audience.[1] In other words, speaking appropriately means choosing words that enhance the connection between you and the members of your audience.

Using appropriate language makes us more effective because it demonstrates that we are adapting successfully to the rhetorical situation. It also demonstrates that we are ethical communicators who respect others, even those who differ from us. If we speak inappropriately, on the other hand, we are likely to offend some listeners and fail to achieve our speech goal. Why? Because from that moment on, listeners are likely to shift their focus to opinions of us as people and stop listening to our message. In this section, we discuss specific strategies that will help you make appropriate language choices.

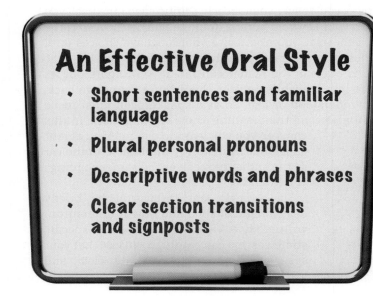

An Effective Oral Style

- Short sentences and familiar language
- Plural personal pronouns
- Descriptive words and phrases
- Clear section transitions and signposts

Use "We" Language

"We" language, the use of plural personal pronouns like "we," "our," and "us" rather than "you" or "they," conveys a sense of connection with your listeners and involves them in the communication event. When used appropriately, "we" language fosters a sense of having a conversation *with* your audience rather than speaking or presenting *in front of* them. As a result, your audience will be more open to listening to you, believing what you say, and remembering your ideas.[2]

Use Bias-Free Language

Another way to create verbal immediacy is by using bias-free language, words that keep an ethical concern for fairness and respect with regard to race, ethnicity, gender, ability, sexual orientation, and diverse worldviews.[3]

1. **Generic language** uses words that apply only to one sex, race, or other group as though they represent everyone. In the past, English speakers used the masculine pronoun *he* to stand for all humans regardless of sex. You can avoid using generic language in one of two ways. First, you can use plurals: "When people shop, they should have a clear idea of what they want to buy." Alternatively, you can use both male and female pronouns: "When a person shops, he or she should have a clear idea of what he or she wants to buy." Research shows that avoiding generic language helps listeners include women in their mental images, thus increasing gender balance in their perceptions.[4] The result is more accurate and bias-free language.

   A second problem of generic language results from the traditional use of the word *man*.[5] Consider the term *policeman*. What this really means is that an individual is a law-enforcement officer, but the underlying tone is that the officer is a male human being. Bias-free alternatives do exist—for instance, *police officer* instead of *policeman*. Bias-free language is not only more appropriate but,

   **Policeman?
   Policewoman?
   Police officer?**

quite frankly, also more accurate.

2. **Nonparallel language** is when terms are changed because of the sex, race, or other group characteristics of the individual. Because it treats groups of people differently, nonparallel language is also belittling. Two common forms of nonparallelism are marking and irrelevant association.

   Marking is the *addition* of sex, race, age, or other group designations to a description. Notice the difference between the following two sentences:

   Jones is a good doctor.

   Jones is a good black doctor.

   In the second sentence, use of the marker "black" is offensive. It has nothing to do with being a doctor. Marking is inappropriate because you trivialize the person's role by introducing an irrelevant characteristic.[6] The speaker may be intending to praise Jones, but listeners may interpret the sentence as saying that Jones is a good doctor for a black person but not that Jones is as good as a good white doctor.

   A second form of nonparallelism is **irrelevant association**, which is when we emphasize one person's relationship to another when that relationship is irrelevant to the point. For example, introducing a speaker as "Gladys Thompson, whose husband is CEO of Acme . . ." is inappropriate. Mentioning her husband's status implies that Gladys Thompson is chairperson because of her *husband*'s accomplishments, not her own.

> **"we" language**
> the use of plural personal pronouns like "we," "our," and "us" rather than "you" or "they"
>
> **bias-free language**
> language that demonstrates through word choices an ethical concern for fairness and respect with regard to race, ethnicity, gender, ability, sexual orientation, and diverse worldviews
>
> **generic language**
> language that uses words that apply only to one sex, race, or other group as though they represent everyone
>
> **nonparallel language**
> language in which terms are changed because of the sex, race, or other group characteristics of the individual
>
> **marking**
> the addition of sex, race, age, or other group designations to a description
>
> **irrelevant association**
> emphasizing one person's relationship to another when that relationship is irrelevant to the point

Adapt to Cultural Diversity

Verbal communication rules and expectations vary from culture to culture. One major theory used to explain similarities and differences in language and behavior is individualism versus collectivism.[7] In general, individualistic cultures emphasize individual goals more than group goals because these cultures value uniqueness. Many individualistic cultures are found in Western Europe and North America. In contrast, collectivistic cultures emphasize group goals more than individual goals because these cultures value harmony and solidarity. Many collectivistic cultures are found in Asia, Africa, and Latin America.[8]

Individualistic cultures tend to use low-context communication, in which information is (a) embedded mainly in the messages transmitted and (b) presented directly. Collectivistic cultures tend to use high-context communication, in which people (a) expect others to know how they're thinking and feeling and (b) present some messages indirectly to avoid embarrassing the other person. Thus, speakers from low-context cultures operate on the principle of saying what they mean and getting to the point. Their approach may be characterized by such expressions as "Say what you mean" and "Don't beat around the bush."[9] In contrast, speakers from high-context cultures form messages with language that is intentionally ambiguous and indirect; to interpret these messages correctly, listeners need to understand not only the message but also the context in which it is uttered.

What does this mean for public speakers? When you are a member of a cultural group that operates differently from that of the majority of your audience members, you need to adapt your language to be appropriate for your audience. It may help to ask someone from the same cultural group as the majority of your audience to listen to your speech and suggest ways to make it more appropriate for that audience.

To read more about how to adapt to audiences from other cultures, go to the CourseMate for SPEAK at www.cengagebrain.com to access **Web Resource 10.1: Speaking to International Audiences**.

Avoid Offensive Humor

Show sensitivity by avoiding offensive humor. Some jokes may not be intended to be offensive, but if some listeners are offended, you will have lost verbal immediacy. Comedian Chris Rock used offensive humor many times during his remarks as host of the 2003 MTV music awards. For example, he introduced entertainment mogul P. Diddy, who had faced several lawsuits recently, as "being sued by more people than the Catholic Church."[10] Some in his audience were probably offended. To be most effective with your formal public speeches, avoid humorous comments or jokes that may be offensive to some listeners. Being inclusive means demonstrating respect for all listeners.

Avoid Profanity and Vulgarity

Appropriate language avoids profanity and vulgar expressions. Fifty years ago, a child was punished for saying "hell" or "damn," and adults used profanity and vulgarity only in rare situations to express strong emotions. Today, "casual swearing"—profanity injected into regular conversation—is epidemic in some language communities, including college campuses.[11] In some settings, even the crudest and most offensive terms are so commonly used that speakers and (as a result) listeners alike have become desensitized, and the words have lost their ability to shock and offend.

Despite the growing, mindless use of crude speech, many people are still shocked and offended by swearing. And people who casually pepper their speech with profanity and vulgar expressions are often perceived as abrasive and lacking in character, maturity, intelligence, manners, and emotional control.[12]

Unfortunately, profanity and vulgarity are habits that are easily acquired and hard to extinguish. If you have acquired a "potty mouth," you're going to have to work very hard to clean up your act because verbal habits are hard to break. For tips on how to "tame your tongue," go to the CourseMate for SPEAK at www.cengagebrain.com to access **Web Resource 10.2: Cuss Control Academy**.

Shun Hate Speech

You've heard the old child's saying, "Sticks and stones will break my bones, but words will never hurt me." As children, we all knew that this statement was a lie. Still, it gave us psychological comfort in the face of cruel name-calling. Unfortunately, name-calling can take on even uglier forms in adult speech. Think of the damage caused by the use of words such as "nigger," "cracker," "kike," or "fag."

Hate speech is the use of words and phrases not only to demean another person or group but also to express hatred and prejudice toward that person or group. Under the U.S. Constitution, people are generally afforded free speech protection. From a communication perspective, however, hate speech is designed to be divisive rather than inclusive and demonstrates extreme lack of respect.

Speaking Accurately

Using accurate language means using words that convey your meaning precisely. On the surface, speaking accurately seems simple enough. If you select words to represent your meaning, won't audience members understand the meaning you wish to convey? In fact, there are four reasons speaking accurately is not that simple.

1. **Language is symbolic.** We use words to represent things, ideas, events, and so forth. Words have no tangible meanings in and of themselves; rather, we attach meaning to them.[13] In communication studies, we often simply say the *word* is not the *thing*. In their influential book *The Meaning of Meaning: A Study of the Influence of Language upon Thought and the Science of Symbolism*, I. A. Richards and C. K. Ogden clarify this idea using the semantic triangle, as depicted in Exhibit 10.1.[14] In the triangle, a "referent" is the *thing* or object we refer to with a word, which is the "symbol" we use to refer to it. Our audience then attaches meaning to that symbol, which is what Richards and Ogden label the "thought of referent." For example, when you hear the word *dog*, what image forms in your mind? Do you visualize a poodle? A sheepdog? A mutt? There is so much variation in what the word *dog* conjures in our minds because the word *dog* is not the actual animal. The word is a symbol you use to represent the animal. So if you use the word *dog* in a speech, each mem-

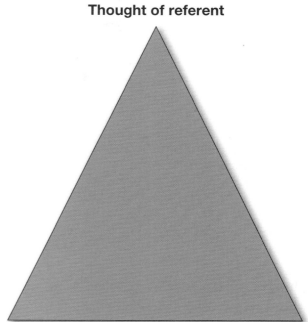

Exhibit 10.1

The Semantic Triangle

Thought of referent

Symbol   **Referent**

ber of your audience may picture something different. Because the *word* is not the *thing*, as a speaker you should use accurate words that most closely match the thing or idea you want your audience to see or understand.

2. **We are not born knowing a language; we must *learn* it.** Moreover, each generation within a language community learns the language anew. We learn much of our language early in life from our families. We then learn more in school, and we continue to learn more throughout our lives. But we do not all learn to use the same words in the same way.

3. **Although every language has a system of syntax and grammar, each utterance of a word is a creative act.** When we speak, we use language to create new sentences that represent our own personal meaning. Although on occasion we repeat other people's sentence constructions to represent what we are thinking or feeling, most of our talk is unique.

hate speech
the use of words and phrases to demean another person or group and to express the speaker's hatred and prejudice toward that person or group

accurate language
words that convey your meaning precisely

4. **Even though two people may know the same words, they may interpret the meanings of the words differently.** When James tells Chrissie that he liked going to the movies with her the previous night, what Chrissie understands James to mean by "liked" depends on how she interprets the message. Did James mean that he thought the movie was entertaining, or did he mean that he enjoyed spending time with Chrissie?

Using accurate language is crucial to effective speaking because it helps you be **intelligible**, or clearly understood. If listeners don't understand you or what you mean, your attempt to communicate is doomed. To help ensure that the language you use in speeches is accurate, let's take a look at three concepts that affect how words are interpreted: denotation, connotation, and dialect.

Denotation

A word's **denotation** is the explicit meaning a language community formally gives a word (i.e., its dictionary definition). So, denotatively, when Melissa said her dog died, she meant that her domesticated canine no longer demonstrates physical life. Keep in mind that in some situations the denotative meaning of a word may not be clear. Why? One reason is that dictionary definitions reflect current and past practices in the language community. Another reason is that dictionaries often offer more than one definition for a given word. And dictionaries use words to define words. The end result is that words are defined differently in various dictionaries and may include multiple meanings that also may change over time.

Moreover, meaning may vary depending on the context in which the word is used. For example, the dictionary definition of *gay* includes both (a) having or showing a merry, lively mood and (b) being homosexual. Thus, **context**—the position of a word in a sentence and its relationship to other words around it—has an important effect on correctly interpreting which denotation is meant. Not only will the other words, the syntax, and the grammar of a verbal message help us understand the denotative meaning of certain words, but so will the situation in which they are spoken. For example, if you're at the beach and you say you are "surfing," you probably mean you're riding the waves. But if you're sitting at your desk in front of your computer, you probably mean you're searching the Internet.

Connotation

A word's **connotation** is the positive, neutral, or negative feelings or evaluations we associate with it. For example, consider how your impression of Dave would differ if someone said he was "cheap" versus "frugal." The denotative meaning of both words indicates someone who doesn't like to spend a lot of money, but for most of us "frugal" has a more positive connotation than "cheap." Thus, our perception of a word's connotation may be even more important than its denotation in how we interpret the meaning of the word.

Ogden and Richards were among the first scholars to consider the misunderstandings that result from the failure of communicators to realize that their subjective reactions to words are a product of their life experiences.[15] For instance, when Melissa told Trish that her dog died, Trish's understanding of the message depends on the extent to which her feelings about pets and death—her connotations of the words—correspond to the feelings Melissa has about pets and death. Whereas Melissa (who sees dogs as truly indispensable friends) may be intending to communicate her overwhelming grief, Trish (who doesn't particularly care for pets in general or dogs in particular) may miss the emotional meaning of Melissa's statement.

I went surfing last night.

Connotations give emotional power to words, so much so that people will even fight and die for them. Consider the connotative meanings people assign to words like *freedom* or *honor* and *right* or *wrong*. For this reason, connotations can be used effectively to increase pathos, which you remember is the emotional appeal of your message. As you consider language options, be sure to consider how predisposed your audience may be about the words you select. Use your audience analysis to help you steer clear of words that arouse unintended connotations, or be sure to explain how you are using a word to avoid negative responses to your message.

Dialect

Dialect, a regional or ethnic variety of a language, can also affect listener understanding of your message. Dialects evolve over time, and the manner in which they differ from the "standard" of the language may be influenced by other languages spoken in the region or by the ethnic group. For instance, in her book *Chicano English in Context*, Carmen Fought details how the English spoken by some Hispanic people in the Los Angeles area differs from Standard English.[16] Regional differences are also reflected in the words used to represent common things. For example, carbonated soft drinks are typically called "pop" in the Midwest, "soda" along the East Coast, and "Coke" in the South. Some dialects also incorporate what is considered non-standard grammar, such as "he don't" or "I says." If your audience doesn't share the dialect you normally speak, using it during your speeches can interfere with the intelligibility of your message. Not only that, it can also affect the audience's perception of your competence and credibility. Because most audiences are diverse, the best way to ensure being understood by all and conveying positive ethos is to use **Standard English** (which is taught in American schools and detailed in grammar handbooks like *Hodges Harbrace Handbook*, 17th ed.[17]).

Speaking Clearly

Speaking clearly results from reducing your use of ambiguous and confusing language. Compare the clarity of the following two descriptions of the same incident:

Some nut almost ran into me awhile ago.

Last Saturday afternoon, an older man in a banged-up Honda Civic ran through the red light at Calhoun and Clifton and came within inches of hitting

my car while I was waiting to turn left.

Speaking clearly decreases ambiguity and audience confusion when we speak. Let's look at four strategies for improving clarity: using specific language, choosing familiar terms, providing details and examples, and limiting vocalized pauses.

dialect
a regional or ethnic variety of a language

Standard English
form of English described in the dictionary or an English handbook

specific language
words that clarify meaning by narrowing what is understood from a general category to a particular item or group within that category

Use Specific Language

Specific language clarifies meaning by narrowing what is understood from a general category to a particular item or group within that category. Often, as we try to express our thoughts, the first words that come to mind are general, abstract, and imprecise. The ambiguity of these words makes the listener choose from many possible images rather than picturing the precise image we have in mind. The more listeners are called on to provide their own images, the more likely they are to see meanings different from what we intend. For instance, if in her speech Nevah refers to a "blue-collar worker," you might picture any number of occupations that fall within this broad category.

How would you describe this person with specific language?

If, instead, she says he's a "construction worker," the number of possible images you can picture is reduced. Now you select your image from the subcategory of construction worker, and your meaning is likely to be closer to the one she intended. If she is even more specific, she may say "bulldozer operator." Now you are even clearer on the specific occupation. To see a video clip of a student speaker using specific language, go to the CourseMate for SPEAK at www.cengagebrain.com to access the Interactive Video Activities for Chapter 10. Select the clip called "Shakespeare."

Choosing specific language is easier when you have a large working vocabulary. As a speaker, the larger your vocabulary, the more choices you have from which to select the word you want. As a listener, the larger your vocabulary, the more likely you are to understand the words used by others. One way to increase your vocabulary is to study one of the many vocabulary-building books on the shelves of almost any bookstore, such as *Word Smart: Building an Educated Vocabulary*.[18] You might also study magazine features such as "Word Power" in the *Reader's Digest*. By completing this monthly quiz and learning the words with which you are not familiar, you could increase your vocabulary by as many as 20 words per month. To take a vocabulary test online, go to the CourseMate for SPEAK at www.cengagebrain.com to access **Web Resource 10.3: Wordsmart Challenge**.

A second way to increase your vocabulary is to take note of words that you read or that people use in their conversations with you that you don't know and look them up. For instance, suppose you read or hear, "I was inundated with phone calls today!" If you wrote down *inundated* and looked it up in a dictionary later, you would find that it means "overwhelmed" or "flooded." If you then say to yourself, "She was inundated—overwhelmed or flooded—with phone calls today," you are likely to remember that meaning and apply it the next time you hear the word.

A third way to increase your vocabulary is to use a thesaurus (a book of words and their synonyms) to identify synonyms that are more specific than the word you may have chosen. But be careful—avoid unfamiliar words that may make you sound intelligent but could reduce your intelligibility. For example, *somnolent* is an interesting word, but most people don't know that it is a synonym for *sleepy*. Go to the CourseMate for SPEAK at www.cengagebrain.com to access **Web Resource 10.4: Merriam-Webster Online**.

Having a larger vocabulary won't help your speaking if you don't have a procedure for accessing it when you speak. So, during practice sessions, you will want to consciously experiment using specific words that precisely reflect your ideas. Suppose you were practicing a speech on registering for classes and said, "Preregistration is awful." If this word isn't quite right, you can quickly brainstorm better words, such as *frustrating, demeaning, cumbersome,* and *annoying*. Then, as you continue to practice, you might say, "Preregistration is a cumbersome process."

Some speakers think that to be effective they must impress their audience with their extensive vocabularies. As a result, instead of looking for precise words that narrow a larger category, they use words that appear pompous, affected, or stilted to the listener. Speaking precisely and specifically does not mean speaking obscurely. The following story illustrates the problem with pretentious words:

A plumber wrote to a government agency, saying that he found that hydrochloric acid quickly opened drainpipes but that he wasn't sure whether it was a good thing to use. A scientist at the agency replied, "The efficacy of hydrochloric acid is indisputable, but the corrosive residue is incompatible with metallic permanence."

The plumber wrote back thanking him for the assurance that hydrochloric acid was all right. Disturbed by this turn of affairs, the scientist showed the letter to his boss, another scientist, who then wrote to the plumber: "We cannot assume responsibility for the production of toxic and noxious residue with hydrochloric acid and suggest you use an alternative procedure."

The plumber wrote back that he agreed. Hydrochloric acid worked fine. Greatly disturbed by this misunderstanding, the scientists took their problem to the top boss. She wrote to the plumber: "Don't use hydrochloric acid. It eats the hell out of pipes."

So, use a more difficult word only when you believe that it is the very best word for a specific context.

You will know that you have really made strides in improving specificity when you find that you can form clear messages even under the pressure of presenting your speeches.

Choose Familiar Terms

Using familiar terms is just as important as using specific words. Avoid jargon, slang, abbreviations, and acronyms unless (a) you define them clearly the first time they are used and (b) using them is central to your speech goal.

Jargon is the unique technical terminology of a trade or profession that is not generally understood by outsiders. We might forget that people who are not in our same line of work or who do not have the same hobbies may not understand the jargon that seems such a part of our daily communication. Limit your use of jargon in speeches to general audiences, and always define jargon in simple terms the first time you use it.

Slang refers to informal, nonstandard vocabulary and nonstandard definitions assigned to words by a social group or subculture. For example, today the word *bad*, which has a standard definition denoting something unpleasant or substandard, can mean quite the opposite in some social groups and subcultures.[19] You should generally avoid slang in your public speeches not only because you risk misunderstanding but also because slang doesn't sound professional and it can hurt your credibility (ethos). Slang is so pervasive that there are special dictionaries devoted to the specialized vocabulary of different communities. You can even find slang dictionaries online. To access one created by a former student of the University of California at Berkeley, go to the CourseMate for SPEAK at www.cengagebrain.com to access **Web Resource 10.5: Slang Dictionary**.

Overusing and misusing abbreviations and acronyms can also hinder clarity. Even if you think the abbreviation or acronym is a common one, to ensure intelligibility, always define it the first time you use it in the speech. For example, in a speech about NASCAR, refer to it initially by the organization's full name and then provide the acronym: "National Association for Stock Car Auto Racing, or NASCAR." Providing the full and abbreviated forms of the name will ensure clarity for all listeners. If you are assuming right now that everyone knows what NASCAR is, it might benefit you to know one of your authors had to look it up to include it in this book!

Provide Details and Examples

Sometimes, the word we use may not have a precise synonym. In these situations, clarity can be achieved by adding details or examples. For instance, Linda says, "Rashad is very loyal." The meaning of *loyal* (faithful to an idea, person, company, or other entity) is abstract, so to avoid ambiguity and confusion, Linda might add, "He defended Gerry when Sara was gossiping about her." By following up her use of the abstract concept of loyalty with this example, Linda makes it easier for her listeners to "ground" their idea of this personal quality in a "real" experience.

Likewise, providing details can clarify our messages. Saying "He lives in a really big house" can be clarified by adding "He lives in a 14-room Tudor mansion on a six-acre estate."

Limit Vocalized Pauses

Vocalized pauses are unnecessary words interjected into sentences to fill moments of silence. Words commonly used for this purpose are "like," "you know," "really," and "basically," as well as "um" and "uh." We sometimes refer to vocalized pauses as "verbal garbage" because they do not serve a meaningful purpose and actually distract listeners from the message. Although a few vocalized pauses typically don't hinder clarity, practicing your speech aloud will help you eliminate them.

Speaking Vividly

Because listeners cannot "reread" what you have said, you must speak in ways that help them remember your message. Speaking vividly is one effective way to maintain your audience's interest and help them remember what you say. Vivid language is full of life—vigorous, bright, and intense. For example, a mediocre baseball announcer might say "Jackson made a great catch," but a better commentator's vivid account might be "Jackson leaped and made a spectacular one-handed catch just as he crashed into the center field wall." The words *leaped*, *spectacular*, *one-handed catch*, and *crashed* paint an intense verbal picture of the action. You can

slang
informal, nonstandard vocabulary and nonstandard definitions assigned to words by a social group or subculture

vocalized pause
unnecessary words interjected into sentences to fill moments of silence

vivid language
language that is full of life—vigorous, bright, and intense

Bull Market?
Sweat Equity?
SWOT Analysis?
NASCAR?
CPU?

make your ideas come to life by using sensory language and by using rhetorical figures and structures of speech.

Use Sensory Language

Sensory language is language that appeals to the senses of seeing, hearing, tasting, smelling, and feeling. Vivid sensory language begins with vivid thought. You are much more likely to express yourself vividly if you can physically or psychologically sense the meanings you are trying to convey. If you feel the "bite of the wind" or "the sting of freezing rain," if you hear and smell "the thick, juicy sirloin steaks sizzling on the grill," you will be able to describe these sensations. Does the cake "taste good"? Or do your taste buds "quiver with the sweet double-chocolate icing and velvety feel of the rich, moist cake"?

sensory language
language that appeals to the senses of seeing, hearing, tasting, smelling, and feeling

rhetorical figures of speech
phrases that make striking comparisons between things that are not obviously alike

rhetorical structures of speech
phrases that combine ideas in a particular way

simile
a direct comparison of dissimilar things using the word *like* or *as*

metaphor
an implied comparison between two unlike things without using *like* or *as*

To develop vivid sensory language, begin by considering how you can re-create what something, someone, or someplace *looks like*. Consider, too, how you can help listeners imagine how something *sounds*. How can you use language to convey the way something *feels* (textures, shapes, temperatures)? How can language re-create a sense of how something *tastes* or *smells*?

To achieve this in your speech, use colorful descriptors. They make your ideas more concrete and can arouse emotions. They invite listeners to imagine details. Here's an example about downhill skiing:

> *Sight: As you climb the hill, the bright winter sunshine glistening on the snow is blinding.*
>
> *Touch and feel: Just before you take off, you gently slip your goggles over your eyes. They are bitterly cold and sting your nose for a moment.*
>
> *Taste: You start the descent and, as you gradually pick up speed, the taste of air and ice and snow in your mouth invigorates you.*
>
> *Sound: An odd silence fills the air. You hear nothing but the swish of your skis against the snow beneath your feet. At last, you arrive at the bottom of the slope. Reality hits as you hear the hustle and bustle of other skiers and instructors directing them to their next session.*
>
> *Smell and feel: You enter the warming house. As your fingers thaw in the warm air, the aroma from the woodstove in the corner comforts you as you drift off into sleep.*

By using colorful descriptors that appeal to the senses, you arouse and maintain listener interest and make your ideas more memorable.

Use Rhetorical Figures and Structures of Speech

Rhetorical figures of speech make striking comparisons between things that are not obviously alike and so help listeners visualize or internalize what you are saying. Rhetorical structures of speech combine ideas in a particular way. Any of these devices can serve to make your speech more memorable as long as they aren't overused. Let's look at some examples.

A simile is a direct comparison of dissimilar things using the word *like* or *as*. Clichés such as "He walks like a duck" and "She's as busy as a bee" are similes. A very vivid simile was used by an elementary school teacher who said that being back at school after a long absence "was like trying to hold 35 corks under water at the same time."[20] This is a fresh, imaginative simile to describe an elementary school teacher's job. Similes can be effective because they make ideas more vivid in listeners' minds. But they should be used sparingly or they lose their appeal. Clichés should be avoided because their predictability reduces their effectiveness.

A metaphor is an implied comparison between two unlike things without using *like* or *as*. Instead of saying that one thing is *like* another, a metaphor says that one thing is another. Thus, problem cars are "lemons," and the leaky roof is a "sieve." Metaphors can be effective because they make an abstract concept more concrete, strengthen an important point, or heighten emotions. Notice how one speaker used a metaphor effectively to conclude a speech: "It is imperative that we weave our fabric of the future with durable thread."[21]

An **analogy** is an extended metaphor. Sometimes, you can develop a story from a metaphor that makes a concept more vivid. If you were to describe a family member as the "black sheep in the barnyard," that's a metaphor. If you went on to talk about the other members of the family as different animals on the farm and the roles ascribed to them, you would be extending the metaphor into an analogy. Analogies can be effective for holding your speech together in a creative and vivid way. Analogies are particularly useful to highlight the similarities between a complex or unfamiliar concept with one that is familiar.

Alliteration is the repetition of consonant sounds at the beginning of words that are near one another. Tongue twisters such as "She sells seashells by the seashore" use alliteration. Used sparingly, alliteration can catch listeners' attention and make the speech memorable. But overuse can hurt the message because listeners might focus on the technique rather than the content of your message.

Assonance is the repetition of vowel sounds in a phrase or phrases. "How now brown cow" is a common example. Sometimes the words rhyme, but they don't have to. As with alliteration, assonance can make your speech more memorable as long as it's not overused.

Onomatopoeia is the use of words that sound like the things they stand for, such as "buzz," "hiss," "crack," and "plop." In the speech about skiing, the "swish" of the skis is an example of onomatopoeia.

Personification is attributing human qualities to a concept or an inanimate object. When Madison talked about her truck, "Big Red," as her trusted friend and companion, she used personification.

Repetition is restating words, phrases, or sentences for emphasis. Martin Luther King Jr.'s "I Have a Dream" speech is a classic example:

I say to you today, my friends, so even though we face the difficulties of today and tomorrow, I still have a dream. It is a dream deeply rooted in the American dream.

I have a dream that one day this nation will rise up and live out the true meaning of its creed: "We hold

these truths to be self-evident: that all men are created equal."

I have a dream that one day on the red hills of Georgia the sons of former slaves and the sons of former slave owners will be able to sit down together at the table of brotherhood.

I have a dream that one day even the state of Mississippi, a state sweltering with the heat of injustice, sweltering with the heat of oppression, will be transformed into the oasis of freedom and justice.

I have a dream that my four little children will one day live in a nation where they will not be judged by the color of their skin but by the content of their character. I have a dream today.[22]

Antithesis is combining contrasting ideas in the same sentence, as when John F. Kennedy said, "Ask not what your country can do for you. Ask what you can do for your country." Speeches that offer antithesis in the concluding remarks are often memorable.

analogy
an extended metaphor

alliteration
repetition of consonant sounds at the beginning of words that are near one another

assonance
repetition of vowel sounds in a phrase or phrases

onomatopoeia
words that sound like the things they stand for

personification
attributing human qualities to a concept or an inanimate object

repetition
restating words, phrases, or sentences for emphasis

antithesis
combining contrasting ideas in the same sentence

THERE ARE EVEN MORE STUDY TOOLS FOR THIS CHAPTER AT WWW.CENGAGEBRAIN.COM

- **Interactive Videos**
- **Speech Builder Express**
- **Printable Flash Cards**
- **Interactive Games**
- **Chapter Review Cards**
- **Online Quizzes With Feedback**
- **Speech Studio available upon instructor request**

Practicing Delivery

LO^1 What are the characteristics of effective delivery? | LO^2 What can you do to use your voice effectively as you deliver your speech? | LO^3 What can you do to use your body effectively as you deliver your speech? | LO^4 Why and how should you rehearse your speech?

When Nadia finished speaking, everyone in the audience burst into spontaneous applause and whistles. "I just don't get it, Maurice. My speech was every bit as good as Nadia's, but when I finished, all I got was the ordinary polite applause that everyone gets regardless of what they've done. Of course, I'm not as hot as Nadia." "Come on, Sylvia, get off it. Yeah, Nadia's pretty, but that's not why the audience loved her. Your speech was good. You had an interesting topic, good information, and it was well organized. But when it comes to delivery, Nadia has it all over most of us, including you."

In leveling with Sylvia, Maurice recognized what has been well known through the ages: Dynamic delivery can make a mediocre speech appear good and a good speech great. Why? Delivery is important because how well the ideas are spoken can have a major impact on the audience's interest, understanding, and memory. In fact, research suggests that listeners are influenced more by delivery than by the content of speeches.[1] A speaker's delivery alone cannot compensate for a poorly researched, organized, or developed speech, but a well-delivered speech can rise above the ordinary and capture an audience. Some people seem naturally gifted in delivering speeches. Other speakers must spend time practicing their speeches to be dynamic. Most of us will need to practice our speeches if we are to capture and hold our audience's attention.

In this chapter, we begin by talking about the characteristics of effective delivery. We then describe the elements of effective delivery: use of voice and use of body. Next, we explain the three types of speech delivery and the settings in which each is most appropriate. Finally, we suggest a process for rehearsing your speech that will prepare you to deliver it in a dynamic, conversational style. We also describe ways to adapt to your audience while giving your speech. At the end of this chapter, we have included a sample speech given by a college student.

What do you think?

A speaker who moves too much during a speech is very distracting.

Strongly Disagree   *Strongly Agree*

| 1 | 2 | 3 | 4 | 5 | 6 | 7 | 8 | 9 | 10 |

ACTION STEP 6:
Practice Oral Language and Delivery Style

B. Practice until the delivery is conversational, intelligible, and expressive.

C. Practice integrating presentational aids until you can do so smoothly and confidently.

D. Continue practicing until you can deliver your speech extemporaneously within the time limit.

Characteristics of an Effective Delivery Style

Think about the best speaker you have ever heard. What made this person stand out in your mind? In all likelihood, how the speaker delivered the speech had a lot to do with your evaluation. So all the work you have done thus far to prepare your speech will be compromised if you cannot deliver it effectively.

delivery
how you use your voice and body to present your message

nonverbal communication
all speech elements other than the words themselves

conversational style
delivery that seems spontaneous, relaxed, and informal and allows the speaker to talk *with*, not *at*, an audience

spontaneity
a naturalness of speech where what is said sounds as if the speaker is really thinking about the ideas *and* the audience as he or she speaks

animated delivery
delivery that is lively, energetic, enthusiastic, and dynamic

Delivery is how a message is communicated orally and visually through your use of voice and body. Effective delivery is both conversational and animated. A conversational style allows each member of your audience to feel as if you are talking with him or her rather than speaking at the group. When your delivery is animated or lively, you create excitement about what you are saying, so it is easier for your audience to pay attention. Your speech content is conveyed through language. Your delivery style, however, is conveyed through your nonverbal behaviors. **Nonverbal communication** includes all speech elements other than the words themselves.[2] These elements include your use of voice (e.g., pitch, volume, rate, quality, articulation, pronunciation, and pauses) and use of body (e.g., facial expressions, eye contact, gestures, body language, and even appearance).

Use a Conversational Style

You have probably witnessed speakers whose delivery was overly dramatic, too formal, or affected. And you've probably heard ineffective speakers who just read their speeches to you. These delivery styles can put off an audience because the speaker appears more interested in performing or reading than in actually talking with the audience. Effective delivery reflects a **conversational style**, meaning that you sound spontaneous, relaxed, and informal, which helps your audience feel you are talking *with*, not *at*, them. The hallmark of a conversational style is spontaneity. **Spontaneity** is the ability to sound natural as you speak—as though you are really thinking about the ideas *and* getting them across to the audience as you speak.

The secret to developing a conversational style is to learn the *ideas* of your speech rather than trying to memorize every *word*. Suppose someone asks you about the route you take to get to work. Because you are familiar with the route, you can present it spontaneously. You have never written out the route, and you've never memorized it—you just know it. You develop a conversational style in public speaking in the same way. Through practice, you get to know the ideas in your speech as well as you know the route you take to work. As you study your outline, you absorb the material you plan to present, and as you rehearse your speech out loud, you can focus on talking about your ideas in an organized, professional, and natural-sounding way.

Be Animated

Have you ever been bored by a professor who reads lecture notes instead of looking at the students and making no gestures besides turning the pages of those notes? Even a well-written speech given by an expert can bore an audience unless its delivery is **animated**, lively, energetic, enthusiastic, and dynamic.

How can you be conversational and animated at the same time? The secret is to focus on conveying the passion you feel about your topic through your voice and body. In everyday life, all of us differ in how animated we are when we speak. Some of us are extroverted and naturally expressive, whereas others are introverted and more circumspect in our verbal and nonverbal expressiveness. And, of course, there are cultural differences in how much animation is appropriate when we speak. Nevertheless, when we are passionate about sharing something with someone, almost all of us become more animated in our delivery. It is this level of liveliness that you want to duplicate when you deliver your speech. To see a video clip of a student speaker with an animated delivery, go to the CourseMate for SPEAK at www.cengagebrain.com to access the speech "Why Pi?" in the Chapter 11 resources.

For most of us, appearing conversational and animated when delivering a speech requires considerable practice. In the next two sections, we'll focus on how you can use your voice and body to deliver your speech effectively.

Effective Use of Voice

Your voice is the sound you produce using your vocal organs (larynx, tongue, teeth, lips, etc.). How you sound should emphasize and reinforce the meaning you intend, but sometimes it can contradict it. As a result, how you use your voice affects how successful you are in getting your ideas across. As you rehearse and deliver your speech, focus on not only *what* you say but also on *how* you sound as you say it. How your voice sounds depends on its pitch, volume, rate, and quality. Your goal is to use your voice so that what you say is both intelligible and vocally expressive. You will be better prepared to do this if you understand the characteristics of your voice.

Characteristics of Voice

The four major characteristics of voice are pitch, volume, rate, and quality.

Pitch is the highness or lowness of the sounds produced in your larynx by the size and vibration of your vocal cords. Just as you can change the pitch of a guitar string by making it tighter or looser, so can you change the pitch of your voice by tightening and loosening the vocal cords.

Volume is how loudly or softly you speak.

Rate is the speed at which you talk. In normal conversations, most people speak between 130 and 180 words per minute. We generally speak faster when we are excited or fearful and slow down when we are explaining difficult material or when we are sad or somber.

Quality is the tone or timbre of your voice and what distinguishes it from the voices of others—it is "how you sound" to others. Voices that are nasal, breathy, harsh, or hoarse can be unpleasant to listen to and may distract from the message.

By effectively varying your pitch, volume, rate, and quality, you can achieve an animated and conversational style that is both intelligible and expressive.

Speak Intelligibly

To be intelligible means to be clearly understandable. All of us have experienced situations in which we couldn't understand what was being said because the speaker was talking too softly or too quickly or had a voice that was compromised in some way. If you're not intelligible, your listeners are bound to struggle with your verbal message. By practicing using appropriate vocal pitch, volume, rate, and vocal quality, you can improve the likelihood that you will be intelligible to your audience.

Most of us speak at a pitch that is appropriate for us and intelligible to listeners. However, some people naturally have voices that are higher or lower in register or become accustomed to talking in tones that are above or below their natural pitch. Speaking at an appropriate pitch is particularly important if your audience includes people who have hearing loss because they may find it difficult to hear a pitch that is too high or too low. As overamplified music has become widespread, hearing loss is becoming a problem even among younger people. Intelligibility is also affected by how much a speaker fluctuates his or her pitch. In normal conversation, pitch fluctuates frequently, and perhaps even a bit more during a speech. Pitch that doesn't fluctuate often hinders intelligibility. For example, in English, a sentence that is meant to be a question is vocalized with rising pitch. If pitch doesn't rise at the end of a question, listeners may interpret the sentence as a statement instead.

Appropriate volume is a key to intelligibility. You must speak loudly enough, with or without a microphone, to be heard easily by audience members seated in the back of the room but not so loudly as to bring discomfort to listeners seated near the front. In addition, you can vary your volume to emphasize important information. For example, you may speak louder

Appropriate volume is a key to intelligibility.

---

voice
the sound you produce in your larynx, or voice box, which is used to transmit the words of your speech to an audience

pitch
the highness or lowness of the sounds produced in your larynx by the size and vibration of your vocal cords

volume
how loudly or softly you speak

rate
the speed at which you talk

quality
the tone, timbre, or sound of your voice and what distinguishes it from the voice of others

intelligible
capable of being clearly understood

© ISTOCKPHOTO.COM/KENNETH C. ZIRKEL

articulation
using the tongue, palate, teeth, jaw movement, and lips to shape vocalized sounds that combine to produce a word

pronunciation
the form and accent of various syllables of a word

accent
the inflection, tone, and speech habits typical of native speakers of a language

vocal expressiveness
variety you create in your voice through changing pitch, volume, and rate, as well as stressing certain words and using pauses strategically

monotone
a voice in which the pitch, volume, and rate remain constant, with no word, idea, or sentence differing significantly in sound from any other

as you introduce each of your main points or when imploring listeners to take action.

The rate at which you speak can determine how intelligible your message is. Speaking too slowly gives your listeners time to let their minds wander after they've processed your message. Speaking too quickly, especially when sharing complex ideas and arguments, doesn't give your listeners enough time to process the difficult information completely. Although your typical rate of speaking may be within the normal range, being nervous when giving a speech can cause you to speak more quickly or slowly. As you practice and then deliver your speech, monitor your speaking rate and slow down or speed up depending on the difficulty of the ideas and the nervousness you feel. To complete a simple test to see if your typical rate of speech is within the range that is intelligible to most people, go to the CourseMate for SPEAK at www.cengagebrain.com and access **Web Resource 11.1: Your Speech Rate**.

In addition to vocal characteristics, articulation, pronunciation, and accent problems can affect how intelligible your message is. **Articulation** is using the tongue, palate, teeth, jaw movement, and lips to shape vocalized sounds that combine to produce a word. Many of us suffer from minor problems in articulation and **pronunciation** (the form and accent of various syllables of a word), such as adding a sound where none appears ("athalete" for *athlete*), leaving out a sound where one occurs ("libary" for *library*), transposing sounds ("revalent" for *relevant*), and distorting sounds ("truf" for *truth*). Exhibit 11.1 lists many common words that people are likely to mispronounce or misarticulate.

Accent is the inflection, tone, and speech habits typical of native speakers of a language. When you misarticulate or speak with a heavy accent during a conversation, your listeners can ask you to repeat yourself until they understand you. But in a speech setting, audience members are unlikely to interrupt to ask you to repeat what you have just said.

Accent is often a major concern for second language speakers or speakers from varying subcultures

Exhibit 11.1

Words Commonly Mispronounced

Word	Incorrect	Correct
arctic	ar'-tic	arc'-tic
athlete	ath'-a-lete	ath'-lete
family	fam'-ly	fam'-a-ly
February	Feb'-yu-ary	Feb'-ru-ary
get	git	get
hundred	hun'-derd	hun'-dred
larynx	lar'-nix	ler'-inks
library	ly'-ber-y	ly'-brer-y
nuclear	nu'-kyu-ler	nu'-klee-er
particular	par-tik'-ler	par-tik'-yu-ler
picture	pitch'-er	pic'-ture
recognize	rek'-a-nize	rek'-ig-nize
relevant	rev'-e-lant	rel'-e-vant
theater	thee-ay'-ter	thee'-a-ter
truth	truf	truth
with	wit or wid	with

or geographic areas. Everyone speaks with some kind of accent, because *accent* means any tone or inflection that differs from the way others speak. Natives of a particular city or region in the United States will speak with inflections and tones that they believe are "normal" spoken English. But when they visit a different city or region, they are perceived as having an accent. If your accent is "thick" or very different from that of most of your audience, practice pronouncing keywords so that you are easily understood, speak slowly to allow your audience members more time to process your message, and consider using visual aids to reinforce key terms, concepts, and important points.

Use Vocal Expressiveness

You achieve **vocal expressiveness** by changing your pitch, volume, and rate, as well as stressing certain words and using pauses strategically. These contrasts clarify the emotional meaning of your message and help animate your delivery. Generally, speeding up your rate, raising your pitch, or increasing your volume reinforces emotions such as joy, enthusiasm, excitement, anticipation, and a sense of urgency or fear. Slowing down your rate, lowering your pitch, or decreasing your volume can communicate resolution, peacefulness, remorse, disgust, or sadness.

A total lack of vocal expressiveness produces a **monotone**—a voice in which the pitch, volume, and rate remain constant, with no word, idea, or sentence differing significantly in sound from any other. Although few people speak in a true monotone, many severely limit themselves by using only two or three pitch levels and relatively unchanging volume and rate. An actual or near monotone not only lulls an audience to sleep but, more important, diminishes the chances of audience understanding.

Creating vocally expressive messages is a complex process. For example, Nick introduced his speech on legalizing marijuana as a painkiller this way:

> Millions of Americans suffer needlessly each year. These people endure unbearable pain needlessly because, although our government is capable of helping them, it chooses to ignore their pain. Our government has no compassion, no empathy, no regard for human feeling. I'm here today to convince you to support my efforts toward legalizing marijuana as a painkiller for terminally ill patients.

To reinforce the emotional elements of anger, disgust, and seriousness, Nick gradually slowed his rate, decreased his volume, and lowered his pitch as he emphasized, "Our government has no compassion, no empathy, no regard for human feeling."

He also used **stress**, an emphasis placed on certain words by speaking them more loudly than the rest of the sentence, to shape his meaning. Read the following sentence from Nick's speech:

> Millions of Americans suffer needlessly each year.

What did Nick intend the focus of that sentence to be? Without hearing it spoken, it is difficult to say because its focus would change depending on which word Nick chose to stress. Read the sentence aloud several times. Each time, stress a different word, and listen to how your stress changes the meaning. If you stress *millions*, the emphasis is on the number of people affected. When you stress *Americans*, the fact that the problem is on a national scale is emphasized. When you stress *suffer*, notice how much more you feel the pain. When you stress *needlessly*, you can sense Nick's frustration with how unnecessary the suffering is. And when you stress *each year*, the ongoing nature of the unnecessary suffering becomes the focus. Thus, the words you stress in a sentence affect your meaning.

Pauses, moments of silence strategically placed to enhance meaning, can also mark important ideas. If you use one or more sentences in your speech to express an important idea, pause before each sentence to signal that something important is coming up, or pause afterward to allow the ideas to sink in.

Pausing one or more times within a sentence can add further impact.

Effective Use of Body

Because your audience can see as well as hear you, how you use your body also contributes to how conversational and animated your audience perceives you to be. The body language elements that affect delivery are eye contact, facial expressions, gestures, movement, posture, poise, and appearance.

Eye Contact

Eye contact is looking directly at the people to whom you are speaking. In speechmaking, it involves looking at people in all parts of the room throughout a speech. As long as you are looking at someone and not at your notes or the ceiling, floor, or window, everyone in the audience will perceive you as having good eye contact with them. Generally, you should look at your audience at least 90 percent of the time, glancing at your notes only when you need a quick reference point. Maintaining eye contact is important for several reasons.

1. **Maintaining eye contact helps audiences concentrate on the speech.** If you do not look at audience members while you talk, they are unlikely to maintain eye contact with you. A break in mutual eye contact often decreases concentration on the message.

2. **Maintaining eye contact bolsters ethos.** Just as you are likely to be skeptical of people who do not look you in the eye as they converse, so too audiences will be skeptical of speakers who do not look at them. In the United States, speakers who fail to maintain eye contact with audiences are perceived almost always as ill at ease and often as insincere or dishonest.[3]

stress
emphasis placed on certain words by speaking them more loudly than the rest of the sentence

pauses
moments of silence strategically placed to enhance meaning

eye contact
looking directly at the people to whom you are speaking

Some cultures however, such as the Hopi, Cherokee, Navajo, and Sioux, believe that indirect eye contact demonstrates humility and respect.[4] Knowing your audience becomes extremely important as you determine what kind of eye contact is most appropriate.

3. **Maintaining eye contact helps you gauge audience reaction to your ideas.** Because communication is two-way, audience members communicate with you while you are speaking to them. In conversation, the audience's response is likely to be both verbal and nonverbal; in public speaking, the audience's response is more likely shown by nonverbal cues alone. Audiences that pay attention are likely to look at you with varying amounts of intensity. Listeners who are bored may yawn, look out the window, slouch in their chairs, and even sleep. By monitoring your audience's behavior, you can adjust by becoming more animated, offer additional examples, or move more quickly through a point. If you are well prepared, you will be better equipped to make the adjustments and adapt to the needs of your audience.

When speaking to large audiences of 100 or more people, you must create a *sense* of looking listeners in the eye even though you actually cannot. This process is called **audience contact**. You can create audience contact using the Z pattern and four- to six-second rule as you focus on different groups of people throughout the speech.

Facial Expressions

Facial expressions are the eye and mouth movements that convey your personableness and good character (bolstering ethos). They can help you animate your speech (bolstering pathos). When you talk with friends, your facial expressions are naturally animated. Your audiences expect your expressions to be similarly animated when you give a speech. Speakers who do not vary their facial expressions during their speech and instead wear deadpan expressions, perpetual grins, or permanent scowls will be perceived as boring, insincere, or stern (hindering ethos). Audiences respond positively to natural facial expressions that appear to spontaneously reflect what you're saying and how you feel about it.

Gestures

Gestures, the movements of your hands, arms, and fingers, can help intelligibility and expressiveness. You can use gestures to describe or emphasize what you are saying, refer to presentational aids, or clarify structure. Some of the most common gestures used by speakers are shown in Exhibit 11.2.

Some people who are nervous when giving a speech clasp their hands behind their backs, bury them in their pockets, or grip the lectern. Unable to pry their hands free gracefully, they wiggle their elbows weirdly or appear stiff, which can distract audience members from the message. As with facial expressions, effec-

One way of ensuring eye contact during your speech is to gaze at various groups of people in all parts of the audience throughout the speech. Try using a Z pattern to divide your audience into small groups and then talk for four to six seconds to each group.

1. Talk with the group in the back left for a few seconds.
2. Glance at people in the far right for a few seconds.
3. Move to a group in the middle.
4. Move to a group in the front left.
5. Move to a group in the front right.

Such a pattern helps you avoid spending a disproportionate amount of your time talking with those in front of you or in the center of the room.

© ISTOCKPHOTO.COM/MATEJ MICHELIZZA

Exhibit 11.2

Common Hand Gestures Used by Speakers

- The supine hand with palm upward to express good humor, frankness, and generalization.

- The prone hand with palm downward to show superposition or the resting of one thing upon another.

- The vertical hand with palm outward to indicate warding off, putting from, or a disagreeable thought.

- The clenched hand to reinforce anger or defiance or to emphasize an important point.

- The index finger to specialize or reinforce the first in a sequence of events.

© CENGAGE LEARNING 2011

tive gestures must appear spontaneous and natural even though they are carefully planned and practiced. When you practice and then deliver your speech, leave your hands free so that they will be available to gesture as you normally do.

Movement

Movement refers to changing the position or location of your entire body. During your speech, it is important to engage only in **motivated movement**, movement with a specific purpose such as emphasizing an important idea, referencing a presentational aid, or clarifying macrostructure. To emphasize a particular point, you might move closer to the audience. To create a feeling of intimacy before you tell a personal story, you might walk out from behind a lectern and sit down on a chair placed at the edge of the stage. Each time you begin a new main point, you might take a few steps to one side of the stage or the other. To use motivated movement effectively, you need to practice when and how you will move until you can do so in a way that appears spontaneous and natural. Ultimately, when you do, you bolster your ethos.

Avoid unmotivated movement such as bobbing, weaving, shifting from foot to foot, or pacing from one side of the room to the other, as unplanned movements distract the audience from your message. Because many unplanned movements result from nervousness, you can minimize them by paying mindful attention to your body as you speak. At the beginning of your speech, stand up straight on both feet. Whenever you find yourself fidgeting, readjust and position your body with your weight equally distributed on both feet.

Posture

Posture refers to the position or bearing with which you hold your body. In speeches, an upright stance and squared shoulders communicate a sense of competence and confidence, which enhances your ethos. Speakers who slouch may give an unfavorable impression of themselves, including the impression of limited self-confidence and an uncaring attitude. To read a thought-provoking discussion of how use of body may affect audience attention during a speech, go to the CourseMate for SPEAK at www.cengagebrain.com to access **Web Resource 11.2: Body Motions and Audience Attention**.

Poise

Poise is a graceful and controlled use of the body that gives the impression that you are self-assured, calm,

movement
changing the position or location of the entire body

motivated movement
movement with a specific purpose

posture
the position or bearing of the body

poise
the graceful and controlled use of the body that gives the impression of self-assurance, calm, and dignity

appearance
the way you look to others

impromptu speech
a speech that is delivered with only seconds or minutes of advance notice for preparation and is usually presented without referring to notes of any kind

and dignified. Mannerisms that convey nervousness, such as swaying from side to side, drumming fingers on the lectern, taking off or putting on glasses, jiggling pocket change, smacking the tongue, or scratching the nose, hand, or arm should be noted during practice sessions and avoided during the speech.

During speech practice sessions, try various methods to monitor or alter your bodily action. Video recording provides an excellent means of monitoring your use of body to determine whether it is enhancing the message or distracting from it. You may also want to practice in front of a mirror to see how you look to others when you speak. Another good method is to get a willing listener to critique your use of body and help you improve. Once you have identified the behavior you want to change, tell your helper what to look for. For instance, you might say, "Raise your hand every time I begin to rock back and forth." By getting specific feedback when the behavior occurs, you can make immediate adjustments.

To see a video clip of a student speaker using effective bodily action, go to the CourseMate for SPEAK at www.cengagebrain.com to access the speech "No More Sugar" in the Chapter 11 resources.

Appearance

Some speakers think that what they wear doesn't or shouldn't affect the success of their speech. But your appearance, the way you look to others, does matter. Studies show that a neatly groomed and professional appearance sends important messages about a speaker's commitment to the topic and occasion, as well as the speaker's credibility (ethos).[5] Your appearance should complement your message, not detract from it. Three guidelines can help you decide how to dress for your speech.

1. **Consider the rhetorical situation.** Dress a bit more formally than you expect the members of your audience will dress. If you dress too formally, your audience is likely to perceive you as untrustworthy and insincere,[6] and if you dress too casually, the audience may view you as uncommitted to your topic or disrespectful of them or the occasion.[7]

2. **Consider your topic and purpose.** In general, the more serious your topic, the more formally you should dress. For example, if you are trying to persuade your audience to be tested for HIV, you will want to look like someone who is an authority by dressing the part. But if you are trying to convince your audience that they would enjoy taking a class at the new campus recreation center, you might dress more casually.

3. **Avoid extremes.** Avoid gaudy jewelry, over- or undersized clothing, or sexually suggestive attire. Remember, you want your audience to focus on your message, so your appearance should be neutral, not distracting.

Delivery Methods

Speeches vary in the amount of content preparation and the amount of practice you do ahead of time. The three most common delivery methods are impromptu, scripted, and extemporaneous.

Impromptu Speeches

At times, you may be asked to speak with little advance warning. An impromptu speech is one that is delivered with only seconds or minutes of advance notice for preparation and is usually presented without referring to notes of any kind. You may have already given an impromptu speech in class, so you know the kind of pressures and problems this type of speaking creates.

Because impromptu speakers gather their thoughts just before and while they speak, it is challenging to carefully organize and develop their ideas. As a result, speakers may leave out important information or confuse audience members. Delivery can suffer as speakers use "ah," "um," "like," and "you know" to buy time as they scramble to collect their thoughts. That's why the more opportunities you have to organize and deliver your thoughts using an impromptu method, the better you'll become at doing so.

Three of the most common rhetorical situations you may find yourself in that will require you to speak using the impromptu method are during employment and performance review interviews, at business meetings, and in the media. In each situation, having practiced organizing ideas quickly and conveying them both intelligibly and expressively will bolster your ethos and help you succeed in business and in life. You can improve your impromptu performances by practicing "mock" impromptu speeches.

Scripted Speeches

At the other extreme, you might carefully prepare a complete written manuscript of the entire speech text and deliver it either word for word from memory or by reading the manuscript from a printed document or a teleprompter. A scripted speech is one that is prepared by creating a complete written manuscript and delivered by reading a written copy or from memory.

Obviously, effective scripted speeches take a great deal of time to prepare and practice. Not only must you prepare an outline, but you must also write out the entire speech, carefully choosing language and sentence structures that sound natural when spoken. Once you've prepared the manuscript, you memorize the script and then rehearse orally, or you rehearse with the written manuscript until you can do so without sounding like you're reading from it. When scripted speeches are memorized, you face the increased anxiety caused by fear of forgetting your lines. When they are read from a printed manuscript or from a teleprompter, you must become adept at looking at the script with your peripheral vision so that you can maintain eye contact with your audience. While politicians, talk show hosts, and television news anchors are usually good at achieving conversational style while reading from printed manuscripts and teleprompters, most speakers sound like they are reading and find it difficult to sound spontaneous and conversational.

Because of the time and skill required to effectively prepare and deliver a scripted speech, they are usually reserved for important occasions that have important consequences. Political speeches, keynote addresses at conventions, commencement addresses, and CEO remarks at annual stockholder meetings are examples of occasions when a scripted speech might be appropriate.

Extemporaneous Speeches

Most speeches, whether in the workplace, in the community, or in class, are delivered extemporaneously. An extemporaneous speech is researched and planned ahead of time, but the exact wording is not scripted and will vary somewhat from presentation to presentation. When speaking extemporaneously, you refer to speaking notes reminding you of key ideas, structure, and delivery cues as you speak.

Extemporaneous speeches are the easiest to give effectively. Unlike impromptu speeches, when speaking extemporaneously, you are able to prepare your thoughts ahead of time and to have notes to prompt you. Yet unlike scripted speeches, extemporaneous speeches do not require as lengthy a preparation and practice process to be effective. In the next section, we describe how to rehearse successfully for an extemporaneous speech.

Rehearsal

Rehearsing is the iterative process of practicing the presentation of your speech aloud. Is it really necessary to practice a speech out loud? Yes. A speech that is not practiced out loud is likely to be far less effective than it would have been had you given yourself sufficient time to revise, evaluate, and mull over all aspects of the speech.[8] Inexperienced speakers often believe they are ready to present the speech once they have finished their outline. In general, try to complete the outline at least three days before you are scheduled to present it to give yourself sufficient time to practice, revise, evaluate, and practice your speech again. Exhibit 11.3 provides a useful timetable for preparing and practicing your speech.

scripted speech a speech that is prepared by creating a complete written manuscript and delivered by reading a written copy or from memory

extemporaneous speech a speech that is researched and planned ahead of time, but the exact wording is not scripted and will vary somewhat from presentation to presentation

rehearsing practicing the presentation of your speech aloud

Exhibit 11.3
Timetable for Preparing a Speech

Date	Task
1/17 (seven days before)	Select topic; begin research
1/18 (six days before)	Continue research
1/19 (five days before)	Outline body of speech
1/20 (four days before)	Work on introduction and conclusion
1/21 (three days before)	Finish outline; find additional material if needed; have all presentation aids completed
1/22 (two days before)	First rehearsal session
1/23 (one day before)	Second rehearsal session
1/24 (due date)	Give speech

speaking notes
a keyword outline with delivery cues and reference citations you will use as you deliver your speech

In the sections that follow, we describe how to rehearse effectively by preparing speaking notes, handling presentational aids, and rehearsing and refining delivery.

Preparing Speaking Notes

Prior to your first rehearsal session, prepare a draft of your speaking notes. Speaking notes are a keyword or phrase outline of your speech, plus hard-to-remember information such as quotations and statistics, as well as delivery cues designed to trigger memory. The best notes contain the fewest words possible written in lettering large enough to be seen instantly at a distance. Although some speakers do so, you should not use PowerPoint slides as speaking notes, because it will result in you and your listeners reading from the screen rather than you communicating a message.

To develop your notes, begin by reducing your speech outline to an abbreviated outline of key phrases and words. Then, if there are details you must cite exactly—such as a specific example, quotation, or set of statistics—add these in the appropriate places. You might also put these on a separate card as a "Quotation Card" you refer to when delivering direct quotations during the speech. Next, indicate exactly where you plan to share presentational aids. Finally, incorporate delivery cues indicating where you want to make use of your voice and body to enhance intelligibility or expressiveness. For example, indicate where you want to pause, gesture, or make a motivated movement. Capitalize or underline words you want to stress. Use slash marks (//) to remind yourself to pause. Use an upward-pointing arrow to remind yourself to increase rate or volume.

Making speaking notes not only provides you with prompts when you are speaking but also helps in two other ways. First, the act of compiling the speaking notes helps to cement the flow of the speech's ideas in your mind. Second, as you prepare your notes, think about key ideas and phrasings. Notes don't include all the developmental material.

For a three- to five-minute speech, you will need no more than three three- by five-inch note cards to record your speaking notes. For longer speeches, you might need one card for the introduction, one for each main point, and one for the conclusion. If your speech contains a particularly important and long quotation or a complicated set of statistics, you can record this information in detail on a separate card. Exhibit 11.4

shows Alyssa's speaking notes for her complete outline, which is shown at the end of this chapter.

During practice sessions, use your actual speech notes. If you will use a lectern, set the notes on the speaker's stand or, alternatively, hold them in one hand and refer to them only when needed. How important is it to construct good note cards? Speakers often find that the act of making a note card is so effective in helping cement ideas in the mind that during practice, or later during the speech itself, they rarely use the notes at all.

Handling Presentational Aids

Some speakers make the mistake of thinking that once they have prepared good presentational aids, they will have no trouble using them in the speech. However, many speeches with good aids have become a shambles because the aids were not well handled. You can avoid problems by following these guidelines.

1. **Carefully plan when to use the presentational aids.** Indicate on your speaking notes/outline exactly when you will reveal and conceal each presentational aid.

2. **Consider audience needs carefully.** As you practice, eliminate any presentational aid that does not contribute directly to the audience's attention to, understanding of, or retention of the key ideas in your speech.

3. **Share a presentational aid only when talking about it.** Because presentational aids will draw audience attention, practice sharing them only when you are talking about them and then concealing them when they are no longer the focus of attention. Because a single presentational aid may contain several bits of information, practice only exposing the portion you are discussing.

4. **Display presentational aids so that everyone in the audience can see and hear them.** It's frustrating not to be able to see or hear an aid. If possible, practice in the space where you will give your speech so you can adjust equipment accordingly. If you cannot practice in the space ahead of time, then arrive early enough on the day of the presentation to practice quickly with the equipment you will use.

5. **Talk to your audience, not to the presentational aid.** Although you will want to acknowledge the presentational aid occasionally, it is important to keep your eye contact focused mainly on your audience. As you

Exhibit 11.4

NOTE CARD 1: Introduction

PLANT FEET . . . . DIRECT EYE CONTACT . . . . POISE/ETHOS! ☺
I. Famous Indian peace activist Mahatma Gandhi: "We must become the change we seek in the world."
   Tall order . . . . We can make a difference right here in Lexington, KY.
II. Think for a moment . . . . child/homework, neighbor/leaves, stranger/ groceries . . . . It's easy for college students like us to get involved.
III. I volunteer at LRM and reaped benefits (SLIDE 1)
IV. Benefits volunteering . . . .
   a. get acquainted
   b. responsibility & privilege
   c. résumé-building skills

BLANK SLIDE, WALK RIGHT, EYE C.: Let's begin by explaining the ways volunteering can help us connect to our local community.

NOTE CARD 2: Body

I. GREAT WAY to become acquainted ☺ ☺
LR: Comforts of home . . . . unfamiliar city . . . . volunteering . . . . easy and quick way . . . .
Natalie Cunningham—May 2nd (Q. CARD #1)
Social issues and conditions
Acc. to a 1991 article published in the *J. of Prevention and Intervention in the Community* by Cohen, Mowbray, Gillette, and Thompson raise awareness . . . .
My experience at LRM (SLIDES 2 & 3)

BLANK SLIDE, WALK LEFT, EYE C.: Not only is volunteering important . . . .familiar and social issues . . . . FRANKLY . . . . dem society . . . .
II. Civic responsibility AND privilege . . . . LR: We benefit college . . . . give back.
   I agree with Wilson and Musick who said in their 1997 article in *Social Forces* **active participation or deprived.** (SLIDES 4 & 5)
   Also a privilege . . . . make a difference . . . . feel good . . . . self-actualization
(SLIDE #6)

NOTE CARD 3: Body & Conclusion

BLANK SLIDE, WALK RIGHT, EYE C: privilege & responsibility . . . .résumé-building . . . .
III. Life skills
   Article "Employability Credentials: A Key to Successful Youth Transition to Work" by I. Charner—1988 issue of the *Journal of Career Development* . . . . (Q. CARD #2)
   Laura Hatfield . . . . leadership, teamwork, and listening skills
   Andrea Stockelman, volunteer (SLIDE #7) (Q. CARD #3)

MY RÉSUMÉ (SLIDE #8)

BLANK SLIDE, WALK TO CENTER, EYE C: Today, we've discussed . . . . get acquainted, responsibility & privilege, résumé-building life skills help after grad.

CL: So, I'm hoping the next time you recall . . . . not distant past. Instead, I hope you'll be thinking bout how you ARE being the change you seek in the world by **volunteering right here //in Lexington///right now!**

PAUSE, EYE CONTACT, POISE, NOD ☺

Quotation Card
#1: "My first group of students needed rides to all the various volunteer sites b/c they had no idea where things were in the city. It was really easy for the students who lived on campus to remain ignorant of their city, but while volunteering they become acquainted with Lexington and the important issues going on here."
#2: "Employers rely on credentials to certify that a young person will become a valuable employee. Credentials that document the experiences and employability skills, knowledge, and attitude."
#3: "I learned that there was a lot more that went into preparing food for the homeless than I ever thougt possible. It was neat to be a part of that process."

practice, resist the urge to stare at your presentational aid.

6. **Resist the temptation to pass objects through the audience.** People look at, read, handle, and think about whatever they hold in their hands. While they are so occupied, they are not likely to be listening to you. If you have handouts or objects, distribute them after the speech rather than during it.

Rehearsing and Refining Delivery

As with any other activity, effective speech delivery requires practice, and the more you practice, the better your speech will be. During practice sessions, you have three goals. First, you will practice language choices so they are appropriate, accurate, clear, and vivid. Second, you will practice your speech aloud until your voice and body convey your ideas conversationally, intelligibly, and expressively. Third, you will practice using presentational aids. As part of each practice, you will want to analyze how well it went and set goals for the next practice session. Let's look at how you can proceed through several practice rounds.

First Practice

Your initial rehearsal should include the following steps:

1. Record your practice session so you can analyze it and make improvements. You may also want to have a friend or relative sit in on your practice.

2. Read through your complete sentence outline once or twice to refresh your memory. Then, put the outline out of sight and practice the speech using only the note cards you have prepared.

3. Make the practice as similar to the public speaking situation as possible, including using the presentational aids you've prepared. Stand up and face your imaginary audience. Pretend that the chairs, lamps, books, and other objects in your practice room are people.

cram all the practices into one long rehearsal time. You may find that a final practice right before you go to bed will be very helpful; while you are sleeping, your subconscious will continue to work on the speech. As a result, you are likely to find significant improvement in your mastery of the speech when you practice again the next day. How many times you practice depends on many variables, including your experience, your familiarity with the subject, and the length of your speech. For beginning speakers, we suggest at least four rehearsal sessions.

4. Write down the time that you begin.

5. Begin speaking. Regardless of what happens, keep going until you have presented your entire speech. If you goof, make a repair as you would if you were actually delivering the speech to an audience.

6. Write down the time you finish. Compute the length of the speech for this first rehearsal.

Analysis

Watch and listen to your recorded performance while reviewing your complete outline. How did it go? Did you leave out any key ideas? Did you talk too long on any one point and not long enough on another? Did you clarify each of your points? Did you adapt to your anticipated audience? (If you had a friend or relative listen to your practices, have him or her help with your analysis.) Were your note cards effective? How well did you do with your presentational aids? Make any necessary changes before your second rehearsal.

Second Practice

Repeat the six steps listed for the first practice. By practicing a second time right after your analysis, you are more likely to make the kind of adjustments that begin to improve the speech.

Additional Rehearsals to Further Refine Your Delivery

After you have completed one full rehearsal session, consisting of two practices and an analysis in between them, put the speech away until that night or the next day. Although you should rehearse the speech at least a couple more times, you will not benefit if you

---

ACTION STEP 6
Activity 6

Rehearsing Your Speech

The goal of this activity is to rehearse your speech, analyze it, and rehearse it again. One complete rehearsal includes (a) a practice, (b) an analysis, and (c) a second practice.

1. Find a place where you can be alone to practice your speech. Follow the six points of the first rehearsal described in the text.

2. Watch and listen to the recording. Review your outline as you do so and then complete a speech evaluation checklist to see how well you presented your speech during this rehearsal. (You can find the Speech Evaluation Checklist: General Criteria on page 12 in Chapter 1, a more detailed checklist in this chapter, and checklists for informative and persuasive speeches in later chapters.)

   List three specific changes you will make in your next practice session.

   One: _____
   Two: _____
   Three: _____

3. Go through the six steps outlined for the first rehearsal again. Then assess: Did you achieve the goals you set for the second rehearsal?

Reevaluate the speech using the checklist, and continue to practice until you are satisfied with all of your presentation.

You can complete this activity online, print copies of this rehearsal analysis sheet, see a student sample of a practice round, and, if requested, e-mail your work to your instructor. Go to the CourseMate for SPEAK at www.cengagebrain.com to access Activity 6.

Adapting to Your Audience as You Give Your Speech: The Rhetorical Situation

Even when you've practiced your speech to the point that you know it inside and out, you must be prepared to adapt to your audience and possibly change course a bit as you give your speech. Remember that your primary goal as a public speaker is to generate shared understanding with your listeners, so pay attention to the audience's feedback as you speak and adjust accordingly. Here are six tips for adapting to your audience.

1. **Be aware of and respond to audience feedback.** As you make eye contact with members of your audience, notice how they react to what you say. If you see quizzical looks on the faces of several listeners, you may need to explain a particular point in a different way. If you notice that many audience members look bored, adjust your voice and try to rekindle their interest by showing your enthusiasm for what you are saying.

2. **Be prepared to use alternative developmental material.** Your ability to adjust to your audience's needs depends on how much additional alternative information you have to share. If you have prepared only one example, you wouldn't be ready if your audience is confused and needs another. As you prepare, try to anticipate where your audience may be confused or already knowledgeable and practice adding or dropping examples and other details.

3. **Correct yourself when you misspeak.** All speakers make mistakes. They stumble over words, mispronounce terms, forget information, and mishandle presentational aids. So expect that you will make a few mistakes—it's normal. What's important is what you do when you make that mistake. If you stumble over a phrase or mispronounce a word, correct yourself and move on. Don't make a big deal of it by laughing, rolling your eyes, or in other ways drawing unnecessary attention to it. If you suddenly remember that you forgot to provide some information, consider how important it is for your audience to have that information. If what you forgot to say will make it difficult for your audience to understand a point that comes later, figure out how and when to provide the information later in your speech. Usually, however, information we have forgotten to share is not critical to

the audience's understanding, and its better to leave it out and move on.

When you make a mistake, remember that your goal is to get your ideas across to the audience. If your mistake will prevent your audience from understanding what you are saying, correct it. Otherwise, go on. Your audience doesn't know what you had planned to say, so as long as what you do say makes sense, your audience won't notice the mistake.

4. **Adapt to unexpected events.** Maintain your composure if something unexpected happens, such as a cell phone ringing or someone entering the room. Simply pause until the disruption ceases and then move on. If the disruption causes you to lose your train of thought or has distracted the audience, take a deep breath, look at your speaking notes, and continue your speech at a point slightly before the interruption occurred. This will allow both you and your audience to refocus on your speech. You might acknowledge that you are backtracking by saying something like, "Let's back up a bit and remember where we were—."

5. **Adapt to unexpected audience reactions.** Sometimes, you'll encounter listeners who disagree strongly with your message. They might show their disagreement by being inattentive, heckling you belligerently, or rolling their eyes when you try to make eye contact with them. If these behaviors are limited to one or only a few members of your audience, ignore them and focus on the rest of your listeners. If, however, you find that your audience analysis was inaccurate and that the majority of your audience is hostile to what you are saying, try to anticipate and address their concerns. You might begin by acknowledging their feedback and then try to persuade your audience to suspend their judgment while they listen.

6. **Handle questions respectfully.** It is rare for audience members to interrupt speakers with questions during a speech. But if you are interrupted, be prepared to deal respectfully with the question. If the question is directly related to understanding the point you are making, answer it immediately. If it is not, acknowledge the question, indicate that you will answer it later, and then do so. In most professional settings, you will be expected to answer questions when you've finished your speech. Some people will ask you to clarify information. Some will ask you for an opinion or to draw conclusions beyond what you have said.

Whenever you answer a question, it is important to be honest about what you know and don't know. If an audience member asks a question you don't know the answer to, admit it by saying something like, "That's an excellent question. I'm not sure of the answer, but I would be happy to follow up on it later if you're interested." Then move on to the next question. If someone asks you to state an opinion about a matter you haven't thought much about, it's okay to say, "You know, I don't think I have given that enough thought to have a valid opinion."

Be sure to monitor how much time you have to answer questions. When the time is nearly up, mention that you'll entertain one more question so as to warn listeners that the question-and-answer period is almost over. You might also suggest that you'll be happy to talk more with individuals one on one later—this provides your more reserved listeners an opportunity to follow up with you.

Although you cannot predict everything that could happen during your speech, you can prepare yourself to be ready for some adjustments. The most important thing to remember is that no speech is perfect. But you will succeed if your audience understands and remembers your message. That's what counts most.

It's important to be aware of, and respond to, the audience's feedback.

Speech Evaluation Form

Check items that were accomplished effectively.

Content

_____ **1.** Was the goal of the speech clear?

_____ **2.** Did the speaker offer breadth and depth to support each main point?

_____ **3.** Did the speaker have high-quality information?

_____ **4.** Did the speaker use a variety of kinds of developmental material?

_____ **5.** Were presentational aids appropriate?

_____ **6.** Did the speaker establish common ground and adapt the content to the audience with listener relevance links?

Macrostructure

_____ **1.** Did the introduction gain attention and establish credibility and listener relevance, as well as state the goal of the speech and preview the main points?

_____ **2.** Were the main points clear, parallel, and meaningful complete sentences?

_____ **3.** Did transitions lead smoothly from one point to another?

_____ **4.** Did the conclusion tie the speech together?

Microstructure

_____ **1.** Was the language appropriate?

_____ **2.** Was the language accurate?

_____ **3.** Was the language clear?

_____ **4.** Was the language vivid?

Delivery

_____ **1.** Was the speaker conversational?

_____ **2.** Was the speaker intelligible?

_____ **3.** Was the speaker vocally expressive?

_____ **4.** Did the speaker look directly at and throughout the audience?

_____ **5.** Did the speaker use appropriate facial expressions?

_____ **6.** Did the speaker have good posture that communicated poise and confidence?

_____ **7.** Were the speaker's gestures and movement appropriate?

_____ **8.** Did the speaker conceal, reveal, and reference the presentational aids effectively?

Based on these criteria, evaluate the speech as (check one):

____ excellent ____ good ____ satisfactory ____ fair ____ poor

You can use the CourseMate for SPEAK at www.cengagebrain.com to access this checklist, complete it online and compare your feedback to that of the authors, or print a copy to use in class.

This section presents a sample informative speech with presentational aids, given by a student and including an adaptation plan, an outline, and a transcript.

Read the speech adaptation plan, outline, and transcript of a speech given by Alyssa Grace Millner. You can access a video clip of Alyssa's speech through the Chapter 11 resources at the CourseMate for SPEAK at www.cengagebrain.com. You can also use the material there to identify some of the strengths of Alyssa's speech by preparing an evaluation checklist and an analysis. You can then compare your answers with those of the authors.

College Student Volunteering and Civic Engagement

By Alyssa Grace Millner, University of Kentucky[9]

Adaptation Plan

1. **Key aspects of audience.** The majority of listeners know what volunteering is in a general sense, but they probably don't know the ways it can benefit them as college students.

2. **Establishing and maintaining common ground.** I'll use personal pronouns throughout the speech, as well as specific examples about volunteering from volunteers right here in Lexington.

3. **Building and maintaining interest.** I'll insert listener relevance links in the introduction and for each main point that point out how volunteering is directly related to improving the lives of college students in some way.

4. **Building credibility.** I will point out right away that I volunteer and that I've done a good deal of research on it. I'll insert examples of my own experiences throughout the speech, as well as cite credible research to support my claims.

5. **Audience attitudes.** Some may be indifferent, but according the research I've found, most will probably be open to the idea of volunteering. They might not know how easy it can be to get started though.

6. **Adapting to audiences from different cultures and language communities.** Although most of my classmates are U.S. citizens, there are a couple of international students in the class. So, when I talk about volunteering being a civic responsibility, I'll make sure to talk about how all of us are reaping benefits of a U.S. education; that's why we are all responsible for giving back in some way. I'll talk about it as an ethical responsibility.

7. **Use presentational aids.** I will show photographs of people engaged in volunteer work throughout the speech. I think this will make my ideas very concrete for the audience and will enhance pathos (emotional appeal). I'll also show some graphs about homelessness in Lexington and the percentage of college students who believe in volunteering. I think these will bolster my ethos as the audience will see I've done research. Finally, I'll show my résumé with elements highlighted that I've been able to include because I've volunteered. I think this will drive home my point about the future benefits for college students who volunteer while still in school.

Outline

General goal: I want to inform my audience.

Specific goal: I want my audience to realize the benefits of volunteering in Lexington while we are students at the University of Kentucky.

Introduction

I. The famous Indian Peace activist and spiritual leader Mahatma Gandhi is known for saying "We must become the change we seek in the world." That sounds at first like an awfully tall order, but today I'd like to show you how each of us can do just that and make a difference right here in Lexington, Kentucky.

Attention getter

II. Think for a moment of a time in your life when you did something kind for someone else. Maybe you helped a child do homework, or a neighbor rake leaves, or even a stranger get groceries from the store to the car. Do you remember how that made you feel? Well, that feeling can be a normal part of your week when you choose to be a volunteer. And for college students like us, it's easy to get involved as volunteers in our local community.

Listener relevance link

III. Personally, I volunteer at the Lexington Rescue Mission and have reaped many benefits by doing so. (*Show slide 1: picture of me volunteering at the Mission.*) I've also done extensive research on volunteering and civic engagement.

Speaker credibility

IV. So, let's spend the next few minutes discussing the benefits volunteering can have for us as college students by focusing on how volunteering helps us get acquainted with the local community, why civic engagement is the responsibility of every one of us, and what volunteering can do to teach us new skills and build our résumés.

Thesis statement with preview

Let's begin by explaining the ways volunteering can connect each of us to our local community.

Transition

Body

I. Volunteering is a great way to become acquainted with a community beyond the university campus.

Listener relevance link

Most college students move away from the comforts of home to a new and unfamiliar city. Not knowing what there is to do or even how to get around can be overwhelming and isolating. Volunteering is an easy way to quickly become familiar with and begin to feel a part of this new city in addition to the campus community.

A. Volunteering allows you to learn your way around town.

1. In an interview I had with Natalie Cunningham, the volunteer coordinator of the Lexington Rescue Mission, she said, "My first group of students needed rides to all the various volunteer sites because they had no idea where things were in the city. It was really easy for the students who lived on campus to remain ignorant of their city, but while volunteering they become acquainted with Lexington and the important issues going on here" (N. Cunningham, personal communication, May 2, 2010).

2. It seems like a silly thing, but knowing your way around town starts to make any city feel like home. Volunteering gets you out into the local area and helps you begin to get acquainted with new people and places.

B. Volunteering can also open your eyes to local social issues and conditions.

1. Many nonprofit organizations strive to raise awareness of important social issues, things like hunger and homelessness (Cohen, Mowbray, Gillette, & Thompson, 1991).

2. The second time I showed up to volunteer at the Lexington Rescue Mission, I served food to the homeless. *(Show slide 2: group of volunteers in the kitchen.)*

    a. I served soup and hung out with other volunteers and local homeless people. One of the "veteran" volunteers explained to me that Lexington has approximately 3,000 homeless people. *(Show slide 3: homelessness statistics in Lexington.)*

    b. I was shocked to learn that we had such a large number of men, women, and children without a regular place to sleep. I wouldn't have known about this problem or the organizations working to end homelessness if I hadn't been a volunteer.

Transition

Not only is volunteering important because it helps us become familiar with a town and its social issues; frankly, as members of a democratic society, volunteering is our civic responsibility.

Listener relevance link

II. Giving back to the community through volunteer work is our civic responsibility and a privilege. Each of us in this room—whether as U.S. citizens or international students—are reaping the benefits of earning college degrees in this democratic society. With that benefit comes the responsibility and privilege of giving back.

    A. Volunteering is our civic responsibility.

        1. Wilson and Musick (1997) explain that, without active participation in the local community, civil society becomes deprived.

        2. I agree. Giving back by volunteering helps the community in so many ways. *(Show slides 4 and 5: volunteers sorting clothes at the mission and then volunteers playing cards with people served at the shelter.)*

    B. Volunteering is also a privilege. Making a difference by volunteering ends up making us feel better about ourselves and our role in the world around us.

        1. In fact, college students aged 16 to 24 represent the largest growth in percentages of volunteers across the country (Corporation for National and Community Service, 2006). *(Show slide 6: bar graph of growth.)*

        2. A study of first-year college students done by the Higher Education Research Institute published in January 2009 revealed that 69.7 percent of students believe it is *essential or very important* to volunteer in order to help people in need (Pryor et al., 2009).

Transition

Certainly, the privilege of giving back as volunteers is our civic responsibility and helps our local community, but we can also reap valuable résumé-building life skills by volunteering.

Listener relevance link

III. Volunteering helps teach us new skills.

These new skills and talents can actually make us more marketable for better jobs once we graduate.

    A. Being a consistent volunteer at a nonprofit organization while attending college can strengthen your résumé.

        1. "Employers rely on credentials to certify that a young person will become a valuable employee. Credentials that document the experiences and employability skills, knowledge, and attitude" (Charner, 1988, p. 30).

        2. Laura Hatfield, director of the Center for Community Outreach at the University of Kentucky, points out that volunteers can include leadership, teamwork, and listening skills on their résumés because they can document the experiences where they had to use them effectively in the real world.

3. Andrea Stockelman, another volunteer at the Lexington Rescue Mission, explained some of the new skills she picked up with volunteering. She said, "I learned that there was a lot more that went into preparing food for the homeless than I ever thought possible. It was neat to be a part of that process" (A. Stockelman, personal communication, April 28, 2010). *(Show slide 7: photo of Andrea preparing food.)*

B. Volunteering at the Lexington Rescue Mission taught me new skills that bolstered my résumé. *(Show slide 8: résumé with skills highlighted.)*

   1. I learned to coordinate the schedules of other volunteers.

   2. I also practiced important people skills such as teamwork, empathy, conflict management, and listening.

Conclusion

I. Today we've discussed why volunteering is beneficial to college students by focusing on how volunteering can connect us quickly and easily to our local community, why it's both our responsibility and a privilege to do so, and how volunteering will benefit us after we graduate.

II. So, I'm hoping the next time you recall a time you really enjoyed making a difference by helping someone, that memory won't come from the distant past. Instead, I hope you'll be thinking about how you are being the change you seek in the world by volunteering right here in Lexington right now.

Thesis statement with main point summary

Clincher

References

Charner, I. (1988). Employability credentials: A key to successful youth transition to work. *Journal of Career Development, 15*(1), 30–40.

Cohen, E., Mowbray, C. T., Gillette, V., & Thompson, E. (1991). Religious organizations and housing development. *Journal of Prevention and Intervention in the Community, 10*(1), 169–185.

Corporation for National and Community Service. (2006). *College students helping America*. Washington, DC: Author.

Pryor, J. H., Hurtado, S., DeAngelo, L., Sharkness, J., Romero, L., Korn, W. S., & Tran, S. (2009). *The American freshman: National norms for fall 2008*. Los Angeles, CA: Higher Education Research Institute.

Wilson, J., & Musick, M. A. (1997). Work and volunteering: The long arm of the job. *Social Forces, 76*(1), 251–272.

Speech and Analysis

The famous Indian peace activist and spiritual leader Mahatma Gandhi is known for saying "We must become the change we seek in the world." That sounds at first like an awfully tall order, but today I'd like to show you how each of us can do just that and make a difference right here in Lexington, Kentucky. Think for a moment of a time in your life when you did something kind for someone else. Maybe you helped a child do homework, or a neighbor rake leaves, or even a stranger get groceries from the store to the car. Do you remember how that made you feel? Well, that feeling can be a normal part of your week when you choose to be a volunteer. And for college students like us, it's easy to get involved as volunteers in our local community. Personally, I volunteer at the Lexington Rescue Mission and have reaped many benefits by doing so. (*Show slide 1: picture of me volunteering at the Mission.*) I've also done extensive research on volunteering and civic engagement. So, let's spend the next few minutes discussing the benefits volunteering can have for us as college students by focusing on how volunteering helps us get acquainted with the local community, why civic engagement is the responsibility of every citizen, and what volunteering can do to teach us new skills and build our résumés. Let's begin by explaining the ways volunteering can connect each of us to our local community.

Volunteering is a great way to become acquainted with a community beyond the university campus. Most college students move away from the comforts of home to a new and unfamiliar city. Not knowing what there is to do or even how to get around can be overwhelming and isolating. Volunteering is an easy way to quickly become familiar with and begin to feel a part of this new city in addition to the campus community.

Volunteering allows you to learn your way around town. In an interview I had with Natalie Cunningham, the volunteer coordinator of the Lexington Rescue Mission, she said, "My first group of students needed rides to all the various volunteer sites because they had no idea where things were in the city. It was really easy for the students who lived on campus to remain ignorant of their city, but while volunteering they become acquainted with Lexington and the important issues going on here." It seems like a silly thing, but knowing your way around town starts to make any city feel like home. Volunteering gets you out into the local area and helps you begin to get acquainted with new people and places.

Volunteering can also open your eyes to local social issues and conditions. According to Cohen,

Notice how Alyssa uses a famous quotation to get the attention of her audience in a way that also piques interest about the topic.

Here, Alyssa establishes listener relevance by pointing out that helping others makes us feel good and volunteering can be easy.

Alyssa mentions that she volunteers, which bolsters ethos and establishes her credibility to speak on the topic.

Notice how Alyssa's thesis with main point preview gives us a sense of the organizational framework for her ideas.

Again, as Alyssa introduces the first main point, she gets us to tune in because we all know how overwhelmed and isolated we can feel when we move to a new place.

Quoting the volunteer coordinator is a great piece of developmental material that encourages us to believe that Alyssa's message is trustworthy. (Note that interviews are not included in the reference section but are cited in the text of the outline.)

Mowbray, Gillette, and Thompson, many nonprofit organizations strive to raise awareness of important social issues, things like hunger and homelessness. The second time I showed up to volunteer at the Lexington Rescue Mission, I served food to the homeless. (Show slide 2: group of volunteers in the kitchen.) I served soup and hung out with other volunteers and local homeless people. One of the "veteran" volunteers explained to me that Lexington has approximately 3,000 homeless people. (Show slide 3: homelessness statistics in Lexington.) I was shocked to learn that we had such a large number of men, women, and children without a regular place to sleep. I wouldn't have known about this problem or the organizations working to end homelessness if I hadn't been a volunteer. Not only is volunteering important because it helps us become familiar with a town and its social issues; frankly, as members of a democratic society, volunteering is our civic responsibility.

Giving back to the community through volunteer work is our civic responsibility and a privilege. Each of us in this room—whether as U.S. citizens or international students—are reaping the benefits of earning college degrees in this democratic society. With that benefit comes the responsibility and privilege of giving back. Volunteering is our civic responsibility. Wilson and Musick explain that, without active participation in the local community, civil society becomes deprived. I agree. Giving back by volunteering helps the community in so many ways. (Show slides 4 and 5: volunteers sorting clothes at the mission and then volunteers playing cards with people served at the shelter.)

Volunteering is also a privilege. Making a difference by volunteering ends up making us feel better about ourselves and our role in the world around us. In fact, research conducted by the Corporation for National and Community Service from 2002 to 2005 shows that college students age 16 to 24 represent the fastest growing demographic of volunteers in this country. (Show slide 6: bar graph showing growth.) Not only that, a study done by the Higher Education Research Institute published in January of 2009 shows that a whopping 69.7 percent of first-year college students believe it is essential or very important to volunteer to help people in need. Certainly, the privilege of giving back as volunteers is our civic responsibility and helps our local community, but we can also reap valuable résumé-building life skills by volunteering.

Volunteering helps teach us new skills. These new skills and talents can actually make us more marketable for better jobs once we graduate. Being a consistent volunteer at a nonprofit organization while attending college can strengthen your résumé.

Alyssa intersperses actual photos of her and others volunteering throughout the speech. Doing so enhances her verbal message but doesn't replace it. The photos also provide pathos, making her ideas more emotionally compelling.

Here and throughout the speech, notice how Alyssa uses effective section transitions to verbally tie the point she is wrapping up with an introduction of the point to come. This makes her speech flow smoothly so listeners can follow her train of thought and bolsters her ethos because she sounds prepared. Alyssa's careful audience analysis reveals itself here as she reminds her audience that even those who are not U.S. citizens are benefiting as students in our educational system and, thus, have a responsibility to give back in some way.

Alyssa's choice to include national statistics of college student volunteers bolsters her credibility and provides listener relevance by reinforcing that college students are doing this, want to do this, and feel good about doing this kind of work.

Students want to know how to market themselves to get good jobs. So this main point will help maintain listener interest at a point when minds might tend to wander.

According to Charner, in the *Journal of Career Development*, "Employers rely on credentials to certify that a young person will become a valuable employee. Credentials that document the experiences and employability skills, knowledge, and attitude." Laura Hatfield, director of the Center for Community Outreach at the University of Kentucky, points out that volunteers can include leadership, teamwork, and listening skills on their résumés because they can document the experiences where they had to use them effectively in the real world. Andrea Stockelman, another volunteer at the Lexington Rescue Mission, explained some of the new skills she picked up with volunteering. She said, "I learned that there was a lot more that went into preparing food for the homeless than I ever thought possible. It was neat to be a part of that process." *(Show slide 7: photo of Andrea preparing food.)*

Volunteering at the Lexington Rescue Mission taught me new skills that bolstered my résumé. *(Show slide 8: résumé with skills highlighted.)* I learned to coordinate the schedules of other volunteers. I also practiced important people skills such as teamwork, empathy, conflict management, and listening.

Today we've discussed why volunteering is beneficial to college students by focusing on how volunteering can connect us quickly and easily to our local community, why it's both our responsibility and a privilege to do so, and how volunteering will benefit us after we graduate. So, I'm hoping the next time you recall a time you really enjoyed making a difference by helping someone, that memory won't come from the distant past. Instead, I hope you'll be thinking about how you are being the change you seek in the world by volunteering right here in Lexington right now.

By including a quotation from another volunteer, we don't have to take Alyssa's word alone.

This very clear thesis restatement with main point summary signals a sense of closure.

Notice how Alyssa ties back to her opening quotation in her clincher. This provides a sense of wrapping up without saying thank you that helps listeners feel like the speech is complete in a memorable way.

THERE ARE EVEN MORE STUDY TOOLS FOR THIS CHAPTER AT WWW.CENGAGEBRAIN.COM

- **Interactive Videos**
- **Speech Builder Express**
- **Printable Flash Cards**
- **Interactive Games**
- **Chapter Review Cards**
- **Online Quizzes With Feedback**
- **Speech Studio available upon instructor request**

Listen Up!

SPEAK *was designed for students just like you—* busy people who want choices, flexibility, and multiple learning options.

SPEAK delivers concise, focused information in a fresh and contemporary format. And ... SPEAK gives you a variety of online learning materials designed with you in mind.

At the CourseMate for SPEAK at **www.cengagebrain.com**, you'll find electronic resources such as **Printable Flash Cards, Interactive Quizzing, Crossword Puzzles, Games, Interactive Video Activities,** and **Audio Study Tools** for each chapter. These resources will help supplement your understanding of core speech communication concepts in a format that fits your busy lifestyle.

Visit the CourseMate for SPEAK at **www.cengagebrain.com** to learn more about the multiple SPEAK resources available to help you succeed!

12

Informative Speaking

Learning Outcomes

LO¹ What is the goal of an informative speaker? | LO² What are the characteristics of effective informative speaking? | LO³ What are the major methods of informing? | LO⁴ What are the two most common informative speech frameworks? | LO⁵ What are the major elements of process speeches? | LO⁶ What are the major types of expository speeches?

The campus had been fortunate to hear a number of excellent speakers at this year's Future of Energy *series, and tonight would be no different. Interested students, faculty, and invited guests took their seats and listened as the speaker was introduced by the director of the university's Center for the Study of the Environment. Now, Susan Cischke, vice president of Sustainability, Environment and Safety Engineering for Ford Motor Company, walked to the microphone to begin her speech titled "Sustainability, Environment, and Safety Engineering."*

This is but one of many scenes played out every day when experts deliver speeches to help others understand complex information. In this chapter, we focus specifically on the characteristics unique to good informative speaking and the methods you can use to develop an effective informative speech.

An **informative speech** is one whose goal is to explain or describe facts, truths, and principles in a way that stimulates interest, facilitates understanding, and increases the likelihood of remembering. In short, informative speeches are designed to educate audiences. Thus, most lectures your instructors give are basically informative speeches. Informative speeches answer questions about a topic, such as who, when, what, where, why, how to, and how does. For example, your informative speech might describe who popular singer-songwriter Lady Gaga is, define what Scientology is, or compare and contrast Twitter and Facebook. Informative speaking differs from other speech forms (such as speaking to persuade, to entertain, or to celebrate) in that your goal is simply to achieve mutual understanding about an object, person, place, process, event, idea, concept, or issue.

In this chapter, we first discuss five distinguishing characteristics of informing. Next, we discuss five methods of informing. And, finally, we discuss two common types of informative speeches and provide examples of each.

What do you think?

I enjoy listening to speeches on topics that I don't know much about.

Strongly Disagree   *Strongly Agree*
1   2   3   4   5   6   7   8   9   10

Characteristics of Effective Informative Speaking

When your goal is to inform, you face some unique challenges to gain and sustain the attention of your listeners, as well as to get them to retain the information. These can be successfully met if you attend to five characteristics of effective informative speaking and develop your speech with these in mind. An effective informative speech is intellectually stimulating, is relevant, is creative, is memorable, and addresses diverse learning styles.

informative speech
a speech whose goal is to explain or describe facts, truths, and principles in a way that stimulates interest, facilitates understanding, and increases the likelihood of remembering

intellectually stimulating information that is new to audience members and is explained in a way that piques their curiosity

creativity the ability to produce original, innovative ideas

productive thinking to contemplate something from a variety of perspectives

Intellectually Stimulating

Your audience will perceive information to be intellectually stimulating when it is new to them and when it is explained in a way that piques their curiosity and excites their interest. By *new*, we mean new information that most of your audience is unfamiliar with or new insights into a topic they are already familiar with.

If your audience is unfamiliar with your topic, you should consider how you might tap their natural curiosity. Imagine that you are an anthropology major who is interested in prehistoric humans, not an interest shared by most members of your audience. You know that in 1991, a 5,300-year-old man, Otzi, as he has become known, was found surprisingly well preserved in an ice field in the mountains between Austria and Italy. Even though the discovery was big news at the time, it is unlikely that your audience knows much about it. You can draw on their natural curiosity by describing scientists' efforts to understand who Otzi was and what happened to him.[1]

If your audience is familiar with your topic, you will need to identify new insight about it. Begin by asking yourself: What about my topic do listeners probably not know? Then, consider depth and breadth as you answer the question. *Depth* has to do with going beyond people's general knowledge of the topic. If you've ever watched programs on the *Food Channel*, that's what they do. Most people know basic recipes, but these programs show new ways to cook the same foods. *Breadth* has to do with looking at how your topic relates to associated topics. Trace considered breadth when he informed listeners about Type 1 diabetes. He discussed not only the physical and emotional effects on a person with diabetes but also the emotional and relational effects on the person's family and friends, as well as the financial effects on society. As you can see, when your topic is one that the audience is familiar with, you will need to explore a new angle on it if you are going to stimulate them intellectually.

So whether your topic is familiar or unfamiliar to the audience, your special challenge is to choose a goal and develop your speech in a way that somehow makes it "new" to them. In doing so, your audience will feel informed rather than bored.

Relevant

A general rule to remember when preparing your informative speeches is this: Don't assume your listeners will recognize how the information you share is relevant to them. Remember to incorporate *listener relevance links*—statements that clarify how a particular point may be important to a listener—throughout the speech. For example, how might the information you share during each main point make audience members happier, healthier, wealthier, and so forth?

Creative

Your audience will perceive your information to be **creative** when it yields original, innovative ideas. You may never have considered yourself creative, but that may be because you have never worked to develop innovative ideas. Contrary to what you may think, **creativity** is not a gift that some have and some don't; rather, it is the result of hard work. Creativity comes from good research, time, and productive thinking.

Creative informative speeches begin with good research. The more you learn about the topic, the more you will have time to think about and develop it creatively. If you have read only one story, located one set of statistics, or consulted one expert, how can you do much more than present this material? Speakers who present information creatively do so because they have given themselves lots of supporting material to work with.

For the creative process to work, you have to give yourself time. If you finish your outline an hour before you are to speak, you are unlikely to come up with creative ideas for maintaining audience interest. Rarely do creative ideas come when we are in a time crunch. Instead, they are likely to come when we least expect it—when we're driving our car, preparing for bed, or daydreaming. So a simple way to increase the likelihood that you will develop creative ideas is to give yourself time by completing your outline several days before you are to speak. Then, you will have time to consider how to present your ideas creatively.

For the creative process to work, you have to think productively. **Productive thinking** occurs when we contemplate something from a variety of perspectives. Then, with numerous ideas to choose from, the productive thinker selects the ones that are best suited to a particular audience. In the article "Thinking Like a Genius," author Michael Michalko describes eight strategies you can use to become a productive thinker. To read this article, go to the CourseMate for SPEAK at www.cengagebrain.com to access **Web Resource 12.1: Thinking Like a Genius**.

© ISTOCKPHOTO.COM/PAVLEN

Now let's look at how productive thinking can help you identify different approaches to a topic. Suppose you want to give a speech on volunteering in the United States, and, in your research, you run across the data shown in Exhibit 12.1.

With productive thinking, you can identify several lines of development for your speech. For instance, notice that in roughly two-thirds of the states, college students volunteer as much as or more than the general adult population. You could investigate why this is so and do a speech about it. Looking at the data from another perspective, you might notice that the percentage of both the general adult and college student populations that volunteer in three states (Minnesota, Nebraska, and Utah) is 40 percent or more. You might examine what types of volunteer work people do in those states and why. Or you might notice that a majority of the states that rank lowest in terms of percentages who volunteer are in the East, and many of the states that tend to rank highest are in the Midwest and mountain West. Again, an interesting speech could be given to explain these differences.

Productive thinking can also help us find alternative ways to make the same point. Again, using the information in Exhibit 12.1, we can quickly create two ways to support the point "On average, about 30 percent of the U.S. general adult population volunteers."

Exhibit 12.1

States' General Adult Population Volunteer Rates Versus States' College Student Volunteer Rates, 2003-2005

State	General adult population		College students, ages 16–24	
	Volunteering rate (in %)	State rank	Volunteering rate (in %)	State rank
Alabama	28.9	32	34.8	16
Alaska	38.9	5	40.1	7
Arizona	24.9	45	30.8	32
Arkansas	25.6	43	31.7	22
California	26.1	40	28.5	38
Colorado	32.8	17	38.3	10
Connecticut	30.8	21	31.5	23
Delaware	26.7	37	26.4	42
District of Columbia	30.8	22	31.0	30
Florida	24.1	48	25.9	43
Georgia	25.9	41	21.4	51
Hawaii	25.4	44	29.6	35
Idaho	35.5	14	44.4	2
Illinois	29.7	28	31.2	27
Indiana	29.5	29	37.3	13
Iowa	39.2	4	31.1	29
Kansas	38.6	8	31.5	24
Kentucky	29.8	27	30.4	33
Louisiana	22.7	49	27.8	40
Maine	33.2	16	31.4	25
Maryland	30.3	25	30.2	34
Massachusetts	27.0	36	24.0	47
Michigan	32.1	18	37.4	12
Minnesota	40.7	3	39.9	8
Mississippi	26.4	39	33.1	20
Missouri	31.9	20	38.9	9
Montana	37.9	10	34.6	17
Nebraska	42.8	2	41.5	5
Nevada	18.8	51	23.6	49
New Hampshire	32.0	19	32.0	21
New Jersey	26.5	38	25.0	45
New Mexico	28.5	33	31.3	26
New York	21.3	50	23.4	50
North Carolina	29.1	30	28.8	37
North Dakota	36.5	13	33.7	19
Ohio	30.7	24	34.4	18
Oklahoma	30.0	26	43.0	3
Oregon	33.6	15	31.1	28
Pennsylvania	30.8	23	35.1	15
Rhode Island	24.9	46	25.8	44
South Carolina	28.0	35	28.3	39
South Dakota	38.8	6	31.0	31
Tennessee	25.9	42	24.0	48
Texas	28.3	34	29.2	36
Utah	48.0	1	62.9	1
Vermont	38.1	9	41.5	4
Virginia	29.0	31	24.6	46
Washington	36.8	12	37.6	11
West Virginia	24.6	47	27.4	41
Wisconsin	37.0	11	36.2	14
Wyoming	38.8	7	40.3	6

Source: Dote, L., Cramer, K., Dietz, N., & Grimm, R. Jr. (2006). *College students helping America*. Washington, DC: Corporation for National and Community Service.

Alternative A: Eighteen of the 50 states plus the District of Columbia had volunteering rates between 25 and 30 percent. Twelve of them had volunteering rates between 30 and 35 percent. In other words, 30 of the 50 states plus DC (or 60 percent) report volunteering rates between 25 and 35 percent.

Alternative B: If we exclude Nevada with its very low volunteering rate of 18.8 percent and Utah, Nebraska, and Minnesota with very high rates of 48 percent, 42.8 percent, and 40.7 percent, respectively, then we see that most states (47) reported volunteering rates between 20 and 40 percent.

Memorable

If your speech is really informative, your audience will hear a lot of new information but will need your help in remembering what is most important. Effective informative speeches emphasize the specific goal, main ideas, and key facts in ways that help audience members remember them. You can use several techniques to emphasize the material you want your audience to remember. For example, as described in Exhibit 12.2, you might use presentational aids, repetition, transitions, humor, or mnemonics. Any of these techniques can pique listener interest as you move through your informative speech.

Diverse Learning Styles

Because the members of your audience differ in how they prefer to learn, effective informative speeches are developed in ways that address diverse learning styles. You can appeal to people who prefer to learn through the feeling dimension by providing concrete, vivid images, examples, stories, and testimonials. You can address the watching dimension by using visual aids and by using appropriate facial expressions and gestures. You can address the thinking dimension through clear macrostructure, as well as definitions, explanations, and statistics. Finally, you can address the doing dimension by providing your listeners with an opportunity to do something during the speech or afterward. Rounding the cycle ensures that you address the diverse learning styles of your audience and make the speech understandable, meaningful, and memorable for all. To help you round the cycle, you might even make note of where and how you address each dimension in your speech outline.

Methods of Informing

Once you have decided that the general goal of your speech will be to inform, you must decide what methods you will use to educate your audience about your topic. We can inform by describing, defining, comparing and contrasting, narrating, and demonstrating. In some cases, you might choose one method of informing as the basis for organizing your entire speech. But in most cases, you will use different methods of informing as you develop each main point.

In this section, we explain each method of informing that you might use in developing your speeches. Later in the chapter,

© ISTOCKPHOTO.COM/DNY59

Exhibit 12.2

Techniques for Making Informative Speech Material Memorable

Technique	Use	Example
Presentational aids	To provide the opportunity for the audience to retain a visual as well as an audio memory of important or difficult material.	A diagram of the process of making ethanol.
Repetition	To give the audience a second or third chance to retain important information by repeating or paraphrasing it.	"The first dimension of romantic love is passion; that is, it can't really be romantic love if there is no sexual attraction."
Transitions	To increase the likelihood that the audience will retain the relationships among the information being presented, including which information is primary and which is supporting.	"So the three characteristics of romantic love are passion, intimacy, and commitment. Now let's look at each of the five ways you can keep love alive. The first is through small talk."
Humor and other emotional anecdotes	To create an emotional memory link to important ideas.	"True love is like a pair of socks: you've got to have two, and they've got to match. So you and your partner need to be mutually committed and compatible."
Mnemonics and acronyms	To provide an easily remembered memory prompt or shortcut to increase the likelihood that a list is retained.	"You can remember the four criteria for evaluating a diamond as the four Cs: carat, clarity, cut, and color."

© CENGAGE LEARNING 2011

we will describe two of the most common organizational frameworks for informative speeches: a process (or demonstration) framework and an expository framework.

Description

Description is a method used to create an accurate, vivid, verbal picture of an object, geographic feature, setting, event, person, or image. This method usually answers an overarching "who," "what," or "where" question. If the thing to be described is simple and familiar, the description may not need to be detailed. But if the thing to be described is complex and unfamiliar, the description will be more exhaustive. Descriptions are of course easier if you have a presentational aid, but verbal descriptions that are clear and vivid can create mental pictures that are also informative. To describe something effectively, you can explain its size, shape, weight, color, composition, age, condition, and spatial organization. Although your description may focus on only a few of these, each is helpful to consider as you create your description.

You can describe size subjectively as large or small and objectively by noting the specific numerical measurements. You can describe shape by reference to common geometric forms, such as round, triangular, oblong, spherical, conical, cylindrical, or rectangular, or by reference to common objects, such as a book or a milk carton. You can describe weight subjectively as heavy or light and objectively by pounds and ounces or kilograms, grams, and milligrams. You can describe color as black, white, red, yellow, orange, blue, green, and brown. Because these eight basic colors will not always describe accurately, a safe way to describe color is to couple a basic color with a common familiar object. You can describe the composition of something by indicating what it is made of, such as a building made of brick, concrete, or wood. At times, you can create the most vivid image of something by describing what it seems like rather than what it is. For example, an object may best be described as "metallic" even if it is made of plastic, not metal. You can describe something by age as old or new and by condition as worn or pristine, either of which helps the audience to visualize what is being described more clearly. Together, descriptions of age and condition can give the audience cues about the worth or value of what is being described. Finally, you can describe spatial organization, going from top to bottom, left to right, or outer to inner. A description of a NASCAR automobile might go from the body to the engine to the interior.

Definition

Definition is a method of informing that explains something by identifying its meaning. There are four ways you can explain what something means.

First, you can define a word or idea by classifying it and differentiating it from similar ideas. Second, you can define a word by explaining its derivation or history. For instance, a vegan is a form of vegetarian who omits all animal products from his or her diet. So where did that come from? At the Vegan Society website, we learn that "the word vegan is made up from the beginning and end of the word VEGetariAN and was coined in the United Kingdom in 1944 when the Vegan Society was founded. The derivation of the word symbolizes that veganism is at the heart of vegetarianism and the logical conclusion of the vegetarian journey in pursuit of good health without the suffering or death of any animal."[2] Offering this etymology will help your audience remember the meaning of *vegan*.

Third, you can define a word by explaining its use or function. For example, in vegan recipes, you can use tofu or tempeh to replace meat and soy milk to replace cow's milk. The fourth and perhaps the quickest way to define something is by using a familiar

description
the informative method used to create an accurate, vivid, verbal picture of an object, geographic feature, setting, event, person, or image

definition
a method of informing that explains something by identifying its meaning

We can inform by describing, defining, comparing and contrasting, narrating, and demonstrating.

synonym or antonym. A synonym is a word that has the same or a similar meaning; an antonym is a word that is directly opposite in meaning. So, you could define *vegan* by comparing it to the word *vegetarian*, which is a synonym, or to the word *carnivore*, which is an antonym.

Comparison and Contrast

Comparison and contrast is a method of informing that explains something by focusing on how it is similar to and different from other things. For example, in a speech on vegans, you might want to tell your audience how vegans are similar to and different from other types of vegetarians. As you will remember, comparisons and contrasts can be figurative or literal. So you can use metaphors and analogies in explaining your ideas as well as making actual comparisons.

Narration

Narration is a method of informing that recounts an autobiographical or biographical event, a myth, a story, or some other account. The narrative method is grounded in narrative theory, which is essentially storytelling. Stories usually have four parts. First, the narration orients the listener by describing when and where the event took place and by introducing the important people or characters. Second, the narration explains the sequence of events that led to a complication or problem, including details that enhance the development. Third, the narration discusses how the complication or problem affected key people in the narrative. Finally, the narration recounts how the complication or problem was solved. The characteristics of a good narration include a strong story line; use of descriptive language and details that enhance the plot, people, setting, and events; effective use of dialogue; pacing that builds suspense; and a strong voice.[3]

Narrations can be presented in a first-, second-, or third-person voice. When you use first person, you report what you have personally experienced or observed using the pronouns "I," "me," and "my" as you recount the events. Your narration will be effective if your audience can identify and empathize with you and the events you describe. When you use second person, you place your audience "at the scene" and use the pronouns "you" and "your." Second-person narration can be effective because it asks the audience to recall an event that has happened to them or to become an "actor" in the story being told. When you use third person, you describe to your audience what has happened, is happening, or will happen to other people. Third-person narration uses pronouns like "he," "her," and "they." The effectiveness of third-person narration will depend on how much your audience can identify with key people in the story.

Demonstration

Demonstration is a method of informing that explains something by showing how it is done by displaying the stages of a process or depicting how something works. Demonstrations range from very simple with a few easy-to-follow steps (such as how to iron a shirt) to very complex (such as demonstrating how a nuclear reactor works). Regardless of whether the topic is simple or complex, effective demonstrations require expertise, a hierarchy of steps, and vivid language and presentational aids.

In a demonstration, your experience with what you are demonstrating is critical. Expertise gives you the necessary background to supplement bare-bones instructions with personally lived experience. Why are TV cooking shows so popular? Because the chef doesn't just read the recipe and do what it says. Rather, while performing each step, the chef shares tips about what to do that won't be mentioned in any cookbook. It is personal experience that allows the chef to say that one egg will work as well as two or that you can't substitute margarine for butter or how to tell if the cake is really done.

In a demonstration, you organize the steps from first to last so that your audience will be able to remember the sequence. Suppose you want to demonstrate the steps in using a touch-screen voting machine. If rather than presenting 14 separate points, you group them under four headings— (a) get ready to vote; (b) vote; (c) review your choices; (d) cast your ballot—chances are much higher that the audience will be able to remember most if not all the items in each of the four groups.

Although you could explain how to do something using only words, most demonstrations involve actually showing the audience the process or parts of the process. If what you are explaining is relatively simple, you can demonstrate the entire process from start to finish. However, if the process is lengthy or

synonym
a word that has the same or a similar meaning

antonym
a word that is directly opposite in meaning

comparison and contrast
a method of informing that explains something by focusing on how it is similar to and different from other things

narration
a method of informing that recounts an autobiographical or biographical event, a myth, a story, or some other account

demonstration
a method of informing that explains something by showing how it is done by displaying the stages of a process or by depicting how something works

complex, you may choose to pre-prepare the material for some of the steps. Although you will show all stages in the process, you will not have to take the time for every single step as the audience watches.

Effective demonstrations require practice. Remember that under the pressure of speaking to an audience, even the simplest task can become difficult—have you ever tried to thread a needle with 25 people watching you? As you practice, you will want to consider the size of your audience and the configuration of the room. Be sure that all of your audience can see what you are doing. You may find that your demonstration takes longer than the time limit you have been given. In that case, you may want to pre-prepare a step or two.

To see a video clip of an effective demonstration from a student informative speech, go to the CourseMate for SPEAK at www.cengagebrain.com to access the video clip "Flag Etiquette" under the Chapter 12 resources.

Now that you understand the methods you can use when your general goal is to inform, we want to explain two speech frameworks that commonly use informative speaking: process speeches and expository speeches.

Common Informative Frameworks

Two of the most common frameworks for organizing the macrostructure of informative speech ideas are process frameworks and expository frameworks.

Process Speeches

The goal of a **process speech framework** is to demonstrate how something is done, is made, or works. Effective process speeches require you to carefully delineate the steps and the order in which they occur. The steps typically become the main points, and concrete explanations of each step become the subpoints. Most process speeches rely heavily on the demonstration method of informing.

For example, Allie is a floral designer and has been asked by her former art teacher to speak on the basics of floral arrangement to a high school art class. The teacher allotted five minutes for her presentation. In preparing for the speech, Allie recognized that in five minutes she could not complete arranging one floral display let alone help students understand how to create various effects. So she opted to demonstrate only parts of the process and bring, as additional presentational aids, arrangements in various stages of completion. The first step in floral arranging is to choose the right vase and frog (flower holder). So she brought in vases and frogs of various sizes and shapes to show as she explained how to choose a vase and frog based on the types of flowers used and the desired visual effect. The second step is to prepare the basic triangle of blooms, so she began to demonstrate how to place the flowers she had brought to form one triangle. Rather than hurrying and trying

process speech framework
a speech that demonstrates how something is done, is made, or works

to get everything perfect in the few seconds she had, however, she also brought out several other partially finished arrangements that were behind a draped table. These showed other carefully completed triangles that used other types of flowers. The third step is placing additional flowers and greenery to complete an arrangement and achieve various artistic effects. Again, Allie actually demonstrated how to place several blooms, and then, as she described them, she brought out several completed arrangements that illustrated various artistic effects. Even though Allie did not perform every step, her visual presentation was an excellent demonstration of floral arranging.

Although some process speeches require you to demonstrate, others are not suited to demonstrations; instead, you can use visual aids to help the audience "see" the steps in the process. In a speech on remodeling a kitchen, it would not be practical to demonstrate the process; however, a speaker would be able to greatly enhance the verbal description by showing pictures before, during, and after the remodeling.

Process Speech Evaluation Form

You can use this form to critique a process speech that you hear in class. As you listen to the speaker, outline the speech. Then, answer the following questions.

Primary Criteria (Content)

_____ 1.   Was the specific goal appropriate for a process speech?

_____ 2.   Did the speaker show personal expertise with the process?

_____ 3.   Did the speaker emphasize the process steps?

_____ 4.   Did the speaker have good presentational aids that helped explain the process?

_____ 5.   If the speaker demonstrated the process, or parts of the process, was the demonstration fluid and skillful?

_____ 6.   Could the audience easily see the presentational aids or demonstration?

_____ 7.   Did the demonstration or presentational aids help you understand the main ideas?

_____ 8.   Did the speaker adequately answer the overarching question of how to do it, how to make it, or how it works?

General Criteria (Structure and Delivery)

_____ 1.   Was the specific goal clear?

_____ 2.   Was the introduction effective in creating interest and introducing the process to be explained?

_____ 3.   Was the macrostructure easy to follow?

_____ 4.   Was the language appropriate, accurate, clear, and vivid?

_____ 5.   Was the conclusion effective in summarizing the steps and clinching?

_____ 6.   Was the speaker's voice conversational, intelligible, and expressive?

_____ 7.   Was the speaker's use of facial expressions, gestures, and movement effective?

Based on these criteria, evaluate the speech as (check one):

_____ excellent _____ good _____ satisfactory _____ fair _____ poor

You can use the CourseMate for SPEAK at www.cengagebrain.com to access this checklist, complete it online and compare your feedback to that of the authors, or print a copy to use in class.

This section presents a sample informative speech given by a student, including an adaptation plan, an outline, and a transcript.

Making Ethanol

By Louisa Greene[4]

Read the speech adaptation plan, outline, and transcript of a speech given by Louisa Greene in an introductory speaking course. You can access a video clip of Louisa's speech through the Chapter 12 resources at the CourseMate for SPEAK at www.cengagebrain.com. You can also find materials there to identify some of the strengths of Louisa's speech by preparing an evaluation checklist and an analysis. You can then compare your answers with those of the authors.

Adaptation Plan

1. **Key aspects of audience.** Most people in my audience have probably heard of ethanol as an alternative to fossil fuels but don't know exactly what it is or how it's produced.

2. **Establishing and maintaining common ground.** I will begin my speech by asking the audience a question. Throughout the speech, I will refer to the audience's previous knowledge and experience.

3. **Building and maintaining interest.** Because my audience is initially unlikely to be interested in how to produce ethanol, I will have to work hard to interest them and to keep their interest through the speech. I will try to gain interest in the introduction by relating the production of ethanol, the fuel, to the production of "white lightning," the illegal alcohol, which might be of more interest to the average college student. Throughout the speech, I will use common analogies and metaphors to explain the complex chemical processes. Finally, I will use a well-designed PowerPoint presentation to capture attention.

4. **Audience knowledge and sophistication.** Because most of the class is not familiar with ethanol, I will introduce them to the four-part process of making ethanol. I believe that by relating the process to that of making alcohol that people can drink, my audience will be more likely to be interested in and retain the information.

5. **Building credibility.** Early in the speech, I will tell the audience about how I got interested in ethanol when I built a still as a science fair project in high school. I will also tell them that I am now a chemical engineering major and am hoping to make a career in the alternative fuel industry.

6. **Audience attitudes.** My audience is likely to be indifferent to my topic, so I need to capture their attention by using interesting examples. I then need to keep them interested by relating the topic to things they're familiar with.

7. **Adapting to audiences from different cultures and language communities.** I will use visual and audiovisual aids in my PowerPoint presentation to help those listeners from different cultures understand what I'm talking about even though English is not their native language.

8. **Using presentational aids to enhance understanding and memory.** Throughout the speech, I will use color-coded PowerPoint slides with headers to reinforce the steps being discussed.

Outline

General goal: To inform

Specific goal: I want my audience to understand the process for making ethanol from corn.

Introduction

Attention getter

I. Did you know that the first Model T cars were originally designed to run on ethanol or that Henry Ford said that ethanol was the fuel of the future? Did you know that in World War II about 75 percent of the German and American military vehicles were powered by ethanol since oil for gasoline was difficult to attain?

Listener relevance link

II. The process for making ethanol is actually very similar to the process used to make moonshine, which may be why—during the first Arab oil embargo in 1978—when Robert Warren built a still to produce ethanol, he called the product "liquid sunshine" (Warren, 2006). Ethanol is an easy-to-make, inexpensive, and nearly pollution-free renewable alternative to gasoline.

Speaker credibility

III. I became interested in ethanol in high school when I built a miniature ethanol still as a science fair project. I'm now a chemical engineering major and hope to make a career in the alternative fuel industry.

Thesis statement with main point preview

IV. Today, I'm going to explain the commercial process that turns corn into ethanol. The four steps include, first, preparing the corn by making a mash; second, fermenting the mash by adding yeast to make beer; third, distilling the ethanol from the beer; and fourth, processing the remaining whole stillage to produce co-products such as animal feed (Ethanol Business, 2004). *(Slide 1. Shows the four-step flow process.)*

Body

I. The first step in the commercial process of making ethanol, preparing the mash, has two parts: milling the corn and breaking the starch down into simple sugars (DENCO, n.d.). *(Slide 2. Title: Preparation. Shows corn flowing from a silo into a hammer mill and then into a holding tank where yeast is added.)*

Listener relevance link

In your saliva, you have enzymes that begin to break the bread and other starches you eat into sugar. In your stomach, you have other enzymes that finish this job of turning starch to simple sugar so your body can use the energy in the food you eat. In the commercial process of making ethanol, a similar transformation takes place.

   A. The corn is emptied into a bin and passes into a hammer mill, where it is ground into coarse flour.

   B. After milling, the corn flour, a starch, must be broken down so that it becomes simple sugar by mixing in water and enzymes to form thick liquid called slurry.

      1. First the water and corn flour are dosed with the enzyme alpha-amylase and heated.

      2. Then the starchy slurry is heated to help the enzyme do its work.

      3. Later gluco-amylase is added to finish the process of turning the starch to simple sugar.

Transition

Once this mixture of sugar, water, and residual corn solids is turned into slurry or mash, it is ready to be fermented.

II. The second step of the commercial process for making ethanol is fermenting the slurry or mash by adding yeast (DENCO, LLC, n.d.). *(Slide 3. Title: Fermentation. Shows yeast added to the mash in a fermenter and carbon dioxide being released to form beer.)*

Listener relevance link

This step works in much the same way yeast is used to make bread dough rise. But in bread the carbon dioxide is trapped in the dough and causes it to rise, and the alcohol is burned off when the bread is baked. In making ethanol, carbon dioxide bubbles out of the mash and is released into the air.

    A. The mash remains in the fermenters for about 50 hours.

    B. As the mash ferments, the sugar is turned into alcohol and carbon dioxide.

    C. The carbon dioxide bubbles out into the air.

    D. What remains after the carbon dioxide is released is called "beer."

Transition

Once the yeast has done its job and the fermentation process is complete, we move on to distillation.

III. The third step of the commercial process for making ethanol is distilling the fermented mash, now called "beer," by passing it through a series of columns where the alcohol is removed from the mash (Tham, 1997–2006). *(Slide 4. Title: Distillation of Ethanol. Animated slide showing beer flowing into distillation tank, heat being applied to the beer, and ethanol vapors being released and captured in a condenser.)*

Listener relevance link

If you've ever seen moonshine cookers in real life or in the movies, that's basically the same process as what I'm explaining here (DENCO, LLC, n.d.).

    A. Distillation is the process of boiling a liquid and then condensing the resulting vapor in order to separate out one component of the liquid.

    B. In most ethanol production, distillation occurs through the use of cooling columns.

    C. Once the ethanol has reached the desired purity or proof, it is denatured to be made undrinkable by adding gasoline to it.

    D. The ethanol is ready to be transported from the plant.

Transition

Once this step is complete, we've successfully produced ethanol, but we aren't done until we complete step 4.

IV. The fourth step in commercial production is converting the remaining whole stillage into co-products (DENCO, n.d.). *(Slide 5. Title: Co-product. Shows a tank with remaining whole solids flowing into a condenser with output flowing into a bin of animal feed.)*

Listener relevance link

Not only is ethanol a renewable resource, but even its byproducts get put to good use!

Conclusion

Thesis restatement with main point summary

I. As you can see, producing ethanol is a simple four-step process: preparing the corn into a slurry or mash, fermenting the slurry into beer, distilling the beer to release the ethanol, and processing the remaining water and corn solids into co-products. *(Slide 6: Same as slide 1.)*

Clincher

II. In 1980, when Robert Warren was operating his still, only 175 million gallons of ethanol were being commercially produced in the United States. Twenty-five years later, 4.85 billion gallons were produced (Renewable Fuels Association, 2007). That's a whopping 2,674 percent increase! And it is a trend that is continuing. With today's skyrocketing gasoline prices and our increasing concerns about preserving our environment, you can see why this simple process of making liquid sunshine is getting more and more popular. I don't know about you, but I'm glad it is!

References

DENCO, LLC. (n.d.) *Tour the plant*. Retrieved from http://www.dencollc.com/DENCO%20WebSite_files /Tour.htm

Ethanol Business and Industry Center. (2004, May). *Module 2: Ethanol science and technology*. Retrieved from http://www.nwicc.com/pages/continuing/business/ethanol/Module2.htm

Renewable Fuels Association. (2007). *Industry statistics: The ethanol industry*. Retrieved from http://www.ethanolrfa.org/industry/statistics/

Tham, M. T. (1997–2006). *Distillation: An introduction*. Retrieved from http://lorien.ncl.ac.uk /ming/distil/distil0.htm

Warren, R. (2006, August). *Make your own fuel*. Retrieved from http://running_on_alcohol .tripod.com/ index.html

Speech and Analysis

Did you know that the first Model T's were designed to run on ethanol and that Henry Ford said that ethanol was the fuel of the future? Or that in World War II about 75 percent of the German and American military vehicles were powered by ethanol since oil for gasoline was difficult to obtain? In 1978, during the first Arab oil embargo, when gas soared from 62 cents a gallon to $1.64, Californian Robert Warren and others built stills to produce what he called—no, not "white lightning"—but "liquid sunshine," which we call ethanol.

I became interested in ethanol in high school when I built a miniature ethanol still as a science fair project. I'm now a chemical engineering major and hope to make a career in the alternative fuel industry. So, today, I'm going to explain to you the simple process that takes corn and turns it into liquid sunshine. Specifically, I want you to understand the process that is used to make ethanol from corn.

According to the Ethanol Business and Industry Center at Northwest Iowa Community College, the four steps in the commercial process of making ethanol are, first, preparing the corn by making a mash; second, fermenting the mash by adding yeast to make beer; third, distilling the ethanol from the beer; and fourth, processing the remaining whole stillage to produce co-products like animal feed. *(Slide 1)*

As this slide taken from the DENCO, LCC, "Tour the Plant" website depicts, the first step in the commercial process of making ethanol, preparing the mash, has two parts: milling the corn and breaking the starch down into simple sugars. *(Slide 2)*

The corn, which has been tested for quality and stored in a silo, is emptied into a bin and passes into

Louisa begins this speech with rhetorical questions designed to pique the audience's interest. At the time she prepared the speech, gasoline prices were again soaring, so these questions—coupled with the example of Warren's solution—provide a provocative introduction to her topic.

At this point, Louisa personalizes the topic with a self-disclosure that also establishes her credibility.

One thing Louisa could do better throughout the speech is to offer listener relevance links that more directly remind the audience of the speech's relevance to them whenever possible.

Notice how Louisa has grouped two steps together, milling and breaking starch into sugars. This grouping keeps the main points at a manageable number and will help her audience remember the steps. Her second slide is simple but effective because it reinforces the two substeps.

a hammer mill, where it is ground into coarse flour. This is done to expose more of the corn's starchy material so that these starches can be more easily broken down into sugar.

In your saliva, you have enzymes that begin to break the bread and other starches you eat into sugar. In your stomach, you have other enzymes that finish this job of turning starch to simple sugar so your body can use the energy in the food you eat. In the commercial production of ethanol, a similar transformation takes place.

To break the milled corn flour starch into sugar, the milled flour is mixed with water and alpha-amylase, the same enzyme that you have in your saliva, and is heated. The alpha-amylase acts as Pac-man and takes bites out of the long sugar chains that are bound together in the starch. What results are broken bits of starch that need further processing to become glucose. So later, gluco-amylase, which is like the enzyme in your stomach, is added, and these new Pacmen bite the starchy bits into simple glucose sugar molecules. Now this mixture of sugar, water, and residual corn solids, called slurry or mash, is ready to be fermented.

The second step in the commercial production of ethanol is to ferment the mash by adding yeast in an environment that has no oxygen and allowing the mixture to "rest" while the yeast "works." *(Slide 3)* This is accomplished by piping the slurry into an oxygen-free tank called a fermenter, adding the yeast, and allowing the mixture to sit for about 50 hours. Without oxygen, the yeast feeds on the sugar and gives off ethanol and carbon dioxide as waste products. Eventually, deprived of oxygen, the yeast dies.

This is similar to what happens when we add yeast to bread dough. But in bread the carbon dioxide is trapped in the dough and causes it to rise, while the alcohol is burned off when the bread is baked.

In ethanol production, the carbon dioxide is not trapped in the watery slurry. Because it is a gas, it bubbles out of the mixture and is captured and released into the outside air. The ethanol, however, remains in the mixture, which is now called "beer," with the water and the nonfermentable corn solids. At the end of the fermentation process, it is the ethanol in the mixture that retains much of the energy of the original sugar. At this point, we are now ready to separate or distill the ethanol from the other parts of the beer.

The third step in the commercial production of ethanol is distillation, which, according to M. T. Tham's book *Distillation: An Introduction*, is the process of purifying a liquid by heating it and then condensing its vapor. So, for example, if you boiled your tap

Louisa helps the audience understand the unfamiliar starch-to-sugar conversion by comparing it to the familiar process of digestion.

The Pacman analogy also helps the audience visualize what occurs during the starch-to-sugar conversion.

The last sentence, mentioning slurry, is an excellent transition between the two main points.

Louisa helps the audience stay with her by using the signpost "second step." Her third slide, a visual of the "fermentation equation," nicely simplifies the complex chemistry that underlies fermentation.

Here she uses an effective transition statement to signal to her audience that she will be moving to the third step.

water and condensed the steam that was produced, you would have purified water with no minerals or other impurities. But distilling ethanol is a bit more complicated since both the ethanol and the water in the beer are liquids and can be vaporized into steam by adding heat.

Luckily, different liquids boil at different temperatures, and since ethanol boils at 173°F while water boils at 212°F, we can use this boiling point difference to separate the two. So to simplify what is really a more complex process (Slide 4), in the commercial distillation of ethanol, a column or series of columns are used to boil off the ethanol and the water and then to separate these vapors so that the ethanol vapors are captured and condensed back into pure liquid ethanol. The liquid ethanol is then tested to make sure that it meets the specifications for purity and proof. At this point, ethanol is drinkable alcohol and would be subject to a $20 per gallon federal excise tax. To avoid this, it is "denatured"—made undrinkable by adding gasoline to it.

After this, the ethanol is ready to be transported from the plant.

The fourth step in the commercial production process is converting the whole stillage into co-products. (Slide 5) One of the greatest things about producing ethanol is that the water and nonfermentable corn solids that are left after the ethanol is distilled aren't just thrown out as waste. Instead, the remaining water and nonfermentable corn solids can also be processed to make co-products that are primarily used as animal feed.

So as you have seen, the process of making ethanol is really quite simple. (Slide 6) One, prepare the corn by milling and breaking its starch into sugar. Two, ferment the mash using yeast. Three, distill off the ethanol from the beer, and four, process the co-products.

In 1980, when Robert Warren was operating his still, only 175 million gallons of ethanol were being commercially produced in the United States. Twenty-five years later, according to the Renewable Fuels Association, 4.85 billion gallons were produced. That's a whopping 2,674 percent increase! And it is a trend that is continuing. With today's skyrocketing gasoline prices and our increasing concerns about preserving our environment, you can see why this simple process of making liquid sunshine is getting more and more popular. I don't know about you, but I'm glad it is!

Her fourth slide is much more elaborate than the others. The animation in the slide helps the audience visualize how distillation works. It would have been more effective had she been able to control the motion so that each stage was animated as she talked about it.

The last sentence serves as an internal conclusion to the third step.

The slide for the fourth main point is so simple that it really isn't needed to aid audience understanding, but it is a visual reinforcement of this step, and the audience has been conditioned to expect one slide per point, so it would seem odd if there were not a slide for this step.

Louisa begins the conclusion with a summary of her main points. The sixth slide, a repetition of the first slide, visually "closes the loop" and reinforces the four steps.

The conclusion includes a circular reference back to Robert Warren, who was introduced at the beginning of the speech. In the conclusion, Louisa uses statistics to drive home the point that ethanol is an important fuel source and that in the near future ethanol may be a fuel used by members of the audience.

Louisa could have offered a better clincher by tying her final sentence back to her introductory comments about Henry Ford. For example, she might have said, "Almost a century later, it seems that what Henry Ford said will be coming true. Look for a green-handled pump coming soon to a gas station near you."

Expository Speeches

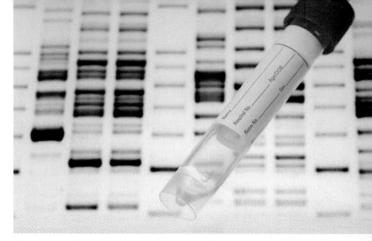

The goal of an **expository speech framework** is to provide carefully researched in-depth knowledge about a complex topic. For example, "The Origins and Classification of Nursery Rhymes" is a topic on which you could give an interesting expository speech. In this section, we describe four kinds of expository speeches.

All expository speeches require that the speaker use an extensive research base for preparing the presentation, choose an organizational pattern that helps the audience understand the material being discussed, and use a variety of informative methods to sustain the audience's attention and comprehension of the material presented.

Even college professors who are experts in their fields draw from a variety of source material when they prepare their lectures. So you will want to acquire your information from a variety of reputable sources. Then, as you are speaking, you will want to cite the sources for the information you present. You do so in the form of **oral footnotes**—oral references to the original source of particular information at the point of presenting it during a speech. In this way, you can establish the trustworthiness of the information you present as well as strengthen your own credibility.

Expository speakers also must choose an organizational pattern that is best suited to the material they will present. Different types of expository speeches are suited to different organizational patterns. It is up to the speaker to arrange the main points of the speech thoughtfully so that they flow in a manner that aids audience understanding and memory.

Finally, a hallmark of effective expository speaking is that it uses various methods of informing for developing material. Within one speech, you may hear the speaker use descriptions, definitions, comparisons and contrasts, narration, and short demonstrations to develop the main points.

Expository speeches include those that explain a political, economic, social, religious, or ethical issue; events or forces of history; a theory, principle, or law; and a creative work.

Exposition of Political, Economic, Social, Religious, or Ethical Issues

In an expository speech, you have the opportunity to help the audience understand the background or context of an issue, including the forces that gave rise to the issue and continue to affect it. You may also present the various positions that are held about the issue and the reasoning behind these positions. Finally, you may discuss various ways that have been presented for resolving the issue.

An expository speech on genetic research needs to present both sides of the issue.

The general goal of your speech is to inform, not to persuade. So you will want to present all sides of controversial issues without advocating which side is better. You will also want to make sure that the sources you are drawing from are respected experts and are objective in what they report. Finally, you will want to present complex issues in a straightforward manner that helps your audience to understand while not oversimplifying knotty issues.

You can identify an issue that you could use for an expository speech by reviewing the list of topics you brainstormed earlier in this course. The following list of topic ideas might stimulate your thinking as you work with your own list:

gay marriage	stem cell research
affirmative action	universal health care
media bias	teen curfews
school uniforms	home schooling
genetic engineering	downloading music

Exposition of Historical Events and Forces

A second important type of expository speech is one that explains historical events or forces. It has been said that those who don't understand history may be destined to repeat it. So an expositional speech about historical events or forces can be fascinating for its own sake, but it can also be relevant for what is happening today. Unfortunately, there are people who think history is boring; we believe this is because many people have learned history from sources that are boring. As an expository speaker, you have a special obligation during your research to seek out stories and narratives that can enliven your speech. And you will want to consult sources that analyze the events you describe so that

expository speech framework
an informative presentation that provides carefully researched in-depth knowledge about a complex topic

oral footnote
reference to an original source made at the point in the speech where information from that source is presented

you can discuss what impact they had at the time they occurred and what meaning they have for us today. Although many of us are familiar with the historical fact that the United States developed the atomic bomb during World War II, an expository speech on the Manhattan Project (as it was known) that dramatized the race to produce the bomb would add to our understanding of the inner workings of "secret" government-funded research projects. It might also place modern arms races and the fear of nuclear proliferation in their proper historical context. The following list of topic ideas might stimulate your thinking about historical topics you speak about:

slavery	the Industrial Revolution
the Papacy	the Ming Dynasty
Irish immigration	the Vietnam War
women's suffrage	the Crusades
Gandhi's movement	the space shuttle *Challenger* explosion
the colonization of Africa	

Exposition of a Theory, Principle, or Law

The way we live is affected by natural and human laws and principles and explained by various theories. Yet there are many theories, principles, and laws that we do not completely understand or don't understand how they affect us. An expository speech can inform us by explaining these important phenomena. The main challenge is to find material that explains the theory, law, or principle in language that is understandable to the audience. You will want to search for or create examples and illustrations that demystify esoteric or complicated terminology. Using effective examples and comparing unfamiliar ideas with those that the audience already knows can help you explain the law. For example, in a speech on the psychological principles of operant conditioning, a speaker could help the audience understand the difference between continuous reinforcement and intermittent reinforcement with the following explanation:

When a behavior is reinforced continuously, each time people perform the behavior they get the reward, but when the behavior is reinforced intermittently, the reward is not always given when the behavior is displayed. Behavior that is learned by continuous reinforcement disappears quickly when the reward is no longer provided, but behavior that is learned by intermittent reinforcement continues for long periods of time, even when not reinforced. You can see examples of how behavior was conditioned in everyday encounters. For example, take the behavior of putting a coin in the slot of a machine. If the machine is a vending machine, you expect to be rewarded every time you "play." And if the machine doesn't eject the item, you might won-

der if the machine is out of order and "play" just one more coin, or you might bang on the machine. In any case, you are unlikely to put in more than one more coin. But suppose the machine is a slot machine or a machine that dispenses instant winner lottery tickets. Now how many coins will you "play" before you stop and conclude that the machine is "out of order"? Why the difference? Because you have been conditioned to a vending machine on a continuous schedule, but a slot machine or automatic lottery ticket dispenser "teaches" you on an intermittent schedule.

The following list of topic ideas might stimulate your thinking about topics for an expository speech on a theory, principle, or law.

natural selection	diminishing returns
gravity	the normal distribution
number theory	psychoanalytic theory
global warming	intelligent design
feminist theory	Maslow's hierarchy of needs
Boyle's law	color theory: complements and contrasts

Exposition of a Creative Work

Courses in art, theater, music, literature, and film appreciation give students tools by which to recognize the style, historical period, and quality of a particular piece or group of pieces. Yet most of us know very little about how to understand a creative work, so presentations designed to explain creative works such as poems, novels, songs, or even famous speeches can be very instructive for audience members.

When developing a speech that explains a creative work or body of work, you will want to find information on the work and the artist who created it. In addition, you will want to find sources that help you understand the period in which this work was created and learn about the criteria that critics use to evaluate works of this type. So, for example, if you wanted to give an expository speech on Frederick

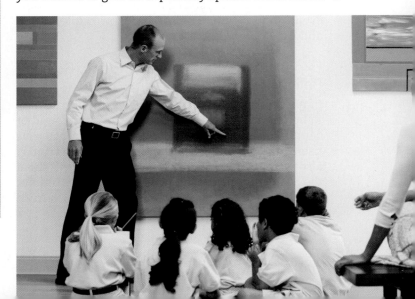

© FUSE/JUPITERIMAGES

Douglass's Fourth of July oration of 1852 in Rochester, New York, you might need to orient your audience by first reminding them of who Douglass was. Then, you would want to explain the traditional expectation that was set for Fourth of July speakers at this point in history. After this, you might want to summarize the speech and perhaps share a few memorable quotations. Finally, you would want to discuss how speech critics view the speech and why the speech is considered "great."

The following list of topic ideas might stimulate your thinking about topics for an expository speech on a creative work:

Spike Lee's *Mo' Better Blues*
a postmodern critique
   of *A Farewell to Arms*
the films of Alfred Hitchcock
The Catcher in the Rye: a
   coming-of-age novel

Impressionist
   painting
hip-hop music
theatre
iconography
inaugural
   addresses

© ISTOCKPHOTO.COM/COGAL

Expository Speech Evaluation Checklist

You can use this form to critique an expository speech that you hear in class. As you listen, outline the speech and identify which expository speech type it is. Then, answer the following questions.

Type of Expository Speech

_____ Exposition of political, economic, social, religious, or ethical issues

_____ Exposition of historical events or forces

_____ Exposition of a theory, principle, or law

_____ Exposition of a creative work

Primary Criteria (Content)

_____ **1.** Was the specific goal of the speech to provide well-researched information on a complex topic?

_____ **2.** Did the speaker effectively use a variety of methods to convey the information?

_____ **3.** Did the speaker emphasize the main ideas and important supporting material?

_____ **4.** Did the speaker use high-quality sources for the information presented?

_____ **5.** Did the speaker use a variety of supporting material?

_____ **6.** Did the speaker present in-depth, high-quality information?

General Criteria (Structure and Delivery)

_____ **1.** Was the specific goal clear?

_____ **2.** Was the introduction effective in creating interest, as well as introducing the topic and main points to be explained?

_____ **3.** Was the macrostructure easy to follow?

_____ **4.** Was the language appropriate, accurate, clear, and vivid?

_____ **5.** Was the conclusion effective in summarizing the main points and clinching?

_____ **6.** Was the speaker's voice intelligible, conversational, and expressive?

_____ **7.** Was the speaker's use of facial expressions, gestures, and movement appropriate?

Based on these criteria, evaluate the speech as (check one):

_____ excellent _____ good _____ satisfactory _____ fair _____ poor

You can use the CourseMate for SPEAK at www.cengagebrain.com to access this checklist, complete it online and compare your feedback to that of the authors, or print a copy to use in class.

This section presents a sample expository speech adaptation plan, outline, and transcript given by a student in an introductory speaking course.

Understanding Hurricanes

Adapted from a speech by Megan Soileau, University of Kentucky[5]

Read the speech adaptation plan, outline, and transcript of a speech given by Megan Soileau in an introductory speaking course. You can access a video clip of Megan's speech, delivered by Chet Harding, through the Chapter 12 resources at the CourseMate for SPEAK at www.cengagebrain.com. You can also use resources at the CourseMate for SPEAK at www.cengagebrain.com to identify some of the strengths of Megan's speech by preparing the Expository Speech Evaluation Checklist and an analysis. You can then compare your answers with those of the authors.

Adaptation Plan

1. **Key aspects of audience.** Because audience members have probably seen television coverage on hurricanes but don't really know much about them, I will need to provide basic information.

2. **Establishing and maintaining common ground.** My main way of establishing common ground will be by using inclusive personal pronouns (*we*, *us*, *our*).

3. **Building and maintaining interest.** I will build interest by pointing out how hurricanes even affect the weather in Kentucky and through the use of examples.

4. **Audience knowledge and sophistication.** Because most of the class has probably not been in a hurricane, I will provide as much explanatory information as I can.

5. **Building credibility.** I will build credibility through solid research and oral citation of sources. Early on, I'll mention where I live on the Gulf Coast and the fact that I have lived through several hurricanes.

6. **Audience attitudes.** I expect my audience to be curious about hurricanes, especially since Hurricane Katrina received so much media attention. So I will give them information to help them become more knowledgeable about them.

7. **Adapt to audiences from different cultures and language communities.** Because hurricanes occur on coasts all over the world, I don't need to adapt to different cultures or language communities. However, I will consider how to make the topic relevant to people who do not live on a coast.

8. **Use presentational aids to enhance audience understanding and memory.** I will use several PowerPoint slides to highlight the effects of hurricanes.

Outline

General purpose: To inform

Speech goal: In this speech, I am going to familiarize the audience with the overall effects of hurricanes: how they work, ways they affect our whole country, and the toll they take on the people who live in their direct paths.

Introduction

I. Think about a time you've been absolutely terrified (whether it was by a person, event, or situation) and all you wanted to do was go home and be with your family and friends. Now imagine the feeling you might have if you were that afraid, but you had no idea if your home would even be there when you arrived.

II. This is the reality for many people living on the coastlines of the United States. Hurricanes affect the lives of those living in their direct paths, but they can also cause spin-off weather that affects the entire country.

III. I have lived about 45 minutes from the Gulf Coast of Texas my entire life and have seen and experienced the destruction caused by hurricanes firsthand, especially in the past three years. *(Slide 1: picture of hurricane that hit my hometown last year.)*

IV. Today I'd like to speak with you about the way hurricanes work, the ways they affect our entire country, and, most importantly, the toll they take on the people who live in their direct paths.

Attention getter

Listener relevance link

Speaker credibility

Thesis statement with main point preview

Body

I. To begin, let's discuss how hurricanes form and the varying degrees of intensity of them. That way, we can be better informed when we watch news broadcasts and read newspaper reports about them.

Listener relevance link

   A. Several basic conditions must be present for a hurricane to form.

      1. According to the award-winning Discovery Communications website HowStuffWorks.com, hurricanes form "when an area of warm, low-pressure air rises and cool, high-pressure air seizes the opportunity to move in underneath it." This causes a center to develop. This center may eventually turn into what is considered a hurricane.

      2. The warm and moist air from the ocean rises up into these pressure zones and begins to form storms. As this happens, the storm continues to draw up more warm, moist air, and a heat transfer occurs because of the cool air being heated, causing the air to rise again.

      3. "The exchange of heat creates a pattern of wind that circulates around a center" (the eye of the storm) "like water going down a drain" (Marshall, Freudenrich, & Lamb, 2008).

      4. The "rising air reinforces the air that is already" being pulled up from the surface of the ocean, "so the circulation and speeds of the wind increase" (Marshall, Freudenrich, & Lamb, 2008).

   B. Classifications of these types of storms help determine their intensity so we can prepare properly for them.

      1. Winds that are less than 38 miles per hour are considered tropical depressions.

      2. Tropical storms are winds ranging from 39 to 73 miles per hour.

      3. And lastly hurricanes are storms with wind speeds of 74 miles per hour and higher.

4. When storms become classified as hurricanes, they become part of another classification system that is displayed by the Saffir-Simpson Hurricane Scale.

    a. Hurricanes are labeled as Categories 1–5 based on their wind-intensity level or speed. *(Slide 2: hurricane scale chart)*

    b. Hurricane Ike was labeled differently at different places. *(Slide 3: map showing the different places Ike was labeled in the different categories)*

Transition

Knowing how and where hurricanes occur helps us determine how our daily lives, even here in Kentucky, may be affected when one hits.

II. A hurricane can affect more than just those living in its direct path.

Listener relevance link

These effects can actually be seen across the country in terms of the environment and the economy.

A. Hurricanes affect wildlife in negative ways.

    1. According to the *Beaumont Enterprise* on October 7, 2008, Christine Rappleye reported that the storm surge (a wall of water) Hurricane Ike brought in was up to 14 feet of water across some parts of Southeast Texas.

    2. Dolphins were swept inland with the surge and then, when the waters flowed back out to sea, dolphins were left stranded in the marsh.

    3. Some were rescued, but not all. This dolphin was rescued from a ditch. *(Slide 4: dolphin being rescued)*

B. Hurricanes also affect the economy as prices climb close to all-time highs when hurricanes hit.

    1. According to economist Beth Ann Bovino, quoted in the September 29, 2005, issue of the *Washington Post*, gas prices skyrocket when a hurricane like Katrina, Rita, or Ike hits.

        a. Paul Davidson said, in a September 12, 2008, article in *USA Today*, that in the anticipation of Hurricane Ike, 12 refineries in Texas were shut down. "This is 17 percent of the U.S. refining capacity," he said.

        b. That's why even residents here in Lexington saw a dramatic spike in gas prices immediately following Ike's landfall.

    2. Energy costs to heat and cool our homes also rise.

        a. When we consumers have to pay more to heat and cool our homes, we also have less to spend eating out at restaurants.

        b. And we have less to spend on nonessentials at the mall.

        c. So, economically we all feel the ripple effect when hurricanes hit.

Transition

So, yes, we all feel the effects of hurricanes, but we should not overlook the dramatic ways in which people who live in the direct path of a hurricane are affected.

III. When a hurricane hits, many of these people become homeless, at least for a while, and suffer emotionally and financially as they evacuate to places all over the country.

Listener relevance link

Yes, many people relocate right here in Kentucky!

A. People who go through hurricanes suffer extreme emotional effects.

    1. Evacuation is stressful because people have to pack up what they can and have no way of knowing if their homes will still be standing or inhabitable when they return. *(Slides 5 and 6: before and after pictures from Hurricane Ike)*

2. Even returning home is emotionally taxing because returning home means rebuilding homes, neighborhoods, and even memories.

3. Though we try to get back to a "normal" life, it can never really be the same as it once was. Instead, it's what Silicon Valley venture capitalist and investor Roger McNamee calls the "new normal" in his book *The New Normal: Great Opportunities in a Time of Great Risk.*

B. Because they have to rebuild their homes and lives, people also go through financial difficulties.

1. People battle with insurance companies about whether a home has wind or water damage as they seek financial assistance. (Insurance companies will often claim that it is the one—wind or water—the homeowner is uninsured for) (Associated Press, 2008).

2. Price gouging is another financial challenge hurricane victims face.

    a. When families and businesses begin the process of rebuilding, people come from outside areas to help with labor and materials and will charge exorbitant fees.

    b. An example of this is when my father needed people to help remove two trees from our home in September 2005 after Hurricane Rita.

Conclusion

I. Hurricanes affect victims who live in their direct path and the country as a whole.

II. To understand these effects, we talked about how hurricanes work, how they affect our country and daily lives, and the impacts they have on the lives of people who live through them.

III. Maybe knowing some of these facts will help each of us appreciate our homes and our families just a little bit more. (*Handout: Hurricane tracking charts*)

Goal restatement
Main point summary

Clincher

References

Associated Press. (2008, October 8). Windstorm costs insurers $550M. *Newark Advocate.*

Bovino, B. A. (2005, September 29). Hurricanes impact national economy. *The Washington Post.* Retrieved from http://washingtonpost.com/wpdym/content/discussion/2005/09/28/D12005092801431.html

Davidson, P. (2008, September 12). Ike blows gasoline prices higher. *USA Today.*

Marshall, B., Freudenrich, C., & Lamb, R. (2008). How hurricanes work. Retrieved from http://www.howstuffworks.com/hurricanes.htm

McNamee, R. (2004). *The new normal: Great opportunities in a time of great risk.* New York, NY: Penguin.

Rappleye, C. (2008, October 7). Hurricane strands marine mammals, damages facility for the stranded. *Beaumont Enterprise.*

Speech and Analysis

Think about a time you've been absolutely terrified, whether it was by a person, event, or situation, and all you wanted to do was go home and be with your family and friends.

Now imagine the feeling you might have if you were that afraid, but you had no idea if your home would even be there when you arrived. This is the reality for many people living on the coastlines of the United States. Hurricanes affect the lives of those living in their direct paths, but they can also affect the entire country.

I have lived about 45 minutes from the Gulf Coast of Texas my entire life and have seen and experienced the destruction caused by hurricanes firsthand, especially in the past three years. *(Slide 1: picture of hurricane that hit my hometown last year)* This is a picture of my hometown when a hurricane hit it last year.

Today I'd like to speak with you about the way hurricanes work, the ways they affect our whole country, and, most importantly, the toll they take on the people who live in their direct paths.

To begin, let's discuss how hurricanes form and the varying degrees of intensity of them so we can be better informed when we watch news broadcasts and read newspaper reports about them.

Several basic conditions must be present for a hurricane to form. According to the award-winning Discovery Communications website HowStuffWorks .com, hurricanes form "when an area of warm, low-pressure air rises and cool, high-pressure air seizes the opportunity to move in underneath it." This causes a center to develop. This center may eventually turn into what is considered a hurricane. The warm and moist air from the ocean rises up into these pressure zones and begins to form storms. As this happens, the storm continues to draw up more warm, moist air, and a heat transfer occurs because of the cool air being heated, causing the air to rise again. "The exchange of heat creates a pattern of wind that circulates around a center" (the eye of the storm) "like water going down a drain." The "rising air reinforces the air that is already" being pulled up from the surface of the ocean, "so the circulation and speeds of the wind increase."

Classifications of these types of storms help determine their intensity so we can prepare properly for them. Winds that are less than 38 miles per hour are considered tropical depressions. Tropical storms have winds that range from 39 to 73 miles per hour. And lastly hurricanes are storms with wind speeds of 74 miles per hour and higher.

When storms become classified as a hurricane, they become part of another classification system

Megan opens by using an analogy to help get her audience emotionally involved in her speech and then quickly introduces her topic.

Notice how Megan establishes her credibility by sharing that she grew up near the Gulf Coast of Texas and has been a hurricane victim herself. The first slide adds emotional appeal to her point.

Megan concludes her introduction by previewing her main points clearly.

Megan does a nice job of incorporating a listener relevance link into her first main point statement.

Here Megan offers an oral footnote to add credibility. Noting that the website is an award-winning one helps her here.

Megan missed a great opportunity to help her audience follow what she was saying. She should have used visual aids here to depict the stages in the hurricane formation process.

that is displayed by the Saffir-Simpson Hurricane Scale. Hurricanes are labeled as Categories 1–5 based on their wind intensity level or speed. (*Slide 2: hurricane scale chart*) Hurricane Ike was labeled differently at different places. (*Slide 3: map showing the different places Ike was labeled in the different categories*)

Knowing how and where hurricanes occur helps us determine how our daily lives, even here in Kentucky, may be affected when one hits.

A hurricane can affect more than just those living in its direct path, and these effects can actually be seen across the country in terms of the environment and the economy.

Hurricanes affect wildlife in negative ways. According to the *Beaumont Enterprise* on October 7, 2008, Christine Rappleye reported that the storm surge, which is basically a wall of water, that Hurricane Ike brought in across some parts of Southeast Texas was about 14 feet in some places. Dolphins were swept inland with the surge and then, when the waters flowed back out to sea, dolphins were left stranded in the marsh. Some were rescued, but not all. This dolphin was rescued from a ditch. (*Slide 4: dolphin being rescued*)

Hurricanes also affect the economy. Prices climb close to all-time highs when hurricanes hit. According to economist Beth Ann Bovino, quoted in the September 29, 2005, issue of *The Washington Post*, gas prices skyrocket when a hurricane like Katrina, Rita, or Ike hits. Paul Davidson said, in a September 12, 2008, article in *USA Today*, that in the anticipation of Hurricane Ike, 12 refineries in Texas were shut down. "This is 17 percent of the U.S. refining capacity," he said. That's why even residents here in Lexington saw a dramatic spike in gas prices immediately following Ike's landfall.

Energy costs to heat and cool our homes also rise. When consumers have to pay more to heat and cool our homes, we also have less to spend eating out at restaurants. And we have less to spend on nonessentials at the mall. So economically we all feel the ripple effect when hurricanes hit.

So, yes, we all feel the effects of hurricanes, but we should not overlook the dramatic ways in which people who live in the direct path of a hurricane are affected.

When a hurricane hits, many of these people become homeless, at least for a while, and suffer emotionally and financially as they evacuate to places all over the country, including Kentucky!

People who go through hurricanes suffer extreme emotional effects. Evacuation is stressful because people have to pack up what they can and have no way of knowing if their home will still be standing or

Showing the hurricane scale chart and the map depicting Hurricane Ike at different categories visually reinforces what Megan describes in her verbal message.

Megan does a nice job tying together the two main points, which makes for a fluent section transition.

Here Megan not only describes the 14-foot-high wall of water Hurricane Ike transported across Texas, but she also reinforces it with the picture on her PowerPoint slide.

By indicating that Beth Ann Bovino is an economist makes this oral footnote stand out as very credible.

Here Megan reminds her audience that even in Lexington, Kentucky, hurricanes have relevance, which is reflected in higher gas prices and energy costs.

Megan could have further developed her main point and maintained audience interest with an example or a concrete story.

Again, Megan offers a clear and fluent section transition.

inhabitable when they return. (*Slides 5 and 6: before and after pictures from Hurricane Ike*)

Even returning home is emotionally taxing because returning home means rebuilding homes, neighborhoods, and even memories. Though we try to get back to a "normal" life, it can never really be the same as it once was. Instead, it's what Silicon Valley venture capitalist and investor Roger McNamee calls the "new normal" in his book *The New Normal: Great Opportunities in a Time of Great Risk*.

Because they have to rebuild their homes and lives, people also go through financial difficulties. People battle with insurance companies about whether a home has wind or water damage as they seek financial assistance. (Insurance companies will often claim that it is the one—wind or water—the homeowner is uninsured for.)

Price gouging is another financial challenge hurricane victims face. When families and businesses begin the process of rebuilding, people come from outside areas to help with labor and materials and will charge exorbitant fees. An example of this is when my father needed people to help remove two trees from our home in September 2005 after Hurricane Rita.

To close, I'd like to remind you that hurricanes affect victims who live in their direct path and the country as a whole. To understand some of these effects, we talked about how hurricanes work, how they affect our country and daily lives, and the impacts they have on the lives of people who live through them. Maybe knowing some of these facts will help each of us appreciate our homes and our families just a little bit more. (*Handout: Hurricane tracking charts*)

Again, Megan makes her emotional appeal stronger by showing before and after pictures.

Megan could have developed this point a bit more, perhaps by giving a specific example of someone whose life was altered.

Megan does a nice job concluding her speech by summarizing her main points and tying back to her introduction.

Notice how Megan waits until the end of her speech to distribute her handout. That way, she kept the focus on her message during the speech.

All in all, this is a well-presented, informative speech with sufficient documentation.

THERE ARE EVEN MORE STUDY TOOLS FOR THIS CHAPTER AT WWW.CENGAGEBRAIN.COM

- **Interactive Videos**
- **Speech Builder Express**
- **Printable Flash Cards**
- **Interactive Games**
- **Chapter Review Cards**
- **Online Quizzes With Feedback**
- **Speech Studio available upon instructor request**

Test coming up? Now what?

With SPEAK you have a multitude of study aids at your fingertips. After reading the chapters, check out these ideas for further help.

Chapter in Review Cards include all learning outcomes, definitions, and summaries for each chapter.

Printable Flash Cards give you three additional ways to check your comprehension of key speech communication concepts.

Other great ways to help you study include **Interactive Quizzing**, **Crossword Puzzles**, **Games**, **Interactive Video Activities**, and **Audio Study Tools**.

You can find it all at the CourseMate for SPEAK at **www.cengagebrain.com**

Understanding Persuasive Messages

Learning Outcomes

LO[1] What is the nature of persuasion? | LO[2] How do people process persuasive messages? | LO[3] What is the role of logos in persuasion? | LO[4] What is the role of ethos in persuasion? | LO[5] What is the role of pathos in persuasion?

Rick loves his golden retriever, Trini. He lives in an apartment right downtown and enjoys taking Trini for walks twice a day, but he wishes there was a place nearby where he could let Trini off her leash to run. He decides to try to persuade the city council to fence off an area of a large inner-city park to turn it into a dog park where owners can let their dogs run free. He learns he needs to circulate a petition about the idea, get at least 500 others to sign it, and collect $1,000 in donations to help pay for the fence. Rick easily gathers more than enough signatures in a few weeks of knocking on doors, but he has raised less than half of the $1,000. He wonders what he can do to persuade more people to actually donate money for the cause.

This scenario is not unusual. As was the case with Rick and the downtown dog park, whenever we attempt to convince others to agree with our position or behave a certain way, we actually construct and present persuasive messages. How successful we are, however, depends on how effectively we employ persuasive strategies in doing so. Persuasion is the process of influencing people's attitudes, beliefs, values, or behaviors. **Persuasive speaking** is the process of doing so in a public speech.

Persuasive messages are pervasive. Whether we are attempting to convince others or others are attempting to influence us, we are constantly involved in influencing or being influenced. Friends persuade us to go to a particular movie or to eat at a certain restaurant, salespeople persuade us to buy a certain sweater or pair of shoes, and advertisements bombard us whenever we turn on the radio or TV, or surf the Internet. It is critical to understand persuasion so you can critically examine and evaluate the persuasive messages you receive, as well as create effective and ethical persuasive messages of your own.

We begin our two-chapter discussion of persuasive speaking by first describing the nature of persuasive messages and the rhetorical strategies used in them. Next, using the Elaboration Likelihood Model (ELM), we explain how people process persuasive messages. Then, we focus specifically on how to use the rhetorical strategies of logos, ethos, and pathos to develop your persuasive messages and offer guidelines for you to consider when evaluating and constructing them.

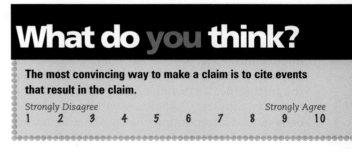

What do you think?

The most convincing way to make a claim is to cite events that result in the claim.

Strongly Disagree   *Strongly Agree*

1   2   3   4   5   6   7   8   9   10

persuasion
the process of influencing people's attitudes, beliefs, values, or behaviors

persuasive speaking
the process of influencing people's attitudes, beliefs, values, or behaviors in a public speech

The Nature of Persuasion

We draw on the work of the Greeks and Romans to define *persuasion* as logical and well-supported arguments developed through rhetorical appeals to logos, ethos, and pathos. In this context, argument is not "to quarrel," but rather means articulating a position with the support of logos, ethos, and pathos.[1] Logos is a means of persuasion in which you construct logical arguments that support your point of view. Ethos is the means of persuasion in which you argue that your competence, credibility, and good character should persuade others to accept your point of view. Pathos is a means of persuasion in which you appeal to the emotions of others so that they accept your point of view.[2]

Throughout this book, we have highlighted the roles logos, ethos, and pathos play in developing effective messages. That's because informing, which we can think of as *teaching*, and persuading, which we can think of as *leading*, are different in purpose but related in process. To remember new information, we have to believe it is factual, relevant, and important, so part of your task when giving an informative speech is to convince your audience about the truthfulness, relevance, and importance of your message. Similarly, before we will be convinced to believe or do something, we must understand (be informed about) what taking that stance or action means.

The speaker's primary goal is to differentiate persuasive messages from informative ones. For example, Susan is a petrochemical engineering student taking a speech course, and she has done significant research on the Deep Water Horizon oil spill. For an informative speech, her goal was to explain the errors that led to the explosion and subsequent oil spill. For a persuasive speech, her goal was to convince the class that the sequence of events that led to the Deep Water Horizon spill could not happen again and that deep water drilling for oil is safe.

While all speakers are expected to behave ethically, persuasive speakers have an extra burden to demonstrate that what they are advocating is in the best interest of the audience. So persuasive speakers must evaluate their message strategies and eliminate those that even begin to violate the ethical principles of truthfulness, integrity, fairness, respect, and responsibility.

Now that you have a basic understanding of the nature of persuasion, let's look more closely at how people think about the persuasive messages they receive.

How People Process Persuasive Messages: The Elaboration Likelihood Model (ELM)

Do you remember times when you listened carefully and thought about something of which someone was trying to convince you? Do you remember consciously thinking over what had been said and making a deliberate decision? Do you remember other times when you only half listened and made up your mind quickly based on your "gut" feeling about the truthfulness of what had been said? What determines how well we listen to and how carefully we evaluate the hundreds of persuasive messages we hear each day? Richard Petty and John Cacioppo developed a model that explains how likely people are to spend time evaluating information (such as the arguments that they hear in a speech) in an *elaborate* way, using their critical thinking skills, rather than processing information in a simpler, less critical manner. Called the Elaboration Likelihood Model (ELM), this theory can be used by speakers to develop persuasive speeches that will be influential with audience members regardless of how they process.

The model suggests that people process information in one of two ways, the central route or the peripheral route. People using the *central route* listen carefully, think about what is said, and may even mentally elaborate on the message. They base their decision to agree with and possibly take action primarily on appeals to logic and reasoning (logos). The *peripheral route* is a shortcut that relies on simple cues such as a quick evaluation of the speaker's competence, credibility, and character (ethos) or a gut check about what the listener feels (pathos) about the message.

The Peripheral Route:
Relies on simple cues or gut checks.

The Central Route:
Listen carefully, think about what is said, mentally elaborate on the message.

According to the ELM, what determines if we use the central or peripheral route is how important we perceive the issue to be for us. When we feel involved with an issue, we are willing to expend the energy necessary for processing on the central route. When the issue is less important, we take the peripheral route. So how closely your audience members will follow your arguments depends on how involved they feel with your topic.

The ELM also suggests that when we form attitudes as a result of central processing, we are less likely to change our minds than when our attitudes have been formed based on peripheral cues. You can probably remember times when in the moment you were swayed by a powerful speaker but on later reflection you regretted your action and changed your mind. Likewise, based on information you have heard and spent time thinking about, you probably have some strongly held beliefs that are not easily changed. If you'd like to learn more about ELM, and persuasion in general, go to the CourseMate for SPEAK at www.cengagebrain.com to access **Web Resource 13.1: Elaboration Likelihood Model.**

Understanding how people process persuasive messages aids you when you are preparing your speeches. Aristotle[3], the Greek philosopher who wrote *The Rhetoric*, defined rhetoric as the ability to discover in a certain case the available means of persuasion. Those available means of persuasion, which we call rhetorical strategies, are logos, ethos, and pathos. So when you prepare a persuasive speech, part of your preparation will entail figuring out the logical arguments, credibility, and emotions related to your topic and fitting them to the audience and occasion (rhetorical situation). Logos strategies will be used by audience members who use the central processing route to decide if they believe you. Ethos and pathos strategies will be used by listeners who process on the peripheral route. Let's now take a closer look at each of these strategies.

reasoning
the mental process of making an argument by drawing inferences from factual information to reach a conclusion
inductive reasoning
arriving at a general conclusion based on several pieces of specific evidence

The Rhetorical Strategy of Logos

Audience members who process on the central route will analyze and evaluate the logic of the arguments you make. So to frame effective arguments, you need to understand the reasoning process and how to build and test the different types of arguments.

Two Types of Reasoning

Reasoning with an audience is making an argument by drawing inferences from factual information to reach your conclusions.[4] Thus, when you show your friend that the engine of his car is "missing" at slow speeds and stalling at stoplights, you can reason that the car needs a tune-up. You can make arguments by reasoning inductively or deductively. **Inductive reasoning** is arriving at a general conclusion based on several pieces of specific evidence. When we reason inductively, how much our audience agrees with our conclusion depends on the number, quality, and typicality of each piece of evidence you offer. For Jim's car, an inductive argument might look like this:

Evidence: Jim's car is missing at slow speeds.

Evidence: Jim's car is stalling at stoplights.

Logical conclusion: Jim's car needs a tune-up.

Sherlock Holmes is famous for using deductive reasoning to solve mysteries.

deductive reasoning
arriving at a conclusion based on a major premise and minor premise

major premise
a general principle that most people agree upon

minor premise
a specific point that fits within the major premise

syllogism
the three-part form of deductive reasoning

claim
the proposition or conclusion to be proven

support
the reason or evidence the speaker offers as the grounds for accepting the conclusion

warrant
the logical statement that connects the support to the claim

Whereas inductive reasoning argues from specific instances to a general conclusion, deductive reasoning is arguing that if something is true for everything that belongs to a certain class (major premise) and a specific instance is part of that class (minor premise), then we must conclude that what is true for all members of the class must be true in the specific instance (logical conclusion). This three-part form of deductive reasoning is called a **syllogism**. For Jim's car, a syllogism might look like this:

Major premise: Cars need a tune-up when the engine misses consistently at slow speeds.

Minor premise: Jim's car is missing at slow speeds.

Conclusion: Jim's car needs a tune-up.

With this introduction to the two types of reasoning, let's now look at how these are used to form and test arguments.

Forming Arguments

Stephen Toulmin, a philosopher and rhetorician, developed a model to explain the form of everyday arguments.[5] His model has three major elements: the claim, the support, and the warrant.

Claim

The claim is the proposition or conclusion to be proven by the speaker. In our simple example, the claim in both the inductive and deductive argument is "Jim's car needs a tune-up." A claim may ask the audience to accept what the speaker is saying as a fact, or as the best policy, or as a superior value.

Support

The support is the reason or evidence the speaker offers as the grounds for accepting the conclusion. You can support a claim with facts, opinions, experiences, and observations. In the car example, the support for the inductive argument includes two reasons, "missing at slow speeds" and "stalling at stoplights."

But if you look closely, you will notice that both of the reasons supporting the claim that Jim's car needs a tune-up are also claims that need to be backed up with specific evidence. For example, while the statement "The car misses at slow speeds" supports the need for a tune-up, without specific evidence, it is simply a claim that may or may not be true. So at times you will need to provide evidence for one of the grounds you have used in justifying your claim. In outline form, our inductive example looks like this:

> **Specific goal:** *I want Jim to believe that his car needs a tune-up because it fits the criteria for cars that need tune-ups. (claim)*
>
> I. *The engine misses at slow speeds. (reason and claim)*
>   A. *On Tuesday, it was missing when driven below 20 mph. (evidence)*
>   B. *On Wednesday, it did the same thing. (evidence)*
> II. *The car stalls at stoplights. (reason and claim)*
>   A. *It stalled three times at lights on Monday. (evidence)*
>   B. *It stalled each time I stopped at a light yesterday. (evidence)*

Warrant

In Toulmin's model, the **warrant** is the logical statement that connects the support to the claim.[6] Sometimes the warrant of an argument is verbalized, but other times it is simply implied. For instance, a person who claims that "the car needs a tune-up" on the basis of "missing" and "stalling at stoplights" may verbalize the reasoning process with the warrant, "Missing at slow speeds and stalling at lights *are common indications, or signs,* that the car needs a tune-up." Or the speaker may just assume you understand that these are signs of a car that needs a tune-up.

Although you may not actually state your warrants during the speech itself, identifying the type of warrants you are planning to use will allow you to build arguments that are persuasive. Similarly, as a listener, your ability to discern warrants will help you evaluate whether or not to agree with the claim.

Using C for claim (*conclusion*), S for support (*reasons and evidence*), and W for warrant (*explanation of the reasoning process*), we can write the reasoning for the proposition in our example in outline form as follows:

> C *I want Jim to believe that his car needs a tune-up.*
>
> S I. *The engine misses at slow speeds.*
>
> S II. *The car stalls at stoplights.*

W *(I believe this reasoning is sound because missing and stalling are major indicators—signs—of the need for a tune-up.)* (The warrant is written in parentheses because it may not be verbalized when the speech is given.)

Types and Tests of Arguments

Although an argument *always* includes a claim and support, different logical relationships can exist between the claim and the support on which it is based. Four types of arguments commonly used in persuasive speeches are sign, example, analogy, and causation.

Arguing From Sign

If certain events, characteristics, or situations always or usually accompany something, those events, characteristics, or situations are signs. You argue from sign when you support a claim by providing evidence that the events that signal the claim have occurred. For instance, your doctor may claim that you have had an allergic reaction because you have hives and a slight fever.

The general warrant for reasoning from sign can be stated as follows: When phenomena that usually or always accompany a specific situation occur, then we can expect that specific situation is occurring (or will occur). So the warrant for the allergy argument can be stated as follows: "Hives and a slight fever are indicators *(signs)* of an allergic reaction."

Let's look at this argument in outline form:

C *You have had an allergic reaction.*

S A. *You have hives.*
B. *You have a slight fever.*

W *(Hives and a slight fever are signs of an allergic reaction.)*

Signs should not be confused with causes; signs accompany a phenomenon but do not bring about, lead to, or create the claim. In fact, signs may actually be the effects of the phenomenon.

Let's consider, for example, Juanita Martinez's campaign for president of the local neighborhood council. If, in analyzing her campaign you notice that she has more campaign workers than all other candidates combined and that a greater number of people from all segments of the commu-

nity are wearing "Juanita for President" buttons, you may reason "Juanita's campaign has the key signs of an election victory."

A speech outline using the sign argument would look like this:

C *Juanita Martinez will be elected.*

S A. *Juanita has more campaign workers than all other candidates combined.*
B. *A greater number of community members are wearing her campaign buttons.*

W *(The presence of a greater number of campaign workers and buttons than the opponents have is a sign/indicator of victory.)*

When arguing from sign, you can make sure that your argument is valid by answering the following questions.

1. **Do the signs cited always or usually indicate the conclusion drawn?** If the data can occur independently of the conclusion, then they are not necessarily indicators. If the signs cited do not usually indicate the conclusion, then you can question the reasoning on that basis.

2. **Are a sufficient number of signs present?** If enough signs are not present, then the conclusion may not follow. If there are insufficient signs, then you can question the reasoning on that basis.

3. **Are contradictory signs in evidence?** If signs usually indicating different conclusions are present, then the stated conclusion may not be valid. If you believe that contradictory signs are evident, then you can question the reasoning on that basis.

Arguing From Example

You argue from example when the support statements you use are examples of the claim you are making. For almost any topic, it is easy to find examples, so you are likely to use arguing from example quite frequently. The warrant for an argument from example—its underlying logic—is, "What is true in the examples provided is (or will be) true in general or in other instances."

Are contradictory signs in evidence?

argue from sign
to support a claim by providing evidence that the events that signal the claim have occurred

argue from example
to support your claim by providing one or more individual examples

argue from analogy to support a claim with a single comparable example that is significantly similar to the subject of the claim

Suppose you are supporting Juanita Martinez for president. One of the reasons you present is the claim that "Juanita is electable." In examining her résumé to find support for this claim, you find several examples of her previous victories. She was elected treasurer of her high school junior class, chairperson of her church youth group, and president of her college sorority. Each of these is an example that gives support to the claim. What would the warrant statement for this argument look like? You could say, "What was true in several instances *(Juanita has been elected in three previous races)* is true or will be true in general or in other instances *(she will be electable in this situation)*."

Let's look at this argument in speech analysis form:

C *Juanita Martinez is electable.*

S *Juanita has won previous elections.*
  A. *Juanita won the election for treasurer of her high school junior class.*
  B. *Juanita won the election for chairperson of her church youth group.*
  C. *Juanita won the election for president of her college sorority.*

W *(Because Juanita Martinez was elected to previous offices, she is electable for this office.)*

When arguing from example, you can make sure your argument is valid by answering the following questions.

I. **Are enough examples cited?** Because the instances cited should represent most or all possibilities, enough must be cited to satisfy the listeners that the instances are not isolated or handpicked.

2. **Are the examples typical?** Typical means that the examples cited must be similar to or representative of most or all within the category. If examples are not typical, they do not support the argument. For instance, because all three of Juanita's successes came in youth organizations, they may not be typical of election dynamics in community organizations. If the examples are not typical, then the logic of the argument can be questioned. As a speaker, you might search for additional examples that are typical.

3. **Are negative examples accounted for?** In searching for supporting material, we may find one or more examples that are exceptions to the argument we wish to make. If the exceptions are minor or infrequent, then they won't invalidate the argument. For instance, in college, Juanita may have run for chairperson of the Sociology Club and lost. That one failure does not necessarily invalidate the argument. If, however, negative examples prove to be more than rare or isolated instances, the validity of the argument is open to serious question.

If you believe that there are not enough examples, that the examples you have found are not typical, or that negative examples are common, then you will have only weak support for the claim and should consider making a different type of argument.

Arguing From Analogy

You **argue from analogy** when you support a claim with a single comparable example that is significantly similar to the subject of the claim. The general statement of a warrant for an argument from analogy is, "What is true for situation A will also be true in situation B, which is similar to situation A" or

© ISTOCKPHOTO.COM/EWG3D

"What is true for situation A will be true in all similar situations."

Let us return to the claim that Juanita is electable for president of the local neighborhood council to see how arguing from analogy works. If you discover that Juanita has essentially the same characteristics as Paula Jefferson, who was elected president two years ago (both are very bright, both have a great deal of drive, and both have track records of successful campaigns), then you can use the single example of Paula to form the reason "Juanita has the same characteristics as Paula Jefferson, who was elected two years ago." This is analogical reasoning.

Let's look at how the Martinez argument would look in outline form:

C *Juanita Martinez is electable.*

S *Juanita has the same characteristics as Paula Jefferson, who was elected two years ago. (This is also a claim, for which A, B, and C below are support.)*
   A. *Juanita and Paula are both very bright.*
   B. *Juanita and Paula both have a great deal of drive.*
   C. *Juanita and Paula both have won other campaigns.*

W *(What was true for Paula will be true for Juanita, who is similar on the important characteristics.)*

So the claim is supported through an analogy; then, additional support is offered to validate the analogy.

When arguing from analogy, you can make sure that your argument is valid by answering the following questions.

1. **Are the subjects being compared similar in every important way?** If the criteria on which the subjects are being compared are not the most important ones, or if they really don't compare well, then you can question the reasoning on that basis.

2. **Are any of the ways in which the subjects are dissimilar important to the outcome?** When dissimilarities outweigh the subjects' similarities, then conclusions drawn from the comparisons may be invalid.

Arguing From Causation

You argue from causation when you support a claim by citing events that have occurred that result in the claim. Reasoning from causation says that one or more of the events cited always (or almost always) brings about, leads to, or creates or prevents a predictable effect or set of effects.

The general warrant for arguments from causation can be stated as follows: If an event comes before another event and is associated with that event, then we can say that it is the cause of the event. "If A, which is known to bring about B, has been observed, then we can expect B to occur."

In researching Juanita's election campaign, you might discover that (a) she has campaigned intelligently and (b) she has won the endorsement of key community leaders. If these two events are usually associated with victory, then you can form the argument that Juanita has engaged in behavior that leads to campaign victories, thus supporting the claim that she is electable. The argument would look like this:

C *Juanita Martinez will be elected.*

S A. *Juanita has campaigned intelligently.*
   B. *Juanita has key endorsements.*

W *(Intelligent campaigning and getting key endorsements lead to [cause] electoral victory.)*

When arguing from causation, you can make sure that your argument is valid by answering the following questions.

1. **Are the events alone sufficient to cause the stated effect?** If the events are truly causes, it means that if these events were eliminated, then the effect would be eliminated as well. If the effect can occur without these events occurring, then you can question the causal relationship.

2. **Do other events accompanying the cited events actually cause the effect?** If other events appear equally or more important in bringing about the effect, then you can question the causal relationship between the data cited and the conclusion. If you believe that other data caused the effect, then you can question the reasoning on that basis.

3. **Is the relationship between the causal events and the effect consistent?** If there are times when the effect has not followed the cause,

argue from causation
to cite events that have occurred that result in the claim

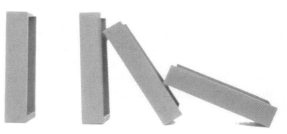

hasty generalization
a fallacy that presents a generalization that is either not supported with evidence or is supported with only one weak example

false cause
a fallacy that occurs when the alleged cause fails to be related to, or to produce, the effect

either-or
a fallacy that argues there are only two alternatives when, in fact, others exist

straw man
a fallacy that occurs when a speaker weakens the opposing position by misrepresenting it in some way and then attacks that weaker position

then you can question whether a causal relationship exists. If you believe that the relationship between the cause and effect is not consistent, then you can question the reasoning on that basis.

Combining Arguments in a Speech

An effective speech usually contains several reasons that are based on various types of arguments. For a speech with the goal "I want my audience to believe that Juanita is electable," you might choose to present three of the reasons we've been working with. Suppose you selected the following:

I. *Juanita has run successful campaigns in the past. (argued by example)*
   A. *Juanita was successful in her campaign for treasurer of her high school class.*
   B. *Juanita was successful in her campaign for chairperson of her church youth group.*
   C. *Juanita was successful in her campaign for president of her college sorority.*
II. *Juanita has engaged in procedures that result in campaign victory. (argued by cause)*
   A. *Juanita has campaigned intelligently.*
   B. *Juanita has key endorsements.*
III. *Juanita is a strong leader. (argued by sign)*
   A. *Juanita has more campaign workers than all other candidates combined.*
   B. *Juanita has a greater number of community members wearing her campaign buttons.*

Just as each of our reasons is presented as an argument, so too is the overall speech. So we need to determine what type of argument we are making. What relationship do all three of these reasons have with the overall claim? How do running successful campaigns in the past, being engaged in procedures that result in victory, and being a strong leader relate to whether Juanita is electable? Are they examples of being electable? Do they cause one to be elected? Are they signs that usually accompany election? Do they distinguish a person who is electable from one who is not? As you study this, you will recognize that the warrant is best stated: "Running successful campaigns in the past, being engaged in procedures

that result in victory, and being a strong leader are all signs of electability." Now you can test the soundness of the overall argument by using the tests of sign argument listed earlier.

Reasoning Fallacies

As you are developing your reasons and the arguments you will make, you should check to make sure that your reasoning is appropriate for the particular situation. This will allow you to avoid fallacies, or errors in reasoning. Five common fallacies to avoid are hasty generalization, false cause, either-or, straw man, and ad hominem arguments.

1. A **hasty generalization** is a fallacy that presents a generalization that is either not supported with evidence or is supported with only one weak example. Because the supporting material should be representative of all the supporting material that could be cited, enough supporting material must be presented to satisfy the audience that the instances are not isolated or handpicked. Avoiding hasty generalizations requires you to be confident that the instances you cite as support are typical and representative of your claim. For example, someone who argued "All Akitas are vicious dogs," whose sole piece of evidence was "My neighbor had an Akita and it bit my best friend's sister," would be guilty of a hasty generalization.

2. A **false cause** fallacy occurs when the alleged cause fails to be related to, or to produce, the effect. Just because two things happen one after the other does not mean that the first necessarily caused the second. Unlike people who blame monetary setbacks and illness on black cats or broken mirrors, be careful that you don't present a coincidental event as a cause unless you can prove the causal relationship. When one event follows another, there may be no connection at all, or the first event might be just one of many causes that contribute to the second.

3. An **either-or** fallacy is the argument that there are only two alternatives when, in fact, others exist. Many such cases are an oversimplification of a complex issue. For example, when Robert argued that "we'll either have to raise taxes or close the library," he committed an either-or fallacy.

4. A **straw man** fallacy is when a speaker weakens the opposing position by misrep-

resenting it in some way and then attacks that weaker (straw man) position. For example, in her speech advocating a seven-day waiting period to purchase handguns, Colleen favored regulation, not prohibition, of gun ownership. Bob argued against that by claiming "it is our constitutional right to bear arms." However, since Colleen did not advocate abolishing the right to bear arms, Bob distorted her position, making it easier for him to refute.

5. An **ad hominem** fallacy attacks or praises the person making the argument rather than addressing the argument itself. For example, if Jamal's support for his claim that his audience should buy an Apple computer is that Steve Jobs, the founder and current president of Apple Computer, is a genius, he is making an ad hominem argument. Jobs's intelligence isn't really a reason to buy a particular brand of computer. TV commercials that feature celebrities using a particular product are often guilty of ad hominem reasoning. For example, Robert De Niro and Jerry Seinfeld have both appeared in American Express commercials, and Gwyneth Paltrow has done ads for Estée Lauder. What makes any of these celebrities experts about the products they are endorsing?

Evaluating Evidence to Support Reasons

Although a reason may seem self-explanatory, before most audience members will believe it, they want to hear evidence that backs it up. As you did your research, you may have discovered more evidence to support a reason than you will be able to use in the time allotted for your speech. So you will have to choose what evidence you will present.

Verifiable factual statements are a strong type of supporting material. Suppose that in a speech whose goal is to convince people that Alzheimer's research should be better funded, you give the reason "Alzheimer's disease is an increasing health problem in the United States." The following would be a factual statement that supported this reason:

ad hominem
a fallacy that occurs when a speaker attacks or praises a person making an argument rather than addressing the argument itself

"According to a 2003 article in the *Archives of Neurology*, 4.5 million Americans had Alzheimer's in 2000 and is expected to affect 13.2 million Americans by the year 2050."

Statements from people who are experts on a subject can also be used as evidence to support a reason. For example, the statement "According to the surgeon general, 'By 2050 Alzheimer's disease may afflict 14 million people a year'" is an expert opinion.

Regardless of whether the evidence is fact based or opinion based, you will want to choose the best evidence you have found to support your point. You can use the answers to the following questions to help you select evidence that is likely to persuade your audience.

1. **Does the evidence come from a well-respected source?** This question involves both the people who offered the opinions or compiled the facts and the book, journal, or Internet source where they were reported. Just as some people's opinions are more reliable than others, so are some printed and Internet sources more reliable than others. Eliminate evidence that comes from a questionable, unreliable, or biased source.

2. **Is the evidence recent and, if not, is it still valid?** Information that was accurate for a particular time period may or may not be valid today. Consider when the evidence was gathered. Something that was true five years ago may not be true today. A trend that was forecast a year ago may have been revised since then. So whether it is a fact or an opinion, you want to choose evidence that is valid today.

For example, the evidence "The total cost of caring for individuals with Alzheimer's is at least $100 billion, according to the Alzheimer's Association and the National Institute on Aging"[7] was cited in a 2003 National Institutes of Health publication. But it is based on information from a study conducted using 1991 data, updated to 1994 data before being published. As a result, we can expect that annual costs would be higher today. If you choose to use this evidence, you should disclose the age of the data in the study and indicate that today the costs would be higher.

3. **Does the evidence really support the reason?** Some of the evidence you have found may be only indirectly related to the reason and should be eliminated in favor of evidence that provides more central support.

4. **Will this evidence be persuasive for this audience?** Finally, you will want to choose evidence that your particular audience is likely to find persuasive. So if you have a choice of two quotations from experts, you will want to use the one from the person your audience is likely to find more compelling.

The Rhetorical Strategy of Ethos

Not everyone will choose the central processing route to make a decision regarding a persuasive message. Some will choose to pay minimal attention to your arguments and will instead use simple cues to decide whether or not to accept your proposal. One important cue people use when they process information by the peripheral route is ethos. So, you will want to demonstrate good character via goodwill. Throughout the speech, you also will want to say and do things to convey competence and credibility.

Conveying Good Character

We turn again to Aristotle, who first observed that a speaker's credibility is dependent on the audience's perception of the speaker's goodwill. Today, we define **goodwill** as a perception the audience forms of a speaker who they believe understands them, empathizes with them, and is responsive to them.[8] In other words, goodwill is the audience's take on the speaker's intentions toward them. When audience members believe in the speaker's goodwill, they are willing to believe what the speaker says.

Let's take a closer look at what goodwill entails. The better you know audience members' experi-ences, circumstances, and desires, the better you will formulate proposals that they will see as in their best interests. A thorough audience analysis will help you. For example, in his speech at the annual conference of the Property Casualty Insurers Association of America (PCI) on November 6, 2006, Julian James, director of Worldwide Markets for Lloyds, demonstrated understanding for the membership by referencing membership facts over the past year:

> I would certainly contend that, following two consecutive record hurricane seasons, we have passed a key financial test. Debate after Katrina was largely about the detail of how we can do things better, and not about whether the industry could survive—as it was after 9/11. Not bad progress for an industry that faced almost double the value of claims from catastrophes in 2005 as it did for 9/11.... If we come out of this year intact, U.S. insurance industry profits in 2006 are forecast to be the best in a generation at $55 to $60 billion.[9]

Not only must you understand your audience, but speakers who show goodwill also empathize with their audience. **Empathy** is the ability to see the world through the eyes of someone else. When we empathize, we put aside our own ideas and feelings and try to experience something from another's point of view. If you do not understand your audience, you will be unable to empathize with them. But empathizing requires you to go beyond understanding to also identify emotionally with your audience members' views.

Your credibility as a speaker depends on the audience's perception.

Empathizing with the views of the audience doesn't mean that you accept their views as your own. It does mean that you acknowledge them as valid. Although your speech may be designed to change audience members' views, the sensitivity you show to audience members' feelings will demonstrate your goodwill. Julian James demonstrates empathy for the reputation of business and industry today:

> So far the industry's finances have rarely looked better. But not everyone is celebrating. With success in business comes greater scrutiny—just ask the oil industry.
>
> In recent weeks we have seen a growing vilification of insurers that is unprecedented and, I believe, wholly unwarranted. Take these recent headlines I came across:
>
>> From USA Today: "Insurance rates pummel Florida homeowners."
>>
>> From Dow Jones Market Watch: "Sweet are the uses of adversity: Are insurers reeling from disaster or reeling in the profits?" (No prizes for guessing which side the authors came down on in that one.)
>>
>> And from the Niagara Falls Reporter: "Insurance companies real villains in Hurricane Katrina's aftermath."
>>
>> If that is the kind of press the industry is getting in Niagara Falls, in upstate New York, you might wonder how we are being portrayed in the Gulf States.[10]

Finally, to demonstrate goodwill, you want to be responsive to the audience. Speakers who are **responsive** show that they care about the audience by acknowledging feedback, especially subtle negative cues. This feedback may occur during the presentation, but it also may have occurred prior to the speech. For example, Julian James reminded this audience about their responses to his speech at a previous PCI convention:

> When I spoke to you at this conference, I posed a challenge and asked, "Do you want to take control of the insurance cycle . . . or do you want to stay a passenger?" The reaction was very interesting. One group said, "That's so obvious, why hasn't anyone said that before?" Others said, "Ah, but you're very young, you don't understand, insurance cycles are a fact of life, and you can't do anything about them." . . . Ladies and gentlemen, four years ago, it may have felt like we were standing at the cliff edge, looking into the abyss.
>
> The good news is that, in the intervening period, we have made important progress.... But we put our future in grave danger if we stop here. . . . The challenges we face today may be different, but the message from 2002 remains the same: "Our thinking and behaviour must change if the insurance industry is to be a stable, secure industry for our policy holders and shareholders of the future." Let's not mess it up again.[11]

Conveying Competence and Credibility

Not surprisingly, we are more likely to be persuaded when we perceive a speaker to be competent and credible. You want your listeners to realize you are well informed about your topic. We propose the following strategies for increasing your audience's perception of your ethos so that your terminal credibility, their perception of your expertise at the end of your speech, is greater than your initial credibility, their perception of your expertise at the beginning of your speech.

1. **Explain your competence.** Unless someone has formally introduced you and your qualifications to your audience, your initial credibility will be low, and as you speak, you will need to tell your audience about your expertise. Sending these types of messages during the speech results in your achieving a level of derived credibility with your audience. You can interweave comments about your expertise into introductory comments and at appropriate places within the body of the speech.[12] If you've done a good deal of research on the topic, say so. If you have personal experience, say so. It's important for the audience to know why they can trust what you are saying.

2. **Establish common ground.** Identify with the audience by talking about shared beliefs and values related to your speech topic.[13] If the topic is controversial or your target audience is opposed to your position, establish common ground by showing empathy for your audience's position before trying to convince them to change. In so doing, you will increase your derived credibility since the audience will feel respected and understood.

3. **Use evidence from respected sources.** If you are not a recognized expert on your subject, you can increase your derived credibility by

responsive
when speakers show that they care about the audience by acknowledging feedback, especially subtle negative cues

terminal credibility
perception of a speaker's expertise at the end of the speech

initial credibility
perception of a speaker's expertise at the beginning of the speech

derived credibility
strategies employed throughout the speech that signal a speaker's expertise

using supporting material from well-recognized, unbiased, and respected sources who are experts. So if you have a choice between using a statistic from a known partisan organization or from a dispassionate professional association, choose the professional association. Likewise, if you can quote a local expert who is well known and respected by your audience or an international scholar with limited name recognition with your audience, use the local expert's opinion.

4. **Use nonverbal elements of delivery to enhance your image.** Your audience establishes its assessment of your initial credibility not only from what it has heard about you before you begin speaking but also from what it has observed about you by looking at you prior to your speech. So how you look and what you do in the few minutes before you speak are important.

Although professional attire enhances credibility in any speaking situation, it is particularly important for persuasive speeches. Research shows that persuasive speakers dressed more formally are perceived as more credible than those dressed casually or sloppily.[14] So your audience will assess your physical appearance in developing its initial judgment about your credibility. That's why it is important to "dress the part."

The audience will also notice how confident you appear as you prepare to address them. From the moment you rise to speak, you will want to convey through your non-

verbal behavior that you are competent. Plant your feet firmly, glance at your notes, and then make eye contact or audience contact with one person or group before taking a breath and beginning to speak. These simple behaviors create a perception of competence and confidence.

Likewise, pause and establish eye contact upon finishing the speech. Just as pausing and establishing eye contact or audience contact before the speech enhance credibility, doing so upon delivering the closing lines of the speech has the same result.

5. **Use vocal expression to enhance your credibility.** Research shows that credibility is strongly influenced by how you sound. Speaking fluently, using a moderately fast rate, and expressing yourself with conviction makes you appear more intelligent and competent.[15] So you will want to practice until you can smoothly and confidently deliver your speech avoiding vocal interrupters like "ums," "uhs," "you knows," and "likes," all of which make you appear unsure of what you are saying and detract from your derived credibility.

The Rhetorical Strategy of Pathos

When we are involved with something, we care about it and have an emotional stake in it. Emotions are the buildup of action-specific energy.[16] We can see simple examples of this when we observe how people's facial expressions change as they receive good or bad news. When people experience the tension associated with any emotion, they look for a way to release the energy. So as a speaker, if you can involve your audience (give them an emotional stake) in what you are saying, they are more likely to use their energy to listen carefully and internalize your speech.[17] Let's look at how research from Robin Nabi shows how you can increase involvement by stimulating both negative and positive emotions in your speeches.[18]

Evoking Negative Emotions

Negative emotions are disquieting, so when people experience them, they look for ways to eliminate them. During your speech, if you can help your audience experience negative emotions, they will be more involved with what you are saying. As a result, they will be motivated to use their energy to listen carefully to you to see if you give them a way to

reduce their feelings of discomfort. There are numerous negative emotions you can tap; in the following discussion, we describe five of the most common.

Fear

We experience **fear** when we perceive that we have no control over a situation that threatens us. We may fear physical harm or psychological harm. Fear is reduced when the threat is eliminated or when we escape. If, as a speaker, you can use examples, stories, and statistics that create fear in your audience, they will be more involved in hearing how your proposal can eliminate the source of their fear or allow them to escape. For example, in a speech whose goal was to convince the audience that they were at risk of developing high blood pressure, the speaker might begin by personalizing the statistics on heart disease:

> One of every three Americans aged 18 and older has high blood pressure. It is a primary cause of stroke, heart disease, heart failure, kidney disease, and blindness. It triples a person's chance of developing heart disease, boosts the chance of stroke seven times, and the chance of congestive heart failure six times. Look at the person on your right; look at the person on your left. If they don't get it, chances are, you will. Today, I'd like to convince you that you are at risk for developing high blood pressure.

Guilt

We feel **guilt** when we personally violate a moral, ethical, or religious code that we hold dear. Guilt is especially keen in situations where the violation is associated with how we believe we should conduct ourselves in relationship to others. We experience guilt as a gnawing sensation that we have done something wrong. When we feel guilty, we are energized or motivated to "make things right" or to atone for our transgression. As a speaker, you can evoke feelings of guilt in your audience so that they pay attention to your arguments. To be effective, your proposal must provide a way for the audience to repair or atone for the damage their transgression has caused or to avoid future violations. For example, in a speech designed to motivate the audience to take their turn as designated drivers, a speaker might evoke guilt like this:

> Have you ever promised your mom that you wouldn't ride in a car driven by someone who had been drinking? And then turned around and got in the car with your buddy even though you both had had a few? You know that wasn't right. Lying to your mother, putting yourself and your buddy at risk . . . (pause) but what can you do? Well, today I'm going to show you how you can avoid all that guilt, live up to your promises to mom, and keep both you and your buddy safe.

Shame

We feel **shame** when we have violated a moral code and it is revealed to someone we think highly of. The more egregious our behavior or the more we admire the person who has found out, the more shame we experience. When we feel shame, we are motivated to "redeem" ourselves in the eyes of that person. Likewise, we can be convinced to refrain from doing something to avoid feelings of shame. If in your speech you can evoke feelings of shame and then demonstrate how your proposal can either redeem someone after a violation has occurred or prevent feelings of shame, then you can motivate the audience to carefully consider your arguments. For example, in a speech advocating thankfulness, the speaker might use a shame-based approach by quoting the old saying, "I cried because I had no shoes until I met a man who had no feet."

Anger

When we are faced with an obstacle that stands in the way of something we want, we experience **anger**. We also experience anger when someone demeans us or someone we love. As with all emotions, the intensity of what we feel varies. We can be mildly annoyed, or we can experience a level of anger that short-circuits the reasoning process and leads to blind rage. Speakers who choose to evoke anger in their audience members must be careful that they don't incite so much anger that reasoning processes are short-circuited.

When we feel anger, we want to strike back at the person or overcome the situation that is thwarting

fear
perceiving no control over a situation that threatens us

guilt
the feeling when we personally violate a moral, ethical, or religious code that we hold dear

shame
the feeling when we have violated a moral code and it is revealed to someone we think highly of

anger
the feeling when we are faced with an obstacle in the way of something we want

our goals or demeaning us. So in your speeches, if you can rouse your audience's anger and then show how your proposal will enable them to prevent the demeaning that has occurred, you can motivate them to listen to you and think about what you have said. For example, suppose you want to convince the audience to support a law requiring the active notification of a community when a sex offender is released from prison and living in the neighborhood. You might arouse the audience's anger to get their attention by personalizing the story of Megan Kanka:

She was your little girl, just seven years old, and the light of your world. She had a smile that could bring you to your knees. And she loved puppies. So when that nice man who had moved in down the street invited her in to see his new puppy, she didn't hesitate. But she didn't get to see the puppy, and you didn't ever see her alive again. He beat her, he raped her, and then he strangled her. He packaged her body in an old toy chest and dumped it in a park. Your seven-year-old princess would never dig in a toy chest again or slip down the slide in that park. And that hurts. But what makes you really angry is she wasn't his first. But you didn't know that. Because no one bothered to tell you that the guy down the street was likely to kill little girls. The cops knew it. But they couldn't tell you. You, the one who was supposed to keep her safe, didn't know. Angry? You bet. Yeah, he's behind bars again, but you still don't know who's living down the street from you. But you can. There is a law pending before Congress that will require active notification of the community when a known sex offender takes up residence, and today I'm going to tell how you can help to get this passed.[19]

Sadness

When we fail to achieve a goal or we experience a loss or separation, we experience **sadness**. Unlike other negative emotions, whose energy is projected outward, when we feel sad, we tend to withdraw and become isolated. Because sadness, like the other negative emotions, is an unpleasant feeling, we look for ways to end it. This can happen through the actions of others when they notice our withdrawal and try to comfort us. Because we withdraw when we are sad,

sadness helps us to focus inward, pondering what has happened and trying to make sense of it. As a result, when we are sad, we are already "looking for answers." So speeches that help us understand and find answers for what has happened can comfort us and help relieve this unpleasant feeling.

Evoking Positive Emotions

Just as evoking negative emotions can cause audience members to internalize what you are saying, so too can you increase audience involvement with your proposal by tapping **positive emotions**, which are feelings that people enjoy experiencing. With negative emotions, our goal is to show how our proposal will help the audience reduce or avoid the feeling. With positive emotions, our goal is to help the audience sustain or develop the feeling. Five of the positive emotions that can motivate the audience to become involved in listening to your arguments are discussed next.

Happiness and Joy

Happiness or joy is the buildup of positive energy we experience when we accomplish something, when we have a satisfying interaction or relationship, or when we see or possess objects that appeal to us. Think of how you felt when you heard that special someone say "I love you" for the very first time. You were happy, maybe even so happy that you were joyous. As a speaker, if you can show how your proposal will lead your audience members to be happy or joyful, then they are likely to listen and to think about your proposal. For example, suppose you want to motivate your audience to attend a couples encounter weekend where they will learn how to "rekindle" their relationship with a partner. If you can remind them about how they felt early in their relationship and then suggest how the weekend can reignite those feelings, they will listen.

Pride

When you experience self-satisfaction and an increase to your self-esteem as the result of something that you have accomplished or that someone you identify with has accomplished, you feel **pride**. "We're number one! We're number one!" is the chant of the crowd feeling pride in the accomplishment of "their" team. Whereas happiness is related to feelings of pleasure, pride is related to feelings of self-worth. So if in your speech you can demonstrate how your proposal will help your audience members to feel good about themselves, they will be more involved in hearing what you have to say. For example, suppose you want to persuade your audience to volunteer on the newest Habitat for Humanity house being constructed in your community. You might involve them by alluding to the pride they will feel when they see the house they have helped to build where there was once a vacant lot.

Relief

When a threatening situation has been alleviated, we feel the positive emotion of **relief**. In relief, the emotional energy that is experienced is directed inward, and we relax and put down our guard. Thus, relief is not usually accompanied by overt action. As a speaker, if you want to use relief as a way to motivate audience members to be involved with your arguments, then you will want to combine it with the negative emotion of fear. For example, suppose your goal is to convince the audience that they are not at risk for high blood pressure. You might use the same personalization of statistics that was described in the example of fear appeals, but instead of proving that the audience is at risk, you could promise relief. Your audience would then listen and evaluate whether they believed your arguments to experience relief from the fear of high blood pressure.

Hope

The emotional energy that stems from believing something desirable is likely to happen is called **hope**. When you yearn for better things, you are feeling hope. Like relief, hope is a positive emotion that has its roots in a difficult situation. Whereas relief causes you to relax and let down your guard, hope energizes you to take action to overcome the situation. Hope empowers. As with relief, hope appeals are usually accompanied by fear appeals. So you can get audience members to listen to you by showing them how your proposal provides a plan for overcoming a difficult situation. In this problem-solution organization, you can embed both fear and hope appeals. For example, if your proposal is that adopting a low-fat diet will reduce the risk of high blood pressure, you can use the same personalization of statistics that were cited in the example of fear but change the ending to state: "Today, I'm going to convince you to beat the odds by adopting a low-fat diet." This offer of hope should influence your audience to listen to and adopt your plan.

Compassion

When we feel selfless concern for the suffering of another person and that concern energizes us to try to relieve that suffering, we feel **compassion**. Speakers can evoke audience members' feelings of compassion by vividly describing the suffering endured by someone. The audience will then be motivated to

listen to see how the speaker's proposal plans to end that suffering. For example, when a speaker whose goal is to have you donate to Project Peanut Butter displays a slide of an emaciated child, claims that 13 percent of all Malawi children die of malnutrition, and states that for $10 you can save a child, he or she is appealing to your compassion.

You can evoke negative emotions, positive emotions, or both as a way to encourage listeners to internalize your message. In the next section, we offer specific guidelines to do so effectively in your content, language, and delivery.

relief
the feeling when a threatening situation has been alleviated

hope
emotional energy that stems from believing something desirable is likely to happen

compassion
the feeling of selfless concern for the suffering of another person and the concern that energizes us to try to relieve that suffering

Guidelines for Appealing to Emotions

As you plan your speech, consider the following guidelines to appeal to emotions.

1. **Tell vivid stories.** Dramatize your arguments by using supporting material such as stories and testimonials that personalize the issue for listeners by appealing to specific emotions. In his speech on bone marrow donation, David Slator simply could have said, "By donating bone marrow—a simple procedure—you can save lives." Instead, he dramatized both the simplicity of the bone marrow donation procedure and the lifesaving impact with a short story designed to heighten audience members' feelings of compassion:

   > When Tricia Matthews decided to undergo a simple medical procedure, she had no idea what impact it could have on her life. But more than a year later, when she saw five-year-old Tommy and his younger brother Daniel walk across the stage of the Oprah Winfrey Show, she realized that the short amount of time it took her to donate her bone marrow was well worth it. Tricia is not related to the boys who suffered from a rare immune deficiency disorder treated by a transplant of her marrow. Tricia and the boys found each other through the National Marrow Donor Program, or NMDP, a national network which strives to bring willing donors and needy patients together. Though the efforts Tricia made were minimal, few Americans made the strides she did. Few of us would deny anyone the gift of life, but sadly, few know how easily we can help.[20]

Notice how David used a compelling example to appeal to his listeners' emotions and personalize the information for them.

2. **Use startling statistics.** Statistics don't have to be boring; instead, when used strategically, they can evoke strong emotions. To provoke emotions, statistics need to be startling. A statistic may surprise because of its sheer magnitude. For example, in a speech urging the audience to attend a local protest march organized by the Mobilization for Global Justice, Cory used the following statistic to shame and anger his audience about the global problem of wealth distribution: "Did you know that the USA has 25.4 percent of the world's wealth? And of that, the top 10 percent of Americans control 71 percent?" Sometimes, by comparing two statistics, you can increase the emotional impact. For example, during his second main point, Cory used the following comparative statistic to highlight wealth disparity. "In the U.S., not only does the top 10 percent control 71 percent of the wealth, but the bottom 40 percent of Americans control less than 1 percent!"

3. **Incorporate listener relevance links.** You can also appeal to emotions by integrating listener relevance links because emotions are stronger when listeners feel personally involved. During a speech on shaken baby syndrome, Ryan appealed to audience emotions through listener relevance. Notice how he brings the problem close to each listener by suggesting the universality of the problem:

   > Jacy Showers, director of the first National Conference on shaken baby syndrome, says "shaking occurs in families of all races, incomes, and education levels" and "81 percent of SBS offenders had no previous history of child abuse." The reason? The offenders were so young, either babysitters or new parents.

4. **Choose striking presentational aids.** Because "a picture is worth a thousand words," consider how you can reinforce your verbal message with dramatic presentational aids. Still pictures and short video clips can at times create an emotional jolt that is difficult to achieve with words. Anton used a 15-second video clip from the DVD *Zoned for Slavery: The Child Behind the Label* to dramatize the problem of child labor in the global textile industry. His goal was to shame his audience members into sending one postcard to the manufacturer of their favorite brand of clothing asking about the working conditions of the workers who manufacture their clothing.

5. **Use descriptive and provocative language.** When developing your speech, include persuasive punch words—words that evoke emotion—where you can. Here's how Ryan used persuasive punch words to strengthen his emotional appeal:

   > The worst of all epidemics is a silent one. With the majority of all victims either infants or young children, shaken baby syndrome can be classified as a stealthy plague. . . . When shaken, the brain is literally ricocheted inside the skull, bruising the brain and tearing blood vessels coming from the neck . . . cutting off oxygen and causing the eyes to bulge.

6. **Use nonverbal elements of delivery to reinforce your emotional appeal.** Even the most eloquently phrased emotional appeal will lose its impact unless the nonverbal parts of delivery heighten and highlight the emotional content of the message. Practice using your voice to emphasize what you are saying with the use of pauses, volume, and pitch to heighten and highlight the emotional content of your message. A dramatic pause before a startling statistic can magnify its emotional effect. Similarly, lowering or raising the volume or pitch of your voice at strategic places can create an emotional response. If you experiment as you practice out loud, you will find a combination of vocal elements that can enhance emotional appeal when delivering your speech.

7. **Use gestures and facial expressions that highlight the emotions you are conveying.** Your message will lose its emotional impact if you deliver it with a deadpan expression or if your demeanor contradicts the emotional content of your message. So if you want your audience to feel angry, you should model this feeling by looking annoyed or livid or furious. You might clench your fists, furrow your brows, and frown. When you want to foster feelings of joy in your audience, you can smile, nod, and use other nonverbal gestures that are natural for you when you experience joy. Remember, as an ethical speaker, you are appealing to emotions that you yourself feel about the situation, so allow yourself to experience these emotions as you practice. Then, when you give your speech, you will be more comfortable displaying your feelings for your audience.

To explore one speaker's use of emotional appeals, go to the CourseMate for SPEAK at www.cengagebrain.com to access **Web Resource 13.2: Terrorism and Islam: Maintaining the Faith**.

© ISTOCKPHOTO.COM/HERMI

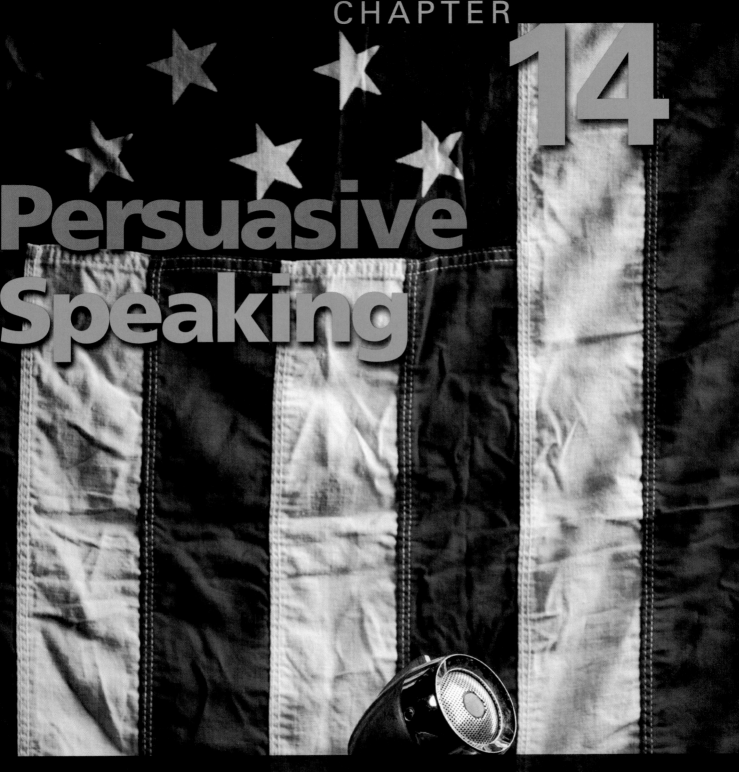

14

Persuasive Speaking

Learning Outcomes

LO¹ Why is it important to consider the initial audience attitude when constructing your persuasive speech goal? | **LO²** How do you phrase a persuasive speech goal as a proposition? | **LO³** What are some dispositional persuasive speech frameworks? | **LO⁴** What are some actuation persuasive speech frameworks? | **LO⁵** What ethical communication guidelines should you follow as a persuasive speaker?

As Steve finished his speech on "Taking Back the Neighborhood: Get Out the Vote!" the audience rose to their feet and began to chant, "No more! No more! No more! No more! . . ." It was clear to him that he had made an impact. Not only had he convinced his audience, but he could also see that they were visibly angry and ready for action. As he was leaving the platform, he heard a member of the audience shout out, "You heard him. It's time! Voting won't do any good. Let's go take what is ours. Take to the streets! Get yours!" In the riot that ensued, three neighborhood shops were ransacked, 10 cars were set on fire, and 23 people were arrested. The next day as he toured the neighborhood and saw firsthand the wreckage his speech had led to, all he could think was, "This wasn't what I meant. This isn't what I wanted."

In the previous chapter, we focused on how persuasive messages employ what Aristotle called the available means of persuasion (logos, ethos, and pathos) to seek agreement or to encourage action. In this chapter, we focus on how to organize those rhetorical appeals into persuasive speeches that are both effective and ethical. In the opening vignette, Steve's speech not only convinced his audience to agree with his point of view, but it also left them so emotionally agitated that when one member of the audience advocated action, the rest followed. And the actions they took went well beyond what Steve wanted the audience to do.

What do you think?

I find it more exciting to talk to an audience that does not agree with me on an issue.

Strongly Disagree ... Strongly Agree

1   2   3   4   5   6   7   8   9   10

Recall that in the previous chapter we introduced you to the Elaboration Likelihood Model (ELM), which illustrates that there are two routes audience members use when they mentally process a persuasive message. If audience members have a personal stake in what you are saying, they are more likely to take the central route and carefully evaluate your arguments and supporting materials. They will also be wary of overt attempts to manipulate their emotions. Audience members who are less involved with your topic—who see it as routine or unimportant—are more likely to take the peripheral route. These listeners are less critical and rely more on a quick assessment of your credibility. They are also more easily swayed by emotional appeals. To be effective with both types of audience members, you must plan your persuasive speeches carefully.

So what do you need to know in order to create effective and ethical persuasive speeches? First, you need to understand where most of the audience members stand on your topic so you can identify whether a speech to convince or to actuate is most appropriate. Then, you need to phrase a proposition, or persuasive speech goal, that is appropriate to the rhetorical situation and choose a suitable persuasive organizational framework. Finally, you need to evaluate your speech plan based on the ethical guidelines you have learned, as well as additional guidelines that are specific to persuasive situations.

Audience Attitude Toward Your Persuasive Topic

Because it is very difficult to convince someone to change his or her mind, what you can hope to accomplish in any one speech depends on where your audience stands on your topic. So as you begin considering your speech, you'll want to understand the current direction and strength of audience members' attitudes about your topic. An **attitude** is "a general or enduring positive or negative feeling about some person, object, or issue."[1] People express their attitudes about something when they give their opinions. So someone who claims "I think physical fitness is important" is expressing an opinion that reflects a favorable attitude about physical fitness.

Assessing your audience's attitudes is part of the audience analysis process, which is Step 2 in the speech-planning process. Recall, you can do this by surveying the audience or by referring to published surveys and extrapolating these polls for the members of your audience. So you will want to begin your persuasive speech preparation by understanding the attitudes your audience is likely to have about your topic. Audience members' attitudes can range from highly favorable to strongly opposed and can be visualized as lying on a continuum like the one pictured in Exhibit 14.1 (the numbers represent the number of audience members who fall into that category).

Even though an audience will include individuals whose opinions fall at nearly every point along the continuum, generally audience members' opinions tend to cluster in one area of it. For instance, the opinions of the audience represented in Exhibit 14.1 cluster around "mildly opposed," even though a few people are more hostile and a few have favorable opinions. That cluster point represents your **target audience**, the group of people you most want to persuade. Based on your target audience, you can classify your audience's initial attitude toward your topic as "in favor" (already supportive of a particular belief), "no opinion" (uninformed, neutral, or apathetic), or "opposed" (against a particular belief or holding an opposite point of view). Given that initial attitude, you can develop a speech goal designed to influence your audience's attitudes in the way you would like. In general, when your target audience is in favor, seek action. When your target audience has no opinion, seek agreement. When your target audience is opposed to your position, seek incremental change.

Opposed

When your target audience is opposed to your goal, it is unrealistic to believe that you will be able to change their attitude from "opposed" to "in favor" in only one short speech. Instead, when dealing with a hostile audience, seek **incremental change**—try to move them only a small degree in your direction—hope for further movement later. For example, if you determine that your audience is likely to be opposed to the goal "I want to convince my audience that gay marriage should be legalized," you might rephrase your goal as "I want to convince my audience that committed gay couples should be able to have the same legal protection afforded to committed heterosexual couples through state-recognized civil unions." Begin by brainstorming objections, questions, and criticisms that might arise, then shape your speech around them.

No Opinion

When your target audience is neutral, you can be straightforward with reasons to support your goal. Still, it might be wise for you to consider whether they are uninformed, impartial, or apathetic about

Exhibit 14.1

Sample Opinion Continuum

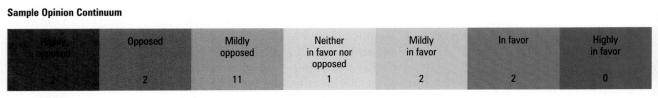

Highly opposed	Opposed	Mildly opposed	Neither in favor nor opposed	Mildly in favor	In favor	Highly in favor
2	2	11	1	2	2	0

your topic. If they are **uninformed**—that is, they do not know enough about the topic to have formed an opinion—you will need to provide the basic arguments and information that they require to become informed. Make sure that each of your reasons is well supported with good information. You may find that your audience is **impartial**—that is, the target audience has some information about the topic but does not really understand why your position is preferred and so still has no opinion. In this case, they are likely to listen objectively and accept sound reasoning if you can demonstrate the superiority of your position to others. Your focus should be on presenting evidence that shows why your position is superior to others. Finally, you may find that your audience members have no opinion because they are **apathetic**. An apathetic audience has no opinion because it is uninterested in, unconcerned about, or indifferent toward your topic. To convince this audience, you will need to provide strong listener relevance links and use evidence that is meaningful to them and their interests.

For more about dealing with audiences who are opposed to or have no opinion about your position, use the CourseMate for SPEAK at www .cengagebrain.com to access **Web Resource 14.1: Dealing With a Hostile Audience** and **Web Resource 14.2: Dealing With a Challenging Audience.**

In Favor

When your target audience is only mildly in favor of your proposal, your task is to reinforce and strengthen their beliefs. An audience whose attitude supports your topic will still benefit from a logical explanation of the reasons for doing so. The audience may also become further committed to an attitude, value, or belief by hearing additional or new reasons and more recent evidence that support it.

When your audience analysis reveals that your listeners strongly agree with your position on the topic, then you can consider a speech goal that moves the audience to act on it. So, for example, if the topic is gay

When dealing with an approving audience, move the audience to act.

When dealing with a hostile audience, seek incremental change.

marriage and your audience poll shows that most audience members strongly favor the idea, then your goal might be "I want my audience to write their state legislators to express their support for gay marriage."

Identifying Your Proposition

In a persuasive speech, you state your specific goal as a proposition. A **proposition** is a declarative sentence that clearly indicates the position you will advocate. For example, "I want to convince my audience that smoking causes cancer" is a proposition. From it, we know that the speaker will present arguments, reasons, and evidence to prove the validity of the proposition.

Notice how a persuasive proposition differs from an informative speech goal on the same subject: "I want to inform my audience about the research on smoking and cancer." In the informative speech, the goal is met if the audience understands and remembers the information the speaker has shared. In the persuasive situation, however, the audience must not only understand what has been said but also agree with it and sometimes even take action. The three major types of persuasive goals are stated as propositions of fact, value, or policy.

A **proposition of fact** is a statement designed to convince your audience that

uninformed
the audience doesn't know enough about a topic to have formed an opinion

impartial
the audience has some information about a topic but does not really understand why one position is preferred and so still has no opinion

apathetic
the audience is uninterested in, unconcerned about, or indifferent toward your topic

proposition
the specific goal of a persuasive speech stated as a declarative sentence that clearly indicates the position the speaker will advocate

proposition of fact
a statement designed to convince the audience that something did or did not exist or occur, is or is not true, or will or will not occur

proposition of value
a statement designed to convince the audience that something is good, bad, desirable, undesirable, fair, unfair, moral, immoral, sound, unsound, beneficial, harmful, important, or unimportant

proposition of policy
a statement designed to convince the audience that they should take a specific course of action

something: (a) did, probably did, probably did not, or did not exist or occur; (b) is, probably is, probably is not, or is not true; or (c) will, probably will, probably will not, or will not occur. It takes a position on something that is generally not known but that can be argued for as true. Propositions of fact can concern the past, present, or future. Although propositions of fact may or may not be true—both positions are arguable—they are stated as true in a persuasive speech. For example, whether or not Lee Harvey Oswald acted alone when he killed President Kennedy is debatable. So you could argue a proposition of fact in two ways: "Lee Harvey Oswald was the lone gunman who shot President John F. Kennedy" or "Lee Harvey Oswald was part of a larger conspiracy to shoot President John F. Kennedy." Examples of propositions of fact concerning the present are "I want to persuade the audience that there is a God," "I want to convince the audience that using cell phones causes brain cancer," and "I want the audience to believe that large numbers of elementary school children are illiterate." Claims of fact concerning the future are predictions. For example, "Thanks to the Internet, paperbound books will eventually cease to exist" and "E-mail will eventually replace traditional postal service" are both propositions of fact concerning the future.

A **proposition of value** is a statement designed to convince your audience that something is good, bad, desirable, undesirable, fair, unfair, moral, immoral,

sound, unsound, beneficial, harmful, important, or unimportant.[2] You can convince your audience that something has more value than something else, or you can convince your audience that something meets valued standards. For instance, "I want to convince my audience that a low-fat diet is actually better than a fat-free diet" is a proposition that will require you to prove that the nutritional value of a low-fat diet meets the American Dietetic Association standards that we value better than a fat-free diet. Similarly, the proposition "I want my audience to believe that multilingual education is beneficial to children" requires you to prove that children who receive multilingual education gain specific educational rewards that we, as a society, value.

A **proposition of policy** is a statement designed to convince your audience that a particular rule, plan, or course of action should be taken. Propositions of policy will implore listeners using words such as "should/should not," or "must/must not." "I want my audience to believe that a public speaking course *should* be required for all students at this university," "I want to persuade the audience that the United States *must* stop deep sea oil drilling," and "I want to convince the audience that home-schooled children *should* be afforded the opportunity to take the standardized tests required of the public school students in their district for free" are all propositions that advocate a specific policy. Similarly, "I want to convince the audience that water packaged in plastic bottles *should* be taxed to pay for the cost associated with recycling empties" and "I want to convince the audience that they *must* stop texting while driving" are propositions of policy.

As you begin working on your persuasive speeches, you can use the Speech Planning Action Steps and

Proposition of Fact
Pharmaceutical companies advertising to consumers increase prescription drug prices.

Proposition of Value
Pharmaceutical advertising of new prescription drugs on TV is better than marketing new drugs directly to doctors.

Proposition of Policy
Pharmaceutical companies should be required to refrain from advertising prescription drugs on TV.

Speech Builder Express to help you organize and develop them, although some of the steps will be modified to provide you with guidance that is particular to persuasive speeches. You can use Activity 1Ep and the sample student response to help you develop a specific goal for a persuasive speech stated as a proposition.

ACTION STEP 1
Activity 1Ep

Speech Planning Action Step for Persuasive Speeches
Writing a Specific Goal as a Persuasive Proposition
1. Tentatively phrase your goal as a proposition.
2. Check whether you believe that your target audience ___ is opposed to, ___ has no opinion of, or ___ is in favor of your proposition. Why?
3. Check whether you believe that ___ the degree of your target audience's attitude makes your goal too difficult to meet or ___ your audience is already convinced of your goal. If you've checked either of these, then rephrase your goal to adapt to that audience attitude.
4. Check whether your proposition, as stated or revised, is one of ___ fact, ___ value, or ___ policy.

You can complete this activity online with Speech Builder Express. Go to the CourseMate for SPEAK at www.cengagebrain.com to access Action Step Activity 1Ep.

{ **Student Response:**
Action Step 1, Activity 1Ep }

Writing a Specific Goal as a Persuasive Proposition
1. Tentatively phrase your goal as a proposition.
   I want to convince members of the audience that they should not download music from the Internet.
2. Check whether you believe that your target audience ___ is opposed to, ✓ has no opinion of, or ___ is in favor of your proposition. Why?
   Although some students may be opposed to or in favor of this proposition, I judge that the majority of the students in class are undecided.
3. Check whether you believe that ___ the degree of your target audience's attitude makes your goal too difficult to meet or ___ your audience is already convinced of your goal. If you've checked either of these, then rephrase your goal to adapt to that audience attitude.
   Because my audience is neutral, my goal seems achievable.
4. Check whether your proposition, as stated or revised, is one of ___ fact, ___ value, or ✓ policy.

Organizational Frameworks for Persuasive Speeches

Once you have identified your speech goal and phrased it as a proposition, you are ready to organize the main points using an appropriate persuasive speech framework. If your proposition focuses on changing or reinforcing your audience's belief or attitude toward your topic, you will give a speech to convince. If your proposition focuses on encouraging your audience to take action, you will give a speech to actuate. There are several different organizational frameworks for each of these types of persuasive speeches.

Common Organizational Frameworks for Speeches to Convince

Most speeches to convince follow one of four organizational frameworks: comparative advantages, criteria satisfaction, refutative, and statement of reasons.

Comparative Advantages

The comparative advantages organizational framework shows that one of two or more alternatives (which may include the status quo) is best. You show that the advantages of your alternative outweigh the disadvantages and that its advantages surpass the advantages of the other options.[3] A comparative advantages approach to a school tax proposition would look like this:

speech to convince
a speech designed to seek agreement about a belief, value, or attitude

speech to actuate
a speech designed to incite action

comparative advantages
an organization that shows that a proposed change has more value than the status quo

Proposition: I want my audience to believe that passing the school tax levy is better than not passing it. (compares the value of change to the status quo)

I. Income from a tax levy will enable schools to reintroduce important programs that had to be cut. (advantage 1)
II. Income from a tax levy will enable schools to avoid a tentative strike by teachers who are underpaid. (advantage 2)
III. Income from a tax levy will enable us to retain local control of our schools, which will be lost to the state if additional local funding is not provided. (advantage 3)

© ISTOCKPHOTO.COM/REBECCA GRABILL

criteria satisfaction
an indirect organization that seeks audience agreement on criteria that should be considered when evaluating a particular proposition and then shows how the proposition satisfies those criteria

refutative
an organization that persuades by both challenging the opposing position and bolstering one's own

Criteria Satisfaction

The criteria satisfaction framework is an indirect organization that seeks audience agreement on criteria that should be considered when evaluating a particular proposition and then shows how the proposition satisfies those criteria. A criteria satisfaction framework is especially useful when your audience is opposed to your proposition because it approaches the proposition indirectly by first focusing on criteria that the audience may agree with before introducing the specific proposition. A criteria satisfaction organization for the school tax proposition would look like this:

Proposition: I want my audience to believe that passing a school tax levy is a good way to fund our schools.

I. We all can agree that a good school funding method must meet three criteria:
   A. A good funding method results in the reestablishment of programs that have been dropped for monetary reasons.
   B. A good funding method results in fair pay for teachers.
   C. A good funding method generates enough income to maintain local control, avoiding state intervention.
II. Passage of a local school tax levy is a good way to fund our schools.
   A. A local levy will allow us to fund important programs again.
   B. A local levy will allow us to give teachers a raise.
   C. A local levy will generate enough income to maintain local control and avoid state intervention.

Refutative

A refutative framework helps you organize your main points to persuade by both challenging the opposing arguments and bolstering your own. This framework is particularly useful when the target audience opposes your position. Begin by acknowledging the merit of opposing arguments and then showing their flaws. Once listeners understand the flaws, they are more receptive to the arguments you present to support your opinion. A refutative organization for the school tax proposition might look like this:

Proposition: I want my audience to agree that a school tax levy is the best way to fund our schools.

I. Opponents of the tax levy argue that the tax increase will fall only on property owners.
   A. Landlords will recoup property taxes in the form of higher rents.
   B. Thus, all people will be affected.
II. Opponents of the tax levy argue that there are fewer students in the school district, so schools should be able to function on the same amount of revenue.
   A. Although there are fewer pupils, costs continue to rise.
      1. Salary cost increases
      2. Energy cost increases
      3. Maintenance cost increases
      4. Unfunded federal and state government mandates add to costs
   B. Although there are fewer pupils, there are many aging school buildings that need replacing or retrofitting for this computer age.

III. Opponents of the tax levy argue that parents should be responsible for the excessive cost of educating their children.
   A. Historically, our nation flourished under a publicly funded educational system.
   B. Parents today are already paying more than our parents did.
      1. Activity fees
      2. Lab fees
      3. Book fees
      4. Transportation fees
   C. Of school-age children today in this district, 42 percent live in families that are below the poverty line and have limited resources.

Proposition: I want my audience to believe that passing the proposed school tax levy is necessary.

I. The income will enable the schools to restore vital programs. (second strongest)
II. The income will enable the schools to give teachers the raises they need to keep up with the cost of living.
III. The income will allow the community to maintain local control and will save the district from state intervention. (strongest)

Statement of Reasons

The statement of reasons is a form of persuasive organization used for confirming propositions of fact in which you present your best-supported reasons in a meaningful order. For a speech with three reasons or more, place the strongest reason last because this is the reason you believe the audience will find most persuasive. You will often place the second strongest reason first because you want to start with a significant point. Place the other reasons in between.

statement of reasons
a straightforward organization in which you present your best-supported reasons in a meaningful order

Speech to Convince Evaluation Checklist

You can use this checklist to critique a speech to convince that you hear in class. As you listen to the speaker, outline the speech. Pay close attention to the reasoning process the speaker uses. Note the claims and supports used in the arguments, and identify the types of warrants used. Then, answer the following questions.

_____ 1. Was the introduction effective in creating interest, involving the audience in the speech, and previewing the main points?

_____ 2. Was the specific goal clear and phrased as a proposition?

_____ 3. Was the speech organized into an appropriate framework?
_____ Comparative advantages _____ Criteria satisfaction _____ Refutative _____ Statement of reasons

_____ 4. Did the speaker use logos effectively?
_____ Strong evidence? _____ Reasoning linked to claims? _____ Fallacies?

_____ 5. Did the speaker use ethos effectively?
_____ Establish expertise? _____ Demonstrate trustworthiness? _____ Convey goodwill?

_____ 6. Did the speaker use pathos effectively?
Appeal to negative emotions? If so, check all that were tapped:
_____ fear _____ guilt _____ anger _____ shame _____ sadness
Appeal to positive emotions? If so, check all that were tapped:
_____ happiness/joy _____ pride _____ relief _____ hope _____ compassion
Were the appeals _____ very effective, _____ somewhat effective, or _____ ineffective?

_____ 7. Was the language appropriate, accurate, clear, and vivid?

_____ 8. Was the use of voice intelligible, conversational, expressive, and convincing?

_____ 9. Was the use of body poised and expressive?

_____ 10. Did the speaker offer a compelling conclusion with thesis restatement and clincher?

Overall evaluation of the speech (check one):
_____ excellent _____ good _____ average _____ fair _____ poor

You can use the CourseMate for SPEAK at www.cengagebrain.com to access this checklist, complete it online and compare your feedback to that of the authors, or print a copy to use in class.

This section presents a sample speech to convince given by a student, including an adaptation plan, an outline, and a transcript.

Hooking Up, Friends-With-Benefits Relationships (FWBRs), or Dating: Not Really a Tough Choice

By Molly Reynolds[4]

Read the speech adaptation plan, outline, and transcript of a speech given by Molly Reynolds in an introductory speaking course. Access the Chapter 14 resources of the CourseMate for SPEAK at www.cengagebrain.com to identify some of the strengths of Molly's speech by preparing an evaluation checklist and an analysis. You can then compare your answers with those of the authors.

Adaptation Plan

1. **Audience attitude.** When I asked people about their feelings concerning hookups and friends-with-benefits relationships (FWBRs), most of them regarded the practices as common and not a big deal. However, very few admitted to their own hookup or FWBRs. Instead, they talked about the involvements that "others" engaged in. Therefore, I determined that the majority of my audience is either undecided or unconcerned about the consequences.

2. **Reasons.** Dating is physically and psychologically healthier, and leads to greater relationship satisfaction.

3. **Organizational framework.** I am going to use a comparative advantages framework. This topic naturally lends itself to demonstrating the comparative advantages that dating has over both hooking up and friends-with-benefits relationships (FWBRs). The three primary advantages are physical health, psychological health, and relationship satisfaction.

Outline

General goal: To persuade

Specific goal: I want to convince my audience that dating relationships are better than hooking up or friends-with-benefits relationships (FWBRs).

Introduction

I. *"Well you know, they travel in threes, and she was not the hot one but she wasn't the fat one either. And it was late, and if I wanted to get laid the choices were getting slim, so—"*

"We were at this party, and I was dancing with this really hot guy. One thing led to another, and I thought, what the heck. He's so hot."

"Josh and I have known each other since grade school, and I've always kind of had a thing for him. Neither one of us was seeing anyone, and one night we were out with friends and dancing, and one thing led to another and we became, you know, 'friends with benefits.' But now I'm really hooked on him and he doesn't know it, and he's started to see someone who he thinks is special. But he wants to keep up our arrangement too because she won't sleep with him."

"I met this really cool girl in my biology class. She's really pretty and smart, and she seems to have a good sense of humor. So I broke the code and asked her out. We took a walk in the park, had dinner, and then went back to her place, and believe it or not, we just talked. It was so weird, but I really enjoyed it. So we've made plans to go to the movies on Saturday. So I won't be going out trolling for a bad girl this weekend. Who knows—I may be out of the action for a while. We'll see."

II. We have all known someone who has engaged in the above-mentioned scenarios. Which of these scenarios appeals most to you? If you had your choice of hooking up with a stranger, having sex with a friend, or going out with someone you found interesting and attractive, what would you prefer?

Listener relevance link

III. As a member of what some call "the hookup generation," I have first-hand knowledge and some experience with the current hookup culture that is so popular on college campuses today. So I was curious about what the research says about these practices, and what I discovered might surprise you as much as it surprised me.

Speaker credibility

IV. Today, I'm here to convince you that hooking up and friends-with-benefits relationships (FWBRs) are poor substitutes for dating relationships.

Thesis statement

V. I will show why dating is the best choice by defining each relationship type and then comparing the physical risks, psychological costs, and feelings of relationship satisfaction among them.

Preview

Body

I. Let's begin by defining each of these three types of relationships.

I'm sure we have all known someone who hooked up and was disappointed when they didn't get a phone call the next day, and someone whose FWBR ended with no benefits and the loss of a friend. And I'm sure we have known friends who grieved the loss of what they thought was a solid dating relationship.

Listener relevance link

A. Before we can examine the risks, we must define what a hookup is.

  1. "Hookups are defined as a sexual encounter which may or may not include sexual intercourse, usually occurring on only one occasion between two people who are strangers or brief acquaintances" (Paul, McManus, & Hayes, 2000, p. 76).

   a. These casual sexual encounters are essentially spontaneous sex between partners who barely had contact with each other before engaging in the sexual act (Winslow, Franzini, & Hwang, 1992).

   b. The nature of the sexual behavior involved is ambiguous and may vary from heavy kissing to intercourse.

  2. Different goals and expectations of those involved can lead to misunderstanding, dissatisfaction, and regret (Carroll, Volk, & Hyde, 1985).

B. Now that we understand the nature of a hookup, what exactly is a friends-with-benefits relationship (FWBR)?

  1. FWBRs are platonic friendships where partners engage in sexual behaviors ranging from kissing to sexual intercourse (Mongeau, Shaw, & Knight, 2009).

    a. FWBRs can include numerous degrees on the intimacy spectrum.

    b. These degrees range from good friends who engage in sexual activity to individuals who engage in serial hookups but have little to no interaction beyond the hookup.

  2. Despite the type of FWBR, individuals usually enter into an FWBR with no intention of it evolving into a romantic relationship (Hughes, Morrison, & Asada, 2005).

    a. Sometimes one partner in an FWBR becomes interested in taking the relationship further, but these feelings aren't always mutual.

    b. Monica and Chandler from the show *Friends* began as friends, moved into an FWBR, and ended up married.

    c. FWBRs rarely have this fairy-tale ending in real life.

C. Now that we understand the nature of hookups and FWBRs, we must define dating relationships.

  1. In dating relationships, individuals spend time getting to know each other and enter into a sexual relationship if and when both partners feel a sense of relational intimacy.

  2. In dating relationships, both people share more intimate thoughts and feelings as trust builds.

  3. Relational success is more likely when partners know each other and date for an extended period before marriage and engage in positive communication (Stafford, 2008).

Transition

Now that we've established a common set of definitions, let's compare these relationships according to how they affect physical health, psychological health, and relationship satisfaction.

II. Let's begin by exploring the physical risks associated with hookups, FWBRs, and dating relationships.

Listener relevance link

Since most of us in this room are not married, we ought to understand the physical risks involved in engaging in these different types of relationships.

A. Because partners often fail to practice safe sex, hookups and FWBRs increase the risk of catching a sexually transmitted disease (STD).

  1. It's true that when you have sex with someone, you also have sex with everyone they have ever had sex with.

    a. Listen to the testimony of someone suffering from pelvic inflammatory disease (PID), a bacterial infection of the uterus, fallopian tubes, and ovaries:

       "I have suffered with pelvic inflammatory disease now for 15 years. I have in the last three years had a full hysterectomy and now suffer worse pain than ever and have severe adhesions and chronic pain. My life is ruined. My PID was silent but deadly—one day no pain; next day I was crippled. PID is a horrible disease—and you don't have to be promiscuous to get it. Just sleeping with someone you don't know and whose sexual past is unknown can put you in jeopardy of this disease."

    b. PID is most frequently caused by gonorrhea and chlamydia, two common STDs.

  2. There are numerous risks associated specifically with hooking up (Downing-Maltibag & Geisinger, 2009).

    a. Students who did not use protection often trusted that their hookup partners were STD-free based on appearance or informal character assessments.

    b. They also tended to rationalize that because there were low rates of HIV/AIDS in the region where they lived, they did not have to protect themselves against it (p. 1204).

3. People aren't any safer in FWBRs.

   a. People who engage in *hookups* report being more careful when engaging in sexual intercourse with unknown or lesser-known individuals than with people they already know (Morr & Mongeau, 2004).

   b. Just because you know someone as a "friend" and have an FWBR with that person does not mean you know what he or she is doing sexually.

      i. FWBRs by their very nature are not meant to be exclusive, so he or she may have other partners who, by association, you are also sleeping with.

      ii. Even if you are both monogamous during your relationship, unless you are both tested prior to having sex, you are still at risk.

   c. In hookups and in FWBRs, the emphasis is on each partner's personal needs for sex and physical satisfaction, so the partner is an "insignificant other."

B. Because partners involved in hookups and FWBRs are less likely to practice safe sex, the likelihood of an unplanned pregnancy also increases.

   1. Listen to the experience of a woman who posted her story on Yahoo! Answers:

   "I was with this guy for a very short time. It pretty much ended up being a one-night stand, even though we texted a little afterwards. When I found out I was pregnant, I decided to tell him, especially since I didn't know what I was going to do yet. But whatever I was going to do was part of his responsibility (i.e., bills for an abortion, child support, or choosing of an adoptive family). When I told him, he just begged me to get an abortion over and over until I finally agreed and told him I had gotten the abortion to get him to stop texting me every five seconds and begging while I could get some quiet time to figure out what I really wanted to do."

   > Notice, guys, it was what she wanted to do. A man who fathers a hookup child is legally responsible for supporting that child until it is an adult. You have no say—it is her body and her decision. So, in addition to your college loans, you may have a significant financial responsibility for the next 18 years. And every time you get a raise, your child gets part of it. It's the risk you take. And if you're morally or religiously opposed to abortion? Tough. Her body, her decision. You can try to change her mind, but if she decides on abortion, there is nothing you can do. And remember, even when condoms are used they are only 95 percent effective as a contraceptive. Think about it.

Listener relevance link

   2. Unintended pregnancy is a risk in any sexual relationship.

      a. But people who are dating and have built some degree of respect and intimacy are more likely to come to a mutual understanding about the woman's choice.

      b. Or they can adjust to co-parenting tasks, even if they choose to end their romantic relationship.

C. While physical risks are inherent in any sexual relationship, dating is physically healthier than either hooking up or engaging in an FWBR.

> *Not only do hookups and FWBRs put you at more risk physically, but they are also more likely to do psychological damage.*

Transition

III. Both hooking up and engaging in FWBRs create psychological distress.

   > How many of you know someone who says they feel more confident and have higher self-esteem following a hookup? After sleeping with their best friend? Not many, right? More often, we listen to our friends express feelings of guilt, shame, and embarrassment. People, it's called a "walk of shame" for a reason.

Listener relevance link

A. People who hook up have lower self-esteem, greater depression, and more feelings of guilt than those who don't (Grello, Welsh, & Harper, 2006; Sprecher, Barbee, & Schwartz, 1995).

   1. Women who engage in hooking up experience more loss of self-esteem and depression than men.

   2. It is not clear whether depression leads to casual sexual behavior or whether casual sexual behavior leads to depression.

   3. Women who engage in casual sex experience feelings of good old-fashioned guilt.

   4. Men don't necessarily feel guilty for hooking up with strangers, but they do feel guilty if they get drunk and hook up with a friend.

B. While breaking up a dating relationship can also lead to depression, research has found that although the first breakup can lead to depression, subsequent breakups are unlikely to do so.

   1. The first act of breaking up seems to "inoculate" us, probably because we figure that there is life after a breakup.

   2. The opposite seems to be true in more casual sexual relationships—the more you do it, the more guilty and depressed you become.

Transition

Because of the many negative physical and psychological consequences of hooking up and FWBRs, dating tends to produce more satisfying relationships in the end.

IV. Hooking up and FWBRs lead to less satisfying relationships than dating.

   A. In a hookup, ideally neither partner wants or expects anything other than sexual satisfaction (Grello, Welsh, & Harper, 2006).

      1. Half of all college students who engage in sexual intercourse during a hookup never see the other person again.

      2. But 18 percent of women view a hookup as stepping stone to a romantic relationship.

   B. In the ideal FWBR, two friends simply become "sex" or "f . . . ing" buddies without damaging the friendship.

   C. According to that famous philosopher Harry Burns in the 1989 movie *When Harry Met Sally*, "Men and women can never be friends because the sex part always gets in the way." Was Harry wrong? Yes and no.

      1. In a 2010 study, Lehmiller and his colleagues found yes:

      "Sex was a more common motivation for men in FWBRs, whereas emotional connection was a more common motivation for women. In addition, men were more likely to hope that the relationship stays the same over time, whereas women expressed more desire for change into either a full-fledged romance or a basic friendship."

      2. This is understandable when you consider the biology of sex, according to sex therapist Dr. Ian Kerner, speaking on the *Today Show* in 2007:

      "During sex, women produce lots of oxytocin, a hormone that stimulates a strong emotional connection. As a result, women are more emotionally integrated when it comes to sex. That's why casual sex and hookups often backfire for lots of women. Guys produce little to no oxytocin, and can easily have sex without any sense of emotional connection. It's sex with no emotional strings attached."

      3. One of the inherent problems in FWBRs is the ambiguity partners can feel about what they can expect. "Euphoria" posted this to the sex forum on womens-health.com:

"We have a very good relationship as friends; we're very close. We've been 'talking' since November, and one night I slept over at his house and it just happened. The thing that bothers me is that he didn't kiss me in the morning and didn't talk to me until the next night. And on New Year's Eve I also slept over his house, along with other people, and I was probably setting myself up for it cause it happened again. I had left early that morning, around eight, and my friend had told me later on that day that he came into the room she was sleeping in and practically woke her up to kiss her. We did agree to be friends with benefits, but I meant that I'm the only one he should be doing it with. Should I say something to him, or do I have no right since we're FWB?"

4. During my research, I came upon an article by Marilyn Murphy on the AskMen.com website that talked about the pros and cons of FWBRs.

   a. Seventy-five percent of the 139 posts responding to the article talked about how an FWBR produced problems.

   b. These problems stemmed from one partner wanting the relationship to evolve into something more serious.

5. But no, Harry wasn't right in one sense—both men and women in an FWBR were ultimately more committed to the friendship than to the sexual aspect of the relationship (Lehmiller, VanderDrift, & Kelly, 2010).

D. Although not all dating relationships lead to "happily ever after," successful dating leads to more satisfactory relationships in terms of intimacy and safe sexual fulfillment.

   1. Dating is the preferred type of relationship for both men and women (Glenn & Marquardt, 2001).

      a. In a national survey of over 1,000 college women published in 2001, 83 percent agreed with the statement "Being married is very important to me."

      b. And 63 percent agreed with the statement "I would like to meet my future husband/wife in college."

      c. Yet 50 percent of the women sampled had had fewer than two dates since starting college.

      d. A 2010 study found that 87 percent of women and 64 percent of men indicated a preference for dating over hooking up, particularly when they might be interested in a long-term relationship (Bradshaw et al.).

   2. As "Bad Reputation" put it in his online post, "There are girls you date and girls you have sex with." So I ask you, ladies: Who do you want to be?

Conclusion

I. Based on analysis, I'm sure you can see that dating, while scary and angst ridden, is still superior to hooking up or having an FWBR.

II. Both hookups and FWBRs have more physical and psychological risks than dating relationships.

III. So, before you go out this weekend, get smashed, and find yourself looking for love in all the wrong places, consider giving that someone you've had your eye on a call and see if you can make a date for a movie, or concert, or just a cup of coffee. While it might not lead to a romantic relationship, who knows—it just might.

Thesis restatement

Main point summary

Clincher

References

Carroll, J. L., Volk, K. D., & Hyde, J. S. (1985). Differences between males and females in motives for engaging in sexual intercourse. *Archives of Sexual Behavior, 14*, 131–139.

Chlamydia–CDC Fact Sheet (2010). *Centers for Disease Control and Prevention*. Retrieved from http://www.cdc.gov/std/chlamydia/stdfact-chlamydia.htm

Cohen, E. (2010). The downside of "friends with benefits," *CNN.com*. Retrieved from http://www.cnn.com/2010/HEALTH/04/15/friends.benefits.stds/index.html

Downing-Maltibag, T. M., & Geisinger, B. (2009). Hooking up and sexual risk taking among college students: A health belief model perspective. *Qualitative Health Research, 19*, 1196–1204.

Glenn, N., & Marquardt, E. (2001). *Hooking up, hanging out, and hoping for Mr. Right: College women on dating and mating today*. A report conducted by the Institute for American Values for the Independent Women's Forum.

Gonorrhea–CDC Fact Sheet (2008). *Centers for Disease Control and Prevention*. Retrieved from http://www.cdc.gov/std/Gonorrhea/STDFact-gonorrhea.htm

Grello, C. M., Welsh, D. P., & Harper, M. S. (2006). No strings attached: The nature of casual sex in college students. *Journal of Sex Research, 43*, 255–267.

Hughes, M., Morrison, K., & Asada, K. J. K. (2005). What's love got to do with it? Exploring the impact of maintenance rules, love attitudes, and network support on friends-with-benefits relationships. *Western Journal of Communication, 69*(1), 49–66.

I'm pregnant, but it was only a hookup. Should I tell him? [Online forum entry]. (2009, November 1). *Yahoo! Answers*. Retrieved from http://answers.yahoo.com/questions/index?qid=20091101094838AAnz4l1

Kerner, I. (2007, September 27). The biggest sex mistakes that men and women make [Video], *The Today Show*. Retrieved from http://www.today.msnbc.msn.com/id/20955254/ns/today-today_relationships//

Lehmiller, J. J., VanderDrift, L. E., & Kelly, J. R. (2010). Sex differences in approaching friends with benefits relationships. *Journal of Sex Research*, *48*(2–3), 275–284. doi:10.1080/00224491003721694.

Monroe, S. M., Rohde, P., Seeley, J. R., & Lewinsohn, P. M. (1999). Life events and depression in adolescence: Relationship loss as a prospective risk factor for first onset of major depressive disorder. *Journal of Abnormal Psychology*, *108*(4), 606–614.

Morr, M. C., & Mongeau, P. A. (2004). First-date expectations: The impact of sex of initiator, alcohol consumption, and relationship type. *Communication Research, 31*(1), 3–35.

Murphy, M. (2009). The pros & cons of casual sex between friends. *AskMen.com*. Retreived from http://www.askmen.com/includes/components/posts/postPage.php?id=910517&p=3

Owen, J. J., Stanley, S. M., & Fincham, F. D. (2010). "Hooking up" among college students: Demographic and psychosocial correlates. *Archives of Sexual Behavior, 39*, 653–663.

Paul, E. L., & Hayes, K. A. (2002). The casualties of "casual" sex: A qualitative exploration of the phenomenology of college students' hookups. *Journal of Social and Personal Relationships, 19*, 639–660.

Paul, E. L., McManus, B., & Hayes, A. (2000). "Hookups": Characteristics and correlates of college students' spontaneous and anonymous sexual experiences. *Journal of Sex Research, 37*, 76–88.

Sprecher, S., Barbee, A., & Schwartz, P. (1995). "Was it good for you too?": Gender differences in first intercourse experiences. *Journal of Sex Research, 32*(1), 3–15.

Stafford, L. (2008). Dating relationships. In Wolfgang Donsbach (Ed.), *The international encyclopedia of communication* (Vol. 3, pp. 1167–1171). Malden, MA: Blackwell Publishing Ltd.

Winslow, R. W., Franzini, L. R., & Hwang, J. (1992). Perceived peer norms, casual sex, and AIDS risk prevention. *Journal of Applied Social Psychology, 22*(24), 1559–1816.

Speech and Analysis

Well you know, they travel in threes, and she was not the hot one but she wasn't the fat one either. And it was late, and if I wanted to get laid the choices were getting slim, so—

We were at this party, and I was dancing with this really hot guy. One thing led to another, and I thought, what the heck. He's so hot.

Josh and I have known each other since grade school, and I've always kind of had a thing for him. Neither one of us was seeing anyone, and one night we were out with friends and dancing, and one thing led to another and we became, you know, "friends with benefits." But now I'm really hooked on him and he doesn't know it, and he's started to see someone who he thinks is special. But he wants to keep up our arrangement too because she won't sleep with him.

I met this really cool girl in my biology class. She's really pretty and smart, and she seems to have a good sense of humor. So I broke the code and asked her out. We took a walk in the park, had dinner, and then went back to her place, and believe it or not, we just talked. It was so weird, but I really enjoyed it. So we've made plans to go to the movies on Saturday. So I won't be going out trolling for a bad girl this weekend. Who knows—I may be out of the action for a while. We'll see.

We have all known someone who has engaged in the above-mentioned scenarios. Which of these scenarios appeals most to you? If you had your choice of hooking up with a stranger, having sex with a friend, or going out with someone you found interesting and attractive, what would you prefer?

As a member of what some call "the hookup generation," I have first-hand knowledge and some experience with the current hookup culture that is so popular on college campuses today. So I was curious about what the research says about these practices, and what I discovered might surprise you as much as it surprised me.

Today I'm here to convince you that hooking up and friends-with-benefits relationships (FWBRs) are poor substitutes for dating relationships. I will show why dating is the best choice by defining each relationship type and then comparing the physical risks, psychological costs, and feelings of relationship satisfaction among them.

Let's begin by defining each of these three types of relationships. I'm sure we have all known someone who hooked up and was disappointed when they didn't get a phone call the next day, and someone whose FWBR ended with no benefits and the loss of a friend. And I'm sure we have known friends who grieved the loss of what they thought was a solid

Molly uses four hypothetical scenarios to grab her audience's attention. Doing so is particularly effective because they are scenarios that most of her classmates can probably relate to.

Here Molly establishes listener relevance by asking a series of rhetorical questions, which engages her audience from the outset.

Molly establishes credibility by pointing out her personal experience with the topic as part of the "hookup generation" and that she was surprised at what she learned from the research.

We clearly understand what Molly's proposition is and how she will organize her arguments to convince us to agree with her about this issue.

Molly realized that she couldn't succeed with her goal unless she knows that her listeners understand the nature of the different types of relationships she's discussing. So she makes this subject her first main point.

dating relationship. Therefore, before we can examine the associated risks, we must begin by defining what a hookup actually is.

According to Paul, McManus, and Hayes in their 2000 article "'Hookups': Characteristics and Correlates of College Students' Spontaneous and Anonymous Sexual Experiences," published in the *Journal of Sex Research*, "Hookups are defined as a sexual encounter which may or may not include sexual intercourse, usually occurring on only one occasion between two people who are strangers or brief acquaintances." Winslow, Franzini, and Hwang explain further in their article published in a 1992 issue of the *Journal of Applied Social Psychology* that these casual sexual encounters are essentially spontaneous sex between partners who barely had contact with each other before engaging in the sexual act. The exact nature of the sexual behavior involved during a hookup is somewhat ambiguous and may vary from heavy kissing to intercourse. Carroll, Volk, and Hyde, in their article "Differences between Males and Females in Motives for Engaging in Sexual Intercourse," published in a 1985 issue of the *Archives of Sexual Behavior*, report that different goals and expectations of those involved can lead to misunderstanding, dissatisfaction, and regret.

Now that we understand the nature of a hookup, what exactly is a friends-with-benefits relationship (FWBR)? Lehmiller, VanderDrift, and Kelly, in their article "Sex Differences in Approaching Friends-with-Benefits Relationships," published in a 2010 issue of the *Journal of Sex Research*, explored the nature of an FWBR as platonic friendships where partners engage in sexual behaviors ranging from kissing to sexual intercourse. The authors found FWBRs can include numerous degrees on the intimacy spectrum, ranging from good friends who engage in sexual activity to individuals who engage in serial hookups but have little to no interaction beyond the hookup.

Despite the type of FWBR, Hughes, Morrison, and Asada reported in their article "What's Love Got to Do with It?" published in a 2005 issue of the *Western Journal of Communication*, individuals usually enter into an FWBR with no intention of it evolving into an romantic one. Sometimes one partner in an FWBR becomes interested in taking the relationship further. However, these feelings aren't always mutual. Some of you probably remember Monica and Chandler from the show *Friends*. They began as friends, moved into an FWBR, and ended up married. Unfortunately, FWBRs rarely have this fairy tale ending in real life.

Now that we understand the nature of hookups and FWBRs, we need to define dating relationships. In dating relationships, individuals spend time getting to know each other and enter into a sexual

Molly bolsters her ethos by using an oral citation. Doing so enhances her credibility, telling the audience that she is informed as well as ethical.

Molly could have elaborated on the findings of this article. As is, listeners are left wondering what the differences are.

Molly does a nice job of using a rhetorical question to verbally tie the point she has finished talking about to the point she is introducing.

Although Molly cites a number of reputable sources for this point, she could improve by integrating a variety of types of evidence, perhaps a testimonial or a personal story.

Molly could improve by offering some kind of warrant to support this claim.

Again, Molly offers a transition that verbally ties her main points together. She also uses inclusive language when she says "we" rather than "I."

relationship if and when both partners feel a sense of relational intimacy. In dating relationships, both people share more intimate thoughts and feelings with each other as trust builds. In her 2008 reference in the *International Encyclopedia of Communication*, Stafford explains that relational success is more likely when partners know each other and date for an extended period before marriage and engage in positive communication.

Now that we've established a common set of definitions, let's compare these relationships according to how they affect physical health, psychological health, and relationship satisfaction. Let's begin by exploring the physical risks associated with hookups, FWBRs, and dating relationships. Since most of us in this room are not married, we ought to understand the physical risks involved in engaging in these different types of relationships.

Hookups and FWBRs increase the risk of catching an STD because partners often fail to practice safe sex. The old saying that when you have sex with someone, you also have sex with everyone they have ever had sex with is true. Listen to the testimony of someone suffering from pelvic inflammatory disease (PID), a bacterial infection of the uterus, fallopian tubes, and ovaries. PID is most frequently caused by gonorrhea and chlamydia, two common STDs that can be devastating. Listen to one sufferer's story:

> I have suffered with pelvic inflammatory disease now for 15 years. I have in the last three years had a full hysterectomy and now suffer worse pain than ever and have severe adhesions and chronic pain. My life is ruined. My PID was silent but deadly—one day no pain; next day I was crippled. PID is a horrible disease—and you don't have to be promiscuous to get it. Just sleeping with someone you don't know and whose sexual past is unknown can put you in jeopardy of this disease.

In their article "Hooking Up and Sexual Risk Taking among College Students: A Health Belief Model Perspective," published in a 2009 issue of the *Qualitative Health Research Journal*, Downing-Maltibag and Geisinger also discovered numerous risks associated with hooking up. Specifically, students who did not use protection often trusted that their hookup partners were STD-free based on appearance or informal character assessments. They also tended to rationalize that because there were low rates of HIV/AIDS in the region where they lived, they did not have to protect themselves against it.

Ironically, people aren't any safer in FWBRs. In fact, according to an article published in *Communication Research* by Morr and Mongeau in 2004, people actually report being more careful when engaging in

Molly could improve by elaborating on this "dating" main point. Perhaps she assumed her listeners already know what a dating relationship is.

Molly attempts to draw her listeners back in by offering an appropriate listener relevance link that proposes why her listeners ought to want to know about the physical risks.

Molly's decision to include a personal testimonial appeals to the feelings of listeners via a rhetorical appeal to pathos.

Some of Molly's listeners might find this fact startling, which will keep their interest focused on learning more.

sexual intercourse with unknown or lesser known individuals than with people they already know. Just because you know someone as a "friend" does not mean you know what they are doing sexually. FWBRs, by their very nature, are not meant to be exclusive, so while you're sleeping with your friend, he or she may also have other partners who, by association, you are also sleeping with. And even if you are both monogamous during your relationship, unless you are both tested prior to having sex, you are still at risk. In hookups and in FWBRs, the emphasis is on each partner's personal needs for sex and physical satisfaction, so the partner is an "insignificant other."

Because partners involved in hookups and FWBRs are less likely to practice safe sex, the likelihood of an unplanned pregnancy also increases. Listen to the experience of a woman who posted her story on Yahoo! Answers:

> I was with this guy for a very short time. It pretty much ended up being a one-night stand, even though we texted a little afterwards. When I found out I was pregnant, I decided to tell him, especially since I didn't know what I was going to do yet. But whatever I was going to do was part of his responsibility (i.e., bills for an abortion, child support, or choosing of an adoptive family). When I told him, he just begged me to get an abortion over and over until I finally agreed and told him I had gotten the abortion to get him to stop texting me every five seconds and begging while I could get some quiet time to figure out what I really wanted to do.

Notice, guys, it was what *she* wanted to do. A man who fathers a hookup child is legally responsible for supporting that child until it is an adult. You have no say—it is her body and her decision. So, in addition to your college loans, you may have a significant financial responsibility for the next 18 years. And every time you get a raise, your child gets part of it. It's the risk you take. And if you're morally or religiously opposed to abortion? Tough. Her body, her decision. You can try to change her mind. But if she decides on abortion there is nothing you can do. And remember, even when condoms are used, they are only 95 percent effective as a contraceptive. Think about it.

While unintended pregnancy is a risk in any sexual relationship, it stands to reason that people who are dating—who have built some degree of respect and intimacy—are more likely to be equipped to come to a mutual understanding about the woman's choice and to adjust to co-parenting tasks, even if they choose to end their romantic relationship.

Molly again uses personal testimony to appeal to pathos in her speech.

Offering this listener relevance link helps males in Molly's audience see how the story of one person's pregnancy relates to them as well.

While physical risks are inherent in any sexual relationship, dating is physically healthier than either hooking up or engaging in an FWBR. Not only do hookups and FWBRs put you at more risk physically, but they are also more likely to do psychological damage. Both hooking up and FWB create psychological distress.

How many of you know someone who says they feel more confident and have higher self-esteem following a hookup? After sleeping with their best friend? Not many, right? More often, we listen to our friends express feelings of guilt, shame, and embarrassment. People, it's called a "walk of shame" for a reason. People who hook up have lower self-esteem, as well as greater depression and feelings of guilt than those who don't. In their 2006 article "No Strings Attached: The Nature of Casual Sex in College Students," published in *The Journal of Sex Research*, Grello, Welsh, and Harper report that women who engage in hooking up experience more loss of self-esteem and depression than men—it is not clear whether depression leads to casual sexual behavior or casual sexual behavior leads to depression. Not only that, women who engage in casual sex experience feelings of good old-fashioned guilt. Men, however, don't necessarily feel guilty for hooking up with strangers, but do feel guilty if they get drunk and hook up with a friend.

While breaking up a dating relationship can also lead to depression, research has found that while the first breakup of a first dating relationship can lead to depression, subsequent breakups are unlikely to do so. The first act of breaking up seems to "inoculate" us, probably because we figure that there is life after a breakup. The opposite seems to be true in more casual sexual relationships. The more you do it, the more guilty and depressed you become. Because of the many negative physical and psychological consequences of hooking up and friends-with-benefits relationships, dating tends to produce more satisfying relationships in the end.

Finally, hooking up and FWBRs lead to less satisfying relationships than dating. In a hookup, ideally neither partner wants or expects anything other than sexual satisfaction. Did you know that, according to that 2006 article by Grello, Welsh, and Harper, half of all college students who engage in sexual intercourse during a hook up never see the other person again? Not only that, 18 percent of women reported in that same study that they consider a hookup to be a stepping-stone toward developing a romantic relationship.

In the ideal FWBR, two friends simply become "sex" or "f...ing" buddies without damaging the friendship. But, according to that famous philosopher, Harry Burns in the 1989 movie *When Harry Met*

One thing Molly does extremely well throughout her speech is provide transitions. With each transition, she uses inclusive "we" language, which enhances a conversational style and helps listeners easily follow along.

Again, Molly uses rhetorical questions in her listener relevance link to keep listeners focused on how this message is important to them.

Here Molly failed to offer an oral citation for the Sprecher research. She missed an opportunity here to bolster her ethos, and she violated the ethic of honesty because failing to cite a source is considered plagiarism.

Citing a quotation from popular culture—in this case the movie When Harry Met Sally— can be an effective strategy for maintaining listener attention, particularly when giving a heavy speech like this one.

Sally, "Men and women can never be friends because the sex part always gets in the way." Was Harry wrong? Well, as it turns out, yes and no.

In their 2010 study published in the *Journal of Sex Research*, Lehmiller and his collegues found yes, and I quote:

> Sex was a more common motivation for men to FWB relationships, whereas emotional connection was a more common motivation for women. In addition, men were more likely to hope that the relationship stays the same over time, whereas women expressed more desire for change into either a full-fledged romance or a basic friendship.

This is understandable when you consider the biology of sex. According to sex therapist Dr. Ian Kerner, speaking on the *Today Show* in 2007:

> During sex, women produce lots of oxytocin, a hormone that stimulates a strong emotional connection. As a result, women are more emotionally integrated when it comes to sex. That's why casual sex and hookups often backfire for lots of women. Guys produce little to no oxytocin, and can easily have sex without any sense of emotional connection. It's sex with no emotional strings attached.

One of the inherent problems in FWBRs is the ambiguity partners can feel about what they can expect. Euphoria posted this to the sex forum on womens-health.com:

> We have a very good relationship as friends; we're very close. We've been 'talking' since November, and one night I slept over at his house and it just happened. The thing that bothers me is that he didn't kiss me in the morning and didn't talk to me until the next night. And on New Year's Eve I also slept over his house, along with other people, and I was probably setting myself up for it cause it happened again. I had left early that morning, around eight, and my friend had told me later on that day that he came into the room she was sleeping in and practically woke her up to kiss her. We did agree to be friends with benefits, but I meant that I'm the only one he should be doing it with. Should I say something to him, or do I have no right since we're FWB?

As I was researching this issue, I came upon an article by Marilyn Murphy on the AskMen.com website that talked about the pros and cons of FWBRs. What I found most interesting was that this article had 139 posts reacting to it. And when I analyzed these posts, 75 percent of them talked about how an FWBR that either the poster or a friend of the poster had been in actually produced problems stemming from one partner wanting the relationship to evolve into something more serious.

Molly's speech tends to rely heavily on academic journal articles. Doing so is fine, but interjecting a few contemporary sources like this one keeps the speech from becoming too academic at the expense of intelligibility and conversationality.

Again, sources like this one—as long as they are only peppered throughout the speech—make it real and potentially more relevant to her audience.

But no, Harry wasn't right in one sense. Lehmiller, VanderDrift, and Kelly, in their 2010 article in the *Journal of Sex Research*, also unexpectedly found that both men and women were ultimately more committed to the friendship than to the sexual aspect of the relationship.

Of course, not all dating relationships lead to "happily ever after" either. However, dating leads to more satisfactory relationships since, if successful, it leads to both intimacy and safe sexual fulfillment. It should come as no surprise that it's the preferred type of relationship of both men and women. In a national survey of over 1,000 college women by Glenn and Marquardt that was published in 2001, 83 percent of them agreed with the statement "Being married is very important to me." And 63 percent agreed with the statement "I would like to meet my future husband/wife in college." Yet 50 percent of the women sampled had had fewer than two dates since starting college. Caroline Bradshaw and her colleagues reported in her 2010 study that 87 percent of women, and even 64 percent of men, indicated a preference for dating over hooking up, particularly when they might be interested in a long-term relationship. As "Bad Reputation" put it in his online post, "There are girls you date and girls you have sex with." So I ask you, ladies, who do you want to be?

Based on analysis, I'm sure you can see that dating, while scary and angst ridden, is still a better choice than hooking up or having an FWBR. Both hookups and FWBRs have more physical and psychological risks than dating relationships.

So, before you go out this weekend, get smashed, and find yourself looking for love in all the wrong places, consider giving that someone you've had your eye on a call and see if you can make a date for a movie, or concert, or just a cup of coffee. While it might not lead to a romantic relationship, who knows—it just might.

Molly could have easily left this statement out, because it contradicts the point she is trying to make. However, including it demonstrates the ethic of fairness.

This survey of both women and men is particularly compelling because it demonstrates not only that research suggests dating is preferred over hooking up or FWBRs, but also that young people themselves prefer dating for initiating long-term relationships.

Molly does a nice job of restating her proposition and providing a clincher that ties back nicely to the opening scenarios.

problem-solution
a persuasive organizational pattern that reveals details about a problem and poses solutions to it

problem-cause-solution
a form of persuasive organization that examines a problem, its cause(s), and solutions designed to eliminate or alleviate the underlying cause(s)

Organizational Frameworks for Speeches to Actuate

Implicit in speeches to actuate is the assumption that there is a problem that audience members can help solve by taking certain actions. As a result, most actuation persuasive speeches follow one of three organizational frameworks: problem-solution, problem-cause-solution, and the motivated sequence.

Problem-Solution

A problem-solution framework explains the nature of a problem and proposes a solution. A problem-solution pattern can be used with any persuasive speech, but it is particularly useful when listeners may be unaware of the problem or how they personally can work toward a solution. A speech to actuate organized in this way usually has three main points. The first examines the problem, the second presents the solution(s), and the third suggests what action the listener should take.

To convince the audience that there is a problem, you will need to explore the breadth and depth of the issue, as well as provide listener relevance links. You provide breadth by showing the scope or scale of the problem—for example, giving the number of people it affects and proving upward trends over time, including forecasted trends if the problem is not solved. You might provide depth by showing the gravity of the problem. Both breadth and depth may be described through stories and startling statistics.

When you describe the solution, you should be detailed enough for the audience to understand how and why it will solve the problem. The call to action should provide your audience with specific steps that they ought to take to help implement the solution(s).

A problem-solution organization for a speech on reducing gun violence might look like this:

I. *Gun-related violence is a serious problem that affects us all.* (statement of the problem)
   A. *Gun-related violence occurs in urban, suburban, and rural communities and across the country.* (breadth)
      1. *Most recent law enforcement statistics on gun-related violence in the United States.*
      2. *Most recent law enforcement statistics on gun violence in Arizona.*
      3. *An example of gun violence right here in Tempe.* (listener relevance link)
   B. *The consequences of gun violence include injury, disability, and death.* (depth)
      1. *Statistics on gun-related injuries.*
      2. *Story of gun-related disability in a person like the audience members.*
      3. *Statistics on gun-related deaths.*
      4. *Story of local family who died in gun-related murder-suicide.*

II. *Our state legislatures and the U.S. Congress should pass measures to reduce gun violence.* (solution)
   A. *Tighten gun ownership requirements.*
      1. *Require background checks at all sales points.*
         a. *Both public and private sales.*
         b. *Checks for both criminal background and evidence of mental illness.*
      2. *Require "proof of competence" testing for gun licensure like vehicle licensure.*
         a. *Evidence of gun safety procedure knowledge.*
         b. *Evidence of marksmanship.*
      3. *Require periodic relicensing of both guns and owners.*
   B. *Increase criminal penalties associated with violation of gun laws.*

III. *You should e-mail, write, or call your state and national representatives to urge them to support measures to reduce gun violence.* (call to action)
   A. *Bills currently pending in the state legislature.*
   B. *Bills currently pending in Congress.*

IMPLICIT IN SPEECHES TO ACTUATE IS THE ASSUMPTION THAT THERE IS A PROBLEM THAT AUDIENCE MEMBERS CAN HELP SOLVE BY TAKING CERTAIN ACTIONS.

Problem-Cause-Solution

The **problem-cause-solution** framework is similar to problem-solution but differs from it by adding a main point that reveals the causes of the problem and then proposes a solution designed to alleviate those causes. This pattern is particularly useful for addressing seemingly intractable problems that have been dealt with unsuccessfully in the past as a result of treating symptoms rather than underlying causes. In speeches to actuate, the problem-cause-solution main points are followed by a fourth main point that calls the audience to a specific action.

Margaret, who lived near a landfill and was concerned about waste overflow, wanted to convince her audience that they should recycle their garbage. As she researched the problem of overflowing landfills, she noticed that recycling was catching on nationally and that, according to 2005 statistics, 32 percent of solid waste was recycled, compared with 54 percent that went into landfills and 13 percent that was burned.[5] She also read articles about communities whose recycling rates were higher than average and concluded that the key to increasing recycling was to make it easy and convenient. So she developed a problem-cause-solution speech to actuate that looked like this:

I. *Solid waste disposal is a problem. (problem)*
   A. *Landfills are overflowing.*
   B. *Recycling, while growing, is not widespread in our community.*
II. *Causes for recycling resistance. (causes)*
   A. *Confusion about proper recycling procedures.*
   B. *Lack of recycling containers.*
   C. *Infrequent recycling pickups.*
   D. *Inconvenience.*
III. *Solutions to overcome recycling resistance. (solutions)*
   A. *Promotional mailers and periodic reminders mailed to each residence to clarify and reinforce local recycling procedures and to communicate changes in local recycling programs.*
   B. *Grade-appropriate educational material used in local classrooms.*
   C. *Free recycling containers delivered to each residential address with additional containers available at convenient locations.*
   D. *Increased frequency of pickups planned for and implemented as recycling becomes more pervasive.*

© ISTOCKPHOTO.COM/NATHAN GLEAVE

   E. *No need to sort recyclables in the home.*
IV. *Audience actions. (call to action)*
   A. *Call your local waste management agency and inquire about recycling policies and procedures.*
   B. *Procure appropriate recycling containers for use in your home.*
      1. *Curbside containers.*
      2. *Containers for in-home use.*
   C. *Educate all family members on proper recycling techniques.*
   D. *Contact local school board members and urge recycling curriculum for your local school district.*

motivated sequence
a form of persuasive organization that combines a problem-solution pattern with explicit appeals designed to motivate the audience

Motivated Sequence

The **motivated sequence** is an organizational framework that combines a problem-solution pattern with explicit appeals designed to motivate the audience. Allan Monroe articulated the motivated sequence as a distinct speech pattern in the 1930s. In the motivated sequence, the normal introduction, body, and conclusion are unified into a five-step sequence described as follows:

1. **The attention step.** The attention step replaces the traditional introduction. Like an introduction, it should begin with a statement that can generate attention. Startling statements, rhetorical questions, quotations, or short narratives will all serve this purpose. Then, you should pique the audience's curiosity by talking about the value of what you are going to say. During the attention step, you might also refer to the knowledge and experiences you have that build your credibility. Finally, just as in a traditional introduction, you will want to clearly identify your purpose stated as a proposition to preview the rest of the speech.

2. **The need step.** The need step explores the nature of the problem that gives rise to the need for change. In it, you will point out

the conditions that are unsatisfactory using statistics, examples, and expert opinion to bolster your argument. Then, you will describe the implications or ramifications of this problem. What is happening because the condition is allowed to continue? Finally, you will allude to how the audience might be instrumental in changing the situation.

3. **The satisfaction step.** Having developed a rational argument that there is a need for change, in the satisfaction step you explain your solution to the problem. In this step, you will show, point by point, how what you are proposing will satisfy each of the needs that you articulated in the previous step. If there are other places where your proposal has been tried successfully, you will want to mention these. In addition, you will want to present and refute any objections to the proposal that you can anticipate.

4. **The visualization step.** In the visualization step, you ask your audience to imagine what will happen if your proposal is implemented and is successful. Alternatively, you can ask the audience to visualize how things will be if your proposal is not adopted, or you can do both and have the audience experience the comparison. Obviously, the more descriptive and graphic your visualization step, the more likely it is to have an impact on the audience.

5. **The action appeal step.** In this final step, you might quickly review your main ideas, but then you will emphasize the specific action(s) you advocate. You will also state or restate your own commitment and action that you have taken. You also offer a direct call to action indicating what your listeners are to do and how. Finally, you will want to conclude with a quote, story, or other element that is emotionally compelling.

Let's look at a short outline of what a speech asking the audience to support a school tax levy would look like if it were organized using the motivated sequence.

Proposition: *I want the audience to vote in favor of the school tax levy that is on the ballot in November.*

I. **Attention step**
   A. *Comparisons of worldwide test scores in math and science show the United States continues to lose ground.*
   B. *I've made an extensive study of this problem, and today I'm going to tell you how you can help stop this decline.*
   C. *I'll start by describing the problem; then, I will tell you what you should do and why it will help.*

II. **Need step:** *The local schools are underfunded.*
   A. *The current funding is insufficient and has resulted in program cuts.*
   B. *Qualified teachers leave because of stagnant wages.*
   C. *A threatened state takeover of local schools would lead to more bureaucracy and less learning.*

III. **Satisfaction step:** *The proposed local tax levy is large enough to solve these problems.*
   A. *Programs will be restored.*
   B. *Qualified teachers will be compensated so they will stay.*
   C. *We will retain local control.*
   D. *You'll once again have pride in your community.*

IV. **Visualization step:** *Imagine the best, and imagine the worst.*
   A. *What it will be like if we pass the levy. How will you feel?*
   B. *What it will be like if we don't. How will you feel?*

V. **Action appeal step:** *Vote "yes" for the levy in November.*
   A. *If you want to see schools improve and the United States catch up to the rest of the world, vote for the levy.*
   B. *Come join me. I'm registered, I'm ready, I'm voting for the levy.*
   C. *It costs to be the best in the world. Where there is pain, there is gain.*
   D. *They say it takes a village, so you can make a difference.*

Speech to Actuate Evaluation Checklist

_____ **1.** Was the introduction effective in creating interest, involving the audience in the speech, and previewing the main points?

_____ **2.** Was the specific goal clear and phrased as a proposition?

_____ **3.** Was the speech organized into an appropriate actuation persuasive speech framework?

_____ Problem-solution _____ Problem-cause-solution _____ Motivated sequence

_____ **4.** Did the speaker use logos effectively?

_____ Strong evidence? _____ Reasoning linked to claims? _____ Fallacies?

_____ **5.** Did the speaker use ethos effectively?

_____ Establish expertise? _____ Demonstrate trustworthiness? _____ Convey goodwill?

_____ **6.** Did the speaker use pathos effectively?

Appeal to negative emotions? If so, check all that were tapped:
_____ fear _____ guilt _____ anger _____ shame _____ sadness

Appeal to positive emotions? If so, check all that were tapped:
_____ happiness/joy _____ pride _____ relief _____ hope _____ compassion

Were the appeals _____ very effective, _____ somewhat effective, or _____ ineffective?

_____ **7.** Was the language appropriate, accurate, clear, and vivid?

_____ **8.** Was the use of voice intelligible, conversational, expressive, and convincing?

_____ **9.** Was the use of body poised and expressive?

_____ **10.** Did the speaker offer a compelling call to action?

Based on these criteria, evaluate the speech as (check one):

_____ excellent _____ good _____ average _____ fair _____ poor

You can use the CourseMate for SPEAK at www.cengagebrain.com to access this checklist, complete it online and compare your feedback to that of the authors, or print a copy to use in class.

SAMPLE ACTUATION PERSUASIVE SPEECH

This section presents a sample speech to actuate given by a student, including an adaptation plan, an outline, and a transcript.

Together, We Can Stop Cyber-Bullying

By Adam Parrish[6]

Read the speech adaptation plan, outline, and transcript of a speech given by Adam Parrish in an introductory speaking course. You can access a video clip of Adam's speech through the Chapter 14 resources of the CourseMate for SPEAK at www.cengagebrain.com. You can also use your CourseMate to identify some of the strengths of Adam's speech by preparing an evaluation checklist and an analysis. You can then compare your answers with those of the authors.

Adaptation Plan

1. **Target audience initial attitude and background knowledge.** My audience is composed of traditional-aged college students with varying majors and classes. Most are from middle-class backgrounds. The initial attitude about bullying for most will be to agree with me already that it's a bad thing. So I will try to get them to take action. My perception is that my audience knows about cyber-bullying but not the nuances of it.

2. **Organizational framework.** I will organize my speech using a problem-cause-solution framework because my audience already agrees that bullying is bad but may not know what they can and should do to help stop it.

3. **Arguments (logos).** I will demonstrate how widespread (breadth) and harmful (depth of effects) cyber-bullying is and why it persists (causes). Once I've convinced my audience, I will propose solutions that must be taken and cite specifically what we must do to help stop this horrible practice.

4. **Building competence, credibility, and good character (ethos).** I will use credible sources to support my claims and cite them using oral footnotes. I will also offer personal stories to create goodwill.

5. **Creating and maintaining interest (pathos).** I will involve my audience by appealing to several emotions, including guilt, sadness, relief, hope, and compassion.

Outline

General goal: To persuade

Specific goal: To convince my audience to take action to help stop cyber-bullying.

Introduction

Attention getter

I. "I'll miss just being around her." "I didn't want to believe it." "It's such a sad thing." These quotes are from the friends and family of 15-year-old Phoebe Prince, who, on January 14, 2010, committed suicide by hanging herself. Why did this senseless act occur? The answer is simple: Phoebe Prince was bullied to death.

Listener relevance link

II. Many of us know someone who has been bullied in school. Perhaps they were teased in the parking lot or in the locker room. In the past, bullying occurred primarily in and around schools. However, with the advent of new communication technologies such as cell phones with text messaging capability, instant messaging, e-mails, blogs, and social networking sites, bullies can now follow their victims anywhere, even into their own bedrooms. Using electronic communications to tease, harass, threaten, and intimidate another person is called cyber-bullying.

Speaker credibility

III. As a tutor and mentor to young students, I have witnessed cyber-bullying firsthand, and by examining current research, I believe I understand the problem, its causes, and how we can help end cyber-bullying.

Thesis statement (stated as a preview)

IV. Cyber-bullying is a devastating form of abuse that must be confronted and stopped.

Preview

V. Today, we will examine the widespread and harmful nature of cyber-bullying, discover how and why it persists, and propose some simple solutions that we must engage in to thwart cyber-bullies and comfort their victims.

Transition

Let's begin by tackling the problem head on.

Body

I. Cyber-bullying is a pervasive and dangerous behavior.

The problem

Many of us have read rude, insensitive, or nasty statements posted about us or someone we care about on social networking sites like MySpace and Facebook. Whether or not those comments were actually intended to hurt another person's feelings, they are perfect examples of cyber-bullying.

Listener relevance link

A. Cyber-bullying takes place all over the world through a wide array of electronic media.

  1. According to an article in the winter 2005 edition of *Reclaiming Children and Youth*, 57 percent of American middle-school students have experienced instances of cyber-bullying ranging from hurtful comments to threats of physical violence (Keith & Martin, 2005).

  2. Females are just as likely as males to engage in cyber-bullying, although women are 10 percent more likely to be victimized (Li, 2007).

  3. While the number of students who are targets of cyber-bullies decreases as students age, data from the Youth Internet Safety Survey indicate that the instances of American high school students being cyber-bullied increased nearly 50 percent from 2000 to 2005 (Ybarra, Mitchell, Wolak, & Finkelhor, 2006).

  4. Quing Li (2007), a researcher of computer-mediated communication, noted that Internet and cell-phone technologies have been used by bullies to harass, torment, and threaten young people in North America, Europe, and Asia.

  5. A particularly disturbing incident occurred in Dallas, Texas, where an overweight student with multiple sclerosis was targeted on a school's social networking page. One message read, "I guess I'll have to wait until you kill yourself, which I hope is not long from now, or I'll have to wait until your disease kills you" (Keith & Martin, 2005, p. 226).

Clearly, cyber-bullying is a widespread problem. What is most disturbing about cyber-bullying, however, is its effects upon victims, bystanders, and perhaps even upon the bullies themselves.

Transition

B. Cyber-bullying can lead to traumatic physical and psychological injuries upon its victims.

  1. According to a 2007 article in the *Journal of Adolescent Health*, 36 percent of the victims of cyber-bullies are also harassed by their attackers in school (Ybarra, Diener-West, & Leaf, 2007).

  2. For example, the Dallas student with MS had eggs thrown at her car and a bottle of acid thrown at her house (Keith & Martin, 2005).

  3. Ybarra et al. (2007) reported that victims of cyber-bullying experience such severe emotional distress that they often exhibit behavioral problems such as poor grades, skipping school, and receiving detentions and suspensions.

  4. Smith, Mahdavi, Carvalho, Fisher, Russel, and Tipett (2008) suggested that even a few instances of cyber-bullying can have these long-lasting and heartbreaking results.

  5. What is even more alarming is that victims of cyber-bullying are significantly more likely to carry weapons to school as a result of feeling threatened (Ybarra et al., 2007). Obviously, this could lead to violent, and perhaps even deadly, outcomes for bullies, victims, and even bystanders.

Now that we realize the devastating nature, scope, and effects of cyber-bullying, let's look at its causes.

Transition

II. Cyber-bullying is perpetuated because victims and bystanders do not report their abusers to authorities.

Think back to a time when you may have seen a friend or loved one being harassed online. Did you report the bully to the network administrator or other authorities? Did you console the victim? I know I didn't. If you are like me, we may unknowingly be enabling future instances of cyber-bullying.

A. Cyber-bullies are cowards who attack their victims anonymously.

1. Ybarra et al. (2007) discovered that 13 percent of cyber-bullying victims did not know who was tormenting them.

2. This is an important statistic because, as Keith and Martin (2005) point out, traditional bullying takes place face to face and often ends when students leave school. However, today, students are subjected to bullying in their own homes.

3. Perhaps the anonymous nature of cyber-attacks partially explains why Li (2007) found that nearly 76 percent of victims of cyber-bullying and 75 percent of bystanders never reported instances of bullying to adults.

B. Victims and bystanders who do not report attacks from cyber-bullies can unintentionally enable bullies.

1. According to De Nies, Donaldson, and Netter of ABCNews.com (2010), several of Phoebe Prince's classmates were aware that she was being harassed but did not inform the school's administration.

2. Li (2007) suggested that victims and bystanders often do not believe that adults will actually intervene to stop cyber-bullying.

3. However, ABCNews.com (De Nies, Donaldson, & Netter, 2010) reports that 41 states have laws against bullying in schools, and 23 of those states target cyber-bullying specifically.

Now that we realize that victims of cyber-bullies desperately need the help of witnesses and bystanders to report their attacks, we should arm ourselves with the information necessary to provide that assistance.

III. Cyber-bullying must be confronted on national, local, and personal levels.

Think about the next time you see a friend or loved one being tormented or harassed online. What would you be willing to do to help?

A. There should be a comprehensive national law confronting cyber-bullying in schools. Certain statutes currently in state laws should be amalgamated to create the strongest protections for victims and the most effective punishments for bullies as possible.

1. According to Limber and Small's (2003) article titled *State Laws and Policies to Address Bullying in Schools*, Georgia law requires faculty and staff to be trained on the nature of bullying and what actions to take if they see students being bullied.

2. Furthermore, Connecticut law *requires* school employees to report bullying as part of their hiring contract (Limber & Small, 2003). Washington takes this a step further by protecting employees from any legal action if a reported bully is proven to be innocent (Limber & Small, 2003).

3. When it comes to protecting victims, West Virginia law demands that schools must ensure that a bullied student does not receive additional abuse at the hands of his or her bully (Limber & Small, 2003).

4. Legislating punishment for bullies is difficult. As Limber and Small (2003) noted, zero-tolerance polices often perpetuate violence because at-risk youth (bullies) are removed from all of the benefits of school, which might help make them less abusive.

5. A comprehensive anti-cyber-bullying law should incorporate the best aspects of these state laws and find a way to punish bullies that is both punitive and has the ability to rehabilitate abusers.

B. Local communities must organize and mobilize to attack the problem of cyber-bullying.

    1. According to Greene (2006), communities need to support bullying prevention programs by conducting a school-based bullying survey for individual school districts. We can't know how to best protect victims in our community without knowing how they are affected by the problem.

    2. It is critical to know this information. As Greene noted, only 3 percent of teachers in the United States perceive bullying to be a problem in their schools (Greene, 2006).

    3. Local school districts should create a Coordinating Committee made up of "administrators, teachers, students, parents, school staff, and community partners" to gather bullying data and rally support to confront the problem (Greene, 2006, p. 73).

    4. Even if your local school district is unable or unwilling to mobilize behind this dire cause, there are some important actions you can take personally to safeguard those you love against cyber-bullying.

C. Take note of these warning signs that might indicate a friend or loved one is a victim of a cyber-bully.

    1. Victims of cyber-bullies often use electronic communication more frequently than do people who are not being bullied.

    2. Victims of cyber-bullies have mood swings and difficulty sleeping (Keith & Martin, 2005).

    3. Victims of cyber-bullies seem depressed and/or become anxious (Keith & Martin, 2005).

    4. Victims of cyber-bullies become withdrawn from social activities and fall behind in scholastic responsibilities (Keith & Martin, 2005).

D. If you see a friend or loved one exhibiting any of these signs, I implore you not to ignore them. Rather take action. Get involved. Do something to stop it.

    1. According to Raskauskas and Stoltz (2007), witnesses of cyber-bullying should inform victims to take the attacks seriously, especially if the bullies threaten violence.

    2. Tell victims to report their attacks to police or other authority figures (Raskauskas & Stoltz, 2007).

    3. Tell victims to block harmful messages by blocking e-mail accounts and cell phone numbers (Raskauskas & Stoltz, 2007).

    4. Tell victims to save copies of attacks and provide them to authorities (Raskauskas & Stoltz, 2007).

    5. If you personally know the bully and feel safe confronting him or her, do so! As Raskauskas and Stoltz (2007) noted, bullies will often back down when confronted by peers.

    6. By being a good friend and by giving good advice, you can help a victim report his or her attacks from cyber-bullies and take a major step toward eliminating this horrendous problem.

So, you see, we are not helpless to stop the cyber-bulling problem as long as we make the choice NOT to ignore it.

Transition

Conclusion

Thesis restatement

Main point summary

Call to action and clincher

I. Cyber-bullying is a devastating form of abuse that must be reported to authorities.

II. Cyber-bullying is a worldwide problem perpetuated by the silence of both victims and bystanders. By paying attention to certain warning signs, we can empower ourselves to console victims and report their abusers.

III. Today, I implore you to do your part to help stop cyber-bullying. I know that you agree that stopping cyber-bullying must be a priority. First, although other states have cyber-bullying laws in place, ours does not. So I'm asking you to sign this petition that I will forward to our district's state legislators. We need to make our voices heard that we want specific laws passed to stop this horrific practice and to punish those caught doing it. Second, I'm also asking you to be vigilant in noticing signs of cyber-bullying and then taking action. Look for signs that your friend, brother, sister, cousin, boyfriend, girlfriend, or loved one might be a victim of cyber-bullying and then get involved to help stop it! Phoebe Prince showed the warning signs, and she did not deserve to die so senselessly. None of us would ever want to say, "I'll miss just being around her," "I didn't want to believe it," "It's such a sad thing" about our own friends or family members. We must work to ensure that victims are supported and bullies are confronted nationally, locally, and personally. I know that, if we stand together and refuse to be silent, we can and will stop cyber-bullying.

References

De Nies, Y., Donaldson, S., & Netter, S. (2010). Mean girls: Cyberbullying blamed for teen suicides. *ABCNews.com*. Retrieved from http://abcnews.go.com/GMA/Parenting/girls-teen-suicide-calls-attention-cyberbullying/story?id=9685026

Greene, M. B. (2006). Bullying in schools: A plea for measure of human rights. *Journal of Social Issues, 62*(1), 63–79.

Keith, S., & Martin, M. (2005). Cyber-bullying: Creating a culture of respect in the cyber world. *Reclaiming Children and Youth, 13*(4), 224–228.

Li, Q. (2007). New bottle of old wine: A research of cyberbullying in schools. *Computers in Human Behavior, 23*, 1777–1791.

Limber, S. P., & Small, M. A. (2003). State laws and policies to address bullying in schools. *School Psychology Review, 32*(3), 445–455.

Raskauskas, J., & Stoltz, A. D. (2007). Involvement in traditional and electronic bullying among adolescents. *Developmental Psychology, 43*(3), 564–575.

Smith, P. K., Mahdavi, J., Carvalho, M., Fisher, S., Russel, S., & Tippett, N. (2008). Cyberbullying: Its nature and impact in secondary school pupils. *Journal of Child Psychology and Psychiatry, 49*(4), 374–385.

Ybarra, M. L., Diener-West, M., & Leaf, P. J. (2007). Examining the overlap in internet harassment and school bullying: Implications for school intervention. *Journal of Adolescent Health, 41*, S42–S50.

Ybarra, M. L., Mitchell, K. J., Wolak, J., & Finkelhor, D. (2006). Examining characteristics and associated distress related to Internet harassment: Findings from the second Youth Internet Safety Survey. *Pediatrics, 118*, 1169–1177.

Speech and Analysis

"I'll miss just being around her." "I didn't want to believe it." "It's such a sad thing." These quotes are from the friends and family of 15-year-old Phoebe Prince, who, on January 14, 2010, committed suicide by hanging herself. Why did this senseless act occur? The answer is simple… Phoebe Prince was bullied to death.

Many of us know someone who has been bullied in school. Perhaps they were teased in the parking lot or in the locker room. In the past, bullying occurred primarily in school. However, with the advent of new communication technologies such as cell phones, text messaging, instant messaging, blogs, and social networking sites, bullies can now follow and terrorize their victims anywhere, even into their own bedrooms. Using electronic communications to tease, harass, threaten, and intimidate another person is called cyber-bullying.

As a tutor and mentor to young students, I have witnessed cyber-bullying firsthand, and by examining current research, I believe I understand the problem, its causes, and how we can help end cyber-bullying. What I know for sure is that cyber-bullying is a devastating form of abuse that must be confronted on national, local, and personal levels.

Today, we will examine the widespread and harmful nature of cyber-bulling, uncover how and why it persists, and pinpoint some simple solutions we must begin to enact in order to thwart cyber-bullies and comfort their victims. Let's begin by tackling the problem head on.

Many of us have read rude, insensitive, or nasty statements posted about us or someone we care about on social networking sites like MySpace and Facebook. Well, whether or not those comments were actually intended to hurt another person's feelings, if they did hurt their feelings, then they are perfect examples of cyber-bullying.

Cyber-bullying is a pervasive and dangerous behavior. It takes place all over the world and through a wide array of electronic media. According to Keith and Martin's article in the winter 2005 edition of *Reclaiming Children and Youth,* 57 percent of American middle-school students had experienced instances of cyber-bullying ranging from hurtful comments to threats of physical violence. Quing Li's article published in the journal *Computers in Human Behavior* noted that cyber-bullying is not gender biased. According to Li, females are just as likely as males to engage in cyber-bullying, although women are 10 percent more likely to be victimized.

While the number of students who are targets of cyber-bullies decreases as students age, data from the *Youth Internet Safety Survey* indicates that the

Adam uses quotes from family and friends of cyber-bullying victim Phoebe Prince to get attention and lead into his proposition.

Here Adam further entices his listeners to pay attention by offering listener relevance that we all can relate to.

Using the vivid term "terrorize," Adam appeals to negative emotions (pathos).

Adam begins to establish ethos by mentioning why he has credibility about this topic. Mentioning that he is a tutor and mentor also conveys goodwill. Listeners are likely to think he must have good character if he volunteers as a tutor and mentor.

Adam does a nice job of previewing his problem-cause-solution organizational framework, but his thesis statement phrased as a proposition is somewhat lost and could be made more overtly here.

Again, Adam's use of a listener relevance helps keep listeners tuned in and interested in hearing more.

Here Adam bolsters his ethos (and avoids plagiarism) by citing an oral footnote for his statistics.

Although this statistic is interesting, it would be more compelling to know more recent statistics and the trends since 2005.

instances of American high school students being cyber-bullied had increased nearly 50 percent from 2000 to 2005. The problem does not exist in the United States alone.

Li noted that Internet and cell-phone technologies have been used by bullies to harass, torment, and threaten young people in North America, Europe, and Asia. However, some of the most horrific attacks happen right here at home.

Notice Adam's word choices (harass, torment, threaten, horrific) to enhance pathos.

According to Keith and Martin, a particularly disturbing incident occurred in Dallas, Texas, where an overweight student with multiple sclerosis was targeted on a school's social networking page. One message read, "I guess I'll have to wait until you kill yourself which I hope is not long from now, or I'll have to wait until your disease kills you." Clearly, the cyber-bullying is a worldwide and perverse phenomenon. What is most disturbing about cyber-bullying is its effects upon victims, bystanders, and perhaps even upon bullies themselves.

This example provides an emotional appeal by offering a real example of a real victim in Dallas, Texas.

Cyber-bullying can lead to physical and psychological injuries upon its victims. According to a 2007 article in the *Journal of Adolescent Health,* Ybarra and colleagues noted that 36 percent of the victims of cyber-bullies are also harassed by their attackers in school. For example, the Dallas student with MS had eggs thrown at her car and a bottle of acid thrown at her house.

This vivid example enhances pathos.

Ybarra et al. reported that victims of cyber-bullying experience such severe emotional distress that they often exhibit behavioral problems such as poor grades, skipping school, and receiving detentions and suspensions. Furthermore, Smith et al. suggested that even a few instances of cyber-bullying can have these long-lasting negative effects.

What is even more alarming is that, according to Ybarra and colleagues, victims of cyber-bullying are significantly more likely to carry weapons to school as a result of feeling threatened. Obviously, this could lead to violent outcomes for bullies, victims, and even bystanders.

Now that Adam has established the breadth of the problem as widespread, he moves into a discussion about the depth of the effects it can have on victims.

Now that we have heard about the nature, scope, and effects of cyber-bullying, let's see if we can discover its causes. Let's think back to a time when we may have seen a friend or loved one being harassed online. Did we report the bully to the network administrator or other authorities? Did we console the victim? I know I didn't. If you are like me, we may unknowingly be enabling future instances of cyber-bullying.

Here Adam helps pique listener interest by pointing out how bystanders could also be hurt if we don't do something to stop this form of terrorism.

Cyber-bullying occurs because of the anonymity offered to bullies by cell phone and Internet technologies, as well as the failure of victims and bystanders to report incidents of cyber-bullying. You see, unlike

Notice how Adam's transition verbally ties the point he is finishing (problem) to the next point (causes) clearly using inclusive "we" language. This, too, bolsters a sense of goodwill and uses a conversational style that keeps listeners engaged.

© ISTOCKPHOTO.COM/KYOSHINO / © ISTOCKPHOTO.COM/TRIGGERPHOTO

schoolyard bullies, cyber-bullies can attack their victims anonymously.

Ybarra and colleagues discovered that 13 percent of cyber-bullying victims did not know who was tormenting them. This devastating statistics is important because, as Keith and Martin noted, traditional bullying takes place face to face and often ends when students leave school. However, today, students are subjected to nonstop bullying, even when they are alone in their own homes.

Perhaps the anonymous nature of cyber-attacks partially explains why Li found that nearly 76 percent of victims of cyber-bullying and 75 percent of bystanders never reported instances of bullying to adults. Victims and bystanders who do not report attacks from cyber-bullies can unintentionally enable bullies.

According to De Nies, Donaldson, and Netter of ABCNews.com, several of Phoebe Prince's classmates were aware that she was being harassed but did not inform the school's administration. Li suggested that victims and bystanders often do not believe that adults will actually intervene to stop cyber-bullying. However, ABCNews.com reports that 41 states have laws against bullying in schools, and 23 of those states target cyber-bullying specifically.

Now that we know that victims of cyber-bullies desperately need the help of witnesses and bystanders to report their attacks, we should arm ourselves with the information necessary to provide that assistance. Think about the next time you see a friend or loved one being tormented or harassed online. What would you be willing to do to help?

Again, Adam does a nice job with his transition.

Cyber-bullying must be confronted on national, local, and personal levels. There should be a comprehensive national law confronting cyber-bullying in schools. Certain statutes currently in state laws should be amalgamated to create the strongest protections for victims and the most effective punishments for bullies as possible.

Notice how Adam gets right to the point about needing to take action on a variety of levels to stop this practice.

Adam gives credence to his policy statement by pointing to several states that have already succeeded in creating such laws.

According to Limber and Small's article titled "State Laws and Policies to Address Bullying in Schools," Georgia law requires faculty and staff to be trained on the nature of bullying and what actions to take if they see students being bullied.

Furthermore, Connecticut law *requires* school employees to report bullying as part of their hiring contract. Washington takes this a step further by protecting employees from any legal action if a reported bully is proven to be innocent. When it comes to protecting victims, West Virginia law demands that schools must ensure that a bullied student does not receive additional abuse at the hands of his or her bully.

Legislating punishment for bullies is difficult. As Limber and Small noted, zero-tolerance polices often perpetuate violence because at-risk youth, i.e., bullies, are removed from all of the benefits of school, which might help make them less abusive. A comprehensive anti-cyber-bullying law should incorporate the best aspects of these state laws and find a way to punish bullies that is both punitive and has the ability to rehabilitate abusers. However, for national laws to be effective, local communities need to be supportive.

Local communities must organize and mobilize to attack the problem of cyber-bullying. According to Greene's 2006 article published in the *Journal of Social Issues*, communities need to support bullying prevention programs by conducting a school-based bullying survey for individual school districts. We can't know how to best protect victims in our community without knowing how they are affected by the problem. It is critical to know this information. As Greene noted, only 3 percent of teachers in the United States perceive bullying to be a problem in their schools.

Local school districts should create a Coordinating Committee made up of administrators, teachers, students, parents, school staff, and community partners to gather bullying data and rally support to confront the problem. Even if your local school district is unable or unwilling to mobilize behind this dire cause, there are some important actions you can take personally to safeguard those you love against cyber-bullying.

There are several warning signs that might indicate a friend or loved one is a victim of a cyber-bully. If you see a friend or loved one exhibiting these signs, the decision to get involved can be the difference between life and death.

According to Keith and Martin's article "Cyber-Bullying: Creating a Culture of Respect in a Cyber World," victims of cyber-bullies often use electronic communication more frequently than do people who are not being bullied. Victims of cyber-bullies have mood swings and difficulty sleeping. They seem depressed and/or become anxious. Victims can also become withdrawn from social activities and fall behind in scholastic responsibilities. If you witness your friends or family members exhibiting these symptoms, there are several ways you can help.

According to Raskauskas and Stoltz's 2007 article in *Developmental Psychology*, witnesses of cyber-bullying should inform victims to take the attacks seriously, especially if the bullies threaten violence. You should tell victims to report their attacks to police or other authorities, to block harmful messages by blocking e-mail accounts and cell phone numbers, and to save copies of attacks and provide them to authorities.

Here Adam points to the need for consequences for bullying behavior when it is caught.

Adam offers specific action steps that communities ought to take to help stop cyber-bullying.

Here Adam gets personal, pointing out that each person in the room has an ethical responsibility to help stop cyber-bullying.

Adam could make this statement more compelling by offering a specific example of what one might tell the police, as well as how to install blockers on e-mail and cell phones.

If you personally know the bully and feel safe confronting him or her, do so! As Raskauskas and Stoltz noted, bullies will often back down when confronted by peers. By being a good friend and by giving good advice, you can help a victim report his or her attacks from cyber-bullies and take a major step toward eliminating this horrendous problem. So, you see, we are not helpless to stop the cyber-bulling problem as long as we make the choice NOT to ignore it.

To conclude, cyber-bullying is a devastating form of abuse that must be reported to authorities. Cyber-bullying is a worldwide problem perpetuated by the silence of both victims and bystanders. By paying attention to certain warning signs, we can empower ourselves to console victims and report their abusers.

Here Adam restates his proposition, but it actually could be more comprehensive (beyond just our need to report bullying to authorities).

Today, I'm imploring you to do your part to help stop cyber-bullying. I know that you agree that stopping cyber-bullying must be a priority. First, although other states have cyber-bullying laws in place, ours does not. So I'm asking you to sign this petition that I will forward to our district's state legislators. We need to make our voices heard that we want specific laws passed to stop this horrific practice and to punish those caught doing it.

Adam reminds us of his specific call to action and even asks listeners to sign a petition today. His approach encourages listeners to follow through with his goal—that is, to actuate.

Second, I'm also asking you to be vigilant in noticing signs of cyber-bullying and then taking action. Look for signs that your friend, brother, sister, cousin, boyfriend, girlfriend, or loved one might be a victim of cyber-bullying, and then get involved to help stop it! Phoebe Prince showed the warning signs, and she did not deserve to die so senselessly. None of us would ever want to say, "I'll miss just being around her," "I didn't want to believe it," "It's such a sad thing" about our own friends or family members. We must work to ensure that victims are supported and bullies are confronted nationally, locally, and personally.

Adam does a nice job with his clincher in terms of tying back to the Phoebe story in his attention catcher. Doing so also appeals to emotions (pathos) in a way that should make his speech memorable.

I know that, if we stand together and refuse to be silent, we can and will stop cyber-bullying.

Ethical Guidelines for Persuasive Speeches

Throughout this book, we have discussed the fundamental behaviors of ethical communicators. At this point, we want to look at five ethical guidelines speakers should follow when their specific goal is to convince the audience to believe a certain idea or to move the audience to action.

1. **Ethical persuasive speeches aim to improve the well-being of the audience by advocating the honest belief of the speaker.** If you have reason to believe that the members of the audience will be hurt or disadvantaged if they believe what you say or do what you ask, then you should not give the speech. At times, we can get excited about seeing what we can do as a devil's advocate—that is, argue for a belief or action that is totally counter to

anything we really believe just to stir up discussion. Although this can be fun when we're dealing with a few friends who just enjoy the spirit of debate, in the real world it is unethical for you to give a speech that calls for the audience to believe something that you do not believe. So, for your persuasive speech, phrase a proposition that you enthusiastically endorse.

2. **Ethical persuasive speeches provide choice.** In any speech, you are free to provide the audience with reasoning that encourages them to evaluate what you have said before making up their own minds. Although it is possible to persuade an audience by manipulating their emotions, using smear tactics to attack opposite points of view (or advocates of those points of view), or coercing them with serious threats, it is unethical.

3. **Ethical persuasive speeches use representative supporting information.** Support your persuasive claims with evidence in the form of statistics, expert opinions, and examples. You can probably find a piece of "evidence" to support any claim, but ethical speakers make sure the evidence they cite is representative of all the evidence that might be used. Although you may use an individual item to show that something is possible, you do not want to give the impression that the item is commonplace. It is unethical to misrepresent what a *body* of evidence (as opposed to a single item) would show if all of it were presented to the audience.

4. **Ethical persuasive speeches use emotional appeals to engage the audience in the rational thought process.** Emotional appeals are a legitimate part of a persuasive speech when

they are used to increase the involvement of the audience so that audience members choose the central processing route to listen to, think about, evaluate, and personally decide whether to believe or act. When excessive emotional appeals are used as the basis of persuasion instead of logical reasons, then, although the speech might be effective, it is unethical.

5. **Ethical persuasive speeches honestly present the speaker's credibility.** Because some audience members will process what you say along a peripheral route, using your credibility as the primary factor that determines what they will believe or how they will act, as an ethical speaker you will want to present your expertise and trustworthiness honestly. It is unethical to act as if you know a great deal about a subject when you do not. In fact, most people believe it is unethical to try to convince others of something on which you are not extremely well informed because you may inadvertently misrepresent the arguments and information. Finally, ethical speakers disclose interests that may have inadvertently biased their arguments and may place their interests and those of their audience at odds. You might say, for example, "I think you should know that I work for the Literacy Project as a paid intern, so even though I will do my best to give you the most accurate information possible on this subject, I may not be totally objective."

As you work on your speech, you will want to continually remind yourself of your ethical responsibilities. It's easy to get caught up in trying to build arguments and lose sight of your bigger ethical responsibility to your audience.

Ethical persuasive speeches use emotional appeals to engage the audience in a rational thought process.

Learning Your Way

89% of students surveyed found the interactive online quizzes valuable.

We know that no two students are alike. SPEAK was developed to help you learn speech communication in a way that works for you.

Not only is the format fresh and contemporary, it's also concise and focused. And, SPEAK is loaded with a variety of supplements, like chapter review cards, printable flash cards, and more.

At the CourseMate for SPEAK at **www.cengagebrain.com**, you'll also find **Interactive Quizzing**, **Crossword Puzzles**, **Games**, **Interactive Video Activities**, and **Audio Study Tools** to test your knowledge of key concepts, and plenty of resources to help you study no matter what learning style you like best!

Ceremonial Speaking: Speeches for Special Occasions

Because Ben didn't know his biological father, his grandfather had been like a father to him. He and his grandfather had spent hours playing ball, fishing, or simply watching television together. Although Ben's grandfather had lived a long and fruitful life, Ben was finding it difficult to say goodbye. Still, he wanted to give the eulogy at the funeral. How could he find the right words to do justice to his grandfather's memory?

On special occasions such as weddings and funerals, we may be called on to "say a few words." On these ceremonial occasions, your audience has distinct expectations for what they will hear. So although the speech plan action steps you have learned will help you prepare your remarks, you also need to understand how the occasion affects how you should shape your speech.

What do you think?

The best ceremonial speeches are usually given spontaneously.

Strongly Disagree   *Strongly Agree*
1   2   3   4   5   6   7   8   9   10

The goal of ceremonial speaking lies somewhere between informing and persuading. In ceremonial speeches, you invite listeners to agree with you about the value of the person, object, event, or place the special occasion revolves around. Another characteristic of most ceremonial speeches is brevity: They are generally—although not always—fewer than five minutes long. This chapter describes six common types of ceremonial speeches given on special occasions: speeches of welcome, introduction, nomination, recognition, acceptance, and tribute. For each speech type, we describe the typical expectations for you to keep in mind as you prepare.

Speeches of Welcome

A speech of welcome is usually a brief, formal ceremonial address that greets and expresses pleasure for the presence of a person or an organization. A speech of welcome is generally not more than two to four minutes long. You can welcome someone on your own, but more frequently, you will give a speech of welcome as the representative of a group. On some occasion, you may be asked to serve as master of ceremonies, an individual designated to welcome guests, set the mood of the program, introduce participants, and keep the program moving. Year-end honorary banquets, corporate dinner meetings, and local charity events typically use someone in this role.

speech of welcome
a brief, formal ceremonial address that greets and expresses pleasure for the presence of a person or an organization

master of ceremonies
an individual designated to welcome guests, set the mood of the program, introduce participants, and keep the program moving

and we raised more than $250,000 last year to support local children's organizations. We hope that our talks here today will lead to closer cooperation between the North Thurston Club and ours here in Yelm.

At times, you may be asked to give a speech that both welcomes and introduces a speaker. When this is the case, the speech can be a bit longer and should also include the type of information described in the next section.

Speeches of Introduction

A **speech of introduction** is a brief ceremonial speech that establishes a supportive climate for the main speaker, highlights the speaker's credibility by familiarizing the audience with pertinent biographical information, and generates enthusiasm for listening to the speaker and topic. Generally, a speech of introduction is not more than three to five minutes long.

Expectations

The goal of a speech of introduction is to establish the credibility of the main speaker by letting the audience know the education, background, and experience of the speaker related to the speech topic and to suggest why the audience should listen. At times, you will be given a résumé or brief biography of the speaker; at other times, you may need to research the speaker's background yourself. Regardless of what you learn, you should also try to contact the speaker and ask what points in the biography the speaker would like you to emphasize.

The beginning of a speech of introduction should quickly establish the nature of the occasion, the body of the speech should focus on three or four things about the person being introduced that are critical for the audience to know, and the conclusion should mention the speaker by name and briefly identify the speaker's topic or the title of the speech. If the person is well known, you might simply say something like, "Ladies and gentlemen, the president of the United States." If the person is less well known, however, then mentioning his or her name specifically during the speech of introduction and especially at the end is imperative.

Speeches of introduction should honestly represent the person being introduced. Do not hype a speaker's credentials or "over-praise" the speaker. If you set the audience's expectations too high, even a good speaker may have trouble living up to them. For instance, an overzealous introducer can doom a

Expectations

You must be familiar with the group that you are representing and the occasion. It is surprising how little some members of an organization, a community, or a college or university really know about their organization or community. As you prepare your welcome, you may need to do some research so you can accurately describe the group and the circumstances or occasion to the person or people you are welcoming.

A speech of welcome invites listeners to agree that the occasion is friendly and their attendance is appreciated. Do this by respectfully catching their attention and, after expressing appreciation on behalf of your group for the presence of the person or people, provide a brief description of the group and setting to which they are being welcomed. The conclusion should briefly express your hope for the outcome of the visit, event, or relationship. A typical speech of welcome might be as simple as this:

speech of introduction
a brief ceremonial speech that establishes a supportive climate for the main speaker, highlights the speaker's credibility by familiarizing the audience with pertinent biographical information, and generates enthusiasm for listening to the speaker and topic

Today, I want to welcome John Sheldon, who is joining us from the North Thurston Club. John, as you are aware, we are a newer club, having been established in 2007. At that time, we had only 10 members. But we had big hopes. Today, we are 127 members strong,

competent speaker by saying, "This man [woman] is undoubtedly one of the greatest speakers of our time. I have no doubt that what you are about to hear will change your thinking." Although this introduction is meant to be complimentary, it does the speaker a grave disservice.

Speeches of Nomination

A **speech of nomination** is a ceremonial presentation that proposes a nominee for an elected office, honor, position, or award. Every four years, the Democratic and Republican parties have speeches of nomination at their national conventions. Those speeches are rather long, but most speeches of nomination are brief, lasting only about two to four minutes.

Expectations

The goal of a speech of nomination is to highlight the qualities that make this person the most credible candidate. To do so, first clarify the importance of the nomination, honor, position, or award by describing the responsibilities involved, related challenges or issues, and the characteristics needed to fulfill it. Second, list the candidate's personal and professional qualifications that meet those criteria. Doing so links the candidate with the nomination, honor, position, or award in ways that make him or her appear to be a natural choice. Finally, formally place the candidate's name in nomination, creating a dramatic climax to clinch your speech.

Speeches of nomination should be brief and should make clear that the nominee is well suited for the nomination, honor, position, or award. Moreover, the nominee is generally most well received when the nominator is a respected member of the organization. A speech of nomination could be as simple and brief as this:

> *I am very proud to place in nomination for president of our association the name of one of our most active members, Ms. Adrienne Lamb.*

speech of nomination
a ceremonial presentation that proposes a nominee for an elected office, honor, position, or award

The 2008 Democratic National Convention in Denver, Colorado

We all realize the demands of this particular post. It requires leadership. It requires vision. It requires enthusiasm and motivation. And, most of all, it requires a sincere love for our group and its mission.

Adrienne Lamb meets and exceeds each one of these demands. It was Adrienne Lamb who chaired our visioning task force. She led us to articulate the mission statement we abide by today. It was Adrienne Lamb who chaired the fund-raising committee last year when we enjoyed a record drive. And it was Adrienne Lamb who acted as mentor to so many of us, myself included, when we were trying to find our place in this association and this community. This association and its members have reaped the benefits of Adrienne Lamb's love and leadership so many times and in so many ways. We now have the opportunity to benefit in even greater ways.

It is truly an honor and a privilege to place in nomination for president of our association Ms. Adrienne Lamb!

Speeches of Recognition

A speech of recognition is a ceremonial presentation that acknowledges someone and usually presents an award, a prize, or a gift to the individual or a representative of a group. Usually, the speech is a fairly short, formal recognition of an accomplishment. You have probably watched speeches of recognition given on shows such as the *Academy Awards*, the *Grammy Awards*, or the *MTV Movie Awards*. Some speeches of recognition are typically quite brief (fewer than three minutes long), but occasionally they are longer.

Expectations

A speech of recognition discusses the nature of the accomplishment or award, including its history, donor, or source, and the conditions under which it is made. Although the tangible award may be a certificate, plaque, trophy, or check symbolizing an achievement, the recognition may have a long history and tradition that you are responsible for recounting.

Because the audience wants to know why the recipient is being recognized, you must know the recognition criteria and how the recipient met them. If the recognition is based on a competition, this might include the number of contestants and the way the contest was judged. If the person earned the award through years of achievement, you will want to describe the specific milestones that the person passed.

Ordinarily, the speech begins by describing what the recognition is for, then states the criteria for winning or achieving the recognition, and finally describes how the person being recognized won or achieved the award. In some cases, the recognition is meant to be a surprise, so you will deliberately omit the name of the recipient in what you say, building to a climax when the name is announced.

There are two special considerations for the speech of recognition. First, as in a speech of introduction, you should refrain from "over-praising"; do not explain everything in superlatives that make the presentation seem to lack sincerity and honesty. Second, in the United States, it is traditional to shake hands with recipients as awards are received. So if you have a certificate or other tangible award that you are going to hand to the recipient, be careful to hold it in your left hand and present it to the recipient's left hand. That way, you will be able to shake the right hand in congratulations. A typical speech of recognition may look like this:

I'm honored to present this year's Idea of the Year Award to Ryan Goldbloom from the installation department. As you may remember, this is an award that we have been giving since 1985 to the employee who has submitted an idea that resulted in the largest first-year cost savings for the company. Ryan's idea to equip all installation trucks with prepackaged kits for each type of job has resulted in a $10,458 savings in the first 12 months. And in recognition of this contribution to our bottom line, I am pleased to share our savings with Ryan in the form of a check for $2,091.60, one-fifth of what he has saved us. Good work, Ryan.

Speeches of Acceptance

A speech of acceptance is a ceremonial speech given to acknowledge receipt of an honor or award. The goal is to sincerely convey to listeners your appreciation for the honor and the recognition and to quickly acknowledge others who have been instrumental in your success. To be effective, the speech should be brief, humble, and gracious. Generally, a speech of acceptance should be no longer than one to two minutes. Remember that the goal in a speech of acceptance is to convey appreciation in a way that makes the audience feel good about you receiving the award.

Expectations

In this speech, speakers should briefly thank the person or group bestowing the honor, acknowledge the competition, express feelings about receiving the award, and thank those who contributed to achieving the honor or award.

Most acceptance speeches are brief. Rarely, as in the case of a politician accepting a nomination, a professional accepting the presidency of a national organization, or a person receiving a prestigious award that is the focus of the gathering, an audience will expect a longer speech. If you have ever watched award programs, you no doubt have observed a winner who gave an overly long or otherwise inappropriate acceptance speech. One of the most famous was in 2003, when Michael Moore used the occasion to chastise the U.S. president by saying "shame on you Mr. Bush, shame on you" rather than to focus on thanking the academy. So, when you have the opportunity to give an acceptance speech, you will want to practice it so that you are confident that you can accomplish your purpose quickly. It is also important that you focus your remarks on the recognition you have been given or on the position you are accepting. It is inappropriate to use an acceptance speech to advocate for an unrelated cause. The following is an example of an appropriate speech of acceptance:

> On behalf of our board of directors, thank you for this award, the Largest Institutional Benefactor in Second Harvest's 1998 Food Drive. It is an honor to be a part of such a worthwhile cause, and it is really our board who should be thanking you, Second Harvest, for all the wonderful work you have done over the years. You continue to collect and distribute food to thousands of needy families and individuals, especially to our senior citizens and single mothers. Without your work, many would otherwise go hungry. You are a model of community sharing and caring.
>
> I would also like to thank our company staff— Juanita Alverez, Su Lin, Al Pouzorek, Linda Williams, and Jesus Washington—for their efforts in organizing the collection of food and money to go to Second Harvest. They were tireless in their work, persistent in their company memos and meetings requesting donations, and consistent in their positive and upbeat attitudes throughout the drive! We could not have won this award without them! Let's give them a round of applause, too.
>
> Finally, thank you, Second Harvest, for this honor— and we hope to be back next year to receive it again!

To see an example of an acceptance speech at a formal occasion, go to the CourseMate for SPEAK at www.cengagebrain.com to access **Web Resource 15.1: Martin Luther King's Nobel Prize Acceptance Speech**.

speech of tribute
a ceremonial speech that praises or celebrates a person, a group, or an event

Speeches of Tribute

A **speech of tribute** is a ceremonial speech that praises or celebrates a person, a group, or an event. You might be asked to pay tribute to a person or persons on the occasion of a birthday, wedding, anniversary, oath of office, retirement, or funeral. There are a variety of special types based on the specific special occasion they are meant for. The goal is to invite listeners to truly appreciate the person, group, or event by arousing their sentiments. This is achieved by focusing on the most notable characteristics or achievements of the person, group, or event with vivid stories, examples, and language that arouses sentiments. Speeches of tribute can vary in length from very brief to lengthy depending on the nature of the occasion. Let's take a closer look at three types of tribute that you are likely to be asked to give.

© HILL STREET STUDIOS/BLEND IMAGES/JUPITERIMAGES

Toasts

A toast is a ceremonial speech offered at the start of a reception or meal that pays tribute to the occasion or to a person. On most occasions, a toast is expected to be very brief, consisting of only a few sentences and focusing on a single characteristic of the person or occasion. Usually, a short example is used to support or illustrate the characteristic. Wedding toasts, given at a rehearsal dinner or reception by a family member or member of the wedding party, are generally longer speeches (three to four minutes) that may use humor but should not embarrass the persons at whom they are directed.

A toast should be sincere and express a sentiment that is likely to be widely shared by those in attendance. The person giving the toast often stands or in some other way separates from the rest of the people. Generally, the person giving the toast and all other attendees have a drink in hand, which they raise and sip from at the conclusion of the toast. So before offering a toast, it is customary to make sure that drinks are refreshed so that all can participate. If particular people are being toasted, the toast is drunk in their honor, so they do not drink.

A typical toast by a daughter given to honor her mother's college graduation might be:

Tonight, I'd like to offer a toast to a woman I admire and respect. My mom has always supported my brother and me. So when she told me that she wanted to go back and finish college, I was worried about how we'd all manage. But I shouldn't have worried. Mom not only finished her degree in less than two years, but she also continued to work full time, and, what's more, she's even had time to coach my brother's Little League team. Here's to you, Mom—you're amazing!

Roasts

One unique type of tribute speech is given as part of a roast, which is an event where family and friends share short speeches in honor of one person. In these short speeches, guests might offer good-natured insults or anecdotes, heartwarming or outlandish personal stories, or uplifting accolades. Some recent celebrities who have been roasted include William Shatner, Pamela Anderson, and Jeff Foxworthy. The key when offering a speech of tribute during a roast is to demonstrate the ethical communication principles of respect and integrity by offering only jokes, stories, and anecdotes that do not offend the featured guest by sharing stories that are too private or too vulgar for a general audience. The point, after all, is to honor and laud the guest.

Eulogies

A eulogy is a ceremonial speech of tribute during a funeral or memorial service that praises someone's life and accomplishments. Your goal is to comfort the mourners by focusing on positive memories of the deceased person. Based on what you know about the person, select three or four positive personal characteristics of the person to use as the main points and then use personal stories you have collected about the person to provide support. Your audience will enjoy hearing new stories that exemplify the characteristics, as well as revisiting widely shared stories. Incidents that reveal how a personal characteristic helped the person overcome adversity will be especially powerful. To see an example of a eulogy, go to the CourseMate for SPEAK at www.cengagebrain.com to access the Interactive Video Activities for Chapter 15. There you can see a video of Oprah Winfrey's eulogy for civil rights activist Rosa Parks. Also access **Web Resource 15.2: Bob Costas's Eulogy for Mickey Mantle.** This tribute speech uses language that enables audiences to understand Mantle's impact, regardless of their knowledge of baseball.

Other Ceremonial Speeches

Other occasions that call for ceremonial speeches include graduations, holidays, anniversaries of major events, and special events. A commencement address, for example, is a ceremonial

© ISTOCKPHOTO.COM/FLOORTJE

speech of tribute praising graduating students and inspiring them to reach for their goals. A **commemorative address** is a ceremonial speech of tribute that celebrates national holidays or anniversaries of important events. A **keynote address** is a ceremonial speech that both sets the tone and generates enthusiasm for the topic of a conference or convention. A **dedication** is a ceremonial speech of tribute that honors a worthy person or group by naming a structure such as a building, monument, or park after the honoree. A **farewell** is a ceremonial speech of tribute honoring someone who is leaving an organization. A **speech to entertain** is a humorous speech that makes a serious point. To learn more about each of these types of ceremonial speeches, go to the CourseMate for SPEAK at www.cengagebrain.com to access "Other Ceremonial Speeches" under the Chapter 15 resources.

THERE ARE EVEN MORE STUDY TOOLS FOR THIS CHAPTER AT WWW.CENGAGEBRAIN.COM

- **Interactive Videos**
- **Speech Builder Express**
- **Printable Flash Cards**
- **Interactive Games**
- **Chapter Review Cards**
- **Online Quizzes With Feedback**
- **Speech Studio available upon instructor request**

commemorative address
a ceremonial speech of tribute that celebrates national holidays or anniversaries of important events

keynote address
a ceremonial speech that both sets the tone and generates enthusiasm for the topic of a conference or convention

dedication
a ceremonial speech of tribute that honors a worthy person or group by naming a structure, monument, or park after the honoree

farewell
a ceremonial speech of tribute honoring someone who is leaving an organization

speech to entertain
a humorous speech that makes a serious point

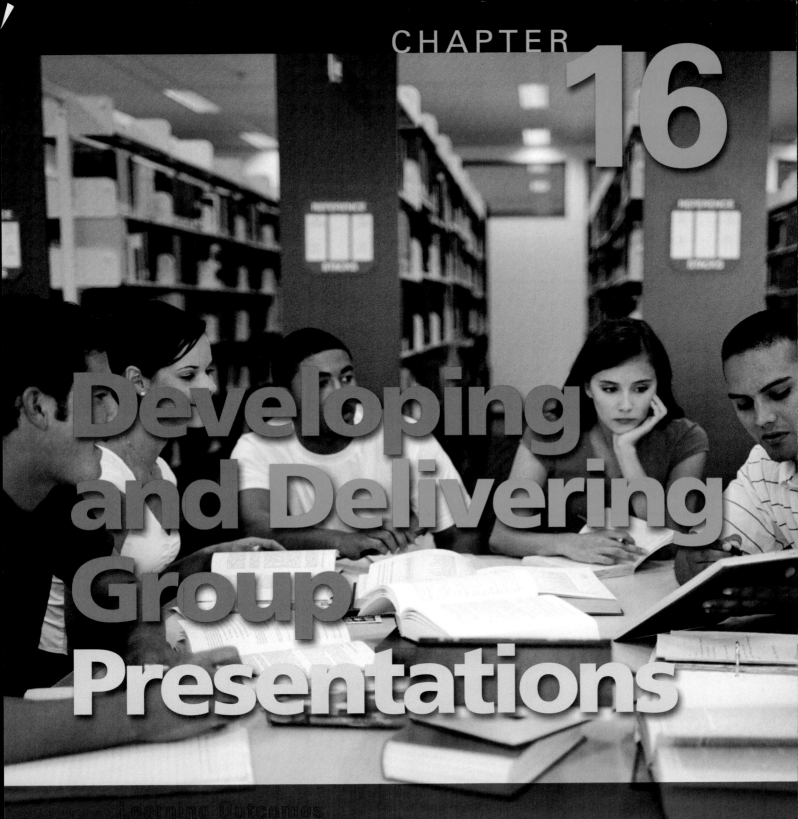

CHAPTER

16

Developing and Delivering Group Presentations

Learning Outcomes

LO¹ Why is teamwork becoming so popular as a means for solving problems? | LO² What does it mean to be a responsible group member? | LO³ How can you solve problems effectively in groups? | LO⁴ How do you prepare a group presentation? | LO⁵ How can you evaluate group work?

WORK SESSION 1: Julio, Kristi, Luke, Bryn, and Nick have been asked to work as a small group to prepare a persuasive presentation that will count for one-third of the grade in the course. As the other members see it, Nick is a troublemaker because he has contradicted the instructor several times during previous class sessions. Their impression might be compounded by the fact that Nick wears fatigues to class and brags about being in a militia. Nick has also been absent several times and seems less than fully committed to earning a good grade. In short, the other members are worried that Nick will cause them to earn a lower grade than they would earn without him in their group.

WORK SESSION 2: After the instructor refused to move Nick to another group, Julio, Kristi, Luke, and Bryn decide to restrict Nick's participation by not asking him for substantive help even though that means he'll get a better grade than he deserves. As the full group begins discussing their topic—an assault weapons ban—Nick explains that he has a lot of material on it since he is a fairly vocal opponent of this proposal. Kristi and Luke become disgruntled because they plan to argue in support of the law, and, as they suspected, Nick opposes it. Kristi asks Bryn, "How do YOU feel about this conflict?" Much to Kristi's surprise, Bryn replies, "Actually, I'd like to hear more from Nick before I decide. Nick, tell us more." Nick goes on to share highly relevant information that would eventually be used to strengthen the group's speech. The group soon realizes the hastiness of their judgments about Nick.

Perhaps you have already been part of a group whose task was to prepare a joint presentation. If so, the opening scenario probably sounds familiar. In fact, when asked to work in small groups on a class or work project, many people respond—as Julio, Kristi, Luke, and Bryn did—with resistance. Their reasons usually focus on concerns that a few members will end up doing most of the work, that the group process will slow them down, that they'll earn a lower grade than if they worked alone, or that they will be forced to work on a topic that they aren't interested in or take a position they don't agree with.

Although working in a group to develop and deliver a presentation has its disadvantages, it is the preferred approach in business and industry.[1] These work teams begin

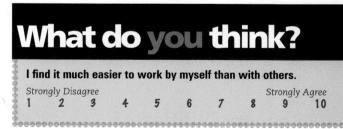

What do you think?

I find it much easier to work by myself than with others.

Strongly Disagree   Strongly Agree

1   2   3   4   5   6   7   8   9   10

problem-solving group
four to seven people who work together to complete a specific task or solve a particular problem

synergy
when the result of group work is better than what one member could have accomplished alone

as problem-solving groups: groups composed of four to seven people that are formed to carry out a specific task or solve a particular problem. Usually at the end of their deliberations, they present their findings and analysis, and recommend solutions to others in the organization. Whether you want to or not, you can expect to work in a group or on a team in your professional life, sometimes in face-to-face settings and often in virtual settings through e-mail, chat rooms, discussion boards, and video conferences.[2] Leaders in business and industry have come to realize that the advantages of work teams far outweigh the disadvantages. The advantages include deeper analysis of problems, greater breadth of ideas and of potential solutions, improved group morale, and increased productivity.

You can also expect to be asked to present group findings in formal presentations whether in the form of a progress report, sales presentation, proposal, or staff report.[3] So it makes sense to learn how to work effectively in problem-solving groups and how to present your group findings orally. In this chapter, we begin by talking about the responsibilities of group members in effective problem-solving groups, paying special attention to managing conflict among members. Then, we describe an effective problem-solving method described by educational philosopher John Dewey. Then, we discuss how to prepare group presentations and describe five public presentation formats. Finally, we explain how you can evaluate your group's effectiveness both in terms of the group process and presentation.

Responsibilities of Group Members

When problem-solving groups work well, the product is better than what any one member could have accomplished alone. This is known as **synergy**. Your goal when working in a small group is to achieve synergy. We believe small groups usually fail when members do not understand or follow through with the ethical responsibilities shown in Exhibit 16.1. When met by all members, these five responsibilities result in shared leadership where every member and his or her contributions are valued and synergy can occur.

1. **Be committed to the group goal.** Being committed to the group goal means finding a way to align your expertise with the agreed-upon goal of the group. In addition to demonstrating responsibility, doing so also conveys both integrity and respect. This might mean working together on a topic that wasn't your first choice. Once the decision has been agreed upon, however, it is no longer appropriate to dredge up old issues that have already been settled.

2. **Keep discussions on track.** It is every member's responsibility to keep the discussion on track by offering only comments that are relevant and by gently reminding others to stay

Exhibit 16.1

Responsibilities of Group Members

Be committed to the group goal

Manage interpersonal conflicts

Keep the discussion on track

Encourage input from all members

Complete individual assignments

focused if the discussion starts to get off track. It is unproductive to talk about personal issues during the team's work time. Moreover, it is unethical to try to get the discussion off track because you disagree with what is being said.

3. **Complete individual assignments on time.** One potential advantage of group work is that tasks can be divided among members. However, each member is responsible for completing his or her tasks thoroughly and on time.

4. **Encourage input from all members.** All too often in problem-solving small groups, quiet members are overshadowed by extroverts. Sometimes, outspoken members interpret their silence as having nothing to contribute or not wanting to contribute. On the contrary, all members have valuable perspectives. If you are an extrovert, you have a special responsibility to refrain from dominating the discussion and to ask others for their opinions. Likewise, if you tend to be an introvert, make a conscious effort to express yourself. You might write down what you want to share or even raise your hand to get the attention of other members in an unobtrusive way. Doing your part to ensure that all opinions and perspectives are heard demon-

strates not only the ethical principle of responsibility but also of fairness.

5. **Manage conflict among members.** All small groups experience some conflict—disagreement or clash among ideas, principles, or people. If managed appropriately, conflict can actually be beneficial to the group goal by stimulating thinking, fostering open communication, encouraging diverse opinions, and enlarging members' understanding of the issues.[4] Doing your part to manage conflict demonstrates the ethical principles of responsibility and respect for others. Because managing conflict effectively is so essential to successful group work, we focus specifically on conflict management and resolution in the next section.

> **conflict**
> disagreement or clash among ideas, principles, or people

Conflict Resolution in Group Settings

As we have already mentioned, all small groups experience some conflict, and, when managed effectively, conflict enhances synergy. In fact, groups that *don't* experience some conflict risk the problem of

groupthink
when group members accept information and ideas without subjecting them to critical analysis

withdrawing
a conflict management style that involves physically or psychologically removing yourself from the conflict

accommodating
a passive conflict management style of accepting others' ideas while neglecting your own, even when you disagree with their views

forcing
a conflict management style that involves satisfying your own needs with no concern for the needs of the others and no concern for the harm it does to the group dynamics or problem-solution process of reaching the best solution

compromising
a conflict management style that involves individuals giving up part of what they want in order to provide at least some satisfaction to other opinions

collaborating
a conflict management style that involves discussing the issues, describing feelings, and identifying the characteristics of an effective solution before deciding what the ultimate solution will be

groupthink—when group members accept information and ideas without subjecting them to critical analysis.[5] Behaviors that signal groupthink include:

- Avoiding conflict to prevent hurting someone's feelings.
- Pressuring members who do not agree with the majority of the group to conform.
- Reaching "consensus" without the support of all members.
- Discouraging or ignoring disagreements.
- Rationalizing a decision without testing it.

So we know that when groups don't experience any conflict, they run the risk of engaging in groupthink. If effective groups actually experience conflict, then how do they manage it effectively? Effective groups do so when all members understand their personal conflict management styles and follow certain guidelines when addressing potentially conflict-arousing situations. Conflict can occur over issues or personalities. Let's look at how we can effectively handle conflicts from each of these sources.

Conflict Over Issues

Research has revealed five common conflict management styles. These are withdrawing, accommodating, forcing, compromising, and collaborating.[6]

Withdrawing involves physically or psychologically removing yourself from the conflict. When a group member engages in withdrawing as a conflict management style, the whole group suffers because everyone is not committed to the group goal and all members' input is not being considered.

Accommodating is a passive conflict management style of accepting others' ideas while neglecting your own, even when you disagree with their views.

When a group member engages in accommodating as a conflict management style, the whole group suffers because not all potential ideas are being weighed in the discussion.

A third style of dealing with conflict is forcing. Forcing means satisfying your own needs with no concern for the needs of the others and no concern for the harm it does to the group dynamics or problem-solution process of reaching the best solution. When one member dominates the group discussion by forcing his or her opinions without considering other views or even allowing them to be expressed, the whole group suffers because input from all group members is not being heard. Researchers say this results in a win–lose solution. If two or more members engage in competing forcing conflict styles, the whole group suffers, not only because all ideas are not being heard but also because the discussion gets off track, interpersonal conflicts are not being managed, and the arguments may even impede the completion of individual assignments.

A fourth way to manage conflict is compromising, which occurs when individuals give up part of what they want in order to provide at least some satisfaction to other opinions. If the group members can't find an ideal time to meet outside of class because they all have busy schedules, they might compromise on a time to meet that isn't particularly ideal for any of them. In terms of coming to a solution, one drawback of this style is that the quality of the decision is probably affected when someone "trades away" a better solution to reach a compromise.

A fifth style for managing conflict is collaborating. When you collaborate, you discuss the issues, describe feelings, and identify the characteristics of an effective solution before deciding what the ultimate solution will be. Researchers describe this as a win–win situation. Your goal in managing conflict is to achieve a win–win solution through collaborative conflict management among members. A win–win solution occurs when input from all members is heard, valued, and evaluated honestly and fairly until the group reaches consensus about how to proceed. Consider the tips in Exhibit 16.2 to achieve effective collaborative conflict management.

Personality Conflicts

Sometimes we experience discord with a certain group member due to a personality conflict. The fact is we will all find ourselves working in groups where we don't necessarily see eye-to-eye with everyone or frankly even want to be friends with everyone. In these situations, manage disagreements by separating the issues from the people involved, keeping your

Exhibit 16.2

Collaborative Conflict Management

Initiating Collaboration	Responding Collaboratively
1. Identify the problem as your own using "I language." "I could really use your help here." 2. Describe the behavior in terms of behavior, consequences, and feelings. "When I see you checking your e-mail, I feel we're missing out on your ideas for the project, and I get frustrated." 3. Refrain from blaming or accusing. 4. Find common ground. "Figuring this out is really tough. I know I feel overwhelmed about it sometimes." 5. Mentally rehearse so you can state your request briefly.	1. Disengage to avoid a defensive response. 2. Respond empathically with genuine interest and concern by first describing the behavior you observe. "I see you checking your e-mail, and I wonder if you're angry or frustrated with something." 3. Paraphrase your understanding of the problem, and ask questions to clarify issues. "Is there something bothering you or something we're overlooking?" 4. Seek common ground. "I know that trying to come to one goal and solution seems impossible at times." 5. Ask the other person to suggest alternative solutions. "What other ideas do you have that we might consider?"

perception checking
a verbal statement that reflects your understanding of another's behavior

paraphrasing
putting into your own words the meaning you have assigned to a message

systematic problem-solving method
an efficient six-step method for finding an effective solution to a problem

emotions in check, and phrasing your comments descriptively, not judgmentally. Rather than calling a particular idea stupid, for example, ask for clarification about why people think or feel the way they do. Seek first to understand. To help you put aside your personal feelings and manage conflicts effectively, employ perception checking or paraphrasing, using "I language" that phrases your interpretations and opinions as your own rather than defense-arousing "you language."[7] In other words, your language needs to reflect the fact that you are responsible for your feelings.[8] Exhibit 16.3 shows some examples of how to change a "you" statement into an "I" statement.

Perception checking is a verbal statement that reflects your understanding of another's behavior. It is a two-step process: (a) In a non-evaluative way, describe what you observed or sensed from someone's behavior, and (b) add to your statement your interpretations of the behavior. **Paraphrasing** is a verbal statement that conveys your understanding of another person's verbal message. It is a four-step process: (a) Listen carefully to the message; (b) notice what images, ideas, and feelings you experience from the message; (c) determine what the message means to you; and (d) create your own message that conveys these images or feel-

ings and asks the other person to confirm what you have understood or correct it. Exhibit 16.4 on page 262 provides examples of perception checking and paraphrasing as they may be applied to avoid personality conflict.

Systematic Group Problem-Solving Method

When you meet with your classmates, teammates at your job, or members of community to work on a project, you will be trying to solve a problem. At school, the problem may be to develop a group presentation for which each of you will receive the same grade, depending on the total group performance. So whether you are in school, at work, or in your community, to be effective, your group will need a concrete approach that arrives at a productive solution in a short amount of time. One effective means for doing this is the **systematic problem-solving method**.[9] Although this method was created nearly a century ago, its staying power is evidenced in classrooms across the country still today.[10] The method consists of six steps.

Exhibit 16.3

Changing "You" Statements Into "I" Statements

"You hurt my feelings."

"You're so irresponsible."

"Don't be so critical."

"I can't believe you said that!"

"I feel hurt when you don't acknowledge what I say."

"I feel my efforts don't matter when you come to the meeting unprepared."

"I feel disrespected when you say my opinion is stupid."

"I feel humiliated when you mention my problems in front of others."

1. **Identify and define the problem.** The first step is to identify the problem or problems and define them in a way all group members understand and agree with. Groups might begin by coming up with a number of problems or needs and then narrow them to a particular one. So your class project group might identify the problems as

Exhibit 16.4

Avoiding Personality Conflict through Perception Checking and Paraphrasing

Situation	Perception Checking	Paraphrase
As you are offering your idea about who the group might interview to get more information on your topic, you notice that Tomika, whom you see as uncommitted to the group, says, "Whatever . . ." and begins reading a message on her cell phone.	Tomika, when you give a dismissive response to my ideas and then start checking your messages, I sense that you don't like my suggestion. Is that an accurate read, or are you just expecting an important message, or is it something else?	From your "whatever" response, I sense that either you don't really agree with my suggestion, you aren't really comitted to the project, or you just don't respect me. Or is it something else?
Over the term, Jose has been quick to volunteer for the easiest assignments and has never taken on a difficult piece of work. Today the group was finalizing who would deliver which part of the group presentation and Jose quickly volunteered, saying, "I'll be the master of ceremonies and introduce our topic and each speaker."	Jose, I have been noticing that you have been quick to volunteer and you usually choose the least time-consuming and simplest tasks, and now you're offering to take a role in the presentation that will again require little effort. Are you really overextended in your other classes or trying to take the easy way out, or is there some other explanation?	Jose, it seems to me like you are again volunteering to do the part of the presentation that will be the least amount of work. Are you really overextended with other courses or not committed to doing your share? Or is there some other reason that you want to be the master of ceremonies?
Today is the day that Madison is supposed to lead the group's discussion, as she was responsible for the research on this part of the group's project. As the group waits for her to begin, she avoids eye contact and rummages through her backpack, finally looking up and saying, "Well, I guess that you all are going to be kind of mad at me."	Madison, I'm noticing you don't seem like you want to get the meeting started, are avoiding eye contact, and have been rummaging around in your bag. I get the sense that you haven't done your homework or lost it. Am I on target, or is it something else?	Madison, from what you said, I understand that you are not prepared to lead the meeting. I'm wondering if you did your homework and lost it. Or is there something else?

developing an effective group presentation, identifying a topic for the presentation, fairly sharing the workload, and so forth. By posing questions, you can also identify and define a problem: What is the problem? What is its history? Who is affected by it, and how does it affect them? How many people are affected, in what ways, and to what degree? These questions help a group realize what kinds of information must be gathered to help define the problem. To ensure that your group is focusing on the problem itself and not just the symptoms of the problem, don't rush through this step.

2. **Analyze the problem.** To analyze the problem, you must find out as much as possible about it. Most groups begin by sharing the information individual members have acquired through their experiences. This process can be described as finding out what we already know. So in your class, you may share stories you have heard from students who have already taken the class, share your ideas for topics, and share your hopes and concerns. Then the group will generate questions regarding what the group members still need to know, which includes questions they still have and experiences they'll want to confirm or reject as typical. So the group

criteria
standards used for judging the merits of proposed solutions

may generate a list of questions to ask the instructor about the assignment. Once the group has identified a topic, members may need to get more information about it by doing research. You might consider using questions to guide you in analyzing the problem: Can the problem be subdivided into a series of smaller problems? Why has the problem occurred? What are the symptoms? What methods already exist for dealing with it? What are the limitations of those methods? One important element of this step when working in problem-solving small groups is to share new information with your other group members as you discover it.

3. **Determine criteria for judging solutions.** Criteria are standards used for judging the merits of proposed solutions—a blueprint for evaluating them. Without clear criteria, groups may select solutions that don't adequately address the real problem or, perhaps, solutions that create a host of new problems. Questions that might guide your thinking about criteria include the following: Exactly what must the solutions achieve? Are there any factors that might limit the choice of solutions (e.g., cost, feasibility, location, complexity, expedience, risk–benefit ratio, etc.)? Once you've established criteria, prioritize the list. Which criteria are most important? Which are least important?

4. **Generate a host of solutions.** At this point, you'll want to brainstorm for possible solutions. Brainstorming, you'll recall, is an uncritical, non-evaluative process of generating alternatives by being creative, suspending judgment, and combining or adapting the ideas of others. It involves verbalizing your ideas as they come to mind without stopping to evaluate their merits. At least one member should record all solutions as they are suggested. To ensure that creativity is not stifled, no solution should be ignored, and members should build on the ideas presented by others. You might come up with 20 or more solutions. As a minimum, try to come up with eight to 10 solutions before moving to the next step. For more on brainstorming, go to the CourseMate for SPEAK at www.cengagebrain.com to access **Web Resource 16.1: Rules for Brainstorming**.

5. **Evaluate the solutions and select the best one based on the criteria.** Here you need to evaluate the merits of each potential solution based on the criteria established by the group. Consider each solution as it meets the criteria, and eliminate solutions that do not meet them adequately. In addition to applying the criteria, the group might also ask questions such as the following: How will the solution solve the problem? How difficult will it be to implement? What problems might be caused as a result of implementing the solution? Once each potential solution has been thoroughly evaluated based on the criteria, the group must select the best one(s). For more resources on evaluating solutions and making decisions, go to the CourseMate for SPEAK at www.cengagebrain.com to access **Web Resource 16.2: Decision Making Methods**.

6. **Implement the agreed-upon solution.** Finally, the group implements the agreed-upon solution or, if the group is presenting the solution to others for implementation, makes recommendations for how the solution should be implemented. The group

has already considered implementation in terms of selecting a solution but now must fill in the details. What tasks are required by the solution(s)? Who will carry out these tasks? What is a reasonable time frame for implementation generally and for each of the tasks specifically?

> **brainstorming**
> an uncritical, non-evaluative process of generating alternatives by being creative, suspending judgment, and combining or adapting the ideas of others

Preparing Group Presentations

Once the group has worked through the systematic problem-solving method, it's time to prepare a group presentation. Doing so involves a five-step process that starts with dividing the topic into areas of responsibility and ends with practicing and then delivering the presentation.

1. **Divide the topic into areas of responsibility.** As a group, determine the thesis and macrostructure for the presentation. Each member can then be responsible for researching and organizing the content necessary to develop a particular main point. If there are more group members than main points, assign more than one person to a main point or assign one person to develop and integrate presentational aids.

2. **Draft an outline of your topic area.** Each group member should construct an outline for his or her main point. Even though the

outline is for only part of the presentation, it must still be thorough, so follow the steps for creating an outline you learned in Chapter 7.

3. **Combine member outlines to form a group outline.** Once the individual outlines are completed, the group is ready to combine them into a single outline. Members should share their individual outlines and then, as a group, develop the transitions between main points and make any other changes needed for continuity and consistency. If no member was responsible for developing the introduction and conclusion, the group should create them now. Likewise, presentational aids should be integrated at this point.

4. **Finalize the details of delivery.** Because this is a group presentation, more than the usual number of decisions must be made about delivery. For example, which presentation format will you use? (The next section in this chapter shows various presentation formats.) Who will speak when? Who will introduce the speakers and when? Where will group members sit when they are not speaking? How will presentational aids be displayed, and who will be responsible for displaying them?

5. **Practice your presentation.** It is crucial to practice both individually and as a group, using the delivery guidelines described in Chapter 11. Because group presentations pose additional complexities, there are more tasks to be done to complete the speech. As a result, there is even more need for practice if you are to succeed at conveying one seamless message to your listeners.

Public Group Presentation Formats

Although your group problem solving will be done in private—without the presence of an onlooking or participating audience—occasionally you will have the opportunity to share your issues in a public forum. At times, this means conducting your group discussion with nonparticipating observers present; at other times, it means presenting your group's conclusions to an audience. As such, public group presentations have much in common with traditional public speaking. Five common formats for public group presentations are the symposium, the panel discussion, the town hall meeting, the electronic conference, and streaming videos and slide shows.

Symposium

A **symposium** is a discussion in which a limited number of participants (usually three to five) present individual speeches of approximately the same length dealing with the same subject. After delivering their planned speeches, the participants in the symposium respond to questions from the audience. Unfortunately, a symposium often omits the interaction necessary for a good discussion. However, if the participants make their prepared speeches short enough to allow sufficient time for questions and answers, a symposium can be interesting and stimulating.

In a symposium, all speakers typically are seated in front of the audience. One person acts as moderator, offering the introductory and concluding remarks and providing transitions between speakers. In a way, the moderator provides the macrostructure for the group presentation. When introduced by the moderator, each speaker moves from his or her seat to the lectern to deliver a speech on the aspect of the topic he or she is covering. Although each speech can stand on its own, all fit together to present the larger picture of the issue. After all speakers have finished, the moderator returns to the lectern to offer concluding remarks and to facilitate the question-and-answer session. Questions can be directed to individuals in the group or to the group as a whole.

The way the group divides the content among speakers depends on how the material was organized. For example, each speaker might focus on one step of the problem-solving process or on one major issue related to the overall topic. If the presentation is persuasive, successive speakers might focus on the problem, the causes, and the solutions. Or one might focus on the need, another on the plan for meeting the need, another on visualization of the future, and another on a call to action. To see a sample persuasive group symposium speech, go to the CourseMate for SPEAK at www.cengagebrain.com to access the Interactive Video Activities for Chapter 16. There you can see the speech prepared by a group of students for their symposium "The Dirty Truth about Antibacterial Products," in which the motivated sequence organizational pattern is used to organize the order of the speeches given by each group member.

Panel Discussion

A panel discussion is a problem-solving discussion in front of an audience. After the formal discussion, the audience is often encouraged to question the participants. Perhaps you've seen or heard a panel of experts discuss a topic on programs like *SportsCenter* or *Meet the Press*. The group is typically seated in a semicircle to allow the audience to see all participants. One person serves as moderator, introduces the topic, and provides the macrostructure by asking a series of planned questions that panelists answer. Their answers and the interaction among them provide the supporting evidence. A well-planned panel discussion seems spontaneous and interactive but requires careful planning and rehearsal to ensure that all relevant information is presented and that all speakers are afforded equal speaking time.

Town Hall Meeting

A town hall meeting is an event in which a large number of people who are interested in a topic convene to discuss, and at times to decide, one or more issues. In the New England states, many small towns use town hall meetings of residents to decide community issues. In a town hall meeting, one person who is respected by other participants is selected to lead the discussion.

The leader announces the ground rules for the discussion, introduces the issues to be discussed, calls on participants for comments, ensures that divergent opinions are expressed, periodically summarizes the discussion, and oversees the decision making. Because town hall meetings involve large numbers of people, the leader strictly controls taking turns. In your public speaking course, your instructor may have the entire class participate in a town hall meeting on a particular topic. You may be asked to consult with other students and as a group to represent a particular type of stakeholder. Your group task will be to research your stakeholder's position and then to represent these ideas in the larger forum.

The Baseball and the Civil Rights Movement Panel Discussion at the National Underground Railroad Freedom Center in Cincinnati, Ohio.

Electronic Conference

Electronic conferencing is a widespread method for individuals to engage in live exchange in real time without being in the same room. The most common forms are teleconferencing, where a group of individuals share information aurally over the telephone, and videoconferencing, where a group of individuals share information aurally and visually over the Internet. Teleconferencing is the most accessible because one only needs a telephone and a group access code provided by the individual or group hosting the meeting. For a successful videoconference, on the other hand, all parties must have access to a computer, webcam, microphone, and the Internet. Many computers today come equipped with webcams and microphones, and software such as Skype, WebEx, and GoToMeeting is downloadable for free or minimal cost. Electronic conferencing can be used to share formal group presentations, as well as for virtual group work sessions. You should follow a few important guidelines to be effective when engaged in electronic conferencing.

1. **Begin with a round of introductions.** Because you can't always see everyone who is present, particularly during teleconferences, a quick round of introductions provides everyone with a clear understanding of who is participating in the interaction.

2. **Reduce potential distractions.** You should turn off anything that could interrupt you or distract you from focusing on your interaction with others at the meeting. This includes radios, TVs, cell phones, e-mail, and social networking sites such as Facebook or MySpace. It is easy to get distracted by these things during face-to-face meetings, and it is even easier during electronic conferences. To resist the temptation to multitask, proper electronic conferencing etiquette is to turn them off.

3. **Be considerate.** Adhere to the five ethical responsibilities of effective group members, discussed on pages 258–259.

4. **Keep an eye on the time.** Typically, time parameters for electronic conferences are determined in advance. And with teleconferences in particular, the conference shuts down at the predetermined end time. So when engaged in these virtual meetings, be sure to stick to the agenda and stay on task to be most productive in achieving what needs to be done.

Streaming Videos and Slide Shows

A streaming video is a pre-recording that is sent in compressed form over the Internet. You are probably familiar with streaming video from popular websites such as YouTube. Streaming videos are a great way to distribute oral reports, symposiums, or panel presentations. A streaming slide show is a series of 15 to 20 slides posted on the Internet, often including voice-over narration. Streaming slide shows may automatically forward after a certain number of seconds or be programmed so the viewer chooses the pace and controls when the next slide appears. Streaming videos and slide shows are useful when it is inconvenient for some or all the people who need to know the results of the group's work to meet at one time or in one place. Unlike real-time and place presentations, viewers can watch streaming videos and slide shows more than once. When preparing streaming videos and slide shows, be sure to follow all the guidelines for effective use of voice, body, and presentational aids. The same rules for effective face-to-face presentations still apply when delivering your messages online.

Evaluating Group Effectiveness

Just as preparing and presenting are a bit different for group speeches than for individual speeches, so is the process of evaluating effectiveness. Evaluations should focus on group dynamics during the preparation process, as well as on the effectiveness of the actual presentation.

Evaluating Group Dynamics During the Preparation Process

To be effective, groups must work together as they define and analyze a problem, generate solutions, and select a course of action. They also need to work together as they prepare their written report, which in some public speaking classrooms is a formal group outline, and practice the oral presentation.

So it is important to evaluate how effectively each member works in the group. This notion of how individuals work together as a team toward a common goal is known as **group dynamics**. You can evaluate group dynamics by judging the merit of each member's efforts in terms of the five group member responsibilities discussed on pages 258–259 earlier in this chapter. In addition, each group member could prepare a "reflective thinking process paper," which details in paragraph form what each member did well and could improve upon in terms of the five member responsibilities. In the final paragraph of the paper, each member should provide a self-evaluation of what he or she did and what he or she could do to improve the group process in future sessions. To complete a reflective thinking process paper online, go to the CourseMate for SPEAK at www.cengagebrain.com to access **Web Resource 16.3: Reflective Thinking Process Paper.**

Like the evaluations business managers make of employees, these evaluations serve to document the efforts of group members. They can be submitted to the instructor, just as they would be submitted to a supervisor. In business, these documents provide a basis for determining promotion, merit pay, and salary adjustments. In the classroom, they can provide a basis for determining one portion of each member's grade.

> **streaming video**
> a pre-recording that is sent in compressed form over the Internet
>
> **streaming slide show**
> a series of 15 to 20 slides posted on the Internet, often including voice-over narration
>
> **group dynamics**
> how individuals work together as a team toward a common goal

Evaluating Effectiveness of the Group Presentation

Effective group presentations depend on quality individual presentations as well as quality overall group performance. So evaluations of group presentations should consist of both an individual and a group component. Exhibit 16.5 (p. 268) shows a form you can use to evaluate the effectiveness of a group presentation.

Evaluating Your Effectiveness

Effective group presentations depend on the combined efforts of individuals. So it's also a good idea to conduct a self-evaluation to determine whether you could be doing something better during the group problem-solving process, while preparing the group presentation, and when giving your portion of the group speech. Exhibit 16.6 (p. 268) is an example of a form used to evaluate your own efforts.

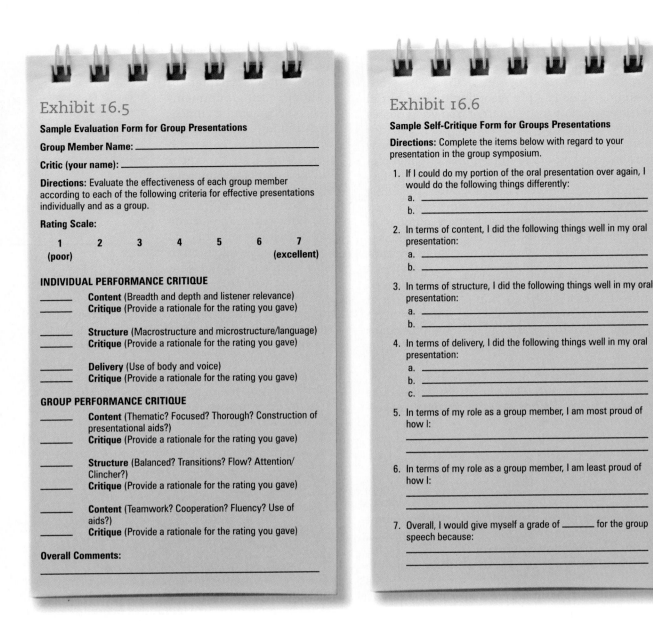

Exhibit 16.5

Sample Evaluation Form for Group Presentations

Group Member Name: _____

Critic (your name): _____

Directions: Evaluate the effectiveness of each group member according to each of the following criteria for effective presentations individually and as a group.

Rating Scale:

1	2	3	4	5	6	7
(poor)						(excellent)

INDIVIDUAL PERFORMANCE CRITIQUE

_____ **Content** (Breadth and depth and listener relevance)
_____ **Critique** (Provide a rationale for the rating you gave)

_____ **Structure** (Macrostructure and microstructure/language)
_____ **Critique** (Provide a rationale for the rating you gave)

_____ **Delivery** (Use of body and voice)
_____ **Critique** (Provide a rationale for the rating you gave)

GROUP PERFORMANCE CRITIQUE

_____ **Content** (Thematic? Focused? Thorough? Construction of presentational aids?)
_____ **Critique** (Provide a rationale for the rating you gave)

_____ **Structure** (Balanced? Transitions? Flow? Attention/ Clincher?)
_____ **Critique** (Provide a rationale for the rating you gave)

_____ **Content** (Teamwork? Cooperation? Fluency? Use of aids?)
_____ **Critique** (Provide a rationale for the rating you gave)

Overall Comments:
_____

Exhibit 16.6

Sample Self-Critique Form for Groups Presentations

Directions: Complete the items below with regard to your presentation in the group symposium.

1. If I could do my portion of the oral presentation over again, I would do the following things differently:
   a. _____
   b. _____

2. In terms of content, I did the following things well in my oral presentation:
   a. _____
   b. _____

3. In terms of structure, I did the following things well in my oral presentation:
   a. _____
   b. _____

4. In terms of delivery, I did the following things well in my oral presentation:
   a. _____
   b. _____
   c. _____

5. In terms of my role as a group member, I am most proud of how I:
   _____
   _____

6. In terms of my role as a group member, I am least proud of how I:
   _____
   _____

7. Overall, I would give myself a grade of _____ for the group speech because:
   _____
   _____

THERE ARE EVEN MORE STUDY TOOLS FOR THIS CHAPTER AT WWW.CENGAGEBRAIN.COM

- **Interactive Videos**
- **Speech Builder Express**
- **Printable Flash Cards**
- **Interactive Games**

- **Chapter Review Cards**
- **Online Quizzes With Feedback**
- **Speech Studio available upon instructor request**

Chapter 1 Foundations of Public Speaking

1. Littlejohn, S. W. (2002). *Theories of human communication.* Belmont, CA: Thomson Wadsworth.
2. Kellerman, K. (1992). Communication: Inherently strategic and primarily automatic. *Communication Monographs, 59,* 288–300.
3. Kellerman, K. (1992). Communication: Inherently strategic and primarily automatic. *Communication Monographs, 59,* 288–300; Knapp, M., & Daly, J. (2002). *Handbook of interpersonal communication.* Thousand Oaks, CA: Sage.
4. Poole, M. S. (1998). The small group should be the fundamental unit of communication research. In J. Trent (Ed.), *Communication: Views from the helm for the twenty-first century* (p. 94). Needham Heights, MA: Allyn & Bacon.
5. Devine, D. J., Clayton, L. D., Phillips, J. L., Dunford, B. B., & Melner, S. B. (1999). Teams in organizations: Prevalence, characteristics, and effectiveness. *Small Group Research, 30,* 678–711.
6. Morreale, S., Hugenberg, L., & Worley, D. (2006). The basic communication course at U.S. colleges and universities in the 21st century: Study VII. *Communication Education, 55*(4), 415–437.
7. Cooper, L. (1932). *The rhetoric of Aristotle.* Englewood Cliffs, NJ: Prentice Hall.
8. Koncz, A. (2008). *Job outlook 2009.* Bethlehem, PA: National Association of Colleges and Employers.
9. Hansen, R. S., & Hansen, K. (n.d.). What do employers *really* want? Top skills and values employers seek from job-seekers. Retrieved from http://www.quintcareers.com/job _skills_values.html
10. Das, S. K. (2003). Plagiarism in higher education: Is there a remedy? Lots of instruction and some careful vigilance could work wonders. *Scientist, 17*(20), 8.
11. What is plagiarism? (n.d.). *PlagiarismdotORG.* Retrieved from http://www.plagiarism.org /learning _center/what_is_plagiarism.html
12. McCullen, C. (2003). Tactics and resources to help students avoid plagiarism. *Multimedia Schools, 10*(6), 40–43.
13. Aristotle. (1960). *On rhetoric* (L. Cooper, Trans., p. 16). New York, NY: Appleton-Century-Crofts.
14. Bitzer, L. F. (1995). The rhetorical situation. In W. A. Covino, & D. A. Jolliffe (Eds.), *Rhetoric: Concepts, definitions, boundaries.* Boston, MA: Allyn & Bacon.
15. Ibid.
16. Exigence. (2009). In *Microsoft Encarta world English dictionary* (North American edition). Retrieved from http://encarta.msn.com /dictionary_1861609760 /exigency.html
17. Cooper, *The rhetoric of Aristotle.*
18. Jensen, V. (1985). Teaching ethics in speech communication. *Communication Education, 34,* 324–330.
19. Decker, B. (1992). *You've got to be believed to be heard.* New York, NY: St. Martin's Press.
20. Treinen, K. *Mirror image.* Unpublished manuscript, North Dakota State University.

Chapter 2 Developing Confidence Through the Speech-Planning Process

1. Hahner, J. C., Sokoloff, M. A., & Salisch, S. L. (2001). *Speaking clearly: Improving voice and diction* (6th ed.). New York, NY: McGraw-Hill.
2. Richmond, V. P., & McCroskey, J. C. (2000). *Communication apprehension, avoidance, and effectiveness* (5th ed.). Scottsdale, AZ: Gorsuch Scarisbrick.
3. Phillips, G. M. (1977). Rhetoritherapy versus the medical model: Dealing with reticence. *Communication Education, 26,* 37.
4. Motley, M. (1997). COM therapy. In J. A. Daly, J. C. McCroskey, J. Ayres, T. Hopf, & D. M. Ayres (Eds.), *Avoiding communication: Shyness, reticence, and communication apprehension* (2nd ed., p. 382). Cresskill, NJ: Hampton Press.
5. Phillips, Rhetoritherapy versus the medical model, 37.
6. Richmond & McCroskey, *Communication.*
7. Behnke, R. R., & Carlile, L. W. (1971). Heart rate as an index of speech anxiety. *Speech Monographs, 38,* 66.
8. Beatty, M. J., & Behnke, R. R. (1991). Effects of public speaking trait anxiety and intensity of speaking task on heart rate during performance. *Human Communication Research, 18,* 147–176.
9. Richmond & McCroskey, *Communication.*
10. Beatty, M. J., McCroskey, J. C., & Heisner, A. D. (1998). Communication apprehension as temperamental expression: A communibiological paradigm. *Communication Monographs, 65,* 200.
11. Richmond & McCroskey, *Communication.*
12. Bandura, A. (1973). *Social learning theory.* Englewood Cliffs, NJ: Prentice Hall.
13. Daly, J. A., Caughlin, J. P., & Stafford, L. (1997). Correlates and consequences of social-communicative anxiety. In J. A. Daly, J. C. McCroskey, J. Ayres, T. Hopf, & D. M. Ayres (Eds.), *Avoiding communication: Shyness, reticence, and communication apprehension* (2nd ed., p. 27). Cresskill, NJ: Hampton Press.
14. White, D. (1998). Smile when you say that. *Working Woman,* 94–95.
15. Motley, COM therapy, 382.
16. Ibid., 380.
17. Ayres, J., & Hopf, T. S. (1990). The long-term effect of visualization in the classroom: A brief research report. *Communication Education, 39,* 77.
18. Ayres, J., Hopf, T., & Ayres, D. M. (1994). An examination of whether imaging ability enhances the effectiveness of an intervention designed to reduce speech anxiety. *Communication Education, 43,* 256.
19. Bourne, E. J. (1990). *The anxiety and phobia workbook.* Oakland, CA: New Harbinger Publications.
20. Friedrich, G., & Goss, B. (1984). Systematic desensitization. In J. A. Daly & J. C. McCroskey (Eds.), *Avoiding communication.* Beverly Hills, CA: Sage.
21. Davis, M., Echelon, E., & McKay, M. (1988). *The relaxation and stress workbook.* Oakland, CA: New Harbinger Publications.
22. Richmond & McCroskey, *Communication.*
23. Ibid.
24. Griffin, K. (1995). Beating performance anxiety. *Working Woman,* 62–65, 76.
25. Kelly, L., Phillips, G. M., & Keaten, J. A. (1995). *Teaching people to speak well: Training and remediation of communication reticence* (p. 11). Cresskill, NJ: Hampton Press.
26. Ibid., 11–13.

27. Dwyer, K. K. (2000). The multidimensional model: Teaching students to self-manage high communication apprehension by self-selecting treatments. *Communication Education, 49*, 79.

28. Richmond & McCroskey, *Communication*.

29. Study shows how sleep improves memory. (2005, June 29). *Science Daily*. Retrieved from http://www.sciencedaily.com/releases/2005/06/050629070337.htm

30. Caplan, H. (Trans.). (1954). *Rhetorica ad herennium*. Cambridge, MA: Harvard University Press.

31. Bitzer, L. (1968). The rhetorical situation. *Philosophy and Rhetoric, 1*(1), 1–14.

32. Aristotle. (1960). *On rhetoric* (L. Cooper, Trans.). New York, NY: Appleton-Century-Crofts.

33. Fisher, W. (1987). *Human communication as narration: Toward a philosophy of reason, value, and action*. Columbia: University of South Carolina Press.

Chapter 3 Listening and Responding Effectively

1. International Listening Association. (1996). Retrieved from http://www.listen.org/

2. Janusik, L. A., & Wolvin, A. D. (2006). *24 hours in a day: A listening update to the time studies*. Paper presented at the meeting of the International Listening Association, Salem, OR.

3. International Listening Association. (2003). Listening factoid. Retrieved from http://www.listen.org/pages/factoids/html

4. DeWine, S., & Daniels, T. (1993). Beyond the snapshot: Setting a research agenda in organizational communication. In S. A. Deetz (Ed.), *Communication yearbook 16* (pp. 252–230). Thousand Oaks, CA: Sage.

5. Salopek, J. J. (1999). Is anyone listening? *Training and Development, 53*(9), 58–60.

6. Millar, D. P., & Irvine, R. B. (1996). *Exposing the errors: An examination of the nature of organizational crisis*. Paper presented at the annual conference of the Speech Communication Association, San Diego, CA.

7. Wolvin, A., & Coakley, C. G. (1996). *Listening* (5th ed.). New York, NY: McGraw-Hill.

8. Ibid.

9. Stephens, M. (1999). The new TV: Stop making sense. In R. E. Hiebert (Ed.), *Impact of mass media: Current issues* (4th ed., pp. 16–22). White Plains, NY: Longman.

10. Dukette, D., & Cornish, D. (2009). *The essential 20: Twenty components of an excellent health care team* (pp. 72–73). Pittsburgh, PA: RoseDog Books; Turning into digital goldfish. (2002, February 22). *BBC News*. Retrieved from http://news.bbc.co.uk/2/hi/science/nature/1834682.stm

11. Sharpening your listening skills. (2002). *Teller Vision*, 0895-1039, 7.

12. Lebauer, R. S. (2000). *Learning to listen, listen to learn: Academic listening and note-taking* (2nd ed., p. 49). White Plains, NY: Longman.

13. Dunkel, P., & Pialorsi, F. (2005). *Advanced listening comprehension: Developing aural and notetaking skills*. Boston, MA: Thomson Heinle; Wolvin & Coakley, *Listening*.

Chapter 4 Selecting an Appropriate Speech Goal

1. Berger, C. R. (1988). Uncertainty reduction and information exchange in developing relationships. In S. Duck, D. Hay, S. Hobfoll, W. Ickes, & B. Montgomery (Eds.), *Handbook of interpersonal relationships: Theory, research, and interventions* (pp. 239–255). New York, NY: Wiley.

2. Callison, D. (2001). Concept mapping. *School Library Media Activities Monthly, 17*(10), 30–32.

Chapter 5 Adapting to Audiences

1. Bates, S. (2005). *Speak like a CEO: Secrets for commanding attention and getting results*. New York, NY: McGraw-Hill.

2. Blumer, H. (1969). *Symbolic interactionism*. Englewood Cliffs, NJ: Prentice Hall.

3. Barbe, W., & Swassing, R. H. (1979). *The Swassing-Barbe modality index*. Columbus, OH: Waner-Bloser; Canfield, A. A. (1980). *Learning styles inventory manual*. Ann Arbor, MI: Humanics Inc.; Dunn, R., Dunn, K., & Price, G. E. (1975). *Learning styles inventory*. Lawrence, KS: Price Systems; Gardner, H. (1983). *Frames of mind: The theory of multiple intelligences*. New York, NY: Basic Books; Kolb, D. (1984). *Experiential learning: Experience as the source of learning and development*. Englewood Cliffs, NJ: Prentice Hall.

4. Kolb, *Experiential learning*.

5. Dewey, J. (1938/1997). *Experience and education*. New York, NY: Macmillan.

6. Ibid.

7. *The world almanac and book of facts* (pp. 798, 850). (2004). New York, NY: World Almanac Books.

Chapter 6 Gathering and Evaluating Information

1. Munger, D., Anderson, D., Benjamin, B., Busiel, C., & Pardes-Holt, B. (2000). *Researching online* (3rd ed.). New York, NY: Longman.

2. Tengler, C., & Jablin, F. M. (1983). Effects of question type, orientation, and sequencing in the employment screening interview. *Communication Monographs, 50*, 261.

3. Biagi, S. (1992). *Interviews that work: A practical guide for journalists* (2nd ed., p. 94). Belmont, CA: Wadsworth.

4. Frances, P. (1994). Lies, damned lies. *American Demographics, 16*, 2.

5. Ibid.

6. Ahladas, J. (1989, April 1). Global warming. *Vital Speeches*, 382.

7. Shalala, D. (1994, May 15). Domestic terrorism: An unacknowledged epidemic. *Vital Speeches*, 451.

8. Howard, J. A. (2000, August 1). Principles in default: Rediscovered and reapplied. *Vital Speeches*, 618.

9. Trachtenberg, S. (1986, August 15). Five ways in which thinking is dangerous. *Vital Speeches*, 653.

10. Durst, G. M. (1989, March 1). The manager as a developer. *Vital Speeches*, 309–310.

11. Becerer, H. (2000, September 15). Enduring values for a secular age: Faith, hope and love. *Vital Speeches*, 732.

12. Opheim, C. (2000, November 1). Making democracy work: Your responsibility to society. *Vital Speeches*, 60.

Chapter 7 Organizing and Outlining the Speech Body

1. Fisher, W. (1987). *Human communication as narration: Toward a philosophy of reason, value, and action*. Columbia: University of South Carolina Press.

Chapter 8 The Introduction and Conclusion

1. Trenholm, S. (1989). *Persuasion and social influence*. Englewood Cliffs, NJ: Prentice-Hall; Crano, W. D. (1977). Primacy versus recency in retention of information and opinion change. *The Journal of Social Psychology, 101*, 87–96.

2. Mackay, H. (2009, July). Changing the world: Your future is a work in progress. *Vital Speeches*, 319–323.

3. Humes, J. C. (1988). *Standing ovation: How to be an effective speaker and communicator*. New York, NY: Harper & Row.

4. Cole, B. (2002, July). The urgency of memory: The arts give us history. *Vital Speeches of the Day*, 563–565.

5. Mason, S. (2007, April). Equality will someday come. *Vital Speeches*, 159–163.

6. Princeton Language Institute (Ed.). (1993). *21st century dictionary of quotations*. New York, NY: Laurel.

7. Aristotle. (1954). *The Rhetoric* (W. Rhys Roberts, Trans.). New York, NY: Modern Library.

8. Mariano, C. (2010, January). Unity, quality, responsibility: The real meaning of the words. *Vital Speeches*, 20–22.

9. Jobs, S. (2005, June 15). "You've got to find what you love," Job says. *Stanford University News*. Retrieved from http://news.stanford.edu/news/2005/june15/jobs-061505.html

10. Cossolotto, M. (2009, December). An urgent call to action for study abroad alumni to help reduce our global awareness deficit. *Vital Speeches*, 564–568.

Chapter 9 Presentational Aids

1. Muren, D. (2009). *Humblefacturing a sustainable electronic future*. Presentation at Ignite Seattle 6. Retrieved from http://www.youtube.com/watch?v=FloU1pemi18

2. Tversky, B. (1997). Memory for pictures, maps, environments, and graphs. In D. G. Payne & F. G. Conrad (Eds.), *Intersections in basic and applied memory research* (pp. 257–277). Hillsdale, NJ: Erlbaum.

3. Gallo, C. (2006, December 5). Presentations with something for everyone. *Bloomberg Businessweek*. Retrieved from http://www.businessweek.com/smallbiz/content/dec2006/sb20061205_454055.htm; Kolb, D. (1984). *Experiential learning: Experience as the source of learning and development*. Englewood Cliffs, NJ: Prentice Hall.

4. Hanke, J. (1998). The psychology of presentation visuals. *Presentations, 12*(5), 42–47.

5. Ayers, J. (1991). Using visual aids to reduce speech anxiety. *Communication Research Reports, 8*, 73–79; Dwyer, K. (1991). *Conquer your speechfright*. Orlando, FL: Harcourt Brace.

6. Booher, D. (2003). *Speak with confidence: Powerful presentations that inform, inspire, and persuade*. New York, NY: McGraw-Hill.

7. Kolb, *Experiential learning*; Long, K. (1997). *Visual-aids and learning*. University of Portsmouth. Retrieved from http://www.mech.port.ac.uk/av/AVInfo.htm

8. Brandt, J. R. (2007, January). Missing the (Power)point: When bullet points fly, attention spans die. *Industry Week*. Retrieved from http://www.industryweek.com; Wahl, A. (2003). PowerPoint of no return. *Canadian Business, 76*(22), 131–133.

Chapter 10 Language and Oral Style

1. Witt, P. L., Wheeless, L. R., & Allen, M. (2007, May). A meta-analytical review of the relationship between teacher immediacy and student learning. Paper presented at the annual meeting of the International Communication Association, San Diego, CA. Retrieved from http://www.allacademic.com/meta/p112238_index.html

2. Edwards, C. C. (2002). Verbal immediacy and androgyny: An examination of student perceptions of college instructors. *Academic Exchange Quarterly, 6*, 180–185; Gorham, J. (1998). The relationship between teacher verbal immediacy behaviors and student learning. *Communication Education, 37*, 40–53; Powell R. G., & Harville, B. (1990). The effects of teacher immediacy and clarity on instructional outcomes: An intercultural assessment. *Communication Education, 39*, 369–379.

3. Braithwaite D., & Braithwaite, C. (1997). Viewing persons with disabilities as a culture. In L. Samovar & R. Porter (Eds.), *Intercultural communication: A reader* (8th ed., pp. 154–164). Belmont, CA: Wadsworth; Treinen, K., & Warren, J. (2001). Antiracist pedagogy in the basic course: Teaching cultural communication as if whiteness matters. *Basic Communication Course Annual, 13*, 46–75.

4. Stewart, L. P., Cooper, P. J., Stewart, A. D., & Friedley, S. A. (2003). *Communication and gender* (4th ed., p. 63). Boston, MA: Allyn & Bacon.

5. Gastil, J. (1990). Generic pronouns and sexist language: The oxymoronic character of masculine generics. *Sex Roles, 23*, 629–643; Hamilton, M. C. (1991). Masculine bias in the attribution of personhood: People = male, male = people. *Psychology of Women Quarterly, 15*, 393–402; Switzer, J. W. (1990). The impact of generic word choices: An empirical investigation of age- and sex-related differences. *Sex Roles, 22*, 69–82.

6. Treinen & Warren, Antiracist pedagogy in the basic course, 13.

7. Gudykunst, W. B., & Matsumoto, Y. (1996). Cross-cultural variability of communication in personal relationships. In W. B. Gudykunst, S. Ting-Toomey, & T. Nishida (Eds.), *Communication in personal relationships across cultures* (p. 21). Thousand Oaks, CA: Sage.

8. Hofstede, G. (1991). *Cultures and organizations: Software of the mind* (p. 67). New York, NY: McGraw-Hill.

9. Levine, D. (1985). *The flight from ambiguity* (p. 28). Chicago, IL: University of Chicago Press.

10. MTV video music awards [Video]. (2003, August 28). Retrieved from http://www.mtv.com/onair/vma/2003/

11. DuFrene D. D., & Lehman, C. M. (2002). Persuasive appeal for clean language. *Business Quarterly, 65*, 48.

12. O'Connor, J. V. (2000). FAQs #1. *Cuss Control Academy*. Retrieved from http://www.cusscontrol.com/faqs.html

13. Duck, S. W. (1994). *Meaningful relationships*. Thousand Oaks, CA: Sage. See also Shotter, J. (1993). *Conversational realities: The construction of life through language*. Newbury Park, CA: Sage.

14. Richards, I. A., & Ogden, C. K. (1923). *The meaning of meaning: A study of the influence of language upon thought and the science of symbolism*. Orlando, FL: Harcourt.

15. Ibid.

16. Fought, C. (2003). *Chicano English in context* (pp. 64–78). New York, NY: Pallgrave MacMillan.

17. Glenn, C., & Gray, L. (2010). *Hodges Harbrace handbook* (17th ed.). Belmont, CA: Cengage Learning.

18. Robinson, A. (2001). *Word smart: Building an educated vocabulary* (3rd ed.). Princeton, NJ: Princeton Review.

19. Rader, W. (2007). The online slang dictionary. Retrieved from http://www.ocf.berkeley.edu/~wrader/slang/b.html

20. Hensley, C. W. (1995, September 1). Speak with style and watch the impact. *Vital Speeches of the Day*, 703.

21. Schertz, R. H. (1977, November 1). Deregulation: After the airlines, is trucking next? *Vital Speeches of the Day*, 40.

22. Reprinted by arrangement with the Estate of Martin Luther King, Jr. c/o Writers House as agent for the proprietor New York, NY. Copyright 1963 Dr. Martin Luther King, Jr., copyright renewed 1991 Coretta Scott King.

Chapter 11 Practicing Delivery

1. Decker, B. (1992). *You've got to be believed to be heard*. New York, NY: St. Martin's Press.

2. Watzlawick, P., Bavelas, J. B., & Jackson, D. D. (1967). *Pragmatics of human communication*. New York, NY: Norton.

3. Burgoon, J. K., Coker, D. A., & Coker, R. A. (1986). Communicative effects of gaze behavior: A test of two contrasting explanations. *Human Communication Research, 12*, 495–524.

4. Chiang, L. H. (1993). *Beyond the language: Native Americans' nonverbal communication*. Paper presented at the annual meeting of the Midwest Association of Teachers of Educational Psychology, Anderson, IN (ERIC Document Services No. ED 368 540).

5. Bates, B. (1992). *Communication and the sexes*. Prospect Heights, IL: Waveland Press; Cherulnik, P. D. (1989). *Physical attractiveness and judged suitability for leadership*, Report No. CG 021 893. Paper presented at the annual meeting of the Midwestern Psychological Association, Chicago, IL (ERIC Document Services No. ED 310 317); Lawrence S. G., & Watson, M. (1991). Getting others to help: The effectiveness of professional uniforms in charitable fund raising. *Journal of Applied Communication Research,*

19, 170–185; Malloy, J. T. (1975). *Dress for success.* New York, NY: Warner; Temple, L. E., & Loewen, K. R. (1993). Perceptions of power: First impressions of a woman wearing a jacket. *Perceptual and Motor Skills, 76*, 339–348.

6. Phillips P. A., & Smith, L. R. (1992). *The effects of teacher dress on student perceptions*, Report No. SP 033 944 (ERIC Document Services No. ED 347 151).

7. Morris, T. L., Gorham, J., Cohen, S. H., & Huffman, D. (1996). Fashion in the classroom: Effects of attire on student perceptions of instructors in college classes. *Communication Education, 45*, 135–148.

8. Menzel, K. E., & Carrell, L. J. (1994). The relationship between preparation and performance in public speaking. *Communication Education, 43*, 23.

9. Used with permission of Alyssa Grace Millner.

Chapter 12 Informative Speaking

1. Otzi, the ice man. (n.d.). *Dig: The archaeology magazine for kids.* Retrieved from http://www.digonsite.com/drdig /mummy/22.html

2. Vegan Society website. Retrieved from http://www.vegansociety.com

3. Based on Baerwald, D., & Northshore School District. Narrative. Retrieved from http://ccweb.norshore.wednet.edu/writingcorner /narrative.html

4. Used with permission of Louisa Greene.

5. Used with permission of Megan Soileau.

Chapter 13 Understanding Persuasive Messages

1. Perloff, R. M. (1993). *The dynamics of persuasion.* Hillsdale, NJ: Erlbaum.

2. Kennedy, G. A. (1980). *Classical rhetoric and its Christian and secular tradition from ancient to modern times.* Chapel Hill: University of North Carolina Press.

3. Aristotle. (1960). *The rhetoric* (L. Cooper, Trans.). New York, NY: Appleton-Century-Crofts.

4. Perloff, *The dynamics of persuasion.*

5. Toulmin, S. (1958). *The uses of argument.* Cambridge, England: Cambridge University Press.

6. Ibid.

7. National Institute on Aging. (n.d.) Alzheimer's disease: A looming national crisis. Retrieved from http://www.nia.nih.gov/Alzheimers /Publications /ADProgress2005_2006/Part1 /looming.htm

8. Labor, R. (1998). Shaken baby syndrome: The silent epidemic. In *Winning orations* (pp. 70–72). Mankato, MN: Interstate Oratorical Association.

9. James, J. (2007, January). No time for complacency. *Vital Speeches of the Day*, 26–29.

10. Ibid.

11. Ibid.

12. Stewart, R. (1994). Perceptions of a speaker's initial credibility as a function of religious involvement and religious disclosiveness. *Communication Research Reports, 11*, 169–176.

13. Perloff, *The dynamics of persuasion*, 145–149.

14. Morris, T. L., Gorham, J., Cohen, S. H., & Huffman, D. (1996). Fashion in the classroom: Effects of attire on student perceptions of instructors in college classes. *Communication Education, 45*, 135–148; Treinen, K. (1998). *The effects of gender and physical attractiveness on peer critiques of a persuasive speech.* Unpublished master's thesis, North Dakota State University, Fargo, ND.

15. Perloff, *The dynamics of persuasion.*

16. Petri, H. L., & Govern, J. M. (2004). *Motivation: Theory, research, and application* (5th ed., p. 376). Belmont, CA: Wadsworth.

17. Eagly, A. H., & Chaiken, S. (1992). *The psychology of attitudes.* Fort Worth, TX: Harcourt Brace; Maloney, S. R. (1992). *Talk your way to the top.* Englewood Cliffs, NJ: Prentice Hall.

18. Nabi, R. L. (2002). Discrete emotions and persuasion. In J. P. Dillard & M. Pfau (Eds.), *The persuasion handbook: Developments in theory and practice* (pp. 291–299). Thousand Oaks, CA: Sage.

19. Cannon, A. (1996, May 13). Megan's law passes, mom promises to fight any judicial appeals. Retrieved from http://www.accessmylibrary.com/coms2 /summary_0286-6368573_ITM

20. Slater, D. (1998). Sharing life. In *Winning orations* (pp. 63–66). Mankato, MN: Interstate Oratorical Association.

Chapter 14 Persuasive Speaking

1. Petty, R. E., & Cacioppo, J. (1996). *Attitudes and persuasion: Classic and contemporary approaches* (p. 7). Boulder, CO: Westview.

2. Hill, B., & Leeman, R. W. (1997). *The art and practice of argumentation and debate* (p. 135). Mountain View, CA: Mayfield.

3. Ziegelmueller, G. W., Kay, J., & Dause, C. A. (1990). *Argumentation: Inquiry and advocacy* (2nd ed., p. 186). Englewood Cliffs, NJ: Prentice Hall.

4. Used with permission.

5. Facts pages: History and statistics of U.S. waste production and recycling. (n.d.). *Tufts Recycles.* Retrieved from http://www.tufts .edu/tuftsrecycles /usstats.html

6. Used with permission.

Chapter 16 Developing and Delivering Group Presentations

1. Katzenbach, J. R., Garvin, D. A., & Wenger E. C. (2004). *Harvard Business Review on teams that succeed.* Boston, MA: Harvard Business School Press; O'Hair, D., O'Rourke, J., & O'Hair, M. (2001). *Business communication: A framework for success.* Cincinnati, OH: South-Western; Snyder, B. (2004). Differing views cultivate better decisions. *Stanford Business.* Retrieved from http://www.gsb .stanford.edu/NEWS/bmag/sbsm0405/feature _workteams_gruenfeld.shtml

2. Tullar, W., & Kaiser, P. (2000). The effect of process training on process and outcomes in virtual groups. *Journal of Business Communication, 37*, 408–427.

3. Lesikar, R., Pettit J. Jr., & Flately, M. (1999). *Basic business communication* (8th ed.). New York, NY: McGraw-Hill.

4. Rahim, M. A. (2001). *Managing conflict in organizations* (3rd ed.). Westport, CT: Greenwood Press.

5. Janis, I. L. (1982). *Groupthink: Psychological studies of policy decision and fiascos* (2nd ed.). Boston, MA: Houghton Mifflin.

6. Conrad, C. (1997). *Strategic organizational communication: Toward the 21st century.* Orlando, FL: Harcourt Brace.

7. Godamer, H. (1989). *Truth and method* (2nd ed., J. Weinsheimer & D. G. Marshall, Trans.). New York, NY: Crossroad.

8. Braithwaite, D. O., & Eckstein, N. (2003). Reconceptualizing supportive interactions: How persons with disabilities communicatively manage assistance. *Journal of Applied Communication Research, 31*, 1–26.

9. Dewey, J. (1933). *How we think.* Boston, MA: Heath.

10. Duch, B. J., Groh, S. E., & Allen, D. E. (Eds.). (2001). *The power of problem-based learning.* Sterling, VA: Stylus; Edens, K. M. (2000). Preparing problem solvers for the 21st century through problem-based learning. *College Teaching, 48*(2), 55–60; Levin, B. B. (Ed.). (2001). *Energizing teacher education and professional development with problem-based learning.* Alexandria, MN: Association for Supervision and Curriculum Development.

Index

Chapter in Review

To help you succeed, we've designed a Review Card for each chapter.

public speaking
a sustained formal presentation by a speaker to an audience

communication
the process of crea...

participants
the individual...
of senders and re...
interaction

Here you'll find the key terms and their definitions in the order in which they appear in the chapter.

senders
participants who form and transmit messages using verbal symbols and nonverbal behaviors

receivers
participants who interpret the messages sent by others

messages
the verbal utterances, visual images, and nonverbal behaviors to which meaning is attributed during communication

meanings
the interpretations participants make of the messages they send and receive

encoding
the process of putting our thoughts and feelings into words and nonverbal behaviors

decoding
the process of interpreting the verbal and nonverbal messages sent by others

feedback messages
messages sent by receivers intended to let the sender know how the receiver made sense of the original message

channels
both the route traveled by a message and the means of transportation

interference/noise
any stimulus that interferes with the process of sharing meaning

feedback
the reactions and responses to messages that indicate to the sender whether and how a message was heard, seen, and interpreted

intrapersonal communication

How to Use This Card:

1. Look over the card to preview the new concepts you'll be introduced to in the chapter.

2. Read the chapter to understand the material.

3. Go to class (and pay attention).

4. Review the card to make sure you've registered the key concepts. Take the Chapter Quiz to test your comprehension.

5. Don't forget, this card is only one of many SPEAK learning tools available to help you succeed in learning.

LO1 How does the communication process work?
Public speaking is important to achieving success in nearly every walk of life. It is one form of human communication, which consists of participants, messages, channels, interference/noise, feedback, and contexts.

LO2 What are the contexts in which communication occurs?
Public speaking occurs within the public communication context. Intrapersonal, interpersonal, small group communicate, and public communication are additional contexts within which we communicate regularly.

LO3 What is public speaking, ...ly?
Effective public speaking skill... ...e for us to enact our civic responsibility to participate actively ...

In this column, you'll find summary points that give an overview of important concepts.

LO4 What does it mean to be an ethical speaker?
To enact our civil responsibility, we must adhere to five essential ethical principles: to be honest, to have integrity, to behave fairly, to demonstrate respect for others, and to act responsibly. Public speaking challenges us to behave ethically.

LO5 How does understanding the rhetorical situation help you prepare a speech?
Public speaking is an audience-centered process that occurs within a rhetorical situation comprised of speaker, audience, and occasion and is guided by exigence.

LO6 What makes a speech effective?
How effective a speech is depends on how well audience members listen to, understand, remember, and are motivated to act on what the speaker has said.

LO7 What process can you use to prepare and make effective speeches?
The audience-centered speaker demonstrates honesty and respect for listeners by employing ethos, pathos, and logos throughout the speech-planning and -presenting process and adhering to principles of effective content, structure, and delivery.

Chapter Quiz

True/False

1. Public speaking can occur in an informal setting.
2. The meaning of what a speaker is saying is almost always easy to interpret.
3. During communication, noise can be due to physical reasons or psychological reasons.
4. Interpersonal communication is another term for self-talk.
5. The participants of a communication process are known as senders and receivers.

Multiple Choice

Newspapers and magazines are...
a. mass communication
b. small group communication
c. interpersonal communication
d. intrapersonal communication
e. targeted communication

Every chapter has a short self-assessment quiz for you to use while reviewing the chapter. You will find the answer key at the end of the quiz.

During a lecture on police training, an audience member raises his hand and asks the speaker to clarify the last point that he made. This is an example of:
a. encoding
b. decoding
c. noise
d. channels
e. feedback

Glossary

mass communication
communication produced and transmitted via media to massive audiences

liberal art
a body of general knowledge and skills needed to participate effectively in a democratic society

ethics
moral principles that a society, group, or individual holds that differentiate right from wrong and good behavior from bad behavior

plagiarism
passing off the ideas, words, or created works of another as one's own by failing to credit the source

rhetorical situation
the composite of the occasion, speaker, and the audience that influences the speech that is given

exigence
some real or perceived need that a speech might help address

speaker
the source or originator of the speech

audience
the specific group of people to whom your speech is directed

audience analysis
a study made to learn about the diverse characteristics of audience members and then, based on these characteristics, to predict how audience members are apt to listen to, understand, and be motivated to act on your speech

occasion
the setting in which the speech is given

speech effectiveness
the extent to which audience members listen to, understand, remember, and are motivated to act on what a speaker has said

audience centered
offering ideas in ways that respond to a felt need, are appropriate to the occasion, reflect careful research, make sense, and sound interesting

ethos
everything you say and do to convey competence and good character

pathos
everything you say and do to appeal to emotions

logos
everything you say and do to appeal to logic and sound reasoning

macrostructure
the overall framework you use to organize your speech content

microstructure
the specific language and style choices you use as you frame your ideas and verbalize them to your audience

rhetorical devices
language techniques designed to create audience attention, hold interest, and aid memory

delivery
how you use your voice and body to present your message

---

8. All of the following are ethical principles speakers should follow EXCEPT:
    a. Ethical communicators are honest.
    b. Ethical communicators are responsible.
    c. Ethical communicators have integrity.
    d. Ethical communicators have little respect for others.
    e. Ethical communicators are fair.
9. The source or originator of the speech is the:
    a. audience
    b. speaker
    c. teacher
    d. professor
    e. research
10. All of the following are elements of the communication process EXCEPT:
    a. messages
    b. channels
    c. criticism
    d. noise
    e. feedback

Answers:
1. F; 2. F; 3. T; 4. F; 5. T; 6. a; 7. e; 8. d; 9. b; 10. c

Speech Snippets

Being Audience Centered

Kris's first speech was a speech of self-introduction. Her audience was her classmates, a diverse group of men and women with a variety of life experiences. In planning what to say, Kris decided to concentrate on how being who she is led to her major. In this way, she hoped to help her audience know her by comparing her academic journey to their own.

Content

Kris decided to talk about how growing up in a resort town influenced her plans to study hospitality management, how being an identical twin contributed to her decision to attend this college, and how she hoped to use her major to work in a ski resort where she could help children with disabilities learn to snowboard. She made sure her content was audience centered by focusing on the importance of pursuing one's dreams when selecting a major and a career goal.

Macrostructure

Kris decided that the most logical way to present her main ideas was chronologically. She would begin by talking about being a twin, then discuss how her upbringing influenced her choice of majors, and then she'd conclude with her dream of teaching kids with disabilities to snowboard. She planned to use people's curiosity about twins to pique interest during her introduction, and she planned a conclusion that would challenge her audience to pursue their passions.

Rhetorical Devices

Kris used the rhetorical device called *hypophora*, when the speaker raises a question to pique the audience's curiosity and then answers it: "Have you ever looked into a mirror and seen your reflection and realized that the reflection in the mirror wasn't really you? I have, many times."

1 Chapter in Review

public speaking
a sustained formal presentation by a speaker to an audience

communication
the process of creating shared meaning

participants
the individuals who assume the roles of senders and receivers during an interaction

senders
participants who form and transmit messages using verbal symbols and nonverbal behaviors

receivers
participants who interpret the messages sent by others

messages
the verbal utterances, visual images, and nonverbal behaviors to which meaning is attributed during communication

meanings
the interpretations participants make of the messages they send and receive

encoding
the process of putting our thoughts and feelings into words and nonverbal behaviors

decoding
the process of interpreting the verbal and nonverbal messages sent by others

feedback messages
messages sent by receivers intended to let the sender know how the receiver made sense of the original message

channels
both the route traveled by a message and the means of transportation

interference/noise
any stimulus that interferes with the process of sharing meaning

feedback
the reactions and responses to messages that indicate to the sender whether and how a message was heard, seen, and interpreted

intrapersonal communication
communicating with yourself (a.k.a. self-talk)

interpersonal communication
communication between two people

small group communication
communication that occurs among approximately three to 10 people

public communication
communication that occurs among more than 10 people where one message is presented to the participants who function as receivers whose own messages are limited primarily to feedback

 LO1 How does the communication process work?

Public speaking is important to achieving success in nearly every walk of life. It is one form of human communication, which consists of participants, messages, channels, interference/noise, feedback, and contexts.

 LO2 What are the contexts in which communication occurs?

Public speaking occurs within the public communication context. Intrapersonal, interpersonal, small group communicate, and public communication are additional contexts within which we communicate regularly.

LO3 What is public speaking, and why is it important to study?

Effective public speaking skills are a liberal art that makes it possible for us to enact our civic responsibility to participate actively as a member of a democratic society.

 LO4 What does it mean to be an ethical speaker?

To enact our civil responsibility, we must adhere to five essential ethical principles: to be honest, to have integrity, to behave fairly, to demonstrate respect for others, and to act responsibly. Public speaking challenges us to behave ethically.

 LO5 How does understanding the rhetorical situation help you prepare a speech?

Public speaking is an audience-centered process that occurs within a rhetorical situation comprised of speaker, audience, and occasion and is guided by exigence.

LO6 What makes a speech effective?

How effective a speech is depends on how well audience members listen to, understand, remember, and are motivated to act on what the speaker has said.

LO7 What process can you use to prepare and make effective speeches?

The audience-centered speaker demonstrates honesty and respect for listeners by employing ethos, pathos, and logos throughout the speech-planning and -presenting process and adhering to principles of effective content, structure, and delivery.

Chapter Quiz

True/False

1. Public speaking can occur in an informal setting.
2. The meaning of what a speaker is saying is almost always easy to interpret.
3. During communication, noise can be due to physical reasons or psychological reasons.
4. Interpersonal communication is another term for self-talk.
5. The participants of a communication process are known as senders and receivers.

Multiple Choice

6. Newspapers and magazines are examples of:
   a. mass communication
   b. small group communication
   c. interpersonal communication
   d. intrapersonal communication
   e. targeted communication
7. During a lecture on police training, an audience member raises his hand and asks the speaker to clarify the last point that he made. This is an example of:
   a. encoding
   b. decoding
   c. noise
   d. channels
   e. feedback

Glossary

mass communication
communication produced and transmitted via media to massive audiences

liberal art
a body of general knowledge and skills needed to participate effectively in a democratic society

ethics
moral principles that a society, group, or individual holds that differentiate right from wrong and good behavior from bad behavior

plagiarism
passing off the ideas, words, or created works of another as one's own by failing to credit the source

rhetorical situation
the composite of the occasion, speaker, and the audience that influences the speech that is given

exigence
some real or perceived need that a speech might help address

speaker
the source or originator of the speech

audience
the specific group of people to whom your speech is directed

audience analysis
a study made to learn about the diverse characteristics of audience members and then, based on these characteristics, to predict how audience members are apt to listen to, understand, and be motivated to act on your speech

occasion
the setting in which the speech is given

speech effectiveness
the extent to which audience members listen to, understand, remember, and are motivated to act on what a speaker has said

audience centered
offering ideas in ways that respond to a felt need, are appropriate to the occasion, reflect careful research, make sense, and sound interesting

ethos
everything you say and do to convey competence and good character

pathos
everything you say and do to appeal to emotions

logos
everything you say and do to appeal to logic and sound reasoning

macrostructure
the overall framework you use to organize your speech content

microstructure
the specific language and style choices you use as you frame your ideas and verbalize them to your audience

rhetorical devices
language techniques designed to create audience attention, hold interest, and aid memory

delivery
how you use your voice and body to present your message

---

8. All of the following are ethical principles speakers should follow EXCEPT:
   a. Ethical communicators are honest.
   b. Ethical communicators are responsible.
   c. Ethical communicators have integrity.
   d. Ethical communicators have little respect for others.
   e. Ethical communicators are fair.
9. The source or originator of the speech is the:
   a. audience
   b. speaker
   c. teacher
   d. professor
   e. research
10. All of the following are elements of the communication process EXCEPT:
   a. messages
   b. channels
   c. criticism
   d. noise
   e. feedback

Answers:
1. F; 2. F; 3. T; 4. F; 5. T; 6. a; 7. e; 8. d; 9. b; 10. c

Speech Snippets

Being Audience Centered

Kris's first speech was a speech of self-introduction. Her audience was her classmates, a diverse group of men and women with a variety of life experiences. In planning what to say, Kris decided to concentrate on how being who she is led to her major. In this way, she hoped to help her audience know her by comparing her academic journey to their own.

Content

Kris decided to talk about how growing up in a resort town influenced her plans to study hospitality management, how being an identical twin contributed to her decision to attend this college, and how she hoped to use her major to work in a ski resort where she could help children with disabilities learn to snowboard. She made sure her content was audience centered by focusing on the importance of pursuing one's dreams when selecting a major and a career goal.

Macrostructure

Kris decided that the most logical way to present her main ideas was chronologically. She would begin by talking about being a twin, then discuss how her upbringing influenced her choice of majors, and then she'd conclude with her dream of teaching kids with disabilities to snowboard. She planned to use people's curiosity about twins to pique interest during her introduction, and she planned a conclusion that would challenge her audience to pursue their passions.

Rhetorical Devices

Kris used the rhetorical device called *hypophora*, when the speaker raises a question to pique the audience's curiosity and then answers it: "Have you ever looked into a mirror and seen your reflection and realized that the reflection in the mirror wasn't really you? I have, many times."

Chapter in Review

public speaking apprehension
the level of fear a person experiences when anticipating or actually speaking to an audience

anticipation phase
the anxiety you experience prior to giving the speech, including the nervousness you feel while preparing and waiting to speak

confrontation phase
the surge of anxiety you feel as you begin delivering your speech

adaptation phase
the period during which your anxiety level gradually decreases

self-talk
intrapersonal communication regarding perceived success or failure in a particular situation

modeling
learning by observing and then imitating those you admire or are close to

reinforcement
learning from personal experiences so that past responses to our behavior shape our expectations about how our future behavior will be received

communication orientation motivation (COM) techniques
designed to reduce anxiety by helping the speaker adopt a "communication" rather than a "performance" orientation toward the speech

performance orientation
viewing public speaking as a situation demanding special delivery techniques to impress an audience aesthetically or viewing audience members as hypercritical judges who will not forgive even minor mistakes

communication orientation
viewing a speech as just an opportunity to talk with a number of people about an important topic

visualization
a method that reduces apprehension by helping speakers develop a mental picture of themselves giving a masterful speech

relaxation exercises
breathing techniques and progressive muscle relaxation exercises that help reduce anxiety

systematic desensitization
a method that reduces apprehension by gradually having people visualize and perform increasingly more frightening events while remaining in a relaxed state

 LO1 What is public speaking apprehension?
Public speaking apprehension is the level of fear a person experiences when speaking. Symptoms include cognitive, physical, and emotional reactions that vary from person to person. The level of apprehension varies over the course of speaking.

LO2 Why do we experience public speaking apprehension?
The main cause of public speaking apprehension is negative self-talk. Research suggests that negative thoughts have three common roots: biologically based temperament, previous experience, and level of skills.

LO3 What can we do to manage public speaking apprehension?
Several methods are available for managing public speaking apprehension. General methods include communication orientation motivation (COM) techniques, visualization, relaxation exercises, systematic desensitization, cognitive restructuring, and public speaking skills training. Specific techniques include allowing sufficient time to prepare, using presentational aids, practicing the speech aloud, dressing up, choosing an appropriate time to speak, using positive self-talk, facing the audience with confidence, and focusing on sharing your message.

 LO4 In what ways does careful planning help reduce public speaking apprehension?
Gaining confidence through effective speech planning reduces public speaking apprehension and increases speaking effectiveness.

LO5 What are the six steps in an effective speech action plan?
An effective speech plan is the product of six action steps. The first step is to select a speech goal that is appropriate to the rhetorical situation. The second step is to understand your audience and adapt to it. The third step is to gather and evaluate information to use in the speech. The fourth step is to organize and develop ideas into a well-structured outline. The fifth step is to choose, prepare, and use appropriate presentational aids. And the sixth step is to practice oral language and delivery style of the speech until you sound confident and fluent.

Exhibit 2.3

Negative Self-Talk Versus Positive Coping Statements

Negative Self-Talk	Positive Coping Statements
I'm afraid I'll stumble over my words and look foolish.	Even if I stumble, I will have succeeded as long as I get my message across.
I'm afraid everyone will be able to tell that I'm nervous.	They probably won't be able to tell I'm nervous, but as long as I focus on getting my message across, that's what matters.
I'm afraid my voice will crack.	Even if my voice cracks, as long as I keep going and focus on getting my message across, I'll succeed at what matters most.
I'm afraid I'll sound boring.	I won't sound boring if I focus on how important this message is to me and to my audience. I don't have to do somersaults to keep the audience's attention, because my topic is relevant to them.

© Cengage Learning 2011

Chapter Quiz

True/False

1. Speaking apprehension may actually make you a better speaker.
2. During the adaptation phase, a speaker's level of anxiety begins to decrease.

cognitive restructuring
a process designed to help you systematically change your intrapersonal communication (self-talk) about public speaking

public speaking skills training
systematic practicing of the skills associated with the processes involved in preparing and delivering an effective public speech with the intention of improving speaking competence and reducing public speaking apprehension

speech plan
a strategy for achieving your goal

canons of rhetoric
five general rules for effective public speeches

speech goal
a specific statement of what you want your listeners to know, believe, or do

audience adaptation
the process of tailoring your speech's information to the needs, interests, and expectations of your listeners

narrative/personal experience speech
a presentation in which you recount an experience or experiences you have had and the significance you attach to it or them

moral
a life lesson about right and wrong

3. One way to reduce public speaking apprehension is to develop a mental picture of giving a great speech.
4. For most speakers, their apprehension results from previous negative experiences in public speaking.
5. Public speaking apprehension only occurs in the moments before giving a speech.

Multiple Choice

6. Which of the following is not a specific technique for managing apprehension?
   a. practicing the speech aloud
   b. relaxation exercises
   c. using positive self-talk
   d. sufficient preparation time
   e. using presentational aids
7. The symptoms of public speaking apprehension can be cognitive, physical, or:
   a. mental
   b. emotional
   c. tactile
   d. intellectual
   e. spiritual
8. The process of tailoring a speech's information to the needs, interests, and expectations of the audience is:
   a. audience analysis
   b. audience interpretation
   c. audience adaptation
   d. audience scanning
   e. audience examination
9. The first step of effective speech planning is:
   a. practicing oral language and delivery style
   b. gathering and evaluating information to use
   c. understanding your audience and adapting to it
   d. selecting a speech goal that is appropriate to the rhetorical situation
   e. choosing, preparing, and using appropriate presentational aids
10. The three phases that most speakers proceed through in dealing with apprehension are:
    a. confrontation, adaptation, and transformation
    b. anticipation, education, and illustration
    c. causation, confrontation, and conciliation
    d. solicitation, conduction, and mentalization
    e. anticipation, confrontation, and adaptation

Answers:
1. T; 2. T; 3. T; 4. F; 5. F; 6. b; 7. b; 8. c; 9. d; 10. e

Do you have to give a speech for this chapter? Use the deck of perforated speech note cards to get ready!

Chapter in Review

hearing
the biological process that occurs when the brain detects sound waves

listening
the process of receiving, attending to, constructing meaning from, and responding to spoken or nonverbal messages

appreciative listening
your goal is to enjoy the thoughts and experiences of others

discriminative listening
your goal is to understand the speaker's meaning conveyed in other ways than the words themselves

comprehensive listening
your goal is to understand, remember, and recall what has been said

empathic listening
your goal is to be a sounding board to help another sort through feelings

critical listening
your ultimate goal is to evaluate the worth of a message

attending
paying attention to what the speaker is saying regardless of extraneous interference

understanding
the ability to assign accurate meaning to what was said

remembering
being able to retain and recall information we have heard

paraphrase
putting into your own words the meaning you have assigned to a message

evaluating
critically analyzing what is said to determine its truthfulness, utility, and trustworthiness

responding
providing feedback to the speaker about what is being said; usually occurs in the form of nonverbal behaviors

constructive critique
an analysis of a speech or presentation that evaluates how well a speaker meets a specific speaking goal while following the norms for good speaking and that recommends how the presentation could be improved

LO1 Why is it important to study listening in a public speaking course?

LO2 What is the difference between listening and hearing?
Listening is the process of receiving, attending to, constructing meaning from, and responding to spoken or nonverbal messages. Listening is not the same as hearing. Hearing is the biological process that occurs when the brain detects sound waves.

LO3 What are five different types of listening?
Scholars have identified five different types of listening based on five different purposes. These are appreciative, discriminative, comprehension, empathic, and critical listening.

LO4 What strategies can you employ to improve your listening skills?
Effective listening is an active process that requires the skills of attending, understanding, remembering, evaluating, and responding. The process of attending to a message is sharpened by getting physically ready to listen, resisting mental distractions while you listen, hearing the speaker out regardless of your thoughts or feelings, and identifying benefits of attending to the speaker. Understanding and remembering are enhanced by determining the speaker's organization, asking questions, silently paraphrasing key information, paying attention to nonverbal cues, and taking good notes. Evaluating is the process of critically analyzing how truthful, useful, and trustworthy you judge a speaker and the speaker's information to be. Critical analysis requires you to judge the quality of the content, structure, and delivery of the speech.

LO5 How can you constructively critique speeches you hear?
In public speaking situations, effective listeners respond nonverbally in the form of smiles, head nods, and applause, as well as verbally by critiquing the speeches of others. Because overall speaking effectiveness is complex, effective critics base their evaluation on how well the speaker meets the specific criteria related to the type of speech that has been given. Constructive critiques cite specific strengths of speeches, suggest ways in which speakers can improve, provide clear explanations of observations, and use nonthreatening "I" language.

Chapter Quiz

True/False
1. One way to be an effective listener is to resist mental distractions.
2. The goal of appreciative listening is to understand and remember what has been said.
3. Note taking is not a good technique to use during a public speech.
4. Someone who is good at hearing is definitely good at listening.
5. Most executives in North America believe that listening is important for the corporate environment.

Multiple Choice
6. During a public lecture on French history, Edward is listening with the goal of evaluating the accuracy of the lecture's content. He is using:
   a. appreciative listening
   b. critical listening
   c. empathic listening
   d. discriminative listening
   e. comprehensive listening
7. While listening to the senator's speech, Jackie pays particular attention to how the senator is using his hands and arms. She is using:
   a. appreciative listening
   b. critical listening
   c. empathic listening
   d. discriminative listening
   e. comprehensive listening

8. All of the following are techniques that can be used to improve understanding and memory, EXCEPT:
   a. Observe nonverbal cues.
   b. Determine the speaker's organization.
   c. Silently paraphrase key information.
   d. Take good notes.
   e. Identify the benefits of attending to the speaker's words.

9. According to research data, about _____ percent of people have had formal training in listening.
   a. 90
   b. 75
   c. 50
   d. 2
   e. 25

10. The process of paying attention to what the speaker is saying, regardless of interference, is:
    a. attending
    b. listening
    c. focusing
    d. realizing
    e. inventing

Answers:
1. T. 2. F. 3. F. 4. F. 5. T. 6. b. 7. d. 8. e. 9. d. 10. a

Exhibit 3.5

General Criteria for a Constructive Critique

1. **Content of the speech**
   • Does the speaker establish common ground and adapt the content to the audience's interests, knowledge, and attitudes?
   • Does the speaker seem to have expertise in the subject areas?
   • Does the speaker have high-quality sources for the information given in the speech?
   • Does the speaker reveal the sources of the information?
   • Are the sources relevant? recent? varied? distributed throughout the speech?
   • Does the information presented explain or support each of the main points?
   • Are presentational aids appropriate and well used?
   • Is each main point supported with breadth? depth? listener relevance?

2. **Structure of the speech**
   • Does the introduction of the speech get attention, establish listener relevance and credibility, and lead into the topic?
   • Has the speaker stated a clear goal for the speech?
   • Are the main points of the speech clearly stated, parallel, and meaningful?
   • Do transitions lead smoothly from one point to another?
   • Does the information presented explain or support each of the main points?
   • Does the speaker use language that is appropriate, accurate, clear, and vivid?
   • Does the speaker use a compelling style?
   • Does the conclusion summarize the main points and end with a clincher?

3. **Delivery of the speech**
   • Does the speaker sound intelligible? conversational? expressive?
   • Is the presentation fluent?
   • Does the speaker look at the audience?
   • Does the speaker use appropriate facial expressions?
   • Were the pronunciation and articulation acceptable?
   • Does the speaker have good posture?
   • Does the speaker have sufficient poise?

4 Chapter in Review

subject
a broad area of expertise, such as movies, renewable energy, or the Middle East

topic
a narrow, specific aspect of a subject

brainstorming
an uncritical, nonevaluative process of generating associated ideas

concept mapping
a visual means of exploring connections between a subject and related ideas

listener relevance links
statements of how and why the ideas you offer are of interest to your listeners

credibility
the perception that you are knowledgeable, trustworthy, and personable

survey
questionnaire designed to gather information directly from people

two-sided items
survey items that force the respondent to choose between two answers, such as yes/no, for/against, or pro/con

multiple-response items
survey items that give the respondent several alternative answers from which to choose

scaled items
survey items that measure the direction and/or intensity of an audience member's feeling or attitude toward something

open-ended items
survey items that encourage respondents to elaborate on their opinions without forcing them to answer in a predetermined way

marginalizing
the practice of ignoring the values, needs, and interests of certain audience members, leaving them feeling excluded from the speaking situation

stereotyping
assuming all members of a group have similar knowledge levels, behaviors, or beliefs simply because they belong to the group

demographic diversity
the range of demographic characteristics represented in an audience

general goal
the overall intent of the speech

specific goal
a single statement that identifies the exact response the speaker wants from the audience

LO1 What strategies can you use to brainstorm for speech topics?

The first step of effective speech preparation is to identify a topic. You begin by selecting a subject that is important to you and that you know something about, such as a job, a hobby, or a contemporary issue that concerns you. To arrive at a specific topic, brainstorm a list of related words under each subject. Then check two or three specific topics under each heading that are most meaningful to you. Finally, develop a concept map to come up with a variety of smaller topic areas and related ideas.

LO2 What should you consider about your audience when determining your speech goal?

LO3 How can you find out about your audience before giving your speech?

The second step is to analyze the audience to decide how to shape and direct your speech. Audience analysis is the study of the intended audience for your speech. You will want to gather demographic data and subject-related data. To ensure that you don't unintentionally marginalize or stereotype your listeners based on demographic characteristics, you may survey your audience using two-sided, multiple-response, scaled, or open-ended questions. You may also gather data through informal observation, by questioning the person who invited you to speak, and by making educated guesses about audience demographics and attitudes. Finally, you'll want to use the information ethically by demonstrating respect for the demographic diversity represented in your audience. You can do so by not marginalizing or stereotyping.

LO4 In what ways might the occasion for your speech influence your speech goal?

The third step is to understand the occasion, which will affect your overall speech plan, by asking such questions as: What are the special expectations for the speech? What is the appropriate length for the speech? How large will the audience be? Where will the speech be given? When will the speech be given? Where in the program does the speech occur? What equipment is necessary to give the speech?

LO5 How should you phrase your specific speech goal?

The fourth step is to choose a topic that is appropriate for the rhetorical situation. The final step is to develop your speech goal statement. The general goal of a speech (the overarching purpose) is to entertain, to inform, or to persuade. The specific goal is a single statement that identifies the exact response the speaker wants from the audience. Writing a specific speech goal involves the following four-step procedure: (1) Write a draft of your general speech goal using a complete sentence that specifies the type of response you want from your audience. (2) Revise the statement (and the infinitive phrase) until it indicates the specific audience reaction desired. (3) Make sure that the goal statement contains only one idea. (4) Revise your statement until it describes the precise focus of your speech (the infinitive phrase articulates the complete response you want from your audience).

Chapter Quiz

True/False

1. Marginalizing is the action of assuming that all members of the audience have similar knowledge, levels, behaviors, or beliefs because they belong to the group.
2. While audience analysis focuses on a study of the intended audience, audience adaptation is the process of tailoring the speech's information to the needs of the audience.
3. Information about members' age, education, gender, and income comprise demographics.
4. A key step for determining a specific speech goal is to understand the speech occasion.
5. Brainstorming is an evaluative, critical process.

Multiple Choice

6. A _____ is a broad area of expertise.
   a. topic
   b. area
   c. motif
   d. theme
   e. subject

7. A yes/no question such as "Do you think social network sites are a waste of time?" is an example of:
   a. multiple-response items
   b. two-sided items
   c. scaled items
   d. response items
   e. open-ended items

8. A speaker who is perceived to be very knowledgeable and personable has a lot of:
   a. personality
   b. ethics
   c. motivation
   d. credibility
   e. intensity

9. When analyzing the occasion of a speech, you should ask all of the following EXCEPT:
   a. What is the appropriate length of the speech?
   b. How large will the audience be?
   c. How much am I being paid for the speech?
   d. What are the special expectations for the speech?
   e. Where will the speech be given?

10. An effective way to minimize stereotyping is to:
    a. Collect audience data related to your subject.
    b. Make the audience homogenous.
    c. Ask the audience to assume the same things.
    d. Tell the audience that they are all equal.
    e. Ignore special needs in the audience.

Answers:
1. F; 2. T; 3. T; 4. T; 5. F; 6. e; 7. b; 8. d; 9. c; 10. a

Speech Snippets

Audience Knowledge

Ian's classmates ranged from first-year traditional-age students to nontraditional-age students, some of them married. Ian realized that to be audience centered in his speech about fire safety, he needed to adapt to the diversity of his audience's knowledge. So he decided to talk about fire safety measures that would be appropriate not only for students in residence halls but also for people who have their own homes.

Audience Interest

Laura wanted to give a speech on the prevalence today of unnecessary hysterectomies. Because her audience included males and females, she took care to make her speech relevant for everyone by talking about how we are all affected by the increases in insurance rates that result from unnecessary operations and how a patient's emotional trauma caused by an unnecessary hysterectomy can have a profound effect on family and friends.

Making Educated Guesses About Your Audience

Karlie was asked to give a speech on universal health care to a local service club composed of business professionals. It wasn't practical for her to gather data about her audience before her speech, but she inferred that most of them probably received medical insurance through the companies they worked for. She made her topic relevant to them by talking about the advantages and disadvantages of universal health care relative to private insurance options. In that way, she was able to acknowledge the value of private insurance for those who have it and then move on to compare the two options for society overall.

5 Chapter in Review

relevance
adapting the information in a speech so that audience members view it as important to them

timeliness
showing how information is useful now or in the near future

proximity
the relevance of information to personal life space

initial audience disposition
the knowledge of and opinions about your topic that your listeners have before they hear you speak

common ground
the background, knowledge, attitudes, experiences, and philosophies audience members and the speaker share

personal pronouns
"we," "us," and "our"—pronouns that directly link the speaker to members of the audience

rhetorical questions
questions phrased to stimulate a mental response rather than an actual spoken response from the audience

credibility
the perception that you are knowledgeable, trustworthy, and personable

knowledge and expertise
how well you convince your audience that you are qualified to speak on the topic

trustworthiness
the extent to which the audience can believe that what you say is accurate, true, and in their best interests

personableness
the extent to which you project an agreeable or pleasing personality

learning style
a person's preferred way of receiving information

transition
a sentence or two that summarizes one main point and introduces the next one

LO1 Why is it important to articulate the relevance of your speech to your audience?

One part of audience adaptation is to help the audience see the relevance of your material by demonstrating timeliness (showing how the information is useful now or in the near future), demonstrating proximity (showing relevance to personal life space), and demonstrating personal impact.

LO2 What should you do if your audience does not share your attitude about the topic of your speech?

The second part of the adaptation process is to acknowledge the audience's initial disposition by framing the speech in a way that takes into account how much audience members know about your topic and what their attitudes are about it. The third part is to develop common ground by using personal pronouns, asking rhetorical questions, and drawing from common experiences.

LO3 What can you do to help your audience see you as trustworthy and knowledgeable about your topic?

The fourth part is to build speaker credibility by demonstrating knowledge and expertise, establishing trustworthiness, and displaying personableness.

LO4 Why is it important to address diverse learning styles in your speech?

The fifth part is to increase audience comprehension and retention of information by creating material that appeals to diverse learning styles, orienting listeners, choosing specific and familiar language, using vivid language and examples, personalizing information, and comparing unknown ideas with familiar ones.

LO5 What can you do to overcome language and cultural differences between you and your audience?

The sixth part is to adapt to cultural differences to be understood and demonstrate respect.

Chapter Quiz

True/False

1. As a speaker, it is important to know the knowledge and opinions that the audience has about a topic before they hear you speak.
2. One way to increase the relevance of information is to make it timely.
3. Rhetorical questions are supposed to have only one answer.
4. In general, adapting to the audience's attitude is important only for persuasive speeches.
5. A great way to establish expertise on a subject is to demonstrate your track record on it.

Multiple Choice

6. In her speech on income taxes that she is giving to a local school board, Courtney shows her audience that a decrease in taxes will harm school funding. She is:
   a. establishing relevance
   b. demonstrating proximity
   c. demonstrating timeliness
   d. adapting to the audience
   e. demonstrating ethics
7. A learning style is the way a person prefers to receive:
   a. criticism
   b. praise
   c. information
   d. encouragement
   e. feedback
8. When an audience finds that a speech is relevant, it means that they consider the information in the speech:
   a. timely
   b. witty
   c. depressing
   d. important
   e. contrasting

9. In order to summarize a main point and move on to the next main point, you should use:
   a. transitions
   b. links
   c. connections
   d. bridges
   e. spans
10. The knowledge, attitudes, and beliefs shared between the audience and speaker is known as:
   a. similarity
   b. commonality
   c. foundation
   d. bridge
   e. common ground

Answers:

1. T; 2. T; 3. T; 4. F; 5. T; 6. b; 7. c; 8. d; 9. a; 10. e

Speech Snippets

Demonstrating Proximity

In her speech about the effects of hurricanes, Megan demonstrated proximity by explaining that hurricanes affect not only those living on the coastlines but also people across the entire country with their spin-off weather.

Demonstrating Personal Impact

To drive home the impact of DWP, J. J. talked about John, his high school friend, who is now paralyzed and wheelchair bound because his girlfriend crashed into another car while she was texting.

Acknowledging Listener Attitudes

In her introductory remarks, Tiffany acknowledged listener attitudes in her speech "Meat Free **and Me**": "With Thanksgiving just around the corner, many of you are probably anticipating a feast complete with a flavorful, juicy turkey as the main course. I am too, but many of you would find my menu bizarre—I'm planning to feast on rice pilaf with grilled vegetables and garlic-roasted tofu." In this way, Tiffany acknowledges that her audience will find her alternative menu for Thanksgiving dinner odd.

Drawing on Common Experiences

In his speech about skydiving, Kyron related the sensation of falling out of a plane to something **most listeners could probably relate to in this way:** "The first thing you feel when you finally jump is that stomach-in-the-mouth sensation that is similar to something we've all experienced when we have lurched because we've missed a step going down a staircase or when we have momentarily gone airborne in a car from approaching the crest of a hill too fast."

Establishing Trustworthiness

Tiffany established trustworthiness in her speech by framing it as an explanation about why she chose to live a vegetarian lifestyle rather than trying to persuade her listeners to make that **same choice:** "In the next few minutes, we'll talk about how I made this choice to live meat-free, some of the family issues I've dealt with as a result of this choice, and some of the specific ways this choice continues to affect my life today."

Rounding the Cycle of Learning

In her speech about hurricanes, Megan appealed to both feeling and watching by showing photos of her own hometown after it was ravaged by a hurricane. She appealed to both watching and thinking by explaining hurricane categories with the help of a scale chart visual aid. And she appealed to doing by having the audience look through a box of hurricane-tossed articles to search for a baby ring.

Demonstrating Direct Expertise

Tiffany demonstrated direct expertise with her topic when she declared, "About five years ago, I made a decision to stop eating meat, which has changed my life in several ways. Living a vegetarian lifestyle is an important aspect of who I am today."

6 Chapter in Review

evidence
any information that clarifies, explains, or otherwise adds depth or breadth to a topic

secondary research
the process of locating information that has been discovered by other people

primary research
the process of conducting your own study to acquire the information you need

credentials
your experiences or education that qualifies you to speak with authority on a specific subject

periodicals
magazines and journals that appear at fixed periods

skimming
a method of rapidly going through a work to determine what is covered and how

abstract
a short paragraph summarizing the research findings

ethnography
a form of primary research based on fieldwork observations

survey
a canvassing of people to get information about their ideas and opinions, which are then analyzed for trends

interview
a planned, structured conversation where one person asks questions and another answers them

interview protocol
the list of questions you plan to ask

primary questions
lead-in questions about one of the major topics of the interview, typically related to the main points for the speech

secondary questions
follow-up questions designed to probe the answers given to primary questions

open questions
broad-based questions that ask the interviewee to provide perspective, ideas, information, or opinions

closed questions
narrowly focused questions that require only very brief answers

neutral questions
questions phrased in ways that do not direct a person's answers

leading questions
questions phrased in a way that suggests the interviewer has a preferred answer

factual statements
information that can be verified

statistics
numerical facts

examples
specific instances that illustrate or explain a general factual statement

LO1 What are the differences between primary and secondary research?
Primary research is the process of conducting your own study to acquire the information you need, while secondary research is the process of locating information that has been discovered by other people.

LO2 Where can you locate information for your speech?
Information for your speech can come from primary research or secondary research. Sources for secondary research include encyclopedias, books, articles in academic journals and magazines, newspapers, statistical sources, biographies, quotation books and websites, and government documents. Primary sources include fieldwork observations, surveys, interviews, original artifacts or document examinations, and experiments.

LO3 How will you evaluate information and sources?
Because your search of secondary sources is likely to uncover far more information than you can use, you will want to skim sources to determine whether or not to read them in full. Skimming is a method of rapidly going through a work to determine what is covered and how. Also, there are four criteria to use when evaluating sources: authority, objectivity, currency, and relevance.

LO4 How will you select and record relevant information for your speech?
As you find the facts, opinions, and elaborations that you want to use in your speech, you need to record the information accurately and keep a careful account of your sources so that they can be cited appropriately during your speech. Although some people try to record information in files on their computers, we propose here a proven method for organizing your information on research cards.

LO5 How and why do you cite sources in a speech?
In your speeches, as in any communication in which you use ideas that are not your own, you need to acknowledge the sources of your ideas and statements. Specifically mentioning your sources not only helps the audience evaluate the content but also adds to your credibility. In addition, citing sources will give concrete evidence of the depth of your research. Failure to cite sources, especially when you are presenting information that is meant to substantiate a controversial point, is unethical. So just as you would provide footnotes in a written document, you must provide oral footnotes during your speech.

Chapter Quiz

True/False

1. A biography about a historical figure is not an appropriate source of secondary information.
2. According to the text, the heart of an effective interview is a list of good questions.
3. Primary research involves looking for information that others have discovered.
4. Because statistics are a great way to present information, a speaker should use as many as possible.
5. In addition to research that others have done, your personal experience can be a good source of information for a speech.

Multiple Choice

6. All of the following are examples of primary sources EXCEPT:
   a. surveys
   b. fieldwork
   c. interviews
   d. a website of famous quotations
   e. experiments
7. The list of questions you plan to ask during an interview is known as the:
   a. interview assessment
   b. interview cards
   c. interview inquiries
   d. interview basics
   e. interview protocol

hypothetical examples
specific instances based on reflections about future events

definition
a statement that clarifies the meaning of a word or phrase

expert opinions
interpretations and judgments made by authorities in a particular subject area

anecdotes
brief, often amusing stories

narratives
accounts, personal experiences, tales, or lengthier stories

comparison
illuminating a point by showing similarities

contrast
illuminating a point by highlighting differences

plagiarism
the unethical act of representing another person's work as your own

oral footnote
reference to an original source made at the point in the speech where information from that source is presented

8. Information that clarifies, explains, or adds depth or breadth to a topic is:
   a. data
   b. evidence
   c. research
   d. findings
   e. support

9. Encyclopedias, newspapers, and scholarly journals are all examples of:
   a. tertiary sources
   b. primary sources
   c. secondary sources
   d. redundant sources
   e. expert sources

10. The four criteria that should be used when evaluating sources are authority, relevance, objectivity, and:
   a. currency
   b. importance
   c. popularity
   d. veracity
   e. origins

Answers:
1. E; 2. T; 3. F; 4. F; 5. T; 6. d; 7. d; 8. b; 9. c; 10. a

Speech Snippets

Establishing Credentials

In his speech on bioluminescence—the light emitted by some living organisms, such as fireflies—Dan established his credentials by drawing on his personal knowledge as a biogenetics major and the fieldwork he had done on fireflies during an eight-week summer internship.

Finding Information on Internet Bulletin Boards

For his speech on bioluminescence, Dan consulted a bulletin board maintained by the Association of Biogenetic Engineers. He was able to quote several issues being debated by experts in the field even before their works had been published. This complemented the information he had located in books, which had not been so up-to-date.

Finding Articles from an Online Database

Lauren typed the subject "prescription drug abuse" into the "subject" prompt on the home page of the EBSCO database. The search revealed 108 references from a variety of highly respected periodicals, including the *National Review*, the *Journal of the American Medical Association*, and *American Medical News*.

Accessing Newspaper Articles

Carl wanted to give a speech on Everglades restoration efforts, so to understand how Floridians viewed this project, Carl accessed the website of the *Miami Herald*, where he found 119 recent articles and more than 3,500 archived articles.

Collecting Observational Information for a Speech

Lauren wanted to know what addicts go through as they undergo treatment, so she arranged to spend a day at a local treatment center, observing to learn firsthand about some of these processes and experiences.

Determining Audience Attitudes with a Survey

For her speech on prescription drug abuse, Lauren wanted to know where people in her community and students attending her school stood on the issue. So she conducted a telephone survey of the community, an Internet survey of students on campus, and a paper-and-pencil survey of her classmates, asking them whether they agreed or disagreed with the statement "Prescription drug abuse is a real problem in our country today." She was then able to tailor her speech to address her classmates' attitudes toward the topic and use the other survey data to inform them about where the campus and community stood regarding the topic.

Scheduling an Interview

For his speech on the vanishing honeybees, Justin looked at the Biology Department website and discovered a faculty member who has actually published two papers on the vanishing honeybees. He read the papers and learned that the phenomenon is referred to as CCD, or Colony Collapse Disorder. He decided to try to set up an interview with the professor to learn more. He telephoned and left this message, which he followed up with an e-mail message:

> Hello, my name is Justin Martin. I am preparing a classroom speech on CCD and know that you are an expert on this subject. If possible, I'd like to make an appointment to talk with you. Would you be available to talk with me for 15 or 20 minutes during the next few days?

Conducting Experiments for Primary Research

Justin had heard that the radio waves of cellular telephones are one reason honeybees become disoriented, cannot make it home to their hives, and then die. He followed the suggestion he read about placing a cell phone in a flower garden to observe what happens. Of course, he only did this long enough to see the bees' reaction, not long enough to cause a lasting result.

Stating the Credentials of the Person You Interviewed

Justin's adviser is a nationally known expert on colony collapse disorder and the vanishing honeybee crisis, so he chose to interview her for his speech. Justin revealed her credentials in his speech by saying, "I have the privilege of having as my adviser one of the nation's leading colony collapse disorder scholars. In an interview with Dr. Susan Stromme, I learned that the radiation emitted from cell phones is one major cause of death for the bees."

Preparing Primary Questions

For his interview with a music producer, Noah prepared his primary questions around the topics of finding artists, the decision process, criteria for signing an artist, and stories of success and failure.

Chapter in Review

main points
complete sentence statements of the two to four central ideas the audience needs to understand for your speech goal to be realized

thesis statement
a one- or two-sentence summary of the speech that incorporates the general and specific goals and previews the main points

speech outline
a sentence representation of the hierarchical and sequential relationships among the ideas presented in the speech

preparation outline
provides a starting point of main points but doesn't specify clearly how each main point is related to the goal

parallel
when wording of points follows the same structural pattern, often using the same introductory words

time order
organizing the main points of the speech in a chronological sequence or by steps in a process

narrative order
organizing the main points of the speech as a story or series of stories

topic order
organizing the main points of the speech by categories or divisions of a subject

logical reasons order
organizing the main points of a persuasive speech by the reasons that support the speech goal

listener relevance link
a statement alerting listeners about how a main point or subpoint relates to them or why they should care about it

supporting material
developmental material that will be used in the speech, including personal experiences, examples, illustrations, anecdotes, statistics, and quotations

transition
a sentence or two that summarizes one main point and introduces the next one

section transitions
complete sentences that show the relationship between, or bridge, major parts of a speech

signposts
words or phrases that connect pieces of supporting material to the main point or subpoint they address

1 Why is it important to limit your speech to two to four main points?
You need to limit the number of main points you present so audience members can easily understand what you are saying, remember the major ideas you present, and understand the speech's importance. The difference between a five-minute speech and a 25-minute speech with the same speech goal is not the number of main points but rather the extent to which each main point is developed.

LO2 Why should you construct a clear thesis statement?
Your thesis statement provides a blueprint from which you will organize the body of your speech.

3 How might you arrange your points in your speech?
A speech outline is a sentence representation of the hierarchical and sequential relationships among the ideas presented in the speech. There are several organizational patterns that can be used: time order, narrative order, topic order, and logical reasons order.

LO4 What are some types of supporting material you can use to elaborate your main points?
A good outline also includes short outline statements of supporting material—developmental material that will be used in the speech—for example, personal experiences, examples, illustrations, anecdotes, statistics, and quotations. You will choose these items to meet the needs of your specific audience.

LO5 Why are transitions important?
Section transitions bridge major parts of the speech and occur between the introduction and the body, between main points within the body, and between the body and the conclusion. Section transitions should be planned and placed in the outline as parenthetical statements where they are to occur. Whereas section transitions serve as the glue that holds together the macrostructural elements of your speech, signposts serve as the glue that holds together the subpoints and supporting material within each main point. Together, these types of transitions serve as a road map for listeners to follow as you present your speech.

Chapter Quiz

True/False
1. The length of a speech is determined primarily by the number of main points.
2. A speaker using narrative order would arrange the main points of a speech through a story or series of stories.
3. The ideal number of central ideas of a speech is two to four.
4. Section transitions help the audience follow the organization of ideas in a speech.
5. In a speech outline, the main points and subpoints should be written as complete sentences.

Multiple Choice
6. A sentence or two that summarizes one main point and introduces the next one is known as a:
   a. subpoint
   b. relevance link
   c. transition
   d. connector
   e. conjunction
7. A one- or two-sentence summary of your speech that previews the main point is called a:
   a. thematic statement
   b. thesis statement
   c. central statement
   d. point statement
   e. motif statement

8. All of the following are ways to organize the main points of a speech EXCEPT:
   a. time order
   b. logical reasons order
   c. narrative order
   d. topic order
   e. intensity order
9. A speech outline is arranged by sequence and:
   a. theme
   b. concern
   c. interest
   d. geography
   e. hierarchy
10. The _____ serves as a basis for the transition from the introduction to the body of the speech.
   a. thesis statement
   b. conclusion
   c. main point
   d. subpoint
   e. listener relevance link

Answers:
1. F; 2. T; 3. T; 4. T; 5. T; 6. c; 7. b; 8. e; 9. e; 10. a

Speech Snippets

Crafting a Thesis Statement

Johanna wanted to create a memorable thesis statement for her speech whose goal was to get her classmates to commit to take action to cut the amount of solid waste they send to the landfill. So she phrased each of her main points so that they began with an "R" and used this mnemonic to help her classmates remember this thesis: "I want my classmates to commit to take action to cut their personal contributions to landfills by practicing the three R's: reduce, reuse, and recycle your waste."

Elaborating on a Subpoint

When discussing her main point on how to reuse materials as a means of reducing solid waste, Johanna planned to elaborate on her subpoint about reusing grocery bags by pointing out that "the home page of ReusableBags.com cited an article in the *Wall Street Journal*, which reported that the United States goes through 100 billion plastic shopping bags annually. An estimated 12 million barrels of oil is required to make that many plastic bags."

Wording Main Points

Darla worded her main points on the methods of disciplining children in this way:

I. First, the Skinner disciplinary method is based on behavioral modification.
II. Second, the Freud disciplinary method is rooted in the concepts of the id, the ego, and the superego.
III. Third, the Spock disciplinary method is based on cognitive reasoning.

Narrative Order

Chaz shared two stories about his friend, Garth, to help his listeners understand how Americans with disabilities were discriminated against prior to the passage of the Americans with Disabilities Act. He talked about trying to help Garth get up a flight of stairs in his wheelchair to attend classes and when Garth was told over the telephone he was the top candidate for a position but was later told the position had been eliminated when he arrived in person in his wheelchair.

Using Section Transitions

In her speech about methods of disciplining children, Darla used this section transition between her first and second main point: "Certainly, the behavioral modification approach based on B. F. Skinner's work can be an effective method for disciplining children. It is not the only method, however, which leads us to a second method, based on Sigmund Freud's work."

Chapter in Review

primacy-recency effect
the tendency to remember the first and last items conveyed orally in a series rather than the items in between

startling statement
a sentence or two that grabs your listeners' attention by shocking them in some way

direct question
a question that demands an overt response from the audience, usually by a show of hands

story
an account of something that has happened (actual) or could happen (hypothetical)

joke
an anecdote or a piece of wordplay designed to be funny and make people laugh

personal reference
a brief story about something that happened to you or a hypothetical situation that listeners can imagine themselves in

quotation
a comment made by and attributed to someone other than the speaker

action
an attention-getting act designed to highlight your topic or purpose

creating suspense
wording an attention getter so that what is described generates initial uncertainty or mystery and excites the audience

clincher
a one- or two-sentence statement in a conclusion that provides a sense of closure by driving home the importance of your speech in a memorable way

appeal to action
a statement in a conclusion that describes the behavior you want your listeners to follow after they have heard your arguments

formal outline
a full sentence outline of your speech that includes internal references and a reference list

 LO1 Why are solid introductions and conclusions so important to effective public speaking?
A speech's introduction and conclusion are important because we are more likely to remember the first and last items conveyed orally in a series than the items in between. Listeners are more likely to remember the beginning and ending of your speech than what you say in the body. Introduction and conclusion are also important because of the need for listeners to grasp quickly your goal and main points as they listen to your speech and to remember them after you've finished.

 LO2 How can you get your audience's attention in your introduction?
An effective speech introduction gets audience attention, establishes listener relevance, establishes credibility and goodwill, and introduces the thesis.

LO3 Why should you summarize your main points again in the conclusion?
A well-designed speech conclusion summarizes the speech goal and main points and leaves the audience with a vivid impression.

 LO4 How might you motivate listeners to remember your speech in your conclusion?
Informative and persuasive speeches may leave an impression with a clincher, a one- or two-sentence statement that provides a sense of closure by driving home the importance of your speech in a memorable way. Two strategies for effective clinchers are using vivid imagery and appealing to action.

LO5 How do you determine which sources to include in your outline and reference list?
Regardless of the type of speech or how long or how short it will be, you'll want to prepare a list of the sources you use in it. This list will enable you to direct audience members to the specific source of the information you have used and will allow you to quickly find the information at a later date.

Chapter Quiz

True/False
1. A good introduction will help the audience quickly grasp the goal and main points of a speech.
2. A good speech introduction should only identify and define the topic quickly.
3. Even though an audience is physically present at a speech, it doesn't mean they are paying attention.
4. According to the primacy-recency effect, we are more likely to remember the first thing we hear rather than the last.
5. The best way to create an introduction is to come up with a single idea and then stick to it.

Multiple Choice
6. While a good introduction previews the main points of the speech, a good conclusion _____ them.
   a. summarizes
   b. repeats
   c. contravenes
   d. reinforces
   e. tells
7. The term _____ refers to appeals to emotions.
   a. ethos
   b. chronos
   c. pathos
   d. logos
   e. kairos

8. An effective way to get the audience's attention is by:
   a. telling a story
   b. using a startling statement
   c. telling a joke
   d. asking a question
   e. All of the above
9. A speaker can achieve a sense of closure in a conclusion by using a:
   a. joke
   b. adumbration
   c. wrap-up
   d. clincher
   e. preview
10. Which of the following is not one of the goals of an effective introduction?
    a. Get audience attention
    b. Demonstrate the speaker's sense of humor
    c. Establish speaker credibility
    d. Identify the thesis statement
    e. Establish listener relevance

Answers:
1. T 2. F 3. T 4. F 5. F 6. d 7. c 8. e 9. d 10. b

Speech Snippets

Introducing a Speech with Rhetorical Questions and a Startling Statement

Lana used a combination of rhetorical questions and a startling statement to get her listeners' attention for her speech on eating disorders:

Who are five of the most important women in your life? Your mother? Your sister? Your daughter? Your wife? Your best friend? Now which one of them has an eating disorder? Before you disregard my question, listen to what research tells us. One in every five women in the United States has an eating disorder.

Getting Attention by Telling a Story

Matt used a short story to get audience attention for his speech about spanking as a form of discipline:

One rainy afternoon, four-year-old Billy was playing "pretend" in the living room. He was Captain Jack Sparrow, staving off the bad guys with his amazing sword-fighting skills. Then it happened. Billy knocked his mother's very expensive china bowl off the table. Billy hung his head and began to cry. He knew what was coming, and sure enough it did. The low thud of his mother's hand on his bottom brought a sting to his behind and a small yelp from his mouth. Billy got a spanking.

Introducing a Speech with a Personal Reference and a Startling Statement

In her speech about binge eating and obesity, Jamie used this personal reference and startling statement to get her audience's attention:

Imagine a table full of all the food you eat in one week. [pause] That's a lot of food, right? Now, imagine eating all that food in one day! Believe it or not, there are people who do this. They consume many thousands of calories more than the suggested intake of 2,000 per day. This is a condition called binge eating, and it's more common than you might think.

Using a Short Quotation to Get Attention

In a speech about the importance of courage and taking risks, Sonja began with Franklin D. Roosevelt's famous quotation, "The only thing we have to fear is fear itself."

Getting Attention through Action

In her speech about acupressure, Andria asked her audience to perform this action as she modeled it for them:

Take the thumb and index finger of your right hand and pinch the skin between the thumb and index finger of your left hand. What you've just done is stimulated a pressure point that can relieve headaches.

Establishing Listener Relevance

Tiffany created a listener relevance link by asking her audience to consider her topic in relation to their own lives:

Although a diet rich in eggs and meat was once the norm in our country, more and more of us are choosing a vegetarian lifestyle to help lower blood pressure, reduce cholesterol, and even help prevent the onset of some diseases. So as I describe my experience, you may want to consider how you could alter your diet.

Establishing Credibility in an Introduction

In his speech about smoking in public places, Eric established his credibility by saying, "I used to smoke cigarettes and have quit, but not before I did a good deal of research about the effects of smoking and secondhand smoke."

Summarizing Your Main Points

For her speech on the benefits of organic food, Courtney offered this summary:

So I hope you now understand how eating organically produced food contributes to physical health, a cleaner environment, and animal welfare.

Ending with a Clincher

Jamie drove home her point about obesity by referring back to her opening story about Tom and then offering an appeal to action:

Without doubt, obesity is a serious problem that must be addressed by examining its causes and then constructing and implementing workable solutions. Together, we can help people like Tom overcome obesity. If we can, we must—before it's too late.

9 Chapter in Review

presentational aid
any visual, audio, audiovisual, or other sensory material used in a speech

visual aid
a form of speech development that allows the audience to see as well as hear the speaker present the information

audio aid
a presentational aid that enhances the speaker's verbal message with additional sound

audiovisual aid
a presentational aid that enhances the speech using a combination of sight and sound through video

other sensory aids
presentational aids that enhance the ideas offered verbally by appealing to smell, taste, or touch

actual object
an inanimate or animate sample of the idea you are communicating

model
a three-dimensional scaled-down or scaled-up version of an actual object

diagram
a type of drawing that shows how the whole relates to its parts

chart
a graphic representation that distills a lot of information and presents it to an audience in an easily interpreted visual format

flowchart
a chart that diagrams a sequence of steps through a complicated process

organizational chart
a chart that shows the structure of an organization in terms of rank and chain of command

pie chart
a diagram that shows the relationships among parts of a single unit

graph
a diagram that presents numerical comparisons

bar graph
a diagram that uses vertical or horizontal bars to show relationships between or among two or more variables at the same time or at various times on one or more dimensions

line graph
a diagram that indicates changes in one or more variables over time

presentation software
a computer program that enables you to electronically prepare and store your visual aids using a computer

flipchart
a large pad of paper mounted on an easel

LO1 Why should you incorporate presentational aids into your speech?
Presentational aids are useful when they help audience members understand and remember important information.

LO2 What are some types of presentational aids you can choose from?
The most common types of visual aids are objects, models, photographs, simple drawings and diagrams, maps, charts, and graphs. Audio aids include recordings of music, speeches, and environmental sounds. Audiovisual aids include clips from movies, TV programs, commercials, and YouTube. Other sensory aids enhance the verbal message by focusing on taste, smell, or touch. Methods that speakers can use to present presentational aids include posters, flipcharts, whiteboards and chalkboards, handouts, and computerized slide shows using a computer, projector, and screen.

LO3 What are some common mistakes speakers make when constructing and using presentational aids?
There are several guidelines to keep in mind to construct and use presentational aids effectively. First, you should limit the reading required of the audience. Second, you should customize presentational aids from other sources. Third, you should use a photo, print, or type size that can be easily seen and a volume and sound quality that can be heard easily by your entire audience. Fourth, you should use a consistent print style that is easy to read. Fifth, you should make sure information is laid out in a way that is aesthetically pleasing. Sixth, you should add pictures or other visual symbols to add interest. Seventh, you should use color strategically. And finally, you should use presentation software to prepare professional-looking presentational aids.

LO4 What are some important considerations to keep in mind when choosing presentational aids?
When choosing presentational aids, you should consider the following questions: What are the most important ideas you want your audience to understand and remember? Are there ideas that are complex or difficult to explain verbally but would be easier to explain with the help of a presentational aid? How many presentational aids should I consider? How large is the audience? Is the necessary equipment readily available? Is the time involved in making or getting the visual aid or equipment cost-effective?

LO5 What are some important considerations to keep in mind when preparing presentational aids?
Take time to design your visual aids with the following principles in mind: Use a print or font size that can be seen easily by your entire audience. Use a font that is easy to read and pleasing to the eye. Use upper- and lowercase type. Try to limit the lines of type to six or fewer. Include only items of information that you will emphasize in your speech. Make sure information is laid out in a way that is aesthetically pleasing. Add clip art where appropriate. Use color strategically.

LO6 What are some important considerations to keep in mind when presenting with your presentational aids?
When you plan to use presentational aids in a speech, make sure you practice using them as you rehearse your speech. Keep the following suggestions in mind: Carefully plan when you will use each aid during your speech. Position the aids and equipment before beginning your speech. Show presentational aids only when talking about them; when you show a video clip or play an audio clip, talk about it before you play it. Display presentational aids so that everyone in the audience can see them. Talk to your audience, not to your presentational aid. Avoid passing objects around the audience. In short, keep your audience focused on *you* as the speaker as well as your presentational aids.

Chapter Quiz

True/False

1. It is effective to show a visual aid even when you are not speaking about it.
2. Presentational aids should appeal primarily to the sense of vision or hearing.
3. Good presentational aids should be easy to carry.
4. A presentational aid and a visual aid are identical.
5. Sometimes, the speaker can use him- or herself as a presentational aid.

LCD multimedia projector
a projection unit that connects to a VCR
player, a DVD player, or a computer and
projects images from them onto a screen

Multiple Choice

6. All of the following are steps you should take to prepare effective presentational aids EXCEPT:
   a. Use a photo that can be easily seen by the entire audience.
   b. Have the audience read a lot of text.
   c. Use a consistent print style.
   d. Add pictures or symbols to add interest.
   e. Use color strategically.

7. Aids that enhance a speech by using a combination of sight and sound are called:
   a. audiovisual aids
   b. visual aids
   c. audio aids
   d. other sensory aids
   e. animate objects

8. If you want an audience to refer to information after a speech, you should use:
   a. flipcharts
   b. document cameras
   c. posters
   d. handouts
   e. chalkboards

9. A(n) _____ uses symbols and lines to diagram a sequence of steps.
   a. line graph
   b. pie chart
   c. flowchart
   d. organizational chart
   e. bar graph

10. Which of the following is not an advantage of using presentational aids?
    a. They enable the speaker to adapt to the audience's knowledge.
    b. They help speakers feel more competent.
    c. They allow speakers to increase the persuasive appeal of the speech.
    d. They help the audience remember information presented in the speech.
    e. They appeal primarily to one learning style.

Answers:
1. E; 2. T; 3. T; 4. F; 5. T; 6. b; 7. a; 8. d; 9. c; 10. e

Speech Snippets

Avoiding Unsafe Presentational Aids

Mike decided to give a demonstration speech on how to safely clean a rifle. At first, he assumed he would just bring his Winchester to class and do an actual demonstration. But after his instructor reviewed his outline, she e-mailed him a reminder that it was illegal to bring a weapon to campus. So he got his wife to videotape him cleaning his rifle instead, and he used clips from this video to demonstrate several of the steps.

Using a Photograph as a Visual Aid

In his speech about global warming, Joey showed photographs of receding glaciers off the coast of Alaska taken in 1990, 2000, and 2010.

Using Audio Aids

In her speech about whales, Emily played a recording of blue whales "singing." Playing the recording not only allowed the audience to better understand her topic, but it allowed her to present information that would have been difficult to describe with words alone.

Using Audiovisual Aids

For his speech on what happens to race horses after they retire, Paul began by playing a short clip he found on YouTube showing SuperSaver winning the 2010 Kentucky Derby.

Using Sensory Aids

For his speech on store-brand foods, Greg argued that store-brand products taste as good as their name-brand counterparts. He demonstrated his point by providing audience members with small samples of both store-brand and name-brand cereals to taste as he spoke.

Being Prepared for Equipment Problems

On his introductory slide, Paul inserted a hyperlink to the Kentucky Derby race video on YouTube to grab audience attention. To be prepared for equipment troubles, however, he also recorded it on his iPod and brought it along to the event.

Using Handouts as Presentational Aids

In his speech on obesity, Tim created a handout of his flowchart that shows how to determine if you are overweight. He created the flowchart on a poster board for reference during his speech, saving the handout to distribute to the audience until after he'd completed his speech.

10

Chapter in Review

speaking notes
a keyword outline with delivery cues and reference citations you will use as you deliver your speech

oral style
the manner in which one conveys messages through the spoken word

speaking appropriately
using language that adapts to the needs, interests, knowledge, and attitudes of the listener and avoiding language that alienates audience members

verbal immediacy
when the language you use reduces the psychological distance between you and your audience

"we" language
the use of plural personal pronouns like "we," "our," and "us" rather than "you" or "they"

bias-free language
language that demonstrates through word choices an ethical concern for fairness and respect with regard to race, ethnicity, gender, ability, sexual orientation, and diverse worldviews

generic language
language that uses words that apply only to one sex, race, or other group as though they represent everyone

nonparallel language
language in which terms are changed because of the sex, race, or other group characteristics of the individual

marking
the addition of sex, race, age, or other group designations to a description

irrelevant association
emphasizing one person's relationship to another when that relationship is irrelevant to the point

hate speech
the use of words and phrases to demean another person or group and to express the speaker's hatred and prejudice toward that person or group

accurate language
words that convey your meaning precisely

intelligible
capable of being clearly understood

denotation
the explicit meaning a language community formally gives a word

context
the position of a word in a sentence and its relationship to other words around it

connotation
the positive, neutral, or negative feelings or evaluations we associate with a word

LO¹ How does oral style differ from written style?
Oral style refers to the manner in which one conveys messages through the spoken word. An effective oral style tends toward short sentences and familiar language. An effective oral style features plural personal pronouns. An effective oral style features descriptive words and phrases that appeal to the ear and are designed to sustain listener interest and promote retention. An effective oral style incorporates clear section transitions and signposts.

LO² How can you word your speech to avoid offending some listeners?
There are a number of strategies that speakers can use to speak appropriately and avoid offending listeners: using "we" language, using bias-free language, adapting to cultural diversity, avoiding offensive humor, avoiding profanity and vulgarity, and shunning hate speech.

LO³ What should you do to make sure your language and style is appropriate?
Being appropriate means using language that adapts to the audience's needs, interests, knowledge, and attitudes and that avoids alienating or offending listeners. Appropriate language demonstrates respect for all audience members. To be appropriate, practice verbal immediacy by using "we" language and bias-free language, as well as adapting to cultural diversity and avoiding offensive humor, profanity, vulgarity, and hate speech.

LO⁴ What should you consider to make sure your word choices will be interpreted accurately by your audience?
Being accurate begins with a realization that words are only representations of ideas, objects, and feelings. Meaning is a product of both denotation (dictionary meaning) and connotation (positive, neutral, and negative feelings and evaluations that words evoke). To ensure that your ideas are interpreted accurately, consider denotation, connotation, and dialect.

LO⁵ What can you do to make sure your message is clear?
Clear language is specific and precise. Specific language clarifies meaning. Precise words are those that narrow down a broad idea. The larger your vocabulary, the more choices you have to select a word you want. Ways to increase your vocabulary are to study vocabulary-building books, to look up meanings of words you don't understand, and to use a thesaurus to identify synonyms. Clarity can also be achieved by providing details and examples.

LO⁶ What are some strategies you can employ to make your ideas vivid?
Vividness means full of life, vigorous, bright, and intense. Increase the vividness of your language by using sensory language, as well as rhetorical figures and structures of speech.

Chapter Quiz

True/False
1. In some situations, it not appropriate to speak with a personal tone.
2. As long as you don't intend to be offensive, the audience will not be offended by jokes you include in the speech.
3. Language is symbolic because it is used to represent things, ideas, and events.
4. The speaking notes should include delivery cues and citations of reference material.
5. The use of transitions and signposts is important to an effective oral style.

Multiple Choice
6. During a speech, Louis uses the word *policemen* to refer to all law enforcement officers. This is an example of:
   a. "we" language
   b. bias-free language
   c. stereotypical language
   d. nonparallel language
   e. generic language

dialect
a regional or ethnic variety of a language

Standard English
form of English described in the dictionary or an English handbook

specific language
words that clarify meaning by narrowing what is understood from a general category to a particular item or group within that category

precise words
words that narrow a larger category

jargon
unique technical terminology of a trade or profession that is not generally understood by outsiders

slang
informal, nonstandard vocabulary and nonstandard definitions assigned to words by a social group or subculture

vocalized pause
unnecessary words interjected into sentences to fill moments of silence

vivid language
language that is full of life—vigorous, bright, and intense

sensory language
language that appeals to the senses of seeing, hearing, tasting, smelling, and feeling

rhetorical figures of speech
phrases that make striking comparisons between things that are not obviously alike

rhetorical structures of speech
phrases that combine ideas in a particular way

simile
a direct comparison of dissimilar things using the word *like* or *as*

metaphor
an implied comparison between two unlike things without using *like* or *as*

analogy
an extended metaphor

alliteration
repetition of consonant sounds at the beginning of words that are near one another

assonance
repetition of vowel sounds in a phrase or phrases

onomatopoeia
words that sound like the things they stand for

personification
attributing human qualities to a concept or an inanimate object

repetition
restating words, phrases, or sentences for emphasis

antithesis
combining contrasting ideas in the same sentence

7. The definition of a word given in the dictionary is known as:
   a. semantic field
   b. denotation
   c. ambiguity
   d. nuance
   e. connotation
8. Which of the following is an example of a vocalized pause?
   a. "For instance"
   b. "Secondly"
   c. "Moreover"
   d. "Uh"
   e. "Let's take a moment to reconsider the last point."
9. An effective oral style:
   a. tends toward short sentences and familiar language
   b. uses "you" and "they"
   c. involves using big, technical terms
   d. delivers content quickly and rapidly
   e. does not depend on the volume of the voice
10. Language that involves words and phrases that demean an ethic group is called:
    a. jargon
    b. slang
    c. hate speech
    d. symbolic language
    e. marked language

Answers:
1. F; 2. F; 3. T; 4. T; 5. T; 6. e; 7. b; 8. d; 9. a; 10. c

Speech Snippets

Using "We" Language

Pete used "we" language to introduce his speech in this way: "Today, we'll see why Tok Pisin of Papua New Guinea should be considered a legitimate language. We'll do this by looking at what kind of language Tok Pisin is, some of the features of the Tok Pisin language, and why this language is necessary in New Guinea."

Using Bias-Free Language

In his speech about the Stanislavski system of method acting, Duane practiced referring to Ellen Burstyn as an "actor" rather than using "actress," which unnecessarily highlights the fact that Burstyn is a woman.

Adjusting for Dialect

As Maren, who is from Minnesota, prepared to practice her speech on the effect that drinking sugared sodas has on childhood obesity, she thought about how her roommate would tease her when she referred to "soda" as "pop." As she practiced, she made notes to always say "soda" during her speech.

Defining Acronyms for Clarity

In her speech about STDs, Larissa first introduced the acronym this way: "According to a 2007 report by the American Social Health Association, one in every two sexually active persons will contract a sexually transmitted disease, or STD, by age 25."

Using Metaphors

Dan decided to use a metaphor to help explain the complex concept of bioluminescence to his listeners. He said that "bioluminescence is a miniature flashlight that fireflies turn on and off at will."

11 Chapter in Review

delivery
how you use your voice and body to present your message

nonverbal communication
all speech elements other than the words themselves

conversational style
delivery that seems spontaneous, relaxed, and informal and allows the speaker to talk *with*, not *at*, an audience

spontaneity
a naturalness of speech where what is said sounds as if the speaker is really thinking about the ideas *and* the audience as he or she speaks

animated delivery
delivery that is lively, energetic, enthusiastic, and dynamic

voice
the sound you produce in your larynx, or voice box, which is used to transmit the words of your speech to an audience

pitch
the highness or lowness of the sounds produced in your larynx by the size and vibration of your vocal cords

volume
how loudly or softly you speak

rate
the speed at which you talk

quality
the tone, timbre, or sound of your voice and what distinguishes it from the voice of others

intelligible
capable of being clearly understood

articulation
using the tongue, palate, teeth, jaw movement, and lips to shape vocalized sounds that combine to produce a word

pronunciation
the form and accent of various syllables of a word

accent
the inflection, tone, and speech habits typical of native speakers of a language

vocal expressiveness
variety you create in your voice through changing pitch, volume, and rate, as well as stressing certain words and using pauses strategically

monotone
a voice in which the pitch, volume, and rate remain constant, with no word, idea, or sentence differing significantly in sound from any other

stress
emphasis placed on certain words by speaking them more loudly than the rest of the sentence

LO1 **What are the characteristics of effective delivery?**
Delivery refers to the use of voice and body to communicate the message of the speech; it is what the audience sees and hears. Effective delivery is conversational and animated.

LO2 **What can you do to use your voice effectively as you deliver your speech?**
By varying the four characteristics of voice (pitch, volume, rate, and quality) and using strategically placed pauses, you can ensure that your speech is intelligible to your audience and is vocally expressive.

LO3 **What can you do to use your body effectively as you deliver your speech?**
During a speech, you can use your body (eye contact, facial expressions, gestures, movement, posture, poise, and appearance) to convey ethos, reinforce the emotional tone of your ideas, and clarify structure.

LO4 **Why and how should you rehearse your speech?**
Between the time the outline is completed and the speech is given, it is important to engage in rehearsal sessions consisting of a practice, an analysis, and another practice. During these rehearsal sessions, you will work on using a keyword outline of your speaking notes, using your presentational aids effectively, and using an effective oral language and delivery style. When you are finally ready to give your speech, remember that your goal is to have your audience understand your message, so be prepared to adapt to your audience during your speech.

Chapter Quiz

True/False

1. It is relatively simple and easy to create a vocally expressive message.
2. The more serious your speech topic, the more formally you should dress.
3. Nonverbal communication includes how the speaker uses the voice and the body.
4. During a speech, maintaining eye contact helps you gauge the audience's reaction to your ideas.
5. It is difficult to sound both conversational and animated at the same time.

Multiple Choice

6. All of the following are characteristics of the voice EXCEPT:
   a. pitch
   b. quality
   c. rate
   d. animation
   e. volume
7. A(n) _____ speech is one that is delivered with only a few minutes advance notice.
   a. scripted
   b. impromptu
   c. spontaneous
   d. extemporaneous
   e. rehearsed
8. _____ refers to how a message is delivered orally and visually.
   a. Mannerisms
   b. Delivery
   c. Articulation
   d. Poise
   e. Stance

pauses
moments of silence strategically placed to enhance meaning

eye contact
looking directly at the people to whom you are speaking

audience contact
creating a sense of looking listeners in the eye when speaking to large audiences

facial expressions
eye and mouth movements that convey personableness and good character

gestures
the movements of your hands, arms, and fingers that help you remain intelligible

movement
changing the position or location of the entire body

motivated movement
movement with a specific purpose

posture
the position or bearing of the body

poise
the graceful and controlled use of the body that gives the impression of self-assurance, calm, and dignity

appearance
the way you look to others

impromptu speech
a speech that is delivered with only seconds or minutes of advance notice for preparation and is usually presented without referring to notes of any kind

scripted speech
a speech that is prepared by creating a complete written manuscript and delivered by reading a written copy or from memory

extemporaneous speech
a speech that is researched and planned ahead of time, but the exact wording is not scripted and will vary somewhat from presentation to presentation

rehearsing
practicing the presentation of your speech aloud

speaking notes
a keyword outline with delivery cues and reference citations you will use as you deliver your speech

9. During his speech, Vince can emphasize certain words by using:
   a. accent
   b. dialect
   c. stress
   d. tone
   e. pace
10. A speaker using a conversational style will, in general, sound:
   a. spontaneous
   b. tense
   c. nonchalant
   d. apathetic
   e. careless

Answers:
1. F; **2.** T; **3.** T; **4.** T; **5.** F; **6.** d; **7.** b; **8.** b; **9.** c; **10.** a

Speech Snippets

Speaking in a Second Language

Yao Mingxin was in her first semester at the university and in the United States and anticipated that her classmates would have trouble understanding her accent. So she prepared several PowerPoint slides that reinforced key terms and ideas. That way, if she mispronounced a key term, her audience would have the visual prompt to help them interpret what she was saying.

Using Vocal Expressiveness

To convey a sense of urgency about prioritizing the capping of the oil leak in the Gulf of Mexico, David increased his volume and rate, and stressed words such as *now*, *today*, and *immediately*.

Appropriate Eye Contact

As a member of the Cherokee nation, Desiree was raised to avoid direct eye contact as a sign of humility and respect. When speaking to her audience made up of people raised in the dominant American culture, however, she made a special effort to make direct eye contact with them throughout her speech.

Using Appropriate Facial Expressions

Nancy furrowed her brows and pursed her lips when she told the story of two young children who were abandoned in a parking lot—her facial expression conveyed seriousness and disgust. Thad, on the other hand, raised his eyebrows and smiled slightly as he talked about the many new forms of entertainment a domed stadium would bring to the city—his expression conveyed joy and excitement.

Using Appropriate Gestures

For emphasis, Marcella repeatedly slammed her right fist into her left palm to emphasize her frustration as she said, "Over and over and over again, we have tried to stop child pornography, but to no avail."

Using Appropriate Movement

Leena ended her speech with a plea for businesses to better support parental leave to care for sick children. She decided to emphasize her call to action by moving forward toward her audience, gesturing with her palms up. Doing so emphasized the urgency of her request.

Speaking Impromptu With the News Media

Frank's efforts to stop the city from replacing a four-way stop sign with a traffic light on the street corner where he lives quickly became front-page news. As he left the city council meeting, a local TV reporter stopped him to ask him about the issue. He quickly organized his thoughts, identifying his primary reason for fighting the battle and three reasons doing so was not in the best interests of the community. Then he looked directly at the camera and shared these with the reporter.

12 Chapter in Review

informative speech
a speech whose goal is to explain or describe facts, truths, and principles in a way that stimulates interest, facilitates understanding, and increases the likelihood of remembering

intellectually stimulating
information that is new to audience members and is explained in a way that piques their curiosity

creativity
the ability to produce original, innovative ideas

productive thinking
to contemplate something from a variety of perspectives

description
the informative method used to create an accurate, vivid, verbal picture of an object, geographic feature, setting, event, person, or image

definition
a method of informing that explains something by identifying its meaning

synonym
a word that has the same or a similar meaning

antonym
a word that is directly opposite in meaning

comparison and contrast
a method of informing that explains something by focusing on how it is similar to and different from other things

narration
a method of informing that recounts an autobiographical or biographical event, a myth, a story, or some other account

demonstration
a method of informing that explains something by showing how it is done by displaying the stages of a process or by depicting how something works

process speech framework
a speech that demonstrates how something is done, is made, or works

expository speech framework
an informative presentation that provides carefully researched in-depth knowledge about a complex topic

oral footnote
reference to an original source made at the point in the speech where information from that source is presented

LO1 What is the goal of an informative speaker?
An informative speech is one whose goal is to explain or describe facts, truths, and principles in a way that stimulates interest, facilitates understanding, and increases the likelihood that audiences will remember. In short, informative speeches are designed to educate an audience.

LO2 What are the characteristics of effective informative speaking?
Effective informative speeches are intellectually stimulating, are relevant, are creative, are memorable, and address diverse learning styles.

LO3 What are the major methods of informing?
We can inform by describing something, defining it, comparing and contrasting it with other things, narrating stories about it, or demonstrating it.

LO4 What are the two most common informative speech frameworks?
Two common informative speech frameworks are process speeches, in which the steps of making or doing something are shown, and expository speeches, which are well-researched explanations of complex ideas.

LO5 What are the major elements of process speeches?
Effective process speeches require you to carefully delineate the steps and the order in which they occur. The steps typically become the main points, and concrete explanations of each step become the subpoints.

LO6 What are the major types of expository speeches?
Types of expository speeches include those that explain political, economic, social, religious, or ethical issues; those that explain events or forces of history; those that explain a theory, principle, or law; and those that explain a creative work.

Chapter Quiz

True/False

1. One of the goals of an informative speech is to present information in a way to help the audience remember it.
2. A synonym of "hot" is "spicy."
3. A speaker who is describing the effects of World War II on the European economy is giving a process speech.
4. In an effective speech, the speaker should not have to explain to the audience how the information is relevant to them.
5. Using presentational aids will help your speech be more memorable.

Multiple Choice

6. The method of informing that explains the meaning of something is called:
   a. description
   b. definition
   c. comparison
   d. narration
   e. contrast
7. The primary goal of an informative speech is to:
   a. entertain
   b. incite
   c. educate
   d. encourage
   e. aggravate

8. According to the text, creativity comes from:
   a. traits
   b. personality
   c. heredity
   d. timing
   e. hard work
9. Information that is new to an audience and piques curiosity is called:
   a. creative
   b. thought provoking
   c. challenging
   d. intellectually stimulating
   e. mind blowing
10. If you were giving a speech on how to make smoked salmon, you would be giving a:
    a. persuasive speech
    b. process speech
    c. ceremonial speech
    d. expository speech
    e. creative speech

Answers:

1. T; 2. T; 3. F; 4. F; 5. T; 6. b; 7. c; 8. c; 9. d; 10. b

Speech Snippets

Choosing an Intellectually Stimulating Informative Topic

Josh, a car buff, decided to give his informative speech on SUVs. Most of his audience knows that SUVs are prone to flip over but not why, so he researched this aspect of his topic in depth to discover an answer. In this way, he made his speech intellectually stimulating for his audience.

Making Your Informative Speech Relevant

In her speech about date rape, Jenny offered a listener relevance link to pique audience interest regarding the statistic that one in four women will be raped at some point in her lifetime. She said, "We can reason, then, that two or three of the eleven women in our classroom will be raped during her lifetime. Not only that, if you have a mother, an aunt, a sister or two, or a daughter, one of them could conceivably be raped in her lifetime."

Addressing Diverse Learning Styles

In his speech about what it is like to do a tour of duty as a soldier in Iraq, Ray rounded the cycle of learning by sharing stories of his own experiences (*feeling*), showing visual aids of the places he has been and the equipment he has used (*watching*), explaining why the days were structured as they were (*thinking*), and asking his audience to respond silently to four questions every soldier must answer "yes" to (*doing*).

Informing by Comparing

In her speech about Islamic traditions, Amanda compared them to Judeo-Christian traditions that her listeners were more familiar with.

13

Chapter in Review

persuasion
the process of influencing people's attitudes, beliefs, values, or behaviors

persuasive speaking
the process of influencing people's attitudes, beliefs, values, or behaviors in a public speech

argument
articulating a position with the support of logos, ethos, and pathos

logos
everything you say and do to appeal to logic and sound reasoning

ethos
everything you say and do to convey competence and good character

pathos
everything you say and do to appeal to emotions

reasoning
the mental process of making an argument by drawing inferences from factual information to reach a conclusion

inductive reasoning
arriving at a general conclusion based on several pieces of specific evidence

deductive reasoning
arriving at a conclusion based on a major premise and minor premise

major premise
a general principle that most people agree upon

minor premise
a specific point that fits within the major premise

syllogism
the three-part form of deductive reasoning

claim
the proposition or conclusion to be proven

support
the reason or evidence the speaker offers as the grounds for accepting the conclusion

warrant
the logical statement that connects the support to the claim

argue from sign
to support a claim by providing evidence that the events that signal the claim have occurred

argue from example
to support your claim by providing one or more individual examples

argue from analogy
to support a claim with a single comparable example that is significantly similar to the subject of the claim

LO1 What is the nature of persuasion?

Persuasion is the process of influencing people's attitudes, beliefs, values, or behaviors, and persuasive speaking is doing so in a public speech. Persuasive messages differ from informative messages in that the primary goal is to seek agreement and sometimes to incite action. Because the goals of persuasion are loftier and the potential implications more acute than informing, both senders and receivers of persuasive messages must pay special attention to the ethical principles of communication when creating and interpreting them.

LO2 How do people process persuasive messages?

The Elaboration Likelihood Model (ELM) describes how audiences process persuasive messages. Understanding this model helps us focus on how to use logos, ethos, and pathos appeals as we construct and deliver persuasive speeches, as well as when we evaluate the worth of the persuasive messages we encounter in our daily lives.

LO3 What is the role of logos in persuasion?

Logos is the means of persuasion devoted to appeals to logic and reasoning. You reason with your audience by making an argument that draws inferences from factual information to support a conclusion. You can reason inductively or deductively by addressing three basic elements of an argument. These are the claim, the support, and the warrant. Four common types of arguments used in persuasive messages are sign, example, analogy, and causation. When creating persuasive messages, it is important to avoid reasoning fallacies, and, when interpreting persuasive messages, it is important to discern them. Some common fallacies are hasty generalization, false cause, either-or, straw man, and ad hominem. Because you will rely on evidence to support your reasons, you must make sure it comes from a well-respected source, is still valid, is relevant to the argument, and is likely to persuade your audience.

LO4 What is the role of ethos in persuasion?

Ethos is the means of persuasion devoted to conveying good character, competence, and credibility. You convey good character by demonstrating goodwill. Your goal is to encourage your audience to believe you understand them, empathize with them, and are responsive to them. You convey competence and credibility by explaining your competence, establishing common ground, using evidence from respected sources, and being nonverbally and vocally expressive in your delivery.

LO5 What is the role of pathos in persuasion?

Pathos is the means of persuasion devoted to emotional appeals. You can appeal to negative emotions such as fear, guilt, shame, anger, and sadness. Or you can appeal to positive emotions such as happiness and joy, pride, relief, hope, and compassion. Some guidelines you can follow to appeal to emotions include telling vivid stories, using startling statistics, incorporating listener relevance links, using striking presentational aids and provocative language, and being vocally and visually expressive when delivering your message.

Chapter Quiz

True/False

1. One way to make an argument in a persuasive speech is to support a claim by linking it to a comparable example.
2. Listeners are more likely to use the central route of processing when they feel that the information in a speech is important to them.
3. A person who is able to see the world through someone else's eyes has empathy.
4. A speaker commits the straw man fallacy when he or she presents a generalization that is not supported with evidence.
5. The two types of reasoning are inductive reasoning and conductive reasoning.

argue from causation
to cite events that have occurred that result in the claim

hasty generalization
a fallacy that presents a generalization that is either not supported with evidence or is supported with only one weak example

false cause
a fallacy that occurs when the alleged cause fails to be related to, or to produce, the effect

either-or
a fallacy that argues there are only two alternatives when, in fact, others exist

straw man
a fallacy that occurs when a speaker weakens the opposing position by misrepresenting it in some way and then attacks that weaker position

ad hominem
a fallacy that occurs when a speaker attacks or praises a person making an argument rather than addressing the argument itself

goodwill
a perception the audience forms of a speaker who they believe understands them, empathizes with them, and is responsive to them

empathy
the ability to see the world through the eyes of someone else

responsive
when speakers show that they care about the audience by acknowledging feedback, especially subtle negative cues

terminal credibility
perception of a speaker's expertise at the end of the speech

initial credibility
perception of a speaker's expertise at the beginning of the speech

derived credibility
strategies employed throughout the speech that signal a speaker's expertise

emotions
the buildup of action-specific energy

negative emotions
disquieting feelings that people experience

fear
perceiving no control over a situation that threatens us

guilt
the feeling when we personally violate a moral, ethical, or religious code that we hold dear

shame
the feeling when we have violated a moral code and it is revealed to someone we think highly of

anger
the feeling when we are faced with an obstacle in the way of something we want

sadness
the feeling when we fail to achieve a goal or we experience a loss or separation

positive emotions
feelings that people enjoy experiencing

Multiple Choice

6. ELM stands for:
   a. Estimated Linkage Model
   b. Elaboration Likelihood Model
   c. Exhibition Landscape Model
   d. Elaborate Listener Model
   e. Extended Localization Model

7. During his speech on Internet privacy, Alan argues that Mark Zuckerberg, the CEO of Facebook, should be ignored as an authority since he never finished college. This is an example of which fallacy?
   a. Hasty generalization
   b. Ad hominem
   c. Straw man
   d. Either-or
   e. False cause

8. A speaker who is appealing to the audience's emotions is using which means of persuasion?
   a. Ethos
   b. Kairos
   c. Pathos
   d. Logos
   e. Cosmos

9. _____ refers to the evidence that a speaker offers as the grounds for accepting the conclusion.
   a. Claim
   b. Warrant
   c. Support
   d. Argument
   e. Criteria

10. When a speaker is describing the suffering of someone, he or she is trying to arouse the audience's:
    a. relief
    b. hope
    c. joy
    d. pride
    e. compassion

Answers:
1. T 2. T 3. T 4. F 5. F 6. b; 7. b; 8. c; 9. c; 10. e

Speech Snippets

Creating an Argument Using Toulmin's Model

Nathan wanted his listeners to agree that people should get six to seven hours of sleep at night. So he developed this argument:

Want listeners to agree that we should try to get six to seven hours of sleep at night.
Sleep produces melatonin, which can prevent cancer.
Sleep reduces stress.
Sleep improves mental alertness and memory.
(I believe these benefits are major reasons to agree that we should strive for at least six hours of sleep at night.)

happiness or joy
the buildup of positive energy we experience when we accomplish something, when we have a satisfying interaction or relationship, or when we see or possess objects that appeal to us

pride
the feeling of self-satisfaction and increased self-esteem as the result of an accomplishment

relief
the feeling when a threatening situation has been alleviated

hope
emotional energy that stems from believing something desirable is likely to happen

compassion
feeling of selfless concern for the suffering of another person and the concern that energizes us to try to relieve that suffering

attitude
a general or enduring positive or negative feeling about some person, object, or issue

target audience
the group of people you most want to persuade

incremental change
attempting to move your audience only a small degree in your direction

uninformed
the audience doesn't know enough about a topic to have formed an opinion

impartial
the audience has some information about a topic but does not really understand why one position is preferred and so still has no opinion

apathetic
the audience is uninterested in, unconcerned about, or indifferent toward your topic

proposition
the specific goal of a persuasive speech stated as a declarative sentence that clearly indicates the position the speaker will advocate

proposition of fact
a statement designed to convince the audience that something did or did not exist or occur, is or is not true, or will or will not occur

proposition of value
a statement designed to convince the audience that something is good, bad, desirable, undesirable, fair, unfair, moral, immoral, sound, unsound, beneficial, harmful, important, or unimportant

proposition of policy
a statement designed to convince the audience that they should take a specific course of action

speech to convince
a speech designed to seek agreement about a belief, value, or attitude

speech to actuate
a speech designed to incite action

comparative advantages
an organization that shows that a proposed change has more value than the status quo

criteria satisfaction
an indirect organization that seeks audience agreement on criteria that should be considered when evaluating a particular proposition and then shows how the proposition satisfies those criteria

refutative
an organization that persuades by both challenging the opposing position and bolstering one's own

LO¹ Why is it important to consider the initial audience attitude when constructing your persuasive speech goal?

Persuasive speeches are designed to influence the attitudes, beliefs, values, or behaviors of audience members. This chapter focuses on creating effective and ethical persuasive speeches. The first step in preparing an effective and ethical persuasive speech is to analyze your target audience to determine where they stand with regard to your topic so you can decide whether a speech to convince or a speech to actuate is most appropriate.

LO² How do you phrase a persuasive speech goal as a proposition?

You can construct a persuasive speech goal phrased as a proposition that is based on the audience's initial attitude toward your topic. An audience may be opposed to the proposition, have no opinion (because they are uninformed, impartial, or apathetic), or be in favor. Generally, if the target audience is opposed to your proposition, seek incremental change. If they have no opinion, seek agreement. If they are in favor, seek action.

LO³ What are some dispositional persuasive speech frameworks?

After formulating a proposition, you will choose an organizational framework. If you seek agreement through a speech to convince, you will likely select from among four frameworks: comparative advantages, criteria satisfaction, refutative, or statement of reasons.

LO⁴ What are some actuation persuasive speech frameworks?

If you seek action, select from among three common frameworks—problem-solution, problem-cause-solution, or motivated sequence—to organize your arguments. One important element in an effective actuation persuasive speech is a call to action that clearly describes actions you want audience members to take.

LO⁵ What ethical communication guidelines should you follow as a persuasive speaker?

Persuasive speakers must evaluate their speech plan based on the ethical guidelines you have learned as well as some additional ones that are specific to persuasive speeches. These include advocating the honest belief of the speaker, providing choice for the audience, using supporting information that is representative, using emotional appeal to engage audiences, and honestly presenting speaker credibility. Persuasive speaking is challenging but can also be extremely rewarding for those who do so effectively and ethically.

Chapter Quiz

True/False

1. The primary goal of a persuasive speech is to seek agreement or encourage action.
2. An audience is neutral only because it does not understand why a speaker prefers a certain position on an issue.
3. A speaker who is describing why young children should not watch more than 30 minutes of TV per day is using a proposition of value.
4. One of the ways that people express their attitude is to give their opinions.
5. The proposition of a persuasive speech should be framed as an exclamatory sentence.

Multiple Choice

6. "The goal of my speech is to convince you that the government should censor websites" is an example of:
   a. proposition of policy
   b. proposition of intent
   c. proposition of fact
   d. proposition of value
   e. proposition of action

statement of reasons
a straightforward organization in which you present your best-supported reasons in a meaningful order

problem-solution
a persuasive organizational pattern that reveals details about a problem and poses solutions to it

problem-cause-solution
a form of persuasive organization that examines a problem, its cause(s), and solutions designed to eliminate or alleviate the underlying cause(s)

motivated sequence
a form of persuasive organization that combines a problem-solution pattern with explicit appeals designed to motivate the audience

7. The term that refers to the group of people that a speaker most wants to persuade is:
   a. core audience
   b. key demographic
   c. target group
   d. target audience
   e. central focus

8. If you wanted to convince an audience that an increase in taxes will lead to job loss, you should use:
   a. proposition of value
   b. proposition of fact
   c. proposition of policy
   d. proposition of legislation
   e. proposition of budget

9. Dorothy wants to give a speech in which she explores the rise in violent crime and makes a proposal for how to address it. She should use the _____ framework.
   a. problem-solution
   b. statement of reasons
   c. problem-cause-solution
   d. motivated sequence
   e. problem-proposal

10. The first step of the motivated sequence organizational pattern is the:
    a. satisfaction step
    b. visualization step
    c. attention step
    d. action appeal step
    e. appeal step

Answers:
1. T; 2. F; 3. T; 4. T; 5. F; 6. a; 7. d; 8. b; 9. a; 10. c

Speech Snippets

Persuading an Audience in Favor of Your Proposition

Adam knew that most if not all of the people in his audience already agreed that bullying is bad, so he decided to focus on a speech that would get them to do their part to help stop cyber-bullying.

Organizing by the Comparative Advantages Framework

Because Molly knew some members of her audience probably engaged in the practice of "hooking up" and others probably didn't care one way or the other, she decided to organize her persuasive speech to convince using a comparative advantages framework.

Organizing by Monroe's Motivated Sequence

Daniel decided to arrange his speech to actuate about ending the practice of deep sea oil drilling using the motivated sequence. He did so because he wanted to spend a good deal of time visualizing a positive and negative future to help persuade his listeners to lobby legislators to create and vote for laws to stop the practice.

15 Chapter in Review

speech of welcome
a brief, formal ceremonial address that greets and expresses pleasure for the presence of a person or an organization

master of ceremonies
an individual designated to welcome guests, set the mood of the program, introduce participants, and keep the program moving

speech of introduction
a brief ceremonial speech that establishes a supportive climate for the main speaker, highlights the speaker's credibility by familiarizing the audience with pertinent biographical information, and generates enthusiasm for listening to the speaker and topic

speech of nomination
a ceremonial presentation that proposes a nominee for an elected office, honor, position, or award

speech of recognition
a ceremonial presentation that acknowledges someone and usually presents an award, a prize, or a gift to the individual or a representative of a group

speech of acceptance
a ceremonial speech given to acknowledge receipt of an honor or award

speech of tribute
a ceremonial speech that praises or celebrates a person, a group, or an event

toast
a ceremonial speech offered at the start of a reception or meal that pays tribute to the occasion or to a person

roast
an event where guests provide short speeches of tribute about the featured guests that are developed with humorous stories and anecdotes

eulogy
a ceremonial speech of tribute during a funeral or memorial service that praises someone's life and accomplishments

commencement address
a ceremonial speech of tribute praising graduating students and inspiring them to reach for their goals

commemorative address
a ceremonial speech of tribute that celebrates national holidays or anniversaries of important events

keynote address
a ceremonial speech that both sets the tone and generates enthusiasm for the topic of a conference or convention

LO1 What should you include in a speech of welcome?

A speech of welcome is usually a brief, formal ceremonial address that greets and expresses pleasure for the presence of a person or an organization. You must be familiar with the group that you are representing and the occasion. A speech of welcome invites listeners to agree that the occasion is friendly and their attendance is appreciated. The conclusion of the speech should briefly express your hope for the outcome of the visit, event, or relationship.

LO2 Why should a speech of introduction be brief?

Speeches of introduction should honestly represent the person being introduced. Do not hype a speaker's credentials or "over-praise" the speaker. If you set the audience's expectations too high, even a good speaker may have trouble living up to them.

LO3 What is your goal in a speech of nomination?

The goal of a speech of nomination is to highlight the qualities that make this person the most credible candidate. To do so, first clarify the importance of the nomination, honor, position, or award by describing the responsibilities involved, related challenges or issues, and the characteristics needed to fulfill it. Second, list the candidate's personal and professional qualifications that meet those criteria. Finally, formally place the candidate's name in nomination, creating a dramatic climax to clinch your speech.

LO4 When might you be expected to give a speech of recognition?

A speech of recognition is a ceremonial presentation that acknowledges someone and usually presents an award, a prize, or a gift to the individual or a representative of a group.

LO5 What are some common types of speeches of tribute?

Common types of speeches of tribute include toasts, roasts, and eulogies.

Chapter Quiz

True/False

1. The goal of a speech to entertain is just to be humorous.
2. Before giving a speech of welcome, you should do some research to become familiar with the group you are representing.
3. During a speech of introduction, it is not very important to mention the main speaker by name.
4. The goal of a ceremonial speech is a hybrid of the goals for informative speeches and persuasive speeches.
5. It is inappropriate to use a speech of acceptance to advocate for an unrelated cause.

Multiple Choice

6. A _____ is a speech given at the start of a reception or meal that pays tribute to the occasion.
   a. roast
   b. dedication
   c. eulogy
   d. toast
   e. keynote address
7. In general, ceremonial speeches should be fewer than _____ minutes long.
   a. ten
   b. twenty
   c. fifteen
   d. five
   e. forty-five

dedication
a ceremonial speech of tribute that honors a worthy person or group by naming a structure, monument, or park after the honoree

farewell
a ceremonial speech of tribute honoring someone who is leaving an organization

speech to entertain
a humorous speech that makes a serious point

8. Adam is assigned to give a speech in which he will present Sam Jones as a candidate as mayor. He should be giving a speech of:
   a. nomination
   b. tribute
   c. introduction
   d. welcome
   e. recognition
9. The main goal of a speech of introduction is to:
   a. make the audience laugh
   b. establish the credibility of the speaker
   c. give a preview of the speech
   d. get familiar with the audience's expectations
   e. set the mood of the program
10. During a ceremony, the _____ is responsible for welcoming guests, introducing participants, and keeping the program moving.
    a. host
    b. lead
    c. entertainer
    d. greeter
    e. master of ceremonies

Answers:
1. F; 2. T; 3. F; 4. T; 5. T; 6. d; 7. d; 8. a; 9. b; 10. e

Speech Snippets

Giving a Speech of Welcome

Marla had been asked to serve as master of ceremonies for the year-end company banquet. She chose to welcome everyone this way:

We have all worked hard, and both the progress and profits our organization has made are evidence of that. I want to congratulate and thank each and every one of you for all you've done to make these results a reality. Because of that, tonight is a night of celebration. So pat yourselves and each other on the back for a job well done. I'll be introducing a number of individuals for special awards after dinner. Until then, enjoy the company of those around you, the good food in front of you, and the music the Melodics String Quartet is here to share with you. Thank you, and enjoy!

Acknowledging the Contributions of Others

When Renee accepted her award for "outstanding community service," she began by acknowledging how much she admired the work of the three other nominees before saying how honored she was to receive the award.

Giving a Eulogy

In the eulogy for his grandfather, "Gramps," Ben highlighted three character traits in Gramps that he admired. One trait was Gramps's patience, which Ben highlighted by telling stories of how Gramps had handled Ben's mistakes during three different incidents: when he tipped the fishing boat at four years old, when he wandered away at the state fair at eight, and when he pouted about a Christmas gift at 13. In each instance, Gramps had taught Ben a life lesson by sharing a story from his boyhood rather than reprimanding him.

16 Chapter in Review

problem-solving group
four to seven people who work together to complete a specific task or solve a particular problem

synergy
when the result of group work is better than what one member could have accomplished alone

conflict
disagreement or clash among ideas, principles, or people

groupthink
when group members accept information and ideas without subjecting them to critical analysis

withdrawing
a conflict management style that involves physically or psychologically removing yourself from the conflict

accommodating
a passive conflict management style of accepting others' ideas while neglecting your own, even when you disagree with their views

forcing
a conflict management style that involves satisfying your own needs with no concern for the needs of the others and no concern for the harm it does to the group dynamics or problem-solution process of reaching the best solution

compromising
a conflict management style that involves individuals giving up part of what they want in order to provide at least some satisfaction to other opinions

collaborating
a conflict management style that involves discussing the issues, describing feelings, and identifying the characteristics of an effective solution before deciding what the ultimate solution will be

perception checking
a verbal statement that reflects your understanding of another's behavior

paraphrasing
putting into your own words the meaning you have assigned to a message

systematic problem-solving method
an efficient six-step method for finding an effective solution to a problem

criteria
standards used for judging the merits of proposed solutions

LO1 Why is teamwork becoming so popular as a means for solving problems?
Today, working and speaking in groups is popular not only in the classroom but also in business and industry. Effective problem-solving groups produce better products than individuals can produce on their own.

LO2 What does it mean to be a responsible group member?
Groups are ineffective when some members fail to fulfill their responsibilities as group members. These responsibilities include being committed to the group goal, keeping the discussion on track, completing individual assignments, encouraging input from all members, and managing conflict among group members.

LO3 How can you solve problems effectively in groups?
Effective groups experience conflict but manage conflicts using collaboration and avoid personality conflict by using the skills of perception checking and paraphrasing. One effective process for solving problems in groups is systematic problem solving. Members work together to identify and define a problem, analyze the problem, determine criteria for judging solutions, generate many solutions, evaluate solutions and select the best one based on the criteria, and implement the agreed-upon solution.

LO4 How do you prepare a group presentation?
Once a group has worked through the problem-solving process, members must work together to prepare the public presentation. Groups can present their findings in a symposium, a panel discussion, a town hall meeting, or electronic conferences, as well as streaming videos and slide shows.

LO5 How can you evaluate group work?
Finally, evaluating group effectiveness includes an evaluation of each individual's public speaking portion of the presentation. It should also include an evaluation of group dynamics and group performance, as well as self-evaluation.

Chapter Quiz

True/False

1. The conflict management style in which you accept others' ideas and neglect your own is known as forcing.
2. One of the advantages of working in a group is that groups can present a greater breadth of ideas and potential solutions.
3. The first step in preparing a group presentation is to draft an outline of the topic area.
4. Synergy occurs when the most talented people in the group do the work that less-talented people can't do.
5. The most effective way to achieve a win–win result in conflict is to collaborate.

Multiple Choice

6. _____ occurs when group members accept ideas without critically analyzing them.
   a. Conformity
   b. Blindness
   c. Acquiescence
   d. Groupthink
   e. Acceptance
7. A problem-solving discussion that occurs in front of an audience is called a/an:
   a. panel discussion
   b. town hall meeting
   c. symposium
   d. conference
   e. streaming video

8. A problem-solving group typically has _____ members.
   a. two to four
   b. five to ten
   c. ten to fifteen
   d. four to seven
   e. more than twenty
9. The first step in the systematic problem-solving method is:
   a. analyze the problem
   b. determine criteria for judging solutions
   c. identify and define the problem
   d. generate a host of solutions
   e. evaluate solutions
10. Which of the following is not a responsibility of a group member?
   a. Keep discussion on track.
   b. Ignore unproductive members.
   c. Be committed to the group goal.
   d. Complete individual assignments on time.
   e. Manage conflict among members.

Answers:
1. F 2. T 3. F 4. F 5. T 6. d 7. a 8. d 9. c 10. b

Speech Snippets

Committing to the Group Goal

Luke wanted to do the group speech on legalizing marijuana for medical purposes. Once his group decided to focus on a different topic, however, he let go of the marijuana idea and supported the agreed-upon goal instead.

Keeping the Discussion on Track

When Luke and Kristi began talking about attending the upcoming football game during the group work session, Bryn gently reminded them that the group had only 30 minutes to figure out how to proceed and assign tasks for the speech that would be due next week.

Encouraging Input From All Group Members

Bryn tends to be quiet during group discussions, yet when Kristi asked for her opinion, Bryn helped the group realize that Nick had a valuable contribution to make.

Implementing Solutions

In their report about gang violence, Matt, Shannon, Pam, and Michelle created implementation plans for parental accountability and for the government to crack down on the illegal gun market. They also provided implementation strategies for churches, businesses, and service groups to offer alternative programs for area youth. Thus, they didn't merely offer solutions; they provided plans for implementing them.

Six Action Steps Toward Effective Speeches

Action Step 1

Select a speech goal that is appropriate to the rhetorical situation. (Chapter 4)

© PHOTOS.COM/JUPITERIMAGES

Action Step 1

Select a speech goal that is appropriate to the rhetorical situation.

A. Brainstorm and concept map for topics.

B. Analyze your audience.

C. Analyze the rhetorical situation.

D. Develop a speech goal statement tailored to your audience and the occasion.

Action Step 2

Understand your audience and adapt to it. (Chapter 5)

© STEWART COHEN/DIGITAL VISION/GETTY IMAGES

Action Step 2

Understand your audience and adapt to it.

A. Understand audience diversity.

B. Understand audience initial interest and attitude.

C. Adjust content to be appropriate for your audience.

D. Determine how you will establish your credibility with the audience.

Action Step 3

Gather and evaluate information to use in the speech. (Chapter 6)

© ISTOCKPHOTO.COM/PHOTOGL

Action Step 3

Gather and evaluate information to use in the speech.

A. Examine what you know already and areas where you need additional information.

B. Locate, evaluate, and select a variety of information types and sources.

C. Prepare research cards.

D. Cite sources.

Action Step 4

Organize and develop ideas into a well-structured outline. (Chapters 7 and 8)

Action Step 5

Choose, prepare, and use appropriate presentational aids. (Chapter 9)

Action Step 6

Practice oral language and delivery style. (Chapters 10 and 11)

Action Step 4

Organize and develop ideas into a well-structured outline.

A. Identify two to four main points.

B. Write a thesis statement with main point preview.

C. Develop your main points.

D. Outline the speech body.

E. Create the speech introduction.

F. Create the speech conclusion.

G. Complete the list of sources used.

H. Complete the formal speech outline.

Action Step 5

Choose, prepare, and use appropriate presentational aids.

A. Consider presentational aids that will clarify, emphasize, or dramatize your message.

B. Use another symbol system (beyond words alone) in your aids.

C. Make sure your visual aids are large enough to be seen.

D. Make sure your audio aids are loud enough to be heard.

E. Plan when to use aids and integrate them during your speech.

Action Step 6

Practice oral language and delivery style.

A. Practice to develop an oral style using language that is appropriate, accurate, clear, and vivid.

B. Practice until the delivery is conversational, intelligible, and expressive.

C. Practice integrating presentational aids until you can do so smoothly and confidently.

D. Continue practicing until you can deliver your speech extemporaneously within the time limit.

Communicating Emotions Nonverbally: Encoding and Decoding Skill and Practice

The Assignment

Your instructor will write a simple sentence on the board that you will recite to your classmates while attempting to convey a particular emotion nonverbally. First, you will use only your voice; then you will use your voice and face; and finally you will use your voice, face, and body. The sentence could be as simple as "I had bacon and eggs for breakfast this morning."

1. To find out the emotion you will convey, draw a card from a stack offered by your instructor. Without letting your classmates see, turn the card over to read what emotion is written on the front. Some possible emotions include *anger, excitement, fear, joy, worry,* and *sadness.* Consider how you will use your voice, face, and body to convey that emotion.
2. When your instructor calls on you, go to the front of the classroom and face the wall (so your classmates cannot see your face). Try to convey that emotion with only your voice while saying the sentence with your back to the class.
3. The class might make some guesses about the emotion you are conveying and give some reasons for their guesses. You should not tell them whether they are correct at this point.
4. Turn around to face your classmates and say the sentence again, this time trying to reinforce the emotion with your face and eyes.
5. The class might again make some guesses.
6. Repeat the sentence once more, this time using your voice, face, and body to convey the emotion.
7. The class might again make some guesses.
8. Tell them the emotion that was on the card and what you did with your voice, face, and body to convey it.
9. Your instructor may lead a discussion about what worked and didn't as well as how you could have made the emotional message more clear.

Critical Listening

The Assignment

Find and attend a formal public presentation that is being given on campus or in your community. Your goal is to listen so that you remember and can critically evaluate what you have heard. Be sure to take notes and record the main ideas the speaker presents. After you have heard the speech, analyze what you heard. You can use the following questions to guide your initial thinking:

- What was the purpose of the speech? What was the speaker trying to explain to you or convince you about?
- Was it easy or difficult to identify the speaker's main ideas? What did you notice about how the speaker developed each point she or he made?
- Did the speaker use examples or tell stories to develop a point? If so, were these typical examples, or did the speaker choose examples that were unusual but seemed to prove the point?
- Did the speaker use statistics to back up what was said? If so, did the speaker tell you where the statistics came from? Did the statistics surprise you? If so, what would you have needed to hear that would have helped you accept them as accurate?
- Do you think the speaker did a good job? If so, why? If not, what should the speaker have done to be more effective?

When you have finished your analysis, follow your instructor's directions. You may be asked to write a short essay about the speech or to present what you learned to the class.

Panel Discussion

The Assignment

Form a small group with three to five classmates. As a group, decide on a social issue or problem you would like to study in depth. Then select one group member to serve as moderator and the others as expert panelists. Members should do research to find out all they can about the issue, why it is a problem, and how it affects people and to what degree as well as potential ideas for solving it. The moderator's role is to come up with four to six good questions to ask the panelists. The panelists should prepare notes about what they discovered in their research.

On the day determined by the instructor, you will engage in a 15- to 20-minute panel discussion in front of your classmates. The moderator will guide the discussion by asking questions of the panelists as well as asking for questions from the class.

Suggested Format

1. Moderator thanks audience for coming and introduces the panelists and the topic.
2. Moderator asks panelists a series of questions, letting a different panelist respond first each time.
3. Moderator asks follow-up questions when appropriate.
4. Moderator asks for questions from the audience.
5. Moderator thanks the panelists and the audience members for participating.

A Persuasive Speech

The Assignment

1. Follow the speech plan Action Steps to prepare a speech to convince, in which you change audience belief. Your instructor will announce the time limit and other parameters for this assignment.
2. Criteria for evaluation include all the general criteria of topic and purpose, content, organization, and presentation, but special emphasis will be placed on the primary persuasive criteria of how well the speech's specific goal was adapted to the audience's initial attitude toward the topic, the soundness of the reasons, the evidence cited in support of them, and the credibility of the arguments.
3. Use the Speech to Convince Evaluation Checklist in Chapter 14 to critique yourself as you practice your speech.
4. Prior to presenting your speech, prepare a complete sentence outline and source list (bibliography). If you have used Speech Builder Express to complete the Action Step activities online, you will be able to print out a copy of your completed outline and source list. Also prepare a written plan for adapting your speech to the audience. Your adaptation plan should address the following issues:
   - How does your goal adapt to whether your prevailing audience attitude is in favor, has no opinion, or is opposed?
   - What reasons will you use, and how will the organizational pattern you select fit your topic and audience?
   - How will you establish your credibility with this audience?
   - How will you motivate your audience?
   - How you will organize your reasons?

SPEECH Studio

Speech Studio™

Practice and *present* with **Speech Studio**—the online video-upload and grading program that improves your public speaking skills.

Speech Studio lets you upload video files of practice speeches or final performances, comment on your peers' speeches, and review your grades and instructor feedback—all within this user-friendly tool.

Check out this SPEAK study tool at
www.cengagebrain.com

Speech Note Cards

To get started with your first class speeches, tear out these perforated cards and use them to create note cards!

Speech Note Cards

To get started with your first class speeches, tear out these perforated cards and use them to create note cards!

Speech Note Cards

To get started with your first class speeches, tear out these perforated cards and use them to create note cards!

Speech Note Cards

To get started with your first class speeches, tear out these perforated cards and use them to create note cards!

Speech Note Cards

To get started with your first class speeches, tear out these perforated cards and use them to create note cards!

Speech Note Cards

To get started with your first class speeches, tear out these perforated cards and use them to create note cards!

Speech Note Cards

To get started with your first class speeches, tear out these perforated cards and use them to create note cards!

Speech Note Cards

To get started with your first class speeches, tear out these perforated cards and use them to create note cards!